DATF

MAR 1 6 2017

9/11/16

Cinematic Narration
and its Psychological Impact

Cinematic Narration
and its Psychological Impact:
Functions of Cognition, Emotion and Play

By

Peter Wuss

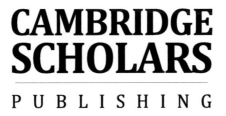

CAMBRIDGE
SCHOLARS
P U B L I S H I N G

Cinematic Narration and its Psychological Impact: Functions of Cognition, Emotion and Play,
by Peter Wuss

This book first published 2009

Cambridge Scholars Publishing

12 Back Chapman Street, Newcastle upon Tyne, NE6 2XX, UK

British Library Cataloguing in Publication Data
A catalogue record for this book is available from the British Library

ISBN (10): 1-4438-0527-0, ISBN (13): 978-1-4438-0527-8

Contents

2.6. Regularities

2.7. Possible Worlds

3. Play in the Regulatory Process of Art

4. Hypotheses Regarding Play Behaviour in the
    Process of Experiencing a Film

    4.1. "As-if" Behaviour and Aesthetic Reaction

    4.2. Dealing with Conflicts

    4.3. Emotive Functions

          4.3.1. Narration

          4.3.2. Empathy

          4.3.3. Genre

    4.4. Functional Pleasure and Hedonistic Function

    4.5. Innovative Function

    4.6. Rules of the Artistic Form

    4.7. Play-Effect and Genre

5. Film Sequences and Stories Based on Play
    Behaviour

CHAPTER IX: NARRATION AND GENRE 247

1. Film Genre as Aesthetic Experience and Cultural
    Instance

2. Theoretical Problems in Dealing with Film Genres

3. The Regulatory Function of Genres

4. Modelling the Ways Classical Genres Achieve
    Effects

    4.1. Estrangement and Comedy

    4.2. Pathos and Drama

    4.3. Catharsis and Tragedy

5. Applications of the Model

    5.1. Summarized Hypotheses on Classical Genres

    5.2. Applications in Regard to Weak Genre
          Tendencies

Preface

A half-century ago, as a pupil on fall break, I left my provincial East-German village to go to Berlin to watch the rehearsals in Brecht's theatre. The dramatist had recently died; but the members of his famous *Berliner Ensemble* did their best to do justice to his intentions and so, in their staging, the question often arose of whether they had "estranged" the performance according to his style and theory or not. When one of the actors interrupted their discussion with the argument that Helene Weigel, Brecht's widow, had just confirmed that this particular scene had been properly estranged, I was deeply amazed. Although I did not doubt the artistic authority of the great actress, I questioned the validity of evaluating an aesthetic impact which had been as carefully and frequently described as "estrangement" based on the subjective opinion of a single person. I thought, in my scientifically-trained pupil's mind, that there should be reliable and objective proof for such effects.

During my media studies at the Film Academy in Potsdam, I began to understand that such attempts to objectify the impact of works of art, and not just estrangement, cannot be realised in a simple way. It dawned on me that to progress in this area, film theory must at least reach out to the field of psychology. In the 1960s, while writing my doctoral thesis on estrangement in the contemporary cinema at the Moscow film institute VGIK, I applied psychological theories of learning, particularly those of Jean Piaget. At this time, I was fortunate enough to hear Piaget's famous lecture at the International Congress of Psychology at the Kremlin, where I had succeeded in sneaking in. This speech emphasized the significance of the cybernetic approach of information processing for the future development of psychology, and I shared the high spirits of the congress participants, who had new hopes that there would soon be remarkable progress in all fields of their discipline. Indeed, at this time the so-called "cognitive revolution" of psychology took place.

I mention these anecdotal reminiscences because they point to the mode of thought and the intentions of this book. At first, there was the practical constraint, accompanied by a certain helplessness, of how to define the aesthetic impact of an artwork, followed by the naive idea that this might best be arranged in conjunction with psychology, and then increasingly raised hopes about new methods and the findings of other disciplines. Thus, the driving force of my activities was a mixture of a practical constraints, a naive reasoning and exaggerated optimism. The limits of such an undertaking were already obvious to me in my youth, but nevertheless, film studies have been searching for a productive approach to analysing the film's aesthetic impact on the viewer to this day.

In the Soviet Union of the 1960s, there already existed different attempts at developing a complex interdisciplinary research of the arts. I was mainly excited by the approaches to a modern analysis of the arts put forth by the Moscow-Tartu School of semiotics, especially Yuri M. Lotman's contributions to a semiotics of culture and theory of literature and the semiotic interpretations of Eisenstein's aesthetics by the versatile linguist Vyacheslav V. Ivanov. These studies often picked up the highly productive ideas which had already been developed in Russia in the 1920s by the exponents of the Formalist school of literary studies and their colleague and foremost critic, Mikhail M. Bakhtin, the film director Sergei M. Eisenstein, and the psychologist Lev S. Vygotsky. During the Stalin era, important writings of these authors were not published and their way of thinking was ostracized, a tendency that, unfortunately, continued for some time in several Eastern-bloc countries. Their theories greatly influenced my view on the arts and their analysis, and I was not surprised that I was able to re-discover—on a new level—many ideas of these early years in the best efforts of the Western scholars of the 1970s and 1980s, for instance in their discourses on the 'Open Work' or 'Cognitive Film Theory'.

After working for a dozen years in film production, I continued my theoretical attempts within the isolation of the Eastern Bloc. In 1986, I published a book on the open work of cinema and, in 1993, another about the analysis of film and psychology using a cognitive approach. These efforts have shown that some of my considerations are very close to the endeavours of my Western colleagues, whereas others are not, as they are based on different traditions of thinking, among them the tradition of the German aesthetics.

The present book develops these ideas. I am trying to outline a complex model which encompasses some important aspects of film's aesthetic impact, which I have, in part, published in separate articles over the last decade. The book is mainly addressed to people who are highly interested in the cinema, particularly in art films, and, of course, to students of audiovisual media who want to know more about the psychological components of film's influence on audiences.

I am also trying to introduce my concept for the first time in an expanded form in the English language, particularly to a circle of colleagues working on Cognitive Film Theory, to whom I owe many of my findings and starting-points. How difficult this attempt would be, I—and my translators—came to realise in those cases where we had to deal with technical terms which, thanks to their different historic origins in German, have a different meaning from the Anglo-American terms. Among them were such central notions as "topic" and "stereotype". Here I had to run the risk of being misunderstood by those readers who are not willing to accept the definitions of these notions given in my study.

This book brings together many ideas that were formulated in lectures at different universities and academic institutions and have since been turned into an academic self-learn course which includes film-sequences on DVD. The present publication attempts to preserve some advantages of this method of learning, thus, a collection of pictures showing parts of film sequences should help to commit to memory the scenes in detail to allow a more thorough analysis. Furthermore, I have focused my attention on a limited number of central film examples. To facilitate the understanding of some psychological arguments for non-psychologists, the text occasionally gives a more thorough explanation of some specific issues in passages which are presented in a smaller font size. This form also allows the reader to leap over these passages without losing the thread of the film studies.

I would not wish to conceal the fact that I should be very pleased if professional psychologists could find an interest in the subject of this book, and use its hypotheses as a starting-point for their own research.

I aimed to anticipate significant effects, emanating from various structures of cinematic narration, in the viewers' mind by using the hypotheses about the films impact on the audience which have been able to be empirically verified by psychological experiments. Fortunately, there already exist some successful endeavours in this direction, but this book is in search of working hypotheses regarding further analyses.

Introduction

1. Why We Go to the Movies

Film provides experience potential. Certainly, there are many reasons why we go to the movies, but foremost among them seems to be the fact that the cinema realizes, broadens and creates human experience, an all-embracing experience which includes psychological as well as cultural and social components.

Moving pictures are made for viewers, for communication with people that assures an actual impact on the audience, a psychologically relevant effect on the viewer's mind with likely and often obvious consequences for cultural aims and social behaviour. Media practice acknowledges this function: The best ideas, pretensions and convictions of filmmakers cannot be realized without the viewer's involvement in the events on the screen, which integrate various processes of thinking, feeling and imagining. Not only the moving picture on the screen, with its artistic devices of performance, but also the proceedings evoked in the spectator's mind, have to be taken into consideration by the student or scholar.

This leads to the main task for film theory today: to study these processes of experience, and to do so on the right level. That means, analysis of the cinema needs to systematically assess the audience's experience, or more precisely, it must, at the very least, bring to bear a modern psychological knowledge about the film's impact on the viewer, a knowledge taking into account different components based on the mental activities of cognition, emotion and imagination.

We have known about this issue for a long time. The first book on film psychology was written by the German-American psychologist Hugo Munsterberg in 1916, and the author already speaks very clearly about these same goals 90 years ago. But the problem is not a simple one. Although the fact that there are more or less regular interrelations between the film's structure and its psychological effect on the viewer seems a matter of course or even a truism, the scholarly analysis of these interrelations turns out to be a task for interdisciplinary research for the future. Both disciplines —film theory and psychology— traditionally have different tasks, different structures and different methods; they use different terminology and are therefore not compatible enough for immediate cooperation. The theorists of the cinema, for instance, are educated in the traditions of the human sciences using the hermeneutic approach, which can be translated as an "art-like" manner of interpretation of the film's meaning using the vaguely defined terminology of aesthetics. Of course, film theorists have a specific professional understanding of what narration, conflict, character, editing, genre and so on are in accordance with the hermeneutic approach common in the theory of art. But what is the essence of these notions in terms of psychology, a discipline with an obvious element of natural science which follows the appropriate kind of experimental method? The crux of an interdisciplinary study already begins with an elementary problem of notification, of understanding one another. Strangely enough, nowadays the film theorist can't ask the psychologist what he thinks about this or that aspect of the film's aesthetic impact. He cannot ask, for example, about the emotional consequences of a specific kind of storytelling, because he is not able to describe different modes of narration in the language of psychology—a description indispensable in order to formulate his question precisely enough. But the issue is not merely one of simple communication or psychological interpretation of an assertion made by film theorists. A fruitful interdisciplinary cooperation needs hypotheses about cinematic structures that lead to data on their significant functions, i.e. moments of impact which are observable through psychology and verifiable experimentally. Finding, for instance, the right form of cinematic storytelling is always a central problem in the filmmaker's creative process, and interdisciplinary research could help by providing assertions regarding the advantages and disadvantages of different modes of narration for a deeper understanding of the various kinds and strategies of storytelling, common as well as innovative ones.

In some respect, the situation of psychology is similar. Although there have been successful attempts to establish a specific media psychology in the last decades regarding the study of different reactions in the auditorium, precise analyses relating to the particular aesthetic effects of the film are lacking to this day. For a long time, research on the influence of art phenomena and aesthetic forms in the cinema rarely took place. Indeed, until the sixties of the last century, psychology had little chance of initiating cooperation because this discipline itself employed many different approaches elaborated by various psychological schools and was therefore not unified as a theoretical system and not capable of posing or answering questions to film theory researchers in an unequivocal language. It was not until the second half of the century that so-called cognitive psychology emerged and founded the various tendencies of psychological research based immediately on the information approach of cybernetics. This afforded new conditions for cooperation between both disciplines, because film theory could follow the same mode of thinking as psychology using the paradigm of information processing. More precisely, these new conditions, in making compatible the two systems of thinking, which for a long time had existed rather theoretically, have over the last 20 years brought noticeable results in interdisciplinary research.

This research, taken on by more or less isolated scholars in different countries, began step by step from both sides, but the bridge between the disciplines has not become a solid and homogenous construction. Rather, there are many thin ropes from one side to the other, and the scholars taking part in this enterprise often have to balance across like tight-rope walkers. And doing so today, they are not better off than their predecessors. Thus, the following study should be read rather as a guide for tight-rope walkers than a manual to an interdisciplinary approach to film studies, because there remain many unsolved problems. For instance: Looking for joint research we have nowhere to start. It requires phenomena of the cinema as subjects for analysis which, on the one hand, are relevant and interesting for film theorists as well as for psychologists and, on the other, can be described easily in the terms of cognitive psychology. Only in such a way can cooperation really be effective and helpful in the future, because the results of the exertions on both sides would stimulate the progress of the whole enterprise as well as the development of each respective discipline.

The subject most suitable as a starting-point for interdisciplinary research seems to be cinematic narration. Filmmakers and theorists

have known for a long time that the principle of narration is
responsible for the connections between the events shown on the
screen. Thanks to narration, situations can be linked and unfolded
into a coherent story. Due to narration the film, which includes
different actions, images and other stimuli, appears as a whole that
can guarantee the continuity of meaning construction in the
viewer's mind and, at the same time, the emotional organisation of
processes of experience. In other words: Narration seems to be a
relevant factor in filmmaking as well as media studies, and without
doubt it has clear consequences for the film's psychological impact
on the spectator. It thus recommends itself as a point on which to
fasten the hook for our rope to the other side.

Attempts at interdisciplinary research actually began with the
psychological modelling of cinematic narration, and until now,
narration has been the central topic of so-called 'Cognitive Film
Theory'. It remains the starting-point for the most important
analyses of film experience. That is so in general and also in my
own efforts. For this reason, this book will focus on this issue. The
chapters are organised in line with an aesthetical theory which
places in the forefront the aspect of narration leading to the film's
psychological impact. This approach is directly linked to the work
of 'Cognitive Film Theory'. While I draw upon the notion of
aesthetic theory to characterize my concept, I do not reject the
highly productive direction modern film theory has taken, but hope
to avoid misunderstandings regarding the interpretation of
"cognitive" which are historically driven. When the cognitive
approach began to prevail in psychology and was adopted by film
theory a quarter century ago, it was based on the abstract
cybernetic model of information processing. This model was very
apt for describing certain processes of information, namely those
connected to comprehension or rational thinking, i.e. consciously
realized mental activities. Cognition, then, was bound to the
criterion of "obligatory consciousness". Meanwhile, psychologists'
interests have shifted to mental activities and kinds of information
processing that are less conscious, and the cognitive approach in
film theory has recently expanded its sphere of action as well. The
traditional understanding of "cognitive" processes, as a result, is no
longer deemed to be adequate. In addition to the more or less
conscious and rational processes of human cognition, new film

studies also try to encompass relatively unconscious ones connected, for instance, with perception, emotion, imagination, fantasy, play, and so on. Artistic forms evoke a whole range of such interacting psychological functions for which suitable terminology is sometimes lacking. These components may, however, be essential to the true attraction and aesthetic value of cinematic experience. When people go to the movies, it is safe to assume that it is not just because of their cognitive value, which is itself reason enough to look more closely at the other aspects of the movie experience.

Unfortunately, my introduction to psychology-oriented film study is not ripe enough for an overarching theory and does not yet include all the necessary steps towards an empirical study of the film's psychological impact on the viewer, but it attempts to offer a blueprint of some elementary models connecting film theory and psychology and, at the same time, focussing on structures of film that probably evoke significant psychological reactions. It is to be hoped that this will be helpful in forging a path for future empirical analysis.

At present, the inclusion of concrete film examples in film studies has merely provided the opportunity to link theoretical ideas with our practical experience regarding individual films in a more palpable way. Nevertheless, the modelling of the aesthetic experience of film that I introduce here has specific advantages. To understand these peculiarities, however, it is necessary to look at some preconditions of their existence.

2. Some Elementary Ideas on Modelling the Aesthetic Experience

The prerequisites of the contemporary development of reception-oriented studies of art, including the cinema, are very complex. They have their roots in different disciplines and are, therefore, often not easy to survey for scholars of other fields of study. They have seldom been explicitly described as basic requirements for scientific progress, although most attempts have promised the greatest possible methodological transparency. Therefore, I would like to delineate some elementary theoretical positions in the development of this approach without which the whole framework could not exist.

The crucial methodological prerequisite for the analysis of art and its experience comes from different results of systems research in aesthetics and studies of art. This method is based on the idea that one can analyse the phenomena of art not only from the inside and by hermeneutically interpreting their spiritual essence, but that one can also view art phenomena as entities, as systems that can be described from the outside in their behaviour as complexes of functional structures. Such a description of functional structures leads to the construction of a scientific model, an artificial system which shows analogies with the researched object and can therefore be temporarily substituted for this original in the research process. Scientific models are not identical with the object, but due to their similarities or behavioural analogies they can systematically provide an approximation to the original and serve as aids in order to gain information about the original in such cases where other ways are not possible or not practical. For instance, one can more easily describe the complicated method of a film's storytelling by using more elementary models of narration.

During the last century, in the history of aesthetics and the theory of art, various different kinds of model were employed: elementary structural ones, semiotic ones, and cybernetic ones, which are mostly based on information processing. Belonging to the integrative sciences, the last-named models in particular systematically provide compatibility of knowledge and make it easier to construct bridges between different disciplines. Although the mentioned types of modelling developed step by step and attained to a certain extent a consecutive status, their central ideas also emerged parallel to one another. Therefore, to delineate briefly the complicated development of the system approach to art seems otiose, but focussing on the steps towards modelling of cinematic narration, I would like to emphasise three central ideas in its development for the purposes of background.

2.1 Art as a Device for Mental Stimulation: Narration as Stimulus

One fundamental approach concerning the analysis of the functions of literature and art comes from the Russian Formalists, whose work began in the 1920s at the former Petrograd/Leningrad. These scholars, particularly Boris Ejkhenbaum, Yury Tynianov and Victor Shklovsky, studied the basic rules for the functioning of art as well as the various modes and aspects of narration found in literature and film. The starting-point for their evaluation of the artwork's influence on the recipient can be characterised as "ostranenie", i.e. "defamiliarization" or "making strange". The term refers to a category of "devices" which enable the work in its entirety, as well as in detail, to intensify its psychological impact on the reader or spectator.

The keyword *ostranenie* has its roots in two terms originating in Broder Christiansen's *Philosophy of Art* (1909): the "difference-quality" (Differenzqualität) of an uncommon or innovative artistic form, which leads to a "difference-sensation" (Differenzempfindung) in the process of aesthetic experience, may be considered as the reason for the intenseness of the reader's or spectator's stimulation by the artwork. This stimulation effect helps, in the opinion of the Formalists, to destroy the tendencies of "automatization" in the recipient's perception of a work and evokes in his mind original feelings and phases of full awareness and increasing consciousness (cf. Shklovsky [1916] 1965, 11ff.).

The Constructivist approach to *ostranenie* turned out to be very productive, because it connected a structural offer to the recipient with a functional one, a decision concerning form with a psychological effect. It returned to the principle of originality dominating the traditional aesthetic ideas of the last centuries, but also employed to a basic conception of psychological stimulation and mental activities. By applying the principle of originality radically to all levels of art analysis, the Formalists upgraded it into an axiom: Striking originality leads to defamiliarization and in this way to aesthetic perception (cf. Wuss 1989a).

One can find a similar model in a recent theory of perception. According to James Gibson (1979, 249), perception is generally based on a "pick-up of information" provoked by so-called "affordances" of reality, mainly of those coming from new or uncommon stimuli patterns. Following this general approach to perception, the accordance of formal difference-quality and psychological difference-sensation of art reception can be seen as a provoked pick-up of information, i.e. as a source or starting-point for mental activities, particularly cognitive ones on the level of perception.

The exponents of Russian Formalism who applied the model of active aesthetic experience to the problem of storytelling tried to describe different modes of narration in literature (cf. Striedter 1988) and film (cf. Beilenhoff 2005), often in order to evaluate peculiarities, historical changes and complete shifts in approaches to narration. In doing so, they stressed the fact that narration, with its specific "devices", is always involved in processes of psychological stimulation.

Of course, in the 1920s, the activities of the mind evoked by artworks were only known insufficiently, and therefore the Formalists' references to psychology remained rather theoretical. But half a century later, the situation had changed. Following its turn to cognitive psychology, this discipline reached a new level of development.

In the same years, it is possible to see parallel progress in the study of art and aesthetics.

2.2 Artwork as "Proposal for Reception": Narration as Structured Reception Proposal

This research temporarily named here 'Reception Theory' covers a wide range of very different activities, including Information Aesthetics (Max Bense, 1954-1960, Abraham Moles, 1958, Helmar Frank, 1959, 1964, 1965), the Constance School of reception aesthetic (Wolfgang Iser, 1972, Robert Jauss, 1970) and their opposite numbers and critics from the Academy of Sciences in East Berlin (Manfred Naumann et. al., 1976); further, the Leningrad School of complex research of art and literature (Boris Mejlach, 1977). Terry Eagleton's (1983) overview of some important positions of this international stream includes also Roland Barthes and Stanley Fish. This list can be extended to include Yuri Lotman and Umberto Eco, scholars whose famous work is linked with the development of 'The Semiotics of Culture'.

The outstanding contributions of these different schools of

reception aesthetics undoubtedly deserve a more careful and detailed acknowledgement than I can give here, but in regard to the genesis of contemporary modelling of cinematic narration, I will elaborate on only a few aspects.

It is important to state here that all of the theories used are more or less explicitly based on the communication model, which allows the study of experience of art as communication and an information process coming from the author and his creative activities of art production, via the artwork and a specific reception phase of the recipient's, i.e. reader's or spectator's, mind (cf. Mejlach 1977, 145).

Focussing on the later relationships in this chain means a revaluation of the reception process and the viewer's mental activities. This is important for a differentiated understanding of the connections between the artwork's performance as well as its psychological impact, because one can study the aesthetic function of an artwork as a process of communication, semiotics or information. The mentioned directions of research sought to do this.

According to Naumann (1976, 35), one can generally regard the artwork as a "proposal for reception" (Rezeptionsvorgabe) structured by the author and programming the response of the viewer. This formula also allows us to describe narration as a central component of these reception proposals in a structured way. In the realm of information theory, one attempted to describe, for instance, the process of storytelling as a message which contains components of innovation as well as of redundancy. Or, according to semiotics, as a pattern, using signs of different codes and hierarchic levels. Such basic structures of narration as the classic plot could be interpreted as so-called "super-signs". The convergence of central ideas of semiotics and information theory made it easier to join them together with the paradigm of 'Information Psychology,' a precursor of contemporary 'Cognitive Psychology'.

For example, simple but of important consequences is the hypothesis of information aesthetics that the mind of the recipient has a limited access capability because the working memory serves as a channel with a specific capacity for information flow from outside to the conscious mind (cf. Frank 1959, 50ff.; 1965, 357). An optimal aesthetic experience depends, probably, on a rate of information flow which ensures that the channel is neither over-utilized nor under-utilized. Certainly, techniques of storytelling have to do with this management of information flow, and consequently the evaluation of structures of narration can be based on rules of information processing. However, these rules are hardly obvious. An important goal of psychological research is connected with the establishment of a theory of learning.

2.3 Reception of Art as a Process of Learning and Cognition: Narration as Generating Cognitive Structures

In the 1960s, psychologists focused on adaptive processes and developed a general concept of learning that could also be used for the modelling of art reception. According to this theory, one can view learning as "the formation or rectification of individual memory store" (Klix 1971, 348).

During a lifelong process within society, an individual will always strive to optimise his or her behaviour in order to best cope with conditions in his/her environment. Individual memory is regarded as an internal model or schema of the world outside, described by Dieter Langer (1962, 14) as follows: "With regard to the totality of environmental occurrences, we look upon our knowledge of 'what is connected with what' and 'what follows after what' as the expression of a pattern of expectations of (what might be called) stochastic nature."

This internal model is normally updated and improved through the individual's confrontations with objective reality, but it can also be updated in modified form by art reception, for instance by watching a film which, being depictive in character, offers a fictional reality. In the case of both practical confrontations with life and fictional confrontations with art, the events depicted are not chaotic, but structured, linked by certain rules to learnable patterns. Therefore, film reception can be seen as a learning process, programmed by the work's structures. These structures can be discerned on many different levels of a film. They constitute a kind of network, sometimes clearly visible and sometimes less so, representing the overall composition. There have been various attempts to use this network for a descriptive model of narration.

The most effective attempt, 'Cognitive Film Theory' as

developed by David Bordwell in the 1980s, relies on a specific type of learnable structures which are particularly clear and obvious, one can also say: highly significant, ratio-morph and given to thinking. Declaring himself in favour of "Neoformalism" (cf. Thompson 1988, 29), Bordwell connects some principles of the Russian school with the new paradigm of cognitive psychology, i.e., the information processing approach. In his famous book *Narration in the Fiction Film* (1985), Bordwell pioneered the cognitive theory of film examining the perceptual and cognitive aspects of film viewing. The basic premise of his treatise is "that narration is the central process that influences the way spectators understand a narrative film" (Buckland 2002, 170). Moreover, he argues "that spectators do not simply absorb a finalized, pre-existing narrative, but must actively construct its meaning" (170). Indeed, Bordwell defines: "In the fiction film, *narration is the process whereby the film's syuzhet and style interact in the course of cueing and channeling the spectator's construction of the fabula*"(1985, 53; emphasis in original). According to Bordwell, the *fabula* is "a pattern which perceivers of narratives create through assumptions and inferences" (49).

Returning to the theory of learning from the 60s, one can say that narration is a process which uses and develops the "patterns of expectation" in the spectator's mind. The spectator wants to know about the direction of events. He wants to foresee the solution of the conflicts. And, involved in this endeavour to anticipate the events, he permanently generates hypotheses and inferences concerning the current dramatic decisions and the flow of the story.

The viewer's expectations are based on his life-experience and particularly on his knowledge, and the most important principle for the construction of expectation patterns seems to be the law of causality. Human beings are not able to survive without an appropriate dealing with the causal relationships in their environment. They have to foresee possible causal chains in order to cope with their situation at different levels. Therefore the principle of causality is highly relevant for storytelling and its understanding, and Bordwell's model of cinematic narration is mainly reliant upon specific cases of causality. Buckland has noted: According to Bordwell, "narrative films cue spectators to generate inferences or hypotheses—but not just any inferences. When comprehending a narrative film, one schema in particular guides our hypotheses—the one that represents the canonical story format" (2002, 170).

This canonical story format has been well-known since the time of Aristotle's *Poetics*. It is the causal chain of situations which creates specific norms or conventions for the construction of classical drama:

Introduction of setting and character — explanation of a state of affairs —complicating action/crisis — ensuing events —outcome—ending.

In the case of the classical plot, the rational schema of linear causality on the screen works together efficiently with the most common experience of the spectator, where cause-and-effect schemata dominate everyday life. Narration has been seen as a process generating specific cognitive structures, which occur as hypotheses and inferences regarding the flow of actions. Thus, the cognitive approach, founded on hypothesis and inference generation, could already explain a very important mode of cinematic narration in the first phase of its development. However, the subject of the analysis was then mostly film comprehension, or more precisely, the consciously perceived structures of storytelling. The advantages of the cognitive approach of this period consisted in the rational transparency of its models. Its limits, however depended on the fact that only certain modes of storytelling were suitable for their adequate representation and modelling, namely those whose structural description was practicable. According to George Mandler (1984a, 112ff.), we become aware of many relationships only through their structural description. In the case of cinematic storytelling, this chance for awareness occurs mainly owing to descriptions of causal connections between events. Where cause-and-effect relations are lacking, an analytical grasp of the process of storytelling becomes very difficult and requires additional efforts. Regarding the opposition between Hollywood's classical narrative and some other forms of storytelling, Bordwell (1989b, 27) points out: "By contrast, the tradition of 'art-cinema' narration encourages the spectator to perceive ambiguities of space, time and causality and then organize them around schemata for authorial commentary and 'objective' and 'subjective' realism (Bordwell 1985). The claim is that in order for films to be composed in the way they are and to produce the effects they do, some such mental representations must underpin spectatorial activity." Yet there are numerous modes of filmic storytelling which develop the aforementioned tradition of art cinema, and some of them have played an important role in the history of film culture.

However, the difficulties in analysing different modes of storytelling cannot be reduced solely to the issue of their structural description. In order to judge narrational processes in a more differentiated way, one should examine them in a closer context to other aspects of film dramaturgy and style, which would lead to a considerable widening of the present cognitive theory of narration.

In addition, the so-called cognitive approach in psychology is now changing, and our cognitive film theory, which is founded on its principles, has come to a shift. Figuratively speaking, the cognitive model was the Trojan horse of the film theorists for invading the viewer's mind. Today, the occupants of the horse's belly are leaving this place to swarm out and explore the unknown areas of perception, emotion, imagination, play and so on. A study of film experience has begun that does more justice to the psychological complexity of its aesthetic impact.

Under these conditions the profile of the cognitive approach is changing entirely. The former explicit rationality of cognitive processes, with their "obligatory consciousness," gives way to a weaker notion that also covers initial stages of conceptualisation and consciousness, connected, for instance, with the viewer's preconscious activities of perception or attention. At the same time, it tends to encroach on the systems of emotion, imagination and play.

At present, it sometimes seems that film psychology should follow the trend of diluting the notion of cognition or even abandoning the cognitive track. But this would be unproductive, insofar as human life is based on rational behaviour, and the mental functions that are subordinated to this purpose can find their optimal description through the model of information processing— the core of the cognitive approach.

As matters stand today, it would be than presumptuous to try to develop our studies of cinematic narration and their different components of impact into a consistent theory. This leads to the issue of how to realise a productive analysis of the subject under the current circumstances.

3. Some Intentions of this Book

My study relies upon a kind of double strategy, insofar as it attempts, on the one hand, to argue as closely as possible to film practice, and, on the other, to follow a heuristics based on a differentiated cognitive approach.

Among the immediate practical issues with which filmmakers and theorists are confronted in their daily work are, for example: How can we objectify our impressions of filmic events of a lower degree of awareness by structural descriptions, and why does it help our understanding of film experience? What is happening in storytelling, and how may we describe the cognitive structure of different modes of cinematic narration? What role does the principle of conflict play for the narrational process, and what are the ensuing consequences of the conflict situations on the screen for the viewers' cognitions and, above all, for their emotions? Further: What is cinematic tension, i.e., suspense, and how do different strategies of narrative tension work in various types of film? What is the essence of the so-called "reality effect" in fiction films and how can it vary in different modes of storytelling? How does the integration of the protagonists' dreams, fantasies and play behaviour work in the course of events for storytelling and also for the development of the viewers' imageries and intentions? And finally: How do film genres function, particularly regarding the viewers' cognition, imagination and emotion?

A deeper understanding of some aspects of dramaturgy should already emerge in the use of a differentiated model of cognitive schema formation which allows the recognition of various structures with a specific narrational function, among them those with lower awareness, which the spectator receives rather pre-consciously or nonconsciously. The cognitive model helps also to explain how conflict situations and discrepancies on the screen engage the viewer in creative thinking and problem-solving. And the emergence of cognitive schemata on the level of stereotyping also renders explicable the way in which genres, which develop in a specific phase of cultural learning or stereotyping, may occur and function in the process of film experience.

The cognitive schema approach is connected with a heuristics that directs attention to the dynamics in the narrational process, insofar as it stresses the principle of innovation manifested in the film's aesthetic message. An aesthetic message has to offer a representation of the world which shows it in a new way, a "difference-quality" from the viewer's prevailing experience. Art experience is always a challenge for the recipient, since it tends to call into question his view of life. It tends to change his internal model of the outer world, and thus, to initiate the jeopardization of the common world-model.

This interpretation of aesthetic stimuli converges with an up-to-date concept of information which seeks its orientation less in the statistical notion developed by Shannon and Weaver (1949) than in the tendency to its "semantic widening" (cf. Bischof 1999, vii ff.). The crucial question is, what significance do the signals have for the receiver with regard to the change in his information store? (cf. Anochin 1963, 150.) Information can be considered as the "change potential" of the message, and definable, for instance, by the length of a program for transformation (cf. Kolmogorov 1965, 7 ff.). Although this concept is close to the trivial understanding of information, despite all simplifications, it does not seem to be misleading. Moreover, in our context, the formula of "change potential" may help to recognize some analogies in different aesthetic theories which should provide bridging-points from art-studies to psychology: Thus, we can already find the principle of "change potential" in the older German aesthetic concept of "originality" (cf. Wuss 1998a); in Christiansen's terms "difference-quality" and "difference-sensation"; in the device of "defamiliarization" developed by the Russian formalists; and also in the central ideas of Bense's and Moles' Information Aesthetics of the 1960s which accentuated the moment of innovation in the functioning of art.

In emphasising this principle of change potential for the understanding of cinematic narration, the book brings strongly into play an approved concept of European studies of theatre and film, which is connected with the notion of "conflict". The experience of conflict situations always has to do with an explicit calling into question of the spectator's view of life, his philosophy and attitudes to action. And at the same time, focusing on conflict situations yields an opportunity to better relate the cognitive approach to the viewers' emotions, because a central supposition of the book sees the source of the viewers' arousals, affections and emotions in the conflicts and discrepancies shown on the screen. The respective chapters on conflict and emotion, narrative tension and suspense, and on the different effects of genres such as comic estrangement, tragic catharsis and dramatic pathos, develop these ideas. The focusing of such effects also provides the chance to verify hypotheses about arousals and emotions elicited by films empirically. In this way, the heuristics, which emphasises the "change potential" of the film, leads to significant alterations in the viewers' mind which are psychologically relevant and often measurable.

Although this study does not elaborate this principle to organize the entire text more systematically, I hope that the occasional references to the above-mentioned analogies may help the reader to independently recognize some connections more closely.

Because of the inadequate general state of research, unfortunately, my considerations on the problem-complex of the viewers' imageries, including their interests, wishes and hopes, must remain fragmentary, though these mental activities play an important role in the experiencing of filmic events and particularly the outcomes of the story. Therefore I have only cautiously begun to approach these subjects from their periphery, via the representation of dreams, the play behaviour of the characters and the construction of possible worlds on which genres are based.

But the central issue among all these considerations and excursions into different thematic fields is the problem of storytelling and its analysis, particularly modes of narration beyond the classical causal chain. We need a deeper understanding of the fact that there are very different ways of storytelling which are based on various narrational structures, all with the potential to be received by the spectator as coherent and meaningful stories.

At the outset, we must recall that modes of storytelling are frequently based on relationships which are less noticeable than the causal chain, and therefore perceived by the viewer on a nearly unconscious level, for instance such types of storytelling as those called "plot-less", "episodic", "epic" or "open". Often they work well, too. Some personal styles and entire group styles in the history of film are dominated by them. The Italian Neorealists, for instance, eschewed the plot story. The "Cinéma du comportement" (J. Daniol-Valcroze, quoted in Leprohon 1964, 128) or "Cinema of behaviour", practised in the 1960s by Michelangelo Antonioni, Alain Resnais, Eric Rohmer and Jacques Rivette, dispensed with striking causal chains; the Documentary Style of fiction film in Eastern European countries rejected the classical plot as well, and likewise some outstanding directors of American Independent Film from John Cassavetes to Jim Jarmusch. It seems that these examples of a plot-less or non-narrative film are also able to achieve a specific kind of coherence as well. Theorists have to acknowledge this fact and examine the reasons for it, i.e. to detect the possibilities of narrative functions beyond the causal chain. This is useful, as well, for analysing another type of film story that does not follow a schema of linearity bound to clearly arranged events, but rather knots, in a complicated manner, phases of real actions and mental occurrences, for instance individual remembrances, spiritual reflections, or dreams.

And finally, there is a huge group of films that submit to a specific genre whose conventions do not rely on the causal chain of events; for example, some sorts of comedy or musical. In the interest of filmmaking and theory, justice must be done to all these different kinds of storytelling. That also means, not to evaluate such films as an inferior kind of movie, but to acknowledge their potential for aesthetic impact. However, to examine the possibilities for coherence based on storytelling beyond the traditional causal chain, one needs a psychological model for the description of the films' structural relations, including those that are inconspicuous and will be received by the spectator in a relatively unconscious manner.

Chapter I: The PCS Model of Filmic Structures

1. Different Phases of Cognition

The psychological model proposed here allows systematic access to all modes of narration based on various interactions between consciously and unconsciously experienced film structures. As previously mentioned, these structures are the result of learning or cognition. The formation or rectification of individual memory store, which psychologists in the 1960s interpreted as a general learning process, was later seen more as generation of cognitive schemata.

David Rumelhart wrote: "According to schema theories, all knowledge is packed into units. These units are the schemata. Embedded in these packets of knowledge is, in addition to the knowledge itself, information about how this knowledge is to be used. A schema, then, is a data structure for representing the generic concepts stored in memory. There are schemata representing our knowledge about all concepts: those underlying objects, situations, events, sequences of events, actions and sequences of actions" (1980, 34).

It is highly important to understand that cognitive schemata are not monolithic entities at the same level of abstraction. The same author pointed out: "Schemata represent knowledge at all levels of abstraction" (Rumelhart/Ortony 1977, 40), and his colleague George Mandler (1984a, 112) emphasised that schemata could vary on a scale from very concrete to very abstract. This distinction is indispensable for understanding human cognition as a process that includes different levels of schema formation.

Since these processes are ongoing in the mind, we cannot usually observe the progress of information processing following the change of levels from a lower to a higher step of abstraction. But a well-known sequence from Antonioni's film *Blow Up* (1966) gives a very impressive illustration of these cognitive processes:

The film shows a young photographer, who, during a shooting in a park, incidentally takes pictures of a middle-aged couple. After having developed the film, he becomes aware that the woman in some pictures is very attentively looking at a place outside the frame, and he begins to search for the reason for her interest. He tries to reconstruct her focal point and her line of sight, which leads to some shrubs; but only after a longer procedure that includes a blow-up of the photo of the shrubs does he discover some strange lines or forms amongst their leaves. An increasing interest in the represented facts prompts him to return to the darkroom, and thanks to a further blow-up, he is able to perceive between the leaves the clear form of a revolver aiming at the woman's partner. After having detected the form of the weapon on the bigger photo, the hero can conceptualise the fact and acknowledge the threat. In this way, the film sequence gives evidence of a dangerous situation in the past, and, at the same time, of the active, step-by-step perceptive process and the subsequent phase in which the conceptualisation of the object takes place in the hero's mind. A series of photographs shows the different phases in the process of cognition (see fig. 1).

An understanding of these steps from sensation and perception to conceptualisation and thinking, from concreteness to abstractness of cognitive schemata, is highly important for the modelling of film reception, because a film does not merely depict structured concrete events: the events depicted are also a product of an artistic abstraction deployed upon the material, which transforms and focuses it in a particular manner and is a product of the particular interest of its author or director. This perspective is in turn a product of learning processes, of schema formation, which has taken place in the creator's own mind.

Every film appears to organise this order purposefully, even if the creator of the work is just as unaware of the overall construction process as she or he is of the result. In general, therefore, one can take the reception process that is triggered by cinematic works of art to entail adapting aspects of reality and learning the real structures with which the viewer is confronted through the artistic image. The human cognition process is like a ladder, with graduated rungs forming hierarchies of structures, and the film is able to fix their levels and to make them objective and observable.

I would like to give another example, a concrete scene of a film, in order to illustrate such rungs of abstraction in cinema: the final sequence of Theodoros Angelopoulos' film *Landscape in the Mist* (*Topio stin omichli*, 1988).

The story of this road movie is clear and simple. Two fatherless children, a girl, aged eleven, and her brother, aged six, are starting a journey. They want to go from a small town in Greece to Germany because their mother told them that their father has been working there for a long time. After a long and hard trip, they come to the border of their own country and hide there for the night to cross the badly-guarded boundary line early in the morning. The morning is foggy, and when the children set out for the other country they cannot see anything. But in search of their aim they notice little by little a grey and vague form like a shadow behind the fog. A moment later, they realize that the grey shadow is the silhouette of a big tree. They walk to the tree and after reaching it they embrace its trunk.

The viewer of this sequence shares the experience of the children. In the first phase he has to make out the object behind the fog in a process of perception. In the second phase he is able to conceptualise the object and to recognize that it is a tree, having a notion of the stimuli configuration. In the third phase the tree acquires a deeper meaning; it becomes a kind of symbol, connected with a well known cultural sign, a stereotype: It seems that in embracing the tree the children embrace the father. The tree becomes the hoped-for father.

2. A Cognitive Model for Description of Cinematic Structures

In this sequence, the configuration of stimuli showing a tree changes the rung of abstraction, its level of cognitive schema formation, its mental status for the viewer. Thereby, the steps of cinematic abstraction follow successively the general principles of schema formation in our mind.

The philosopher's epistemological approach also differentiates between levels of abstraction, as evidenced in its division of the formation of invariants in our cognitive apparatus into three levels of abstraction: There are formations of cognitive invariants (1) on the level of perception, (2) on the level of thought (based on concepts) and (3) on the level of conventionalised or standardised imageries such as moral norms (cf. Klaus 1966, 65)—or cultural stereotypes.

Accordingly, it is useful to attempt to identify the corresponding processes of schemata formation in the realm of film analysis if one wants to describe the nature of an entire work as stimulus configuration. The processing of information operates along one of three different paths, depending on which of the following applies:

(1) the external structure caught on film is to be appropriated by the viewer's internal model in the context of his own perceptual formation of invariants;

(2) the external structure has already had sufficient mental representation that it can be submitted to thought; or

(3) its shape has long since been formed and conventionalised into a stereotype by frequent communicative use.

It is along these lines of differentiation that three types of filmic structure may be distinguished, each corresponding to a different phase in the formation of schemata:

(1) perception-based structures;

(2) conception-based structures; and

(3) stereotype-based structures.

The sequence described shows these three types of cinematic structure in the same order. Beginning with the perception-based structure, it leads to the conception-based and later to the stereotype-based structure successively, and because they share the same configuration of stimuli, i.e. the tree, there are no clear boundaries between the three levels of abstraction or schema formation, but the tendency to stereotyping is obvious.

One can find these three types of cinematic structure everywhere in film, at the level of visual form linked, for instance, with pictures of objects in landscapes or situations, but also at the level of dramaturgy connected, for example, with conflict situations or the characters' activities. The hero's way of acting is always the basic subject of storytelling. The characters' actions form each small situation and limited sequence of a film as well as the impetus of the whole story. Therefore, they have a fundamental influence on the structuring of narration. Since the mental status of the characters' actions can vary, it is also possible to describe different structures and strategies of cinematic narration by using the three-rungs model of film reception, the PCS model (P for perception, C for conceptualisation, S for stereotyping) (cf. Wuss 1993).

At this point we arrive at the crucial point of our considerations: One can approximate different methods of storytelling by a cognitive description of the characters' actions, beginning with small situations and sequences and ending with the modelling of the entire story construction. The principle of description is the same. But before giving a theoretical explanation to the modelling of the narrative structure of a whole film, I would like to describe 3½ minutes of a famous Polish film in order to illustrate through a short scene what is meant by this description. In doing so, I want to demonstrate that the structuring of cinematic narration can be realized not solely at the same level of schema formation but in parallel and in a synchronic order at different ones, for instance on all three rungs of the PCS model.

The opening scene from Andrzej Wajda's *Ashes and Diamonds* (*Popiół i diament*, 1958) depicts an event which takes place at the end of the Second World War, more precisely in the first hours of peace in May 1945. To understand the scene, you have to know that during the war two military groups of Polish soldiers fought against the Germans: one was the People's Army, with headquarters in Moscow and connected with the Soviet Red Army; the other, the Homeland Army, with its headquarters in London, which fought under the leadership of the exiled group of the bourgeois National Polish government and was linked with the Western Allies. During the first years of the war, both Polish armies had the same aim, to conquer the army of Nazi Germany, and therefore they cooperated well; but at the time of victory their opposing political interests concerning the future of Poland became obvious, and the two military groups became enemies in a sort of civil war. The opening scene of the film shows such a civil war situation. Three men, soldiers in the Homeland Army, but dressed in plain clothes, attempt to assassinate the District Secretary of the communist Workers' Party. How can this sequence be described using the PCS model?

2.1 From Conception-based Filmic Structures to the Causal Chain of Narration

One can begin with the types of structure which are most evident and therefore have been included most often in more traditional models proposed by film theorists. I refer to the conception-based structures commonly termed "the causal chain" of events.

They constitute the main development of the action. In the sequence in question, the three soldiers of the Homeland Army, attempting to assassinate the party official, kill the passengers in an off-road vehicle. Seemingly, a conflict between two politically opposing groups is at issue here. The collision of interest leads to a process which the viewer notes and becomes conscious of, and retains in his long-term memory. This happens not only on the basis of the crude form of the events—the brutal physical extermination of the opponent—but also because a cyclic unity of actions with a clearly defined goal has become apparent. An attack is planned and then carried out—putting to death the passengers of the car one after another.

Certain plot points are thus marked and constitute the turning-points of the action. The film marks these with the blood of those who have been murdered. It is at these points that the intensity of the story increases, since certain points of resistance within the conflict become apparent to the viewer. On the other hand, the plot points emphasise phases in the viewer's problem-solving process concerning the conflict decisions on the screen, and initiate cognitive activity in his mind. Thus stable patterns of expectation come into being and lead to the creation of firm hypotheses regarding the unfolding of future events in the story, which in turn lead to a conceptualisation of the entire process and its phases. In retrospect a strong causal chain of significant events seems to have been formed. It is perceived consciously, is passed on to thought processes and is easily recalled from memory.

The conflict between the political enemies not only occupies the centre of this opening sequence, it perpetuates itself, in that the assassins did not shoot their political opponents but rather a group of workers who happened to pass through. Thus they must repeat the attack under new historical conditions, a development which forms the plot of the rest of the film.

The film in its entirety shows how its protagonist Maciek, a young soldier of the Homeland Army, continues to follow the law of war and the commands of this Army on the first day of peace, and murders—in spite of doubts and misgivings—the communist functionary, until he himself is killed.

If a conceptualised causal chain of significant events is extended throughout an entire film, it becomes a basic structure of narration.

As early as 1769, the German playwright Lessing, making reference to Aristotle, termed processes such as these "chains of cause and effect" (1954, 65), which make up the *fabula* of a work. The mode of narration based on this classical causal chain fabula, which in the Aristotelian sense is made up of the beginning, middle and ending of a story, leads to the so-called plot and is still considered by many filmmakers a necessary condition of cinematic narration.

From Aristotle's *Poetics* to Hollywood's mainstream productions the plot seems to be the most important mode of narration or even the only one. But there are also other possibilities of storytelling based on relationships which are less noticeable and therefore perceived by the viewer on a less conscious level.

2.2 From Perception-based Filmic Structures to Topic Lines

We now come to less apparent and almost unconsciously or preconsciously perceived relationships, those of the perception-based structures which can lead to a basic structure of narration, the topic line.

In the sequence in question, topic lines may be located primarily in the "microstructures of narration". The events are broken down into shots which express the repeated disruption of purposeful action. Nearly all parts of this scene have one thing in common: goal-oriented actions are hindered, discontinued, or require reorientation (see: fig. 2).

- During the soldiers' preparations for the bloody attack, a little girl holding flowers suddenly appears and asks them to help her.
- When one of the men tries to help the child who is bringing the flowers into the chapel, the door is closed and the action is interrupted.

- While the man helps the child to put the flowers above the door, he suddenly hesitates because a car is approaching.
- When the protagonist wants to pick up his machine gun from the grass, his attention is distracted by ants crawling on the gun.
- While the men are looking for the best positions for shooting, the little girl is waiting near the chapel as a disturbing factor in the brutalised event, and the soldiers drive her away.
- After having fired on the car, the killers search for documents in the pockets of a dead victim, but there is nothing to be found.
- While the protagonist is shooting at another occupant of the car, he has to change the magazine of his gun, which had not been loaded properly.
- When the third assassin, who seems to be unarmed, wants to stop the runaway, he fails and performs ridiculous movements with his arms like a farmer scaring away a chicken.
- And when the protagonist finally shoots his victim at the chapel's front door, he does so in such an unrestrained manner that his companions must push his gun up to stop him from firing.
- It is more than mere coincidence that one of the men loses his hat as they leave the scene of the action (not unlike the manner of a slapstick comedy), for nothing occurs in this scene that is not marked by disturbance or interruption.

In this three-minute sequence one can detect nearly a dozen such disturbances, and similar patterns of disturbance continue throughout the entire film.

Through the continual repetition of specific patterns of behaviour, the presence of a predominant contradiction is articulated: it becomes apparent that it is not possible to perform purposeful actions at this particular historical junction. To make this clear to the viewer on a perceptual level, it is necessary that the same sensory pattern or stimuli configuration should be repeated numerous times in a single given film in order to allow the formation of cognitive invariants on the level of perception.

As a result of the viewer's continual confrontation with similar filmic structures, i.e. complex patterns of stimuli, cognitive invariants on a perceptual level are formed, leading to meaning construction. I call these structures "filmic topics" and "filmic topic lines" respectively because, for the cinematic narration, the topics function only in a serial manner—that is, by the repetition of similar patterns at certain intervals. Analogously to the plot lines of classical causal chains, the topic lines organize the narrative process, though on a lower level, of the cognitive schema formation. Since these notions are not common as technical terms in the framework of media studies and can therefore be misunderstood, particularly by Anglo-American readers, I would like to clarify their theoretical background, which I have described elsewhere in more detail (Wuss 1993, 137–139).

The chosen terms are in accordance with the notion of "topic" used by Umberto Eco, Roland Barthes and other authors in the framework of linguistics and the theory of literature. Eco (1987, 109) pointed out the dual roots of his term, explaining that it is based on the English synonym for "theme" and also on the Greek word "topos" for "place," which denotes a category of ancient rhetoric. Years earlier, Roland Barthes (1994, 64–66) had introduced a modern interpretation of the term *topos* which also refers to its plural form. What is meant are the *topoi*, certain places or points in a speech returning repeatedly to a similar theme for reasons of better rhetorical argumentation and the coherence of the entire address.

Eco, who dealt with the issue of topic regarding verbal texts in several papers, assumed that a text follows the directions of various topics:

"It is imprudent to speak of *one* textual topic. In fact, a text can function on the basis of various embedded topics. There are first all *sentence* topics; *discursive* topics at the level of short sequences can rule the understanding of microstructural elements, while *narrative* topics can rule the comprehension of the text at higher levels. Topics are not always explicit. Sometimes these questions are manifested at the first level, and the reader simply cooperates by reducing the frames and by blowing up the semantic properties he needs. Sometimes there are topic-markers such as titles. But many other times the reader has to guess where the real topic is hidden. Frequently, a text establishes its topic by reiterating blatantly a series of sememes belonging to the same semantic field (*key words*). In this case these sememes are obsessively reiterated throughout the text. At other times, on the contrary, these sememes cannot be statistically detected because, rather than being abundantly distributed, they are *strategically located*. In these cases the sensitive reader, feeling something unusual in the *dispositio*, tries to make abductions (that is, to single out a hidden rule or regularity) and to test them in the course of his further reading" (1979, 26). The author continues: "In either case the topic directs the right amalgamations and the organization of a single level of sense, or isotopy. Greimas (1970) calls *isotopy* 'a redundant set of semantic categories which make possible the uniform reading of a story' (p.188)." Following Eco (1979, 27) "topics are means to produce isotopies."

According to the topic, the reader decides whether he has to blow up or to narcotize the semantic properties of the lexemes of the given text; thus he defines a level of "interpretative coherence" named isotopy (Eco 1987, 114).

In my opinion, one can modify this notion of topic for film studies: Filmic topics are elements of entire topic lines which lead to the construction of meaning by the repetition of similar structures or stimulus patterns. On the one hand, these topics contribute to the establishment of cognitive schemas on the level of perception; on the other hand, analogously to the principle of isotopy in verbal texts, they provide semantic linking and interpretative coherence between the single elements of the topic line. This can be considered as the construction of a narrative relationship, as the establishing of a possible basic structure of narration with specific functions and characteristics—as will be discussed in the next chapter. I have quoted Eco's ideas at some length in order to emphasise that there are several analogies between the organization of topics in verbal and filmic texts. Both deal with the construction of meaning by the formation of individual elements and whole series of them, both can be used synchronically in multiple parallel arrangements, and both can exist in a different manner with more obvious topics as well as hidden elements which the reader or spectator has to find out by abductions.

Following van Dijk, Eco (1987, 114) calls the topic an "aboutness", i.e. revolving about something, and he interpretes the "topic" in a trivial manner: "The topic is a hypothesis which depends on the activities of the reader who formulates it in an undifferentiated manner as a question ('What the hell is it about?') and consequently translates it in a proposal for a temporary expression ('Probably it is about this and that')."

The disturbances in Wajda's film are such topics, which lead to a focussing of attention and the renewed cognitive activation of the viewer, causing him to search progressively for further topics—an entire topic line—in the film.

Although this is the case in Wajda's film, here the topic line plays a more complementary role alongside the causal chain, in that the topic line emphasises the disturbances of the particular historical moment. The perception-based structures are fully embedded in the construction of meaning realised by the concept-based ones and remain, therefore, more or less unnoticed by the audience. Cooperating semantically, both types of structure serve to strengthen each other, and in such cases their distinct description often makes no sense for the analyst.

But the description of similar perception-based structures and the modelling of topic lines can be of crucial importance for a film analysis when traditional plot-oriented narration is dissolved and there is no narrative structure based on a causal chain. This is particularly true in modes of storytelling termed "episodic", "epic", "open" or "plot-less".

In this way, the viewer's attention follows a series of similar stimuli configurations which construct invariants of perception in his mind. These invariant structures are not striking and their experience remains more or less unconscious to the viewer, but, nevertheless, their analogical "semantic gesture" (Mukařovský 1974, 49) is always at work and thus the structures become more obvious and more conscious with frequent repetition.

The psychologist James Gibson defines perception as "learning what to attend to", focusing on the "pick-up of invariants". At these points perceptual learning begins, which Gibson refers to as a "continuous practice" that "purposefully directs attention to the information contained in the stimuli" (1973, 329). In my opinion, the topic line prepares systematically such a pick-up of invariants of perception in the process of film reception—and we will see later that the so-called "perceptual cycle" (Neisser 1976, 20ff.) works to create a cognitive activation that helps to link filmic events without causal relationships. Since a conception-based causal chain is absent or scarcely evident, the viewer's attentiveness and his expectations are drawn towards the same "aboutness". Thus, the basic structure of narration, the "topic line", can generate coherence.

2.3 From Stereotype-based Filmic Structures to Stereotypes of Narration

The third type of structure is the filmic stereotype. In the opening sequence of Wajda's film one first notices separate shots or stereotypical images. The film begins with the idyllic image of a chapel in the spring sunshine with the song of a lark and the sounds of an ocarina in the background—not to mention the flower-picking child. And the sequence ends with a farmer ploughing his fields.

Each of these images conforms to certain familiar notions which the viewer has acquired in the process of acculturation, before the film presents them to him once again. Such familiar conceptualised forms have been repeated often in communicative usage and have thus acquired a sign-like character. They are stored in the type of long-term memory termed tertiary memory (Schmidt/Thews 1985, 180) and apparently cannot be forgotten. Therefore they call up standardized subprograms of mental reaction, rigid expectations, stereotypical patterns, stable emotions or even conventionalised evaluations of the events.

In our cultural system the visual stereotypes mentioned above function to signify profound peace, which is interrupted by the assassination. When shots are fired at the fleeing men, this happens to take place in front of the chapel. The door to the chapel is thrown open by the gunfire revealing the image of the Madonna behind the dead, declaring the events a sacrilege. In spite of the self-evidence of the stereotypes, which construct a clear opposition (peace vs. violence), the viewer only perceives them inadvertently or unconsciously.

The term "stereotype" is applied here in a neutral manner. It denotes the result of an advanced phase of information processing or cognitive schema formation which can be achieved through various stimulus patterns used in the field of media communication. From these, then, emerge larger units of information and effects of redundancy. Insofar as one can describe structural patterns in film corresponding with the above-mentioned mental and cultural state within the different aspects of their shaping, it makes sense to model them as cinematic stereotypes at the levels of formation of character, conflict, photography, sound, montage and, of course, narration.

Film practice and theory has known of these phenomena for a long time, but mostly under different names, for instance, under the term of "archetype" developed by C.G. Jung (1990). Thus, Federico Fellini quite consciously, in *8½* (1963) (see chapter VII), employed the archetypes of "the child", "the earth-mother", "the maiden" (Kore). In my understanding, the archetype is a specific kind of stereotype.

Another specific case is the social type that one can find in the early films of Eisenstein *Strike* (*Stachka*, 1925), *The Battleship Potemkin* (*Bronenosets Potyomkin*, 1925) and *October* (*Oktyabr*, 1928).

Historic persons such as Spartacus and Robin Hood, Nero and Hitler can become stereotype characters of the movies, and there are fictional characters of mass culture such as Sherlock Holmes, Tarzan, Superman or James Bond that have gained this status. Hollywood has developed a whole group of "stock characters" (see Loukides/Fuller 1990).

Conflicts can function in a comparable way. There are archetypic conflict situations such as "imprisonment" or "unequal fight" (David vs. Goliath), but also those based on real conflicts as between generations, classes or races, including historic events such as wars or revolts.

In regard to camera work, the process of stereotyping creates key images. When in *The Battleship Potemkin* a woman holds her mortally wounded son on the "Odessa Steps", the biblical image of the Pietà comes to the spectator's mind. When the child protagonists in the finale of *Landscape in the Mist* embrace the tree the viewer associates it with the image of the father.

The dominant and repeated use of low-key lighting led to the emergence of the famous dark images of the *film noir.*

And there are particular types of sound which signify danger and horror and are used therefore in corresponding film genres, just as there are kinds of stock music expressing harmony or euphoria.

Standardised figures of montage such as crosscutting found their place in the making of wild-chase scenes or last-minute rescue sequences.

Other than these stereotype-based filmic structures, which refer to limited aspects of film form, there exist very complex structures which apply to conventionalised successions of actions that organise the narrative process. Myths and sagas, for instance the Orpheus myth, the Passion of Jesus Christ, or the Golden Nail (cf. Schweinitz 2006, 93ff.) exemplify this. But there are also archetypical situations such as "the escape", "the setting-out for the promised land", "the love triangle" and others, which Eco (1989b, 295–300) has noticed in Michael Curtiz' *Casablanca* (1942) in a cluster.

If stereotype-based clusters of events are superimposed upon an entire film, it too becomes a basic structure for narration, a stereotype of narration. Referring to the Greek tragedies, which were based on familiar myths, the dramatist Dürrenmatt said: "The audience knew what was going on, they were not as curious about the subject-matter as they were about the way it was treated" (1955, 13). This is an extremely salient description of the principle of cerebral efficiency behind the use of stereotypes: when the sub-program is set in motion, it is easier to gain access to the information in an entire drama or film. At the same time, stereotype structures generate coherence of narration.

We commonly encounter such structures in the form of myths or "canonical stories" which give form to the conventions of narration used by classical or popular genres. They are familiar to the viewer even before he actually views a work of this kind. Following Bakhtin, literary theory calls genre "the representative of creative memory in the process of literary development" (1972, 179). It is certainly true that literary genres (and theatre and cinema will not be much different) are relatively stable in their structure and function. Thus one can regard the entire phenomenon of genre as a stereotype of a higher degree, integrating more elementary stereotyped structures of dramaturgy or visual style during a longer cultural process.

Wajda's film makes use of a narrative stereotype derived from a classical genre, the character-based tragedy. Besides the external conflict between the two groups of people who represent different political tendencies, the film's story unfolds an intra-personal conflict located in the personality of the protagonist. It consists of the young soldier's desire to remain true to himself, even though the historical conditions defining the context of action have changed. On the first day of peace he can no longer use his weapon without pangs of doubt. The director Wajda (1964, 357) considers Maciek's conflict unresolvable in that the hero, at the hour of historical change, can neither follow the rules of war nor those of peace. When he finally shoots the communist functionary, in spite of his own reservations, he is unavoidably brought to the brink of tragedy. In accordance with the genre of tragedy, this stereotype of narration leads to a catastrophe, and the audience perceives this outcome of the conflict as preordained and therefore as predictable. But the viewer can also understand that the protagonist fails in his decision to follow the commands of an army whose goals have become questionable because they lead the tormented people into civil war. In seven different situations during the film it is apparent that the hero is not able to resolve his inner conflict and is thus "cracking up". Already the endless spray of bullets towards the victim in front of the chapel in the very first sequence suggests that he is not quite sane.

Other genres direct their narrative stereotypes towards a positive solution, a happy ending. But I would like come back to these strategies of narration in a later chapter, because they are connected with problems of emotion and imagination that need a further explanation.

3. Description of Opening Sequences of Other Film Examples

Since the cognitive process always has the same phases of information processing, in general one can find in all works of the cinema structures representing the three levels of abstraction used for the descriptive model. This means one is able to describe each film by using the PCS model.

Of course, the structuring of the films depends on the cognitive attempts of the filmmaker, his personal way of thinking, the film's subject, the individual style of expression and so on. Therefore the clearness of the "pattern of cognitive invariance" produced by the filmmaker's articulation varies widely from one work to another. There are many formless films with, respectively, amorphous or chaotic patterns, too. Usually, however, the cognitive patterns are more or less articulated and they also function in the films' communication. In particular, opening sequences often show patterns of relative clearness. Since the opening of a film has the function of programming the information processing of the whole reception process, the first sequences serve as a kind of priming. They formulate the aesthetic rules for the following course of experience. Therefore, they vary for purposes of aesthetic originality and creative diversification.

The opening sequence of the Finnish director Aki Kaurismäki's *Ariel* (1988) shows an obvious conflict situation articulated in a conception-based structure: A mine is to be shut down and the miners are leaving their workplace. An older foreman gives the pitman Taisto, the protagonist, his car keys as a present, then commits suicide. Taking to heart the foreman's advice, Taisto takes his belongings and drives to Helsinki. But after arriving at the capital he becomes the victim of a robbery.

Besides these significant events that lead to a conceptualised causal chain as a basic structure of narration, the opening sequence shows a careful series of micro-actions with invariant perception-based structures forming a kind of topic line. All these micro-actions follow the same principle. They are marking a situation of "the game is up!", of "to be at an end", of "definitely being out" (see: fig. 3):

- Miners coming from the pit switch off the lamps;
- They take away the fuse;
- They ignite the explosives for closing the pit;
- Taisto casts off his tools;
- The miners leave the grounds;
- They lock the mines' door;
- The foreman shoots himself;
- Taisto closes his suitcase;
- At the moment of his driving away, the garage collapses;
- Taisto closes his account;
- Taisto leaves the region forever.

The spectator can always see the same signal. His perspective response is repetitive, and he can feel more and more intensely the same "semantic gesture" in different situations. But aside from the foreman's death and the garage's collapse, the viewer hardly becomes fully aware of these cues. They remain at an almost unconscious level of experience. Nevertheless, the cues are very important for the telling of this story because they hint at the likelihood of "being at an end". Indeed, the opening sequence poses the question of how the protagonist can survive in this society, and this leads to a similar plot because in Helsinki Taisto's situation will further deteriorate.

The opening sequence also includes stereotype-based structures which are obvious and form a clear sign for the viewer. Some of them are connected with specific genres. In the last phase of the sequence in particular one can find cues that the film tends to a hybrid genre, mixing the patterns and narrative structures of the social report and the road movie with tragicomedy. Often hints of actions in the realm of specific genres are sufficient for the viewers' understanding. When the foreman, after his bitter statement, loads his revolver and leaves the bistro in anger and Taisto hears a gunshot, the consequence of this series of events is so evident that Kaurismäki does not have to show the dead man at the end of the scene. The narrative stereotypes of the social report work here to ensure the right interpretation of stimuli patterns. Later, the sudden and ridiculous destruction of the garage follows in its grotesque way the stereotypes of a sub-genre of comedy. In the robbery scene at the transition to the next sequence the viewer can foresee the sad consequences of Taisto's contact with the robbers very easily because their behaviour is performed in a demonstrative and estranging way. And the end of the sequence has a touch of a road movie. While the protagonist is driving the foreman's old road cruiser, a hit-song comments on the situation. Later episodes in the capital will follow that are similar to the stations of a journey: situations of day-labourer's work, of a night-shelter, of love and family life, of prison and escape. The film uses conventionalised places and events including the viewer's expectations linked with different genre-stereotypes. In other words, all three types of cinematic structures are represented here. They are identifiable without effort and each of them seems to be pronounced.

The opening sequence of Michelangelo Antonioni's *The Passenger* (*Professione: reporter*, 1975) barely shows a conceptualised structure able to give a clear direction to the viewer concerning the goal of the protagonist's actions. A stereotype-based structure coming, for instance, from a well-known genre seems absent as well. Nevertheless, on the level of perception-based stimuli patterns the sequence is carefully structured as a series of episodes with the same invariant core:

- The film's action begins with an English journalist arriving in an African village in a jeep. He walks into a workshop containing several natives, but one after another they leave the room, evidently wanting to avoid speaking with the stranger.
- One of the Africans who has remained to receive a cigarette also leaves as the reporter looks for his lighter.
- Outside, the journalist then approaches another man who also wants to scrounge something to smoke. He, however, is no more prepared to talk than the others.
- The protagonist speaks in English and subsequently in French to a boy who has climbed into the jeep. Vague gestures in response to his questions as to the right direction only lead into a barren landscape where the boy then leaves him.
- While the journalist waits in the desert on his own, a bedouin passes by on a camel—but the rider pretends he has not seen the stranger and rides by without saying a word.
- Later, a native comes out of his nearby dwelling and takes the protagonist into the mountains. The only thing he says about the destination is that it is a kind of military camp, but he is not willing to give any more information.
- When the two have climbed a rock face and caught sight of a caravan down in the valley—something the guide had evidently not expected—they make their way back again without exchanging a word.
- The sequence ends with the hapless reporter, whose jeep is stranded in the desert. The protagonist swears at his situation—but nobody is able to hear his words.
- After having returned to the hotel, he knocks on the door of the room next to his, but there is no answer. When he enters the room, however, he sees that his neighbour lies motionless on the

bed. He turns him over as if wanting to speak to him, but a conversation is not possible because the other man is dead.

The remarkable thing about this opening sequence is that it initially consists of a situation in which viewers find it very difficult to orient themselves because they can only divine from the reporter's questions to his companion that he wants to make contact with the African Liberation Front. Although the hero's enterprise has a goal, the viewers are nevertheless kept in the dark for a long time about what the protagonist actually intends to do. In spite of this irritating situation, the viewer will be confronted again and again with episodes following the same principle: The desired communication will be disturbed, is not accomplished, comes to nothing. The semantic gesture of all these episodes expresses the same idea: The protagonist's attempts to establish contact with the natives is doomed (see fig. 4). Of course, this semantic gesture is important for the content of the story, about a reporter who, after a phase of strong engagement in the Africans' issues, loses his interest in them and becomes a sort of irresponsible passenger gambling with their vital problems.

Within the described sequence, there are instances in which this conflict situation is so evident that it begins to be conceived as a structural pattern within the film's action, for instance when the bedouin who comes riding along on his camel ignores the greeting and looks right through the lonely European in the desert. The formation of invariants of perception proceeds to the level of invariants of thought, to that of the concept-based cinematic structures that enables a much easier intellectual reflection of events. Later, one will notice that the film's story even serves standardized expectations of the audience and tends to the adventure genre by using the respective stereotypes of narration. But during the first ten minutes of the opening sequence, the storytelling is mainly based on a series of similar patterns at the level of perception, forming a kind of topic line.

4. Definitions of Three Filmic Structures: The PCS Model

The described sequences show that one can find various filmic structures representing a specific level of abstraction, a different phase of learning or cognitive schema formation, which leads to a different mental status of stimuli configuration. Three of these levels can be approximated by a model for cinematic response and filmic structures in general:

(1) perception-based, (2) conception-based and (3) stereotype-based structures, which form together the previously mentioned PCS model for hypothetical description of a film's structuring via its function in the process of experience.

Any given film may be reproduced in an approximate manner through the description of a net of structural relationships, which include, potentially, each of these three types, and one can analyse numerous phenomena of the moving image by using this three-rung model of description because film form and dramaturgy always have to do with stimuli configurations based on a specific level of cognitive schema formation. We will see later that the structures may differ (1) in their distribution, their respective form and (2) their dominance, and they may also (3) be either complementary or conflicting in their semantic tendencies.

Accordingly, this model is suitable for an approximation to different ways of storytelling, particularly for the description of various modes of narration.

In every fiction film it is possible to detect an underlying net of cinematic structures of various types, a network with—so to speak—varying sizes of mesh which can differ according to their respective combination of conspicuousness, degree of consciousness, semantic stability, the manner in which they are retained in memory and the learning strategies employed in the process of reception. But their clearest marker seems to be their different strategies regarding the principle of repetition: Perception-based structures require frequent repetition throughout the same work, while conception-based structures usually do not require any kind of repetition. Stereotype-based structures depend on the inter-textual repetition of the same form in many different works within the same cultural context.

The various structures interact with one another and thus

together form the content of the whole work, or, in other words, each functions semantically—but in a different way.

4.1 Perception-based Filmic Structures

The perception-based structures which correspond to the formation of cognitive invariants of perception are of minimal conspicuousness and can only be received preconsciously by the spectator. They are implanted in his mind at an early phase of adaptation using a process of autocorrelation or probability learning which presupposes the intra-textual repetition of similar structures. In this process of information pick-up, the minimal conspicuousness of the stimulus configuration increases only incrementally without reaching its maximum, so that no conscious experience ensues. It is not stored in the spectator's long-term memory, and the retention of the structures in the working memory makes possible a recall of information for only a very short time after watching the film. In the art-semantic process of film experience, the perception-based structures are not stable; the spectator permanently has to find out the "aboutness" of the stimuli. Nevertheless, due to the unconscious cognitive activities of the spectator, the structures have a remarkable sensuous power with consequences for meaning construction.

4.2 Conception-based Filmic Structures

The conception-based structures which correspond to the formation of cognitive invariants of thought are very conspicuous and can be consciously received by the spectator. They are the result of a progressed phase of adaptation by the spectator's mind where he disposes of enough pre-information to a represented phenomenon in order to recognise it via classified stimuli and to integrate it in his mind through learning, by free combination or spiritual reflection, in the course of which a singular appearance of a stimulus configuration is sufficient. The structure is stored in the spectator's long-term memory and can be recalled for a very long time after the film reception. In the art-semantic process of film experience, the concept-based structures are stable; they enable the spectator to derive the meaning from the stimulus configuration more or less automatically. In such a way, conception-based structures become a leading factor for the comprehension of film.

4.3 Stereotype-based Filmic Structures

From the epistemological point of view, stereotype-based structures correspond with the construction of invariants on the level of complex motifs which are the result of a progressed individual and, at the same time, social learning process, a post-adaptive state of cultural learning. At the time of reception, the spectator possesses a high grade of pre-information concerning the represented phenomena, since they are already conceptualised and their stimulus configurations are used for communication several times in the current cultural repertoire or of a previous development of arts. Owing to this inter-textual repetition, the respective stimulus pattern has become a stable cultural sign with a certain meaning which is, for specific groups of spectators, connected with standardised sub-programs of impacts, i.e. of complex mental behaviour including patterns of perception, thought, emotions, imageries and values. The learning processes of stereotypes are little researched; commonly, they show a coexistence of free combination or reflection and probability learning. Stored in the long-term memory, stereotype-based structures can hardly be forgotten, especially as a current inter-textual repetition can actualise their stimuli. Nevertheless the extent of their conspicuousness and consciousness has a wide range of variation. Commonly, a concrete stimulus pattern has reached its maximum of conspicuousness at the mental state of conceptualisation and shows, in the phase of stereotyping, a declining conspicuousness. Although stereotypes are the result of a long cognitive process, the spectator receives some of them rather casually and nonconsciously, perhaps due to a kind of habituation in respect to the used stimuli. These properties probably also have consequences for the varying semantic stability of the filmic stereotypes.

4.4 Details Concerning the Psychological Background of the Model

In order to define the PCS model that describes the different cinematic structures, film attributes, which are typically applied to individual works or entire group styles of film, are used. These attributes, formulated into everyday language, are subjected to a psychological interpretation and described into a more schematic manner that aims to facilitate the differentiation and comparison of certain aspects of their impact. Although these interpretations have a limited scope, they provide sufficient detail. The reader who is interested in detailed psychological arguments may take careful note of the following explanations, but for the understanding of the discussed film problems, one can dispense with them and pass on to the next paragraph.

4.4.1. Degree of conspicuousness
Thus, the conspicuousness of a stimulus can be represented mathematically by the degree of unexpectedness (Frank 1965, 352–355). There are experiments with elementary stimuli—an ensemble of pearls of the same colour on a background of pearls of other colours—which show, for instance, that the conspicuousness of the former increases proportionally to their relative frequency in the whole from 0 to 38 % of the entire amount, but paradoxically declines in case of a higher proportion (Frank 1964). One can find a similar curve diagram in regard to a specific filmic structure within the ensemble of others. If the spectator is confronted more frequently with the same structure, then at first its conspicuousness increases until reaching a maximum, but thereafter declines. Possibly the curve diagram corresponds to the mental status of the P, C, and S structures. The conspicuousness or unexpectedness of the same stimulus does increase until a maximum is reached—which should be in the phase of conceptualisation—and then triggers the spectator's habituation connected with the phase of stereotyping. Certainly, filmic stereotypes possess a wide range of conspicuousness. There are very striking stereotypes, yet there are also those which remain nearly invisible.

4.4.2. Degree of consciousness
The level of conspicuousness seems to be closely connected with the degree of consciousness gained by a filmic structure. Unfortunately, psychology does not have generally accepted terms for the various qualities in the scale between conscious and unconscious. In order to differentiate the corresponding qualities of the filmic structures described by the PCS model, I have used the terms: (1) "preconscious", (2) "conscious", (3) "nonconscious".

The clearest suggestion should be possible regarding concept-based structures. The spectator receives these filmic structures consciously according to the working definition of Farthing (1992, 6): "Consciousness is the subjective state of being currently aware of something, either within oneself or outside oneself. In this case, being aware or having awareness refers to cognizance or knowing. Consciousness is always about something." The same author writes: "In cognitive psychological models, consciousness may be equated with working memory (Baars, 1988). This consciousness system may be attributed with certain functions, such as interpreting perceptual inputs, making decisions, or sharing information among various specialized subsystems." (Farthing 2000, 268–269).

Using the framework of information approach, the receiving of P structures ensues as a kind of "preconscious processing". "Preconscious processing refers to the early stages of perceptual processing that occur before an object or event reaches consciousness" (Farthing 2000, 269).

Proceeding from Farthing's (2000, 270) assumption "that nonconscious contents exist on a continuum of retrievability into consciousness, with some contents being easily accessible, some accessible with difficulty, and some inaccessible", stereotype-based filmic structures should be able to reactivate such nonconscious contents, which are more or less "easily accessible" because they can fall back upon the declarative knowledge in long-term memory, which can be actualised by inter-textual repetition of the same stimulus configuration or structure. If this iteration does not happen, or does not work often enough, then even stereotypes become inaccessible or unapproachable.

(It is unfortunate that the terms used here are not unambiguous, indeed less so since Sigmund Freud's famous book *The Interpretation of Dreams* ([1900] 1953) developed a similar terminology a century ago, which differs in some respects from Farthing's version, yet is very popular to this day, and thus leads to confusion. Freud's system included a "preconscious mind", "which contains information (such as personal memories) that is not currently the topic of consciousness, but which can easily be retrieved to consciousness" (Farthing 2000, 269). And his concept of "unconscious mind" "contains hidden desires and repressed memories that cannot be retrieved to consciousness and reported", a fact that hampers cognitive psychology's inclusion of the term "unconscious" in its framework.)

4.4.3. Recall and memory

Experience has shown that the different structures described by the PCS model are not recallable for the spectator in the same manner, which can be interpreted as meaning that they are stored in our memory in a different way. Concerning P structures, the spectator is at best able to recall them immediately after having watched the film, but not for longer than one or two hours. C structures he can recollect for a longer period, sometimes for years, and regarding stereotypes one has the impression that they can be recalled for decades or are hardly forgotten at all. In the 1960s, there were attempts to relate such different spans for a recall to the notions of short-term and long-term memory (and even a so-called tertiary memory). Later, the understanding of memory changed insofar as the notion of short-term memory was increasingly replaced by the concept of working memory, which tried to do justice to the information processing of more complex stimuli by a multi-component model. The working memory can be considered as a mental space with limited capacity which mediates between the pick-up of information and the long-term memory (Baddeley 1986, 2003a, 2003b; Hagendorf 2006). It works as a system of controlled attention (Engle 2002) used to select information from various provenances—i.e. from perception, long-term memory or working processes—with the aim of an efficient processing of tasks (Cowan 1995), and seems to be more and more an emergent property of our consciousness (Postle 2006). Although the new theories of memory did not deliver available arguments regarding the information storage of the different filmic structures, they are not contradictory of the mentioned hypotheses that the three types of filmic structures have very different chances to be stored in the spectators memory. Thus, one can suggest that P structures cannot be stored in the long-term memory in spite of their intra-textual repetition; C structures have the potential to be stored there without any repetition, and for S structures, in spite of their storage in the long-term memory an inter-textual repetition can help to stabilise their efficacy in the communication. In any case, one can find similar arguments in numerous studies on memory.

4.4.4. Modes of learning

As mentioned above, the theory of learning played an important role in the early development of cognitive psychology. This led to attempts at modelling art reception as a learning process in which redundancy is produced by information processing in the spectator's mind. At this time, the intuitively comprehended differences in spectators' art reception could be interpreted with respect to certain basic forms of learning behaviour which were described in the so-called redundancy theory of learning (Cube 1965, 99–144). This theory differentiated, for instance, between "learning by autocorrelation", "probability learning" and "learning by free combination or conscious reflection" Although today these theories are obsolete, some analogies between types of learning and the structuring of film may still elucidate the film experience. For instance, the analogies between the reception of P structures and "probability learning," because these two processes have to do with the repetition of similar stimulus configurations. The "perceptual learning" described by Gibson (1973, 330) is based on the same regularities. The transition from preconscious to conscious information processing, which leads to the formation of invariants of thought and conducts to C structures, nowadays seems to be rather fluid because it is based on complicated interactions between both levels. Nevertheless, consciously comprehended filmic structures make possible for the spectator a sort of free combination of their meanings. The reception of filmic stereotypes, however, rather allows the coexistence of probability learning and learning by conscious reflection and free combination respectively.

4.4.5. Semantic stability

Of course, the art-semantic processes are specific ones, and their differentiation in the framework of the PCS model is rather theoretical. But nevertheless, their various stability or communicative efficacy seems obvious. Thus, the P structures are in their initial phases semantically very unstable—with the consequence that nobody is able to discover their "aboutness". The C structures, however, are stable in their meaning and lead to an unequivocal content which can be—but is not necessarily—lost in the phase of stereotyping, which depends obviously on the reactivation of the corresponding stimuli configurations through the cultural repertoire.

5. On the Application and Psychological Differentiation of the PCS Model

Since the three types of cinematic structure that make up the PCS model stand for the three different phases of human cognition, which form an endless process, one can find in every film structural offers that include these three states of "affordances" (Gibson). However, these structures do not always appear in the same manner. Sometimes, their description is difficult or even impossible because they have not been set up in the film in question, since the author or director lacks the talent or the will (or even both) for their successful aesthetic articulation. In other cases, the analyst is unable to recognize particular structures, for instance, perception-based ones, because they are concealed beneath the representation of life-phenomena. That, for example, the hero of *Ashes And Diamonds* is restrained from the taking-up of his machine gun by ants seems entirely coincidental and without any meaning. But in the context of a multitude of similar disturbing actions which occur in this period of upheaval, the perception of the disturbance by the protagonist and the spectator becomes a "semantic gesture" and obtains a meaning function. Nevertheless, the analyst can fail to notice this. And he can also overlook the stereotypical images at the very beginning of the sequence since the idyllic setting with the chapel can be perceived as a natural location rather than an intentionally designed film set. But the little girl with the flowers stresses the fact that the director aimed for a conventionalised arrangement with symbolic power.

Quite apart from the mentioned difficulties in the analyst's subjective perception process, even a cursory inspection of specific films shows that the three types of structure can also be set up objectively using varying degrees of formal development, distribution and dominance. There are individual films, but also whole groups of films, that show an equal kind of formal clarity, as well as an equal distribution and value of all three types as evidenced in the opening sequences of *Ashes And Diamonds* and *Ariel*. In other cases, however, the perception-based structures especially are set up in carefully-realised, pronounced, closely-packed series, and are correspondingly dominant. This applies to the Cinema of Behaviour of Western Europe, particularly to Michelangelo Antonioni's tetralogy *L'Avventura* (1960), *La Notte* (1960), *L'Eclisse* (1962) and *Il Deserto rosso* (1964) of the first half of the 1960's, and to a substantial part of the works of Rohmer and Rivette, but also to the whole *œuvre* of Ozu from Japan and the early productions of such representatives from different phases of the American Independent Cinema as Cassavetes or Jarmusch. These films permanently confront the spectator with series of homologue forms, for instance similar micro-actions and patterns of the characters' behaviour, by setting into motion specific activity of cinematic perception in which our mind constructs invariants of perception in a preconscious but nevertheless vital process. In this way meaning is generated, and the spectator realizes the connection between similar stimulus patterns, i.e. phenomena which agree with the expectations of the audience. This reception process, which complies with the rules of "perceptual learning" (Gibson 1973, 330) requires an active spectator, who willingly processes the observations of mostly tiny actions that the camera has captured and the editing has brought inconspicuously to a new order.

A related film-historical occurrence that developed in the former Socialist countries of Eastern Europe during the 1960's is the so-called Documentary Style of Fiction Film. The corpus of this group style includes such works as Milos Forman's *Black Peter* (*Černý Petr*, 1964) and *The Loves Of A Blonde* (*Lásky jedné plavovlásky*, 1965), Vera Chytilová's *A Bagful Of Fleas* (*Pytel blech*, 1962) and

Something Different (*O necem jinem*, 1963), Marlen Khutsiyev's *I am Twenty* (*Mne dvadtsat let*, 1964) and *July Rain* (*Iyulskiy dozhd*, 1967), Vasili Shukshin's *There Is Such a Lad* (*Zhivyot takoy paren*, 1964) and *Strange People* (*Strannye lyudi*, 1969), Otar Iosseliani's *Falling Leaves* (*Giorgobistve*, 1967) and *Once Upon a Time There Was a Singing Blackbird* (*Iko shashvi mgalobeli*, 1970), Krzysztof Zanussi's *The Structure Of Crystal* (*Struktura krysztalu*, 1969) and *Illumination* (*Iluminacja*, 1973).

Although stereotypes have played a role in the cinema since its beginnings, their significance grew during the 1980's. Not only in individual works, but also in filmmaking tendencies as a whole, such as the production of series for cinema (in James Bond) or TV, and in group styles such as the postmodern film, they became more pronounced, at closer intervals and of greater importance for the construction and impact of the whole work. This dominance of stereotypes led to a kind of second-hand culture for the cinema which uses stimuli patterns that are well-known because of their inter-textual distribution more emphatically and even playfully.

One can note this tendency within the *œuvres* of such directors as Peter Greenaway, David Lynch or Pedro Almodóvar. Again and again you can find in the works of these filmmakers structures that the spectator knows from other films or artworks. They occur in new combinations and contexts, with the result that the structure in question does not seem redundant for the communication process because it demands further information processing from the spectator.

Of course, the approximation of the complicated and complex formal system of an artwork by such a three-step model amounts to a significant simplification of the described patterns. But, on the one hand, it allows empirical analysis by psychologists that leads to a higher level of research in the future; and it opens the way, on the other hand, to further differentiation of findings about the film's effects. Thus, for instance, M. Suckfüll (1997) clarified the impact of the different structures of Jane Campion's film *The Piano* (1993) psycho-physiologically by testing the changes of the spectators' heartbeats and electrodermal activities according to the PCS model and looking for a cognitive interpretation of the effects. Here, the clearness of the PCS model was helpful for the verification of initial hypotheses regarding the film's impact. And, of course, there is no reason to renounce further attempts to examine and hermeneutically interpret further nuances in film experience.

Moreover, the application of the model is not a mechanical act. Although the elementary framework given by the principle of repetition lays down that P structures need an intra-textual repetition of the same structure whereas C structures dispense with repetition and S structures need intertextual repetition, these necessary conditions for their function are not sufficient alone. That is, the evidence of an intra-textual repetition, for instance, does not lead to the inverse conclusion that we are necessarily dealing with a P structure only. In fact it is possible that C and S structures may also be repeated in the same film, and likely they will have other functions than the perceptual ones, which the analysis must take into consideration. For instance, in films like Nagisa Oshima's *In the Realm of the Senses* (*Ai no corrida*, 1976), Patrice Chéreau's *Intimacy* (2001) or Michael Winterbottom's *9 Songs* (2004), the motif of sexual activity is repeated in a very obvious manner. In these cases, one cannot speak of a perception-based structure regardless of the shown variations of the same action.

Another deviation from the elementary scheme appears in cases where the series of P structures includes single stimulus configurations of the same semantic gesture which have, beyond doubt, the status of a C or S structure. Thus, I have temporarily neglected, in my description of the initial sequences of *The Passenger* and *Ariel*, that the line of obvious P structures also includes single C structures. If the above-mentioned Bedouin ignores the solitary protagonist in the desert, then this event attains the status of a conceptualised filmic structure. And also the suicide of the foreman in *Ariel* is obvious, and can be received therefore as a C structure. It makes the spectator conscious of the protagonist's fatal situation. A careful analysis of individual films has to do justice to these nuances.

In general, the PCS model functions well only where one takes into account the differentiated characteristics of the three types of structure concerning, for instance, the variations in their degree of conspicuousness and consciousness, their mode of learning behaviour and chances for recall, and also their semantic stability. Unfortunately, we are not yet able to systematically represent these functions using a consistent theory, but nevertheless past experience has shown that some special traits of the structures can help to discriminate them.

6. Opening Sequences and Priming

With regard to the "cognitive dramaturgy" of film beginnings, Britta Hartmann (2008, 365) points out: "The film beginning seems to be an almost unavoidable starting point for an investigation of how films are comprehended. Nowhere else can the activity of understanding be more easily grasped, nowhere else can one see as clearly how films stage and direct the viewer's expectations, inferences, and construction of hypotheses or how they strategically integrate his or her knowledge and experience into the process of reception. The way the narrative teaches the viewer how to understand it becomes most obvious at this point where all the registers and levels of the text are set up, where the viewer enters into the fictional world and gets to know the possibilities and probabilities that govern it. The description of the processes of initiation of film thus aims more generally at showing the conditions for the possibility of understanding and experiencing a film and at the forms in which this goes on."

The specific interaction of various filmic structures, which organises the process of the spectator's experience at the beginning, often continues in the further phases of storytelling by using similar rules—with respect to an effective aesthetic function of the corresponding stimulus configurations. It seems to be the case that filmmakers intuitively follow the initially proposed cognitive formation and appoint a structural pattern or pattern of invariants working specifically for each film and leading to its unique aesthetic code.

Decades ago, Meir Sternberg (1978; 1990) and David Bordwell (1985, 37) pointed out that the opening of a film plays a very important role in the spectator's anticipations and establishment of hypotheses regarding the development of a story. Thus Bordwell (1985, 38) writes: "The sequential nature of narrative makes the initial portions of a text crucial for the establishment of hypotheses. [...] Sternberg borrows a term from cognitive psychology, the 'primacy effect', to describe how initial information establishes 'a frame of reference to which subsequent information [is] subordinated as far as possible'. A character initially described as virtuous will tend to be considered so even in the face of some contrary evidence; the initial hypothesis will be qualified but not demolished unless very strong evidence is brought forward."

What is said here about the strength of a limited conceptualised scheme should apply to the more extensive cluster of schemata in the shape of cognitive invariant patterns, because not only the conception-based filmic structures follow an activating cognitive scheme but the two other structures as well. Rumelhart (1980, 51) has pointed out: "Perception is goal directed. We do not passively wait for some stimuli to arrive and then at the later date attempt an interpretation. Instead, we actively seek information relevant to our current needs and goals." Therefore perception-based structures also take part in the process of the spectator's priming, i.e. "the effect in which recent experience of a stimulus facilitates or inhibits later processing of the same or a similar stimulus." (VandenBos 2007, 731)

The initial pattern of cognitive invariants probably becomes a priming pattern for the perception of the whole film. In any case, a comparison of the opening sequences of different films shows that the relationship of the various types of filmic structures often effects the structuring of the entire film, especially the structuring of narration. Every successful film seems to have been provided with its own unmistakable combination of said filmic structures, i.e., its own priming pattern, specified for the entire work.

Although these considerations are only hypothetical, every experienced filmmaker knows that the formation of a successful opening sequence—besides the exposition of characters with their interests and conflicts, which allows hypotheses about possible developments of the events—must also prepare the spectator for a specific way or style of film perception that leads to the aesthetic code of the artwork here called its "priming pattern". Probably, the different mental states of filmic structures lead to different primacy effects, and the combination of various filmic structures in the priming pattern in the films' opening sequences creates certain conditions for further narration. Today, their rules are still a mystery, but priming has become an important subject for cognitive psychology and neuroscience.

Recent studies in neuroscience (Schacter et al. 2004; 2007), for instance, show that there are even analogous interests in research into the specification of priming processes: "Priming is a nonconscious form of memory that involves a change in a person's ability to identify, produce or classify an item as a result of a previous encounter with that item or a related item. One important question relates to the specificity of priming—the extent to which priming reflects the influence of abstract representation or the retention of specific features of a previous episode. Cognitive neuroscience analyses provide evidence for three types of specificity: stimulus, associative and response" (Schacter/Dobbins/ Schnyer 2004, 843). Of course, the concrete intentions and research methods in these disciplines are different, but the general tendency to look for differentiation of the characters of stimuli, including the evoked information processing one, can be found there as well.

There is no doubt that priming as "a nonconscious form of memory in which an encounter with a stimulus influences the subsequent identification, production or classification of the same or a related stimulus" (Schacter/Wig/Stevens 2007, 171) has consequences for the receiving of a film by the spectator, particularly for the information processing caused by the filmic structures, which organise the strategy of storytelling in such a way that the different types of structure prepare the viewers' mind for a subsequent stimulation. Thus, priming seems to be an important component of the processes of cinematic narration.

Chapter II: Cinematic Narration and Its Basic Structures

1. The Richness of Forms of Narrative as a Challenge for Analysis

"Numberless are the world's narratives. First of all in a prodigious variety of genres, themselves distributed among different substances, as if any material were appropriate for man to entrust his stories to it [...]. Further, in these almost infinite forms, narrative occurs in all periods, all places, all societies; narrative begins with the very history of humanity; there is not, there has never been, any people anywhere without narrative; all classes, all human groups have their narratives, and very often these are enjoyed by men of different, even opposing culture: narrative never prefers good to bad literature: international, transhistorical, transcultural, narrative is there, like life", as Roland Barthes (1994, 95) maintains in one of his famous essays.

The cinema perpetuates this age-old cultural tradition with its own specific means. As early as 1894, during the period when moving pictures were being invented, Paul and Wells defined their essence in a patent application as "telling stories by means of moving pictures" (quoted in Montagu 1964, 34). Today it is considered indisputable that films thrive on narration and that audio-visual media have developed into the storytellers of our times.

When spectators grasp what films show or represent, they usually do so in terms of narration, and thus perceive and judge it according to such expectations. The analysis of cinematic narration is therefore extremely important for the critical evaluation of films. Of course, this is also connected to the contents of the various artistic messages, since their interpretation is central. But in artistic films, these are never separable from the way they are conveyed, from the form of their aesthetic representation, and thus from the form of narration.

New contents sometimes lead to new, previously non-existing narrative structures, but in many cases formal means may also be employed that are similar to well-known ones. The mode of narrative sets up a decisive framework for psychological effects and therefore provides the central frame of reference for all analytic approaches to the aesthetic effects of films. In fact, there is no aspect of film form whatsoever that is not connected with narration. In practical work with the medium it has been clear from the first that the choice of a narrative mode has a lot to do with achieving successful communication as well as creating an aesthetic experience, and can even be crucial for the commercial success of a film.

The relevance of narrative represents an important challenge and responsibility for film theory: theory must guarantee that analysis pays due attention to the vitality and diversity involved in the creative effort of telling stories. Theory must consider the possible developments and changes in forms of narration and account for innovation as well as the stability of traditional formal patterns.

Even though no general theory of narration has been developed and such a theory might not even be justifiable, it does seem sensible to pay attention to experience gained by the study of narratives that existed before the cinema arose. Various forms of narrative are found in cultural practices: mimetic (based on imitation or direct representation) and diegetic (based on indirect representation), artistic and non-artistic, fictional and non-fictional.

The development of various art forms and technical media has led these phenomena to interact with one another, thus leading to a variety of combinations. Mimetic narrative is dominant in film, based on the communicative forms and codes of showing, but without abstaining from the diegetic devices of telling. And while most examinations of film tend to concentrate on artistic, fictional narratives, the complete range of material available in the cinema and in audiovisual media also includes narratives that are intentionally neither artistic nor fictional. Theory must pay attention to this entire field if it is to be able to do justice to the specificities of form and effects of a work.

2. What is Narrative?

It is difficult to define what a narrative is, and thus it is necessary to try to approach its most important characteristics by means of working hypotheses:

(1) One can safely presuppose that narrative is a form of cultural communication that has to do with passing on original human experience in such a way that communicated contents take the form of closed entities or units, i.e. narratives.

(2) Human experience is not imparted abstractly, but rather depicted by means of processes of iconic signification, in which complex events are represented in such a way that they appear compatible with the real world.

(3) Narratives always encompass a structured course of events, which includes the temporal organization of what is communicated, resting in part on the representation of events in terms of processes and in part on the temporal duration of reception.

(4) Narration takes on the function of transmitting meaning in the communicative process. Someone who wants to tell a story must have something to say or to show, and this should offer the recipient some new information (in the sense of a potential change of consciousness). That is, the narrative must communicate a message.

(5) Narratives search for coherence. Events and their connections must be organized so that their structural interrelation also provides the recipient with a coherent meaning.

(6) Particularly in the case of artistic narratives, the meaning is made accessible by a specific artistic-semantic process, which cannot be reduced to conscious, rational processes of understanding, but also involves a whole complex of pre-conscious or unconscious effects and components, such as those of perception, emotion, and imagination.

3. Verbal Synopses as a Descriptive Model of Narratives

In analyzing a narrative it seems advisable to focus on this coherence of meaning and thus pay attention primarily to those factors that are relevant to the creation of its aesthetic message. According to Aristotle, who in his *Poetics* (or rather in the part of the text that has come down to us) concentrates on analyzing stage tragedy, narrative "should be a representation of a unitary and complete action; and its parts, consisting of the events, should be so constructed that the displacement or removal of any one of them will disturb and disjoint the work's wholeness" (Aristotle 1987, 40). The phenomenon that Aristotle called "mythos" served as an orientation to guarantee the unity of action in theory and practice. Latin translation refers to this as "fabula," German as "Fabel"; the English equivalent is "plot structure." Aristotle emphasized: "And so, the plot-structure is the first principle and, so to speak, the soul of the tragedy" (38), for which the "structure of events" (37) is of primary importance.

Aristotle sets "standards of probability or necessity" (40) as criteria for a proper connection between events. Particularly causal relationships were meant, and this principle of connection took on a normative character. Thus in the *Poetics* Aristotle states: "Of simple plot-structures and actions the worst are episodic. I call an 'episodic' plot-structure one in which the episodes follow in a succession which is neither probable nor necessary" (41). Aristotle comments: "[...] for it makes a great difference whether things happen *because* of another, or only *after* one another." (42) The criterion is clear. The causal chain was established as a necessary condition of narration.

In the following centuries the concept of plot developed into an aesthetic or dramaturgical category, and working out events and the connections between them became a central part of analyzing works in the performing arts, at least in western culture. This is particularly true for the construction of verbal synopses.

In theatrical theory and practice it has been proved effective to begin analyzing a work by reducing it to its most relevant factors of meaning. However, this should not be done abstractly, but rather through concrete descriptive models that set up analogies to the work. This leads to the construction of mini-narratives, iconic signifying systems that can represent the complex and extensive artistic work during the process of thinking about it and thus make it easier to examine. Film studies has employed this method by creating verbal synopses or plot summaries to express the story line and the drift of its meaning.

It can be helpful to extract certain events and their logical connections from the planned or sketched-out plot and to summarize them during the creative process as well. Modelling the plot line in this way can take on a heuristic function. The director Andrzej Wajda (1987, 16ff.) wrote of this:

"The long months during which the script is being written blur the real contours of the conflict that one is trying to depict on the screen with the help of various characters. […] For me, the best method is to summarize again and again what I am trying to stage, to tell it to myself. When I summarize, I am forced to leave out the details. I concentrate on what I think is important. […] Such a résumé has to be done by memory. Whatever memory does not hold onto is negligible. You can delete it from the script. The scriptwriter should be able to summarize the theme in a few sentences."

Wajda emphasizes that such a summary helps him to better articulate the central theme and the meaning of individual scenes as well as of the whole work.

Academic analysis regularly requires similar summaries, verbal synopses that describe the plot in terms of its central events which—through their temporal order and logical connections—can make the meaning and coherence of the whole work evident.

For most journalistic uses and as a preliminary hypothesis for scholarly studies, it is advisable to formulate the synopsis so that it is clear not only *what* happens in what order and with what consequences, but also *how* and through which specific aesthetic means this is achieved and what effects are intended on the viewers. This leads to the triple question: What is narrated? How is it narrated? Why, i.e. with what intention, is it narrated?

4. Constructing Verbal Synopses as a Problem of Evaluating Stimuli

Writing an accurate synopsis of a story is not a mechanical procedure, since the plot as a model of the complete work is not a miniaturized copy of the whole work like a slide in comparison to the projected image on the screen, which reproduces the proportions of the represented objects in a strictly analogous way. Instead, it is the result of complicated processes involving abstraction and the evaluation of stimuli. Anyone who writes a synopsis is confronted with a multitude of decisions as to which elements of the action are relevant and have to be mentioned and which are irrelevant and can be played down or even fully ignored. Such decisions can be very hard to make in concrete cases. The aesthetic value of individual formal elements or details depends not only on external parameters such as their weight or particular place in the overall composition of the work. Rather, it depends on how they are bound into the complete structure of the work in very complex ways. Thus there are good reasons why newer theories in aesthetics and literature emphasize that the author's ideas are realized in particular artistic structures and cannot be separated from them (cf. Lotman 1977, 11). With regard to artistic texts, Lotman writes: "The artistic text is an intricately constructed thought. All its elements are meaningful elements" (Lotman 1977, 12). Roland Barthes also states that "[...] we believe on the contrary that all the actions of a narrative, however minute they may seem, should be analyzed, integrated into an order which it is our obligation to describe: in the text (contrary to oral narrative) no feature of speech is insignificant" (Barthes 1994, 137).

Roland Barthes notes with reference to the analysis of fairy tales that after having discerned the basic plot elements "[...] there remains a host of minor actions, apparently trivial and more or less mechanical (*knocking at a door, engaging in a conversation, making an appointment etc.*)" (Barthes 1994, 137; emphasis in original), which cannot simply be neglected by the analysis or dismissed as self-evident.

The problems of analyzing narrative which arise when drawing up a verbal synopsis generally become even more difficult not only in cases when minor actions increase in importance in the plot, but also when the story as a whole veers away from using causal chains as its organizing principle, for example if it disintegrates into episodes or tends toward open forms. Such tendencies in prose and drama became obvious by the beginning of the twentieth century at the latest. The method of analysis that was practised from Aristotle onwards—starting the analysis of a work with causal chains of central actions—thus became problematic or even impossible. It is common knowledge that the tendencies referred to in literary criticism as plotlessness became apparent in film by the beginning of the 1960s.

Usually, it is no less complicated to work out the relevant elements of the narrative process in films than it is in literary texts. One key difficulty is that the mimetic details of images, which can lead to innumerable small and miniature actions, may be difficult to relate to what Barthes has referred to as "the major actions, the primordial articulations of the story" (Barthes 1994, 137). In the early days of the cinema, the director and theoretician Urban Gad already called film a "narrative in pictures […] a hybrid form between two forms of art," which therefore could not be compared with any previous form of art and also should not be judged according to the rules that apply to them (1920, 279).

Cognitive film theory has faced up to this challenge. Recent theories of film narration search for a functional link between the macro-structures of the plot and those elements of the film that belong more closely to the mimetic processes of showing. Bordwell (1985) shows that the *fabula*, i.e. the story, of a fiction film must be seen as a construct resulting from the viewer's active mental processes, in which various constituents are involved. He notes: "It would be an error to take the fabula, or story, as the profilmic event.[...] The fabula, writes Tynianov 'can only be guessed at, but it is not a given.'" (Bordwell 1985, 49ff.). For Bordwell, "The fabula is thus a pattern which perceivers of narratives create through assumptions and inferences." (1985, 49). In the definition already quoted, he states: "In the fiction film, *narration is the process whereby the film's syuzhet and style interact in the course of cueing and channelling the spectator's constructions of the fabula*" (53, emphasis in original).

Bordwell uses the term "syuzhet," which was adopted from Russian Formalism and can be translated as "plot," to describe the

dramatic structure of a film and "style" to describe elements of
technique: "The syuzhet embodies the film as a 'dramaturgical'
process; style embodies it as a 'technical' one." (50). Thus "style"
simply refers to the systematic use that the film makes of formal
cinematic devices (50). It is the dynamic relationship between the
two systems of "syuzhet" and "style" that first leads to the
construction of the "fabula" as the result of a mental process.
Bordwell introduces an additional third system, which he calls
"excess" and which Kristin Thompson defines as "materials which
may stand out perceptually but which do not fit either narrative or
stylistic patterns" (1985, 53).

   Thus it is not only the dramaturgical structure of the *syuzhet*
that is responsible for what is narrated, rather it works together
with moments of cinematic stimulus in the area of visual style,
which are perceived as well, even if more often as "cues," i.e. in
terms of having a referential or supplementary function. A major
advantage of Bordwell's approach lies in the positive reevaluation
of the role of such stimuli in the narrative process. This is why the
model has been an enormous help in analyzing certain types of
cinematic narration more precisely, for instance the classical
Hollywood style. That it has had little effect in dealing with more
open forms of narration may have to do with the fact that the term
"syuzhet," taken from Russian formalism, has not lost the
ambivalence that representatives of the Formal School already gave
it. On the one hand, they used *syuzhet* within the relationship
syuzhet-fabula to denominate the events in the order and
connections in which they appear in the work, as opposed to *fabula*
as the totality of interconnected events that the work depicts, and
on the other hand, *syuzhet* appears to be one term of a binary
typology differentiating forms of narrative "with" or "without
syuzhet." In distinction from the first binary, in which nothing is
said of the structure of the connections between events, here the
syuzhet is defined by causal chains. Thus narration is then
connected to having a plot as a necessary condition. Further
complications may arise through the translation of the ambivalent
Russian concept of *syuzhet* into English, since the idea of plot and
with it causal chains have traditionally had a normative value in
British and American usage. In that Bordwell's definition of film
narration suggests a translation of *syuzhet* as plot, it appears to be

essentially bound to the organizational structure of causal chains.
Edward Branigan, who is quite close to Bordwell on this point, notes: "*...narrative is a perceptual activity that organizes data into a special pattern which represents and explains experience.* More specifically, narrative is a way of organizing spatial and temporal data into a cause-effect chain of events with a beginning, middle, and end that embodies a judgment about the nature of the events as well as demonstrates how it is possible to know, and hence to narrate, the events" (1992, 3; emphasis in original).

In practice it proves to be quite difficult to use this model analytically with regard to sample material that does not conform to the pattern of a plot. The consequence is that the model cannot simply be applied to modernist cinema, for example the various versions of the European *cinéma d'auteur*, which tend toward openness, even though precisely these films would seem to demand new analytic models. Many viewers, including connoisseurs of the métier, consider these works to be narratives, since they do communicate human experience through the representation of series of events that formulate a message. These are not just a handful of films, but entire tendencies in film form, including historically important stylistic movements.

In what follows I will try to sketch a descriptive model of narrative structures that retains the major advantages of Bordwell's approach but can be applied more easily to narrative forms that go beyond the structure of causal chains. This model will in part formalize Bordwell's "cues" and give them an even more important role as basic structures of narration.

5. Three Basic Structures of Film Narration and Their Functions

5.1 Models of Film Structure and Forms of Narration

Since the classic model of narration, which rests on the basic narrative structure of causal chains, is not or at most only partially applicable to a number of films, and thus cannot be used to analyze their specific characteristics, I would like to suggest considering that not just one but several basic structures of narrative may exist, which co-exist on an equal basis and can potentially serve as the agency of the process of narration.

As a continuation of the description of film stimuli beyond the three-step PCS model, this hypothesis shall be used to differentiate narrative structures, as has already been suggested. If the three types of film structure are effective throughout the film, from the beginning to the ending, then they form three different basic structures of narration.

(1)   Structures based on perception lead to topic lines of narration,

(2)   Conceptually-based structures produce causal chains of narration,

(3)   Structures based on stereotypes form narrative stereotypes.

These basic structures govern the process of narration, in particular by jointly organizing the entire area of macro-structures within the individual works. In a manner similar to that in which cinematic structures form a sequence, the basic structures can differ strongly from one another according to their prominence, distribution, and correlation within the framework of the whole work, and this then affects the relative dominance of the various structures. In many cases one of the structural forms is clearly dominant, thus causing the story to tend toward a certain kind of narration, which brings out the specificities of the structures and functions particularly well.

In regard to the reception of literary narratives, Umberto Eco remarks, "The *fabula* is not produced once the text has been definitely read: the *fabula* is the result of a continuous series of abductions made during the course of reading. Therefore the *fabula* is always experienced step by step." (Eco 1979, 31). He continues: "To expect means to forecast: the reader collaborates in the course of the fabula, making forecasts about the forthcoming state of affairs. The further states must prove or disprove his hypotheses [...]. The end of the text not only confirms or contradicts the last forecasts, but also authenticates or inauthenticates the whole system of long-distance hypotheses hazarded by the reader about the final state of the fabula." (Eco 1979, 32).

Similar processes probably go on during the reception of film narratives. The narrative structures lead the viewers to set up expectations or hypotheses about the rest of the course of action, and these then lead to abductions. How strong the hypotheses are depends on the kind of basic structures involved in the narrative. Series of topics formed on the basis of perceptions tend to produce diffuse and latent expectations, while conceptualised causal chains tend to form clearly defined goal-oriented expectations or perceptual dispositions. Narrative stereotypes lead to standardized and conventionalized patterns of expectation about coming events. In each case the expected links between events correspond to Aristotle's demand for inner "probability or necessity," but differing criteria apply to these different forms.

In the following I will describe each of the basic structures (1) narrative topic lines, (2) causal chains, and (3) narrative stereotypes separately and show their ideal way of functioning. Then I will turn to possible interactions among them.

Since causal chains are the easiest form to describe and generally have the strongest effects in ordinary film reception, I will begin with them.

5.2 Basic Narrative Structures in Film

5.2.1 Causal Chains and Closed Narration

The basic narrative structure of causal chains is easy to recognize in that it links individual events according to the principle of cause and effect so that they are clearly joined into a dynamic process, which leads to a definite goal and in doing so effects significant changes in the situation depicted.

Aristotle differentiated four kinds of causality in his *Metaphysics* and it was not without reason that he viewed two of them as decisive for the understanding of storylines—the "causa efficiens," the *efficient cause* as the source of change or movement, and the "causa finalis," the *final cause* as purposeful or goal-directed causality. Both types of causality make it possible to shape the narrated course of events so that the events appear to have "necessary or probable connections with one another" (Aristotle 1987, 40) and thus form a unified whole.

Anyone analyzing a play or film, no matter whether for practical and artistic or for academic purposes, is thus well advised to begin investigating the whole work by means of imaginatively reconstructing the causality of the course of events, the "cause-effect chain of events" (Branigan 1992, 3).

Anglo-American theory of the novel developed the concept of plot, which Shaw's (1972, 289) *Dictionary of Literary Terms* defined in distinction to story as follows: "A plot is different from a story or story line (the order of events as they occur). This distinction has been made clear by E.M. Forster, the English novelist: 'We have defined a story as a narrative of events arranged in their time sequence. A plot is also a narrative of events, the emphasis falling on a causality. [...] 'The king died and then the queen died' is a story. 'The king died, and then the queen died of grief' is a plot."

Like the other two basic structures, causal chains can be found in every kind of film narrative, and to a certain extent, they usually are. They make up the dominant form in "classical" or "dramatic" and "closed" narration, to which terms taken from various languages including plot, *syuzhet*, or *intrigue* are applied.

Causal chains can serve as an appropriate descriptive model for these forms of narration, which—at least within western cultures—have developed into the ideal type of narrative. The film industry values this kind of narrative above all others. Hollywood studios favored it from the beginnings of the cinema and established it as the standard form for their products. According to an often-quoted anecdote, an important producer led a guest to his safe, telling him that the important script drafts were stored there and he wanted to show him one. The guest was surprised to see just a single sheet of paper instead of a thick book. But the producer was convinced that a successful idea for a film could be judged from a short sketch. And he was probably right, at least in the case of classical closed narratives.

A closed story based on causality has a number of characteristics that make it particularly easy for spectators to consume. It is simple for the viewer to gain an overview of the entire course of action, since the narrative is organized in terms of a process that is constituted by a series of phases of action which advance a major conflict between differing interests of the main characters toward a resolution. Thus it can be understood both in terms of individual steps and the achieved results. Furthermore, it can easily be interpreted as leading to a message or meaning. The focus on a central conflict, which leads to a series of situations linked by the principle of cause and effect, helps the viewer understand the story. He or she pays attention to certain processes of change and experiences phases of development, which often also mark the escalation of the protagonist's problematic situation, as turning points in the course of action, i.e. as plot points. Much has been written about the techniques that scriptwriters use to steer these processes by emphasizing conflicts, bringing them to a head, and finally causing them to lead to a resolution. A series of operations, which prepare and serve as a foundation for such central narrative processes, are also highly important. In order to understand the plot as a whole, one must not only grasp the conflicts and the rough course of actions, but also the characters' interests and motives, which provide the basis for the plot. This has consequences for characterization, arrangements of characters, and dialogue in the classical narrative mode. Using the example of classical Hollywood cinema, Bordwell (1986) has shown what decisive effects these elements of form can have on the cognitive process of film reception.

At this point we could list a large number of well-known films from different film cultures in which the basic causal chain structure is dominant, making them adhere more or less closely to this particular ideal typus of cinematic narration. They all have a clear pattern of conflicts and a correspondingly clear plot structure, and all express a certain kind of dynamic action. This has to do with the fact that the action centers on something new, on "an 'instance', an event, something which has not happened before, or should not have happened (it is no accident that the name of a kind of plot text, '*novella*', comes from the word for 'news')" (Lotman 1976, 65). This is connected with a certain, and definitely significant, degree of activity for the characters; for the protagonists it often represents overcoming the bounds of the given order or even "the crossing of a prohibition boundary" (Lotman 1976, 66), which can have consequences for the audience's understanding of their life.

Examples of Films with Dominant Causal Chains

In Sergei M. Eisenstein's *The Battleship Potemkin* (*Bronenosets Potyomkin*, 1925), massive social conflicts between the oppressed crew and the Czarist officers lead to the mutiny on a Russian warship, during which the sailors eliminate their tormentors, gain power over the ship, and use its cannons to support the people of the port city Odessa, who are being massacred by Czarist troops after having shown their sympathy for the ship's crew. When the *Potemkin* then sails out to meet other ships of the fleet, their crews also refuse to shoot at the insurgents and open the way for them. The causal chain is connected in this case to a process of social upheaval and also appeals to the audience to change its picture of the world.

In Josef von Sternberg's *The Blue Angel* (*Der blaue Engel*, 1930) an elderly schoolteacher follows some of his wayward pupils to a nightclub and then falls in love with the cabaret singer Lola-Lola, who is appearing there. He abandons his previous bourgeois life and accompanies the woman on her tour. When the troupe comes back to his hometown one day, he experiences it as a profound humiliation. Even when he debases himself by taking part in her appearances in a clown's costume, he is unable to win back her favor, since she has discarded him for another man. In his despair, he attacks her physically and then kills himself in his former classroom. The causal chain of events in this story serves to depict a certain kind of transgression, that is the protagonist's emotionally motivated stepping across the borders of barren bourgeois existence, but without achieving a real alternative, leading instead to a fatal ending.

In Fred Zinnemann's *High Noon* (1952), Bill Kane has served as marshal in a small town for years when he learns that a notorious bandit is planning to return to the town after having been released from prison. The bad guy and his accomplices are seeking revenge on Kane, who had put them in prison, and plan to re-establish their reign of terror in the region. Although Kane has just quit his job and is planning to leave town with his young wife, he decides to stay and face the bandits. The citizens of the town, who had first appeared to support him, desert him one by one and he is left to face the villains alone. After he has won his difficult fight against the bandits, he throws his marshal's star away and leaves. Here, too, the strict causal construction of the events serves to tell an original story that helps to evaluate the protagonist as well as the attitudes and behavior of the townsmen.

In Grigori Chukhrai's *The Forty-First* (*Sorok pervyy*, 1956), which is set during the Russian Civil War in the Karakum Desert, a Red Army sharpshooter's bullet hits an officer of the White Army, but it is not as lethal as her last 40 shots. The injured man, apparently an important courier, is captured and is to be brought to headquarters. But while crossing the stormy Aral Sea, the ship is wrecked and the male guards are killed, so that the female Red Army soldier suddenly finds herself alone with the officer on a deserted island. He falls very ill and she takes care of him. Alone, and far away from the war, they begin a kind of Robinson Crusoe story and fall in love with each other. But when a White Army ship approaches the island and the officer joyfully runs toward his comrades, the girl shoots her lover, before collapsing on top of him.

The film *Woman in the Dunes* (*Suna no onna*, 1964) by the Japanese director Hiroshi Teshigahara tells the story of a frustrated teacher, who has traveled to the seacoast to collect insects in the sand dunes. He arrives at a strange village, where the houses are located in deep pits in the sand and can only be reached by means of rope ladders. When he sleeps in one of the houses, he finds the next day that the ladder has been pulled away and he is unable to get out of the pit. The house belongs to a single woman, who is constantly occupied with shoveling away the sand that steadily sifts down, and she wants her visitor to help her. He refuses, however, and tries to get away, but he is unable to escape the sand pits. Finally he is willing to help her with her laborious work, and his initial hatred of her is gradually replaced by fondness. He even appears to discover an alternative to his previous bourgeois existence in the constant fight against difficult surroundings, since he no longer tries to take advantage of possibilities of escape, but rather stays there.

In Francis Ford Coppola's *Apocalypse Now* (1979), which is set during the Vietnam War, an American captain is sent into the border region of Cambodia on a special CIA mission to find, bring back, or—if necessary—liquidate the former leader of an elite unit, Colonel Kurtz, who is no longer following orders from the army. The more the captain becomes acquainted with the biography of the renegade colonel, the more acceptable his opinions and arguments seem to him. However, when he finally arrives in the area where Kurtz rules over a local tribe like a godly despot, he overcomes the doubts he had begun to have about his mission and kills Kurtz. Here, again, an unusual case is in the middle of the events, and the protagonist has to make decisions in regard to the pathological actions of an individual, brought about by the war, that put his entire understanding of the world into question.

The Celebration (*Festen*, 1998) by the Danish director Thomas Vinterberg, tells how Christian, the grown-up eldest son of a hotel owner, travels from France to his father's birthday party. During the celebration he makes a speech in front of all the guests, accusing his father of having sexually abused him and his sister, who recently committed suicide. The guests are unwilling to take the accusation seriously and treat it as the fantasy of a psychologically unstable man. Christian is so upset by the general reaction that he almost gives up his attempt to reveal the truth, until his sister's suicide note turns up and confirms his accusations. The unheard-of incident at the center of the story is not only that a son publicly accuses his father of a crime at his birthday celebration, which is a transgression of the given order, but that the guests and family members try to avoid listening to or taking his accusations seriously, or even simply ignore them.

Characteristics of the Basic Narrative Structure of Causal Chain

If we look at findings with classic narration and the dominant structure of causal chains in it and try to relate them hypothetically to the cognitive processes of reception, we find a number of characteristics which explain some relations:

(1)   In terms of cognitive psychology, the basic narrative structure of a causally linked chain of events serves to provide a cinematic structure at the level of conceptualisation. Thanks to their causal connections, significant events build up a coherent, closed action with a beginning, a middle, and an end, which can be comprehended as a unit of information and can become effective within the artistic and semantic process. This functions as a singular case.

(2)   Conceptualisation is achieved above all in that the plot is driven forward by strong conflicts among the characters. The viewer is led to orient him or herself in relation to the characters' actions, which are determined on the one hand by

clear goals, and on the other collide with one another, and thus lead to conflicts that push towards decisions. Focusing the action on certain conflicts makes these noticeable and conscious for the viewers, who understand their development as a unified course of action. Since they try to formulate hypotheses about the conflicts and their probable resolution during the narrative, the experience of watching the film is not only connected to processes of comprehension in terms of learning through reflection, building hypotheses, and inferences, but also with problem-solving as a higher form of productive thinking (whereby this touches on subjects which we will not be able to deal with more fully until later).

(3) Stories that are structurally based on causal chains generally have to do with a special case, an unheard-of event, something novel in the world, which is connected to dynamic changes in life that demand creative thinking from the viewers.

(4) The individual phases of this dynamic action differ considerably from one another in terms of their characteristics. They are functionally differentiated and are not interchangeable in their order, but rather firmly integrated into the plot as a whole. The narrative organizes the plot elements that are structurally heterogeneous but still dependent on one another in such a way that they form a closed chain. Thus they usually lead to a distinct and clear-cut ending.

(5) Sequences of actions of this sort require correspondingly active and dynamic characters that are able to overstep the bounds of the given order. If the spectators go along with them, they are also able to gain the experience of possibly transgressing the given order. In this way they can experience in an exemplary way how certain models of the world function and can even be called upon to accept new models of the world, including social ones. The formation of a causal chain is then not just an end in itself, but serves to plausibly explain possible changes in people's lives that are brought about by powerful conflicts and difficult decisions.

(6) After having seen a film with this kind of basic narrative structure, the spectators can easily understand the

conceptualised course of events and also store it in their long-term memory. Therefore, they can easily recapitulate it, and even a complicated and complex story can be reduced to a linear and causal course of action, the meaning of which can be understood without too much effort.

(7)   All these factors have contributed to the fact that films in which this basic structure is dominant have proven to be semantically stable in communication processes. They are considered to be the ideal type of cinematic narration, at least within Western culture, and to be especially suited to a mass audience. This last point in particular is probably why closed film stories which follow a causal chain of events have taken on the character of a standard, not only for Hollywood cinema.

According to Lotman (1976, 65), stories with a plot based on the structure of causality are a kind of text that "answer the question, 'how did it happen?' ('in what manner did it take place?')." This kind of text could be contrasted to the plotless type that answers "the question 'what is it?' (or 'how is it put together?')"

This typology is similar to the linguistically-founded typology that Tzvetan Todorov (1972, 60ff.) developed for episodic forms in literature. He differentiates between a dynamic type of episode, which is suited to describe the transformation from one state of being to another and which makes use of actions that take place only once, and a more static type, which describes one and the same condition (of equilibrium or disequilibrium) and has an iterative character insofar as the same kinds of event happen over and over. According to Todorov, the two types can be compared to two classes of words, verbs and adjectives. This dichotomy of characteristics can be applied to the basic narrative forms. Since the dynamic form has been described thus far, now it is time to turn to the static one.

5.2.2   Topic Lines and the Open Form of Narration

The basic narrative form of a topic line is recognizable in that it repeats invariant, meaningful complexes of stimuli in the form of structurally similar processes intratextually, i.e. within a single work.

Their existence can often only be proven through exact

observation and careful structural comparisons between certain passages of a film. Their narrative function is often only barely apparent. It can even be impossible to explain it as such. The problem is made even more difficult by the fact that this basic narrative structure has not led to any unified ideal types of narrative, even in cases when it is dominant. Thus there are no identifiable patterns from which one could orient oneself, but rather a broad field of different forms of narration, often referred to by terms such as "episodic," "epic," "lyric," or "open."

The film industry has always had great difficulties with works of this kind, since they tend to show events without clear causal links between them and sometimes dispense with any clear temporal order such as chronology. Some works do not even contain anything that one can recognize as clearly contoured events, but instead are made up of apparently random observations of the filmmaker and often create the impression that they are not narrative at all. It is often difficult to recognize any principle that could connect the events through an inner "probability or necessity."

Many critics refer to these films as "plotless" or even as "non-narrative." In doing so, they define the phenomenon *ex negativo*, but that only refers to what is not present in the structure of the works and abstains from a positive definition of any rules that may exist in them. Decades ago, literary criticism used catchwords like "the loss of plot" or the "dissolution of story", which aimed in a similar direction and often revealed a capitulation in the face of the difficulty of the problem.

Despite the deficiencies that have been noted, connoisseurs of this material—and sometimes even an appreciative audience at art house cinemas—have noticed that many of these works do have an inner order and regularity in the configuration of the stimuli they offer. Thus they are potentially able to articulate meaning. They do so through similar, recurring complexes of meaningful stimuli, series of perceptual topics, which can become effective in constructing a narrative. However, it is not immediately clear what such works are about, and the viewers can only arrive at what Eco referred to as "aboutness" in the course of a long process or reception of the often apparently diffuse and insignificant events of a film. A successful analysis of such works must describe the regularities at work within an individual film and search for an explanation of how and in what way they can function within a process of narration and the transmission of meaning.

To achieve this, the descriptive model of series of topics, which is based on the repetition of similar, meaningful complexes of stimuli, is to be brought together with the hypothesis that topics make use of perceptual cycles in order to cause the viewers to develop expectations that certain configurations of stimuli will probably occur. Through this cognitive activity they can create narrative coherence.

In the early period of cognitive psychology, Ulric Neisser developed a functional model for processes of visual perception, which he referred to as the "perceptual cycle." This model seems to be more generally applicable and has lost none of its heuristic value (cf. Dörner 1999, 144). Neisser (1976, 20ff.) points out: "In my view, the cognitive structures crucial for vision are the anticipatory schemata that prepare the perceiver to accept certain kinds of information rather than others and thus control the activity of looking. Because we can see only what we know how to look for, it is these schemata (together with the information actually available) that determine what will be perceived. Perception is indeed a constructive process, but what is constructed is not a mental image appearing in consciousness where it is admired by an inner man. At each moment the perceiver is constructing anticipations of certain kinds of information, that enable him to accept it as it becomes available. Often he must actively explore the optic array to make it available, by moving his eyes or his head or his body. These explorations are directed by the anticipatory schemata, which are plans for perceptual actions as well as readinesses for particular kinds of optical structure. The outcome of the explorations—the information picked up — modifies the original schema. Thus modified, it directs further exploration and becomes ready for more information."

According to this principle, certain characteristics of a stimulus are stored in a person's memory the first time they are noticed. They can then form a sort of hypothesis, which is tested as to whether or not it applies. In the case that the same configuration of stimuli occurs again, the hypothesis is confirmed or can be optimized, and a perceptual pattern comes to exist in the viewer's mind and to correspond more closely to the real object of perception. Through cyclical repetition, the invariant elements of the phenomenon are learned, as it were, and they become fixed as invariants of perception. The viewers are often barely aware of this process and its results.

A sequence of recurring motifs or topics simulates this process, in that it intentionally organizes the perception of periodically repeated patterns of stimuli and makes use of them in the narrative process. When a film again and again observes a certain contradictory pattern of behavior in a character's everyday life or shows a repeated, unchanging relationship between characters in the entire story, the viewers by autocorrelation develop certain expectations as to the further course of the perceptual process. They then consider it to be probable that the film will soon confront them with similar elements again. The formation of such hypotheses occurs almost unconsciously within the framework of probability learning. If at all, it will most likely take a long process of learning to bring the spectator to formulate expectations at a conscious, conceptual level. It is usually very difficult to notice or recapitulate such expectations verbally. Practically, this hinders the articulation of coherent meanings and leads to problems of understanding, which make themselves noticeable, for instance, in the inability to summarize the film in words.

Series of topics can be created in very different ways in films, and they can be related in different ways to other basic structures. In cases where neither causal chains nor narrative stereotypes are to be found, sequences of perception can replace these semantically more stable narrative structures and even serve to support the whole process of narration.

Examples of Films with Dominant Topic Lines

In contrast to stories based on causal chains, no ideal type of narration based on series of topics has developed. Intra-textual repetition of similar patterns of stimuli, which form such topic series, can instead be found in a broad range of different forms of narrative.

The dominant use of this technique is to be found in a film style that became prominent in France and Italy around the beginning of the 1960s: the tendency within the Western European *cinéma d'auteur* that was evocatively called the "*cinéma du comportement*" (cinema of behavior).

Using a number of films of Michelangelo Antonioni, in particular *L'avventura* (1960), *La notte* (1961), *L'eclisse* (1962), and *Il deserto rosso* (1964), as examples, Umberto Eco observes: "And yet there have been a few movies that have definitely broken away from the traditional structures of plot to depict a series of events totally devoid of conventional dramatic connections—stories in which nothing happens, or, rather, where things happen not by narrative necessity but, at least in appearance, by chance." (Eco 1989, 115ff.)

In these films, which Eco (1989a) categorized as "open works," the dissolution of plot or the abandonment of causal chains as a connecting principle for the plot events is not the result of the artist's inability, but rather fully intentional, in the case of *L'avventura* even in a quite provocative manner. During a Mediterranean cruise a girl disappears without a trace on a deserted island, where the yacht has stopped. Such an incident would normally mean that a film narrative would head toward a dramatic conflict. But nothing of the sort happens here. After searching for a long time, her friends, including her fiancé and her best friend, begin to forget about her, and even the director seems to lose track of her, since we are never told what has happened. It is left open whether she has committed suicide, had an accident, or is experimenting with her friends by pretending to disappear. Instead of a central dramatic plot line, which would extend throughout the entire film and link its incidents, other elements seem to become more important: for example, a series of observations of extremely similar forms of behavior by all the other characters from the protagonists to the minor characters. Antonioni finds these constant or invariant forms of behavior to be worth representing in his film, since they represent a socially symptomatic "illness of the emotions" (Antonioni 1964, 83). A common pattern of behavior, which corresponds to this symptom, can be found in the characters' eroticism, a confusion in their erotic aims, for example when the fiancé and the friend of the missing girl become involved with one another during the search, not out of love, but rather for no particular reason, just as a matter of habit. Motifs of eroticism are to be found throughout the film and form a series of topics, which lead the viewers to form corresponding expectations and serve to create coherence in the story. Another sequence of repeated motifs is built up around the characters' behavior in the same film: the characters suffer due to their own inner situation, talk about their feelings, and thus are aware of their unhappy state, but despite their knowledge, they do nothing to change it, instead persisting in their old condition. The film repeats contradictory and even paradoxical twists within extremely small actions. In general, the examples of the *cinéma du comportement* are able to make such moments visible and gradually even conspicuous and conscious for the viewers by observing analogous moments of crisis in their lives. Repetition of topics helps to transmit meaning in a specific way, limited to insinuations, and to create interest in particular aspects of life, which then can be seen and questioned in a new way.

During the exposition of *L'Eclisse* a young woman tells her partner that she is determined to leave him. The man does not want to accept this immediate separation after a long relationship and asks her for the reasons for her decision. Even though the woman's explanations reveal her own inability to enter into a lasting relationship more than his fault and the discussion becomes protracted, she finally leaves his apartment and wrests herself free of him after he first follows her in his car and then accompanies her on foot to the door of her own house. In this sequence, a certain form of behavior of the two is choreographed for the viewer during a period of around 13 minutes, in which their positions confront one another. We pay particular attention to the woman's behavior, because on the one hand she shows her desire for change, but on the other a degree of frustration and fatigue becomes apparent, which gives little hope for a decisive change in the circumstances. The further course of the film confirms this impression. The woman becomes involved in another relationship, which however suffers from the same inability of her partner to commit himself to a lasting relationship. Through the periodical repetition of similar forms of behavior, the film leads the viewer to expect the plot to go on in certain ways and to question the characters' way of life. These questions are not developed rhetorically, but rather arise out of the ambiguity of the situations shown in the film. Eco has pointed out that so-called open work in modern art intentionally promotes a fundamental ambiguity in the message, which is based on a certain polysemy and indeterminacy in "the very elements that are combined in it." (Eco 1989a, 39f.) "This second degree of openness to which contemporary art aspires could also be defined as the growth and multiplication of the possible meanings of a given message" (42). In my opinion, this higher level of ambiguity, which can tend to make some viewers insecure, must not be confused with arbitrariness.

A similar narrative strategy can be found in Western European art films such as Ingmar Bergman's *The Silence* (*Tystnaden*, 1962), or even more strongly in most of the films of Eric Rohmer and Jacques Rivette. In *Out One* (1972), Rivette probably created the longest open series of episodes revolving around an invariant center in film history. Not least because series of topics often cannot become effective until they have repeated a motif a number of times, the film runs for about 13 hours. Decades earlier, the Japanese filmmaker Yasujiro Ozu had already anticipated aspects of the *cinéma du comportement*, in that his films are all based on the intratextual repetition of similar patterns of behavior.

Certain analogies to the Western European 'behavioral' films also made themselves noticeable in the 1960's and 70's in the Documentary Style of Fiction Films in Eastern Europe. This was a transnational group style, which I will discuss in detail later.

More recently, American independent films have come to use similar episodic narrative structures, in which the spectators have to filter out the topics by perceiving invariant patterns in the everyday behaviour of the characters. Examples are Jim Jarmusch's *Stranger than Paradise* (1984) and *Down By Law* (1986) or Harmony Korine's *Gummo* (1997). *Stranger than Paradise* is made up of three relatively autonomous episodes that depict two men from the American suburbs and a young woman, the cousin of one of them, who has just arrived from Hungary. We see them in everyday situations, all of which reveal a similar pattern of behavior: the protagonists seem to be frustrated, relatively incapable of communication, and often appear as slackers, but they also prove to be vigorous, in that they refuse to let themselves be used by anyone. A recurring situation unites the episodes: the missed chance. Again and again, the protagonists prove to be incapable of changing their attitude towards each other and thus of changing the cheerless situation they are caught in.

An episodic structure and repeated perceptual patterns also

play a role in those forms of cinematic narration that critics have called character-driven stories, differentiating them from the more common action-driven stories. In fact, there is a sufficiently large selection of such film stories, including older ones such as Karel Reisz' *Saturday Night and Sunday Morning* (1960), as well as newer ones like Robert Zemeckis' *Forrest Gump* (1994) or Amos Kollek's *Sue* (1997). These films often show strong but contradictory characters in various situations that reveal their individual and social features but do not develop a goal-oriented, dramatic storyline that would necessarily involve decisions. Instead, they utilize the episodic form and observe the characters as they live through various events that are not necessarily causally linked. Each character reacts in his or her own way. The invariance in behavior that is made evident through repetition appears in these cases not to be the result of stylization as much as a natural trait of the characters, as an "adjective" in Todorov's sense. Perhaps the iterative principle of series of topoi is grounded in the portrayal of people, in the careful creation of characters whose behavior in many situations is intended to express the unmistakable individuality as well as the stability of a personality.

A common variation on the character-driven story is that instead of one main character there are two antithetic characters who act in a series of episodes, thus focusing the viewers' expectations in a particular way. Even if the plot does not culminate in a traditional climax, the contrasting characters serve to dramatize the individual episodes to some extent. This is the case in Mihalis Kakogiannis' *Zorba the Greek* (*Alexis Zorbas*, 1964), Mikhail Romm's *Nine Days in One Year* (*9 dney odnogo goda*, 1962), and Krzysztof Zanussi's *The Structure of Crystal* (*Struktura krysztalu*, 1969).

The great epics of the cinema found it useful to employ the iterative principle of the topic line in order to maintain narrative coherence within their voluminous and highly ramified episodes. Works like D.W. Griffith's *Intolerance* (1916), Andrei Tarkovsky's *Andrey Rublyov* (1969), and Bernardo Bertolucci's *1900* (*Novecento*, 1976) manifest such topics in varying degrees of conspicuousness and conceptualisation. With the rhetorically formulated intertitles in *Intolerance*, Griffith makes sure that the common theme in the six episodes—as different as they may be in terms of time, setting, and characters—can easily be reduced to the single concept of the title. In contrast, the shared structural characteristics in the large blocks of events in *1900* are hardly noticeable at first. However, upon closer investigation, one discovers that they are not only developed through the periodic mutual appearances of the two main characters, but also through the paradoxical friendship between the son of a farm laborer and the son of a landowner, which the film observes over the course of time. The poor man always refutes this friendship, but in the decisive moment when he could deprive the other of power, he feels himself bound by it. The property owner often speaks of this friendship, but betrays it when he could protect the other man from the Fascist assaults.

Thematic invariance, or at least structural similarity between the links in a series of topics, seems to be a necessary prerequisite for coherence in thoroughly episodic films. This becomes particularly evident, for example, in works that unite actions which happen in different places and are carried out by different ensembles of characters. Roberto Rossellini's *Paisà* (1946), Akira Kurosawa's *Dreams* (1990), Jim Jarmusch's *Mystery Train* (1989) and *Night on Earth* (1991), Chantal Akerman's *A Whole Night/All Night Long* (*Tout une nuit*, 1982), Robert Altman's *Short Cuts* (1993), and Paul Haggis's *Crash* (2004) are among such films.

The six episodes of *Paisà*, which present a chronicle of the Allied advance in Italy and sketches an almost documentary picture of the last days of the war, can be grasped as a narrative unit to a large part because in each case changes in the behavior of the main characters are shown that would not have been possible in this form without the events of the war and the contacts between Allied soldiers and Italians. Rossellini's first sketch for the film is revealing for the conceptual coherence among the episodes, which rely both on plot structures and the principle of invariance: a cross on a grave, the sign of a fallen Allied soldier, was planned to be shown at the end of each episode.

Well-known examples of European art cinema such as Alain Resnais's *Hiroshima mon amour* (1959) and *Last Year at Marienbad* (*L'Année dernière à Marienbad*, 1961), Federico Fellini's *8½* (1963), or Andrei Tarkovsky's *The Mirror* (*Zerkalo*, 1975), which were at the time often referred to as "mise en conscience" because of their mixtures of real events and mental ones like memories, dreams, or fantasies, are almost impossible to analyze unless one investigates the series of topics that serve to give them coherence. The same goes for many fictional experimental films such as the so-called video diaries of the last few years.

The application of a modified topic model also makes sense for the study of a newer phenomenon of storytelling. In American independent film, but as well in the international art cinema of the late 1980s and 1990s, there sometimes occurred films applying a similar strategy of narration named more generally "multi-draft narratives" (Nichols 2002), or, rather specifically, "parallel lines" (M. Smith 2001), "forking-path narratives" (Bordwell 2002; 2006), "forking plots" (Branigan 2002), "modular narratives" (Cameron 2006) or "decentred dynamics of narration" (Tröhler 2006). In order to characterize the narrational strategy "based around several parallel story lines" using a kind of prototype, Murray Smith (2001, 155) describes a sequence at the heart of Quentin Tarantino's JACKIE BROWN (1997) showing an elaborate money-switch. "The switch—involving an exchange of shopping bags in the changing rooms of a clothing store in a mall—is not narrated to us in a linear fashion, tracking the actions of a particular character or set of characters. Nor is the action related to us through cross-cutting, flicking back and forth between their various parties [...] as they pursue their goals. Instead, the action is played out a full three times, on each occasion from the perspective of a different key figure in the switch [...] laying the parallel sequence out in succession, end on end at is were. This is a curious and striking choice."

Since that time, kindred strategies of storytelling have been noticed by different scholars in numerous other films, which led to an extensive corpus of examples that includes its precursors and can be followed up to the present time. To the well-known films of the mentioned type should belong Jim Jarmusch's *Mystery Train*, Wong Kar-wai's *Chungking Express* (*Chung Hing sam lam*, 1994), Quentin Tarantino's *Pulp Fiction* (1994), and *Jackie Brown*, David Lynch's *Lost Highway* (1997) and *Mulholland Dr.* (2001) and Tom Tykwer's *Run, Lola, Run* (*Lola rennt*, 1998).

In film studies, the definition of this corpus is already difficult because of the variability of some important dimensions of formal decisions. Therefore, the common understanding of this type of storytelling seems to be based more or less on a definition *ex negativo*. One can notice an obvious loss of the elementary conditions of narration in the traditional understanding, for instance a loss of the chronological order of events, of the continuity of action space or of the presence of the same central figures in the story's events—all this in very different combinations. But in wondering why a coherence in the best of these stories can be established in spite of the various artists' attempts at deconstructing the traditional rules of narration, one becomes aware of the tendency towards the formation of analogical structures and their recurrence in the present corpus. Again and again one may notice that the description model of perception-based filmic structures is fitting here. But instead of the linear succession of similar structures which are given to the perception cycle in clearly arranged lines of "affordances" of information (cf. Gibson 1979), here multi-layered structural offers, organized in entire networks of topic lines, are at work.

With regard to the decentred dynamics of narration, Margrit Tröhler (2006, 104) points out that "narrative motion which is inevitably pressing on, resembles an 'unfocused chain' (Branigan 1992, 12), in that the episodes, in a manner of speaking, are paratactically lined up and organized spatially rather than according to time, following in this scarcely a unified action scheme. Parallelism, simultaneity, circularity and, as the case may be, seriality dominate the extremely weak causal relationships which can appear among the episodes of characters. By that means, traverse, previous and back references and also 'structural kinships' can be facilitated." Speaking about a "network of analogies" which passes through all levels of narration, Tröhler is building on the remarks of Barbara M. Stafford (1999, 8), who characterizes a structuring of newer artworks by the formation of analogies as "the webworking strategy *par excellence*." She argues concerning their functioning: "Most fundamentally, analogy is the vision of ordered relationships articulated as similarity-in-difference.[...] We should imagine analogy [...] as a participatory performance, a ballet of centripetal and centrifugal forces lifting gobbets of sameness from one level or sphere to another. Analogy correlates originality with continuity, what comes after with what went before, ensuing parts with evolving whole" (Stafford 1999, 9).

Characteristics of the Basic Narrative Structure of Topic Line

(1) From the perspective of cognitive psychology, a series of topics, which is based on a sequence of similar stimuli, motifs, or complete episodes with related thematic tendencies, is derived in terms of structure and function from the principle of the creation of perceptive invariants. Similar configurations of stimuli in the actions or contents of a film, which the viewer may not consciously notice at first, are repeated periodically in the course of a film and thus create latent expectations in the viewer's mind in relation to analogous patterns of perception and meanings they may create. Here I am proposing the hypothesis that it is intratextual repetition that is responsible for the formation of structural coherence that can potentially take on a narrative function.

(2) Neisser's principle of perceptual cycle may be of use in understanding the function of this model. According to this idea, a person explores the world through his or her perceptions and draws on particular cognitive schemata that have been built up through past experience and that he or she then applies to the current situation as hypotheses to be tested and confirmed or corrected. With topic-based narratives, the hypotheses that were set up as reactions to stimuli in the beginning are periodically confirmed in the course of reception through processes of perceptual and probability learning. These processes and their results often go on in a relatively unconscious way for the viewer, who may not be able to grasp them conceptually. Since the production of meaning that occurs is always connected to a cognitive activation of the viewer, the goal-oriented reception of stimuli tends to insist on the creation of narrative coherence. However, the narrative structure remains semantically unstable as a result of the relatively weak hypotheses. This is also true when the individual topics are based on conceptualised actions, since in this case, too, the viewer has to work out the common elements in the events of the whole series.

(3) In general, the contents of topics result from repeated observation of similar phenomena, for instance analogous human behavior, relationships between characters, situations,

or more extensive series of actions. Series of topics tend to show people and their life-world, including their social environment, in terms of a state of conditions, that is, as static and as a status quo, as is characteristic of stagnating situations. The minimal changes in life that they reveal appear in film as "movements regularly and correctly repeated and always equal to themselves" (Lotman 1976, 65).

(4) As topic lines favor the repeated representation of similar phenomena, the principle of stringing together more or less equal, functionally similar elements tends to govern their narrative construction. The order of the elements often seems fairly arbitrary, since they tend to be relatively independent of the course of development of the whole story. The cumulative linking of elements allows the construction of open, unlimited series (cf. Lotman 1976, 70). In fact, films of this kind are often very long and seldom lead to a clear-cut ending.

(5) Processes of this sort require relatively static protagonists. They rarely allow major changes to occur in themselves or their surroundings. They are recognizable not so much through unmistakable actions as through recurrent patterns of behavior. Such perceptual patterns are often linked to the observation of contradictory phenomena, in particular to ones in which conflicts first become apparent but have not yet led to outright confrontations or to transgressions of the existing order. New models of the world cannot be created in this way, but the observation of life can cause the viewer to begin to question the world that is shown because of the conflicts, discrepancies and incongruities in it and thus become critical of the usual model of the world.

(6) Since the processing of information in topics usually remains at the perceptual level, it is difficult to reflect on them consciously or to interpret their meaning. Furthermore, we can assume that the observation of the film goes on in short-term or working memory and is not stored in the viewer's long-term memory. This means that the viewer can only remember the stimuli for a short time after having watched the film. This is also why viewers rarely have the impression that the perceptual topics form a unified and closed story. The film

seems to be open and its meaning ambiguous.

(7)   Even if a film does not provide any semantically more stable structures such as causal chains or narrative stereotypes to go along with the perceptual topics, it still may fulfill their traditional function and create narrative coherence by substituting for narrative structures. The narration will, however, be of a different—"open"—kind. It takes an active and sensitized spectator to be able to communicate about this kind of narrative.

5.2.3   Narrative Stereotypes and Genre Storytelling

Another basic narrative structure that makes up a third important organizational principle of film stories is that of narrative stereotypes that refer to film stereotypes. This basic structure is never found in just one film, but rather is based on intertextual repetition of the same structures in many works within cinema or the other arts.

A film narrative never invents all its plot devices anew, no matter how original it may be, but can always draw on the long cultural experience of storytelling (and now on a special tradition of audiovisual forms), and thus can draw on specific patterns of narration that were invented long ago and have proven themselves in communicative practice. These narrative structures can be empirically verified by determining intertextual repetition of certain formal elements. Thus we can recognize narrative stereotypes in configurations of stimuli that have a narrative potential and have been employed in a large number of films. These narrative patterns can be found recurring in a long historical line of tradition just as much as in the contemporary ensemble of media within a certain culture. These patterns make up a unit of information during reception and thus create coherence and make it easier to grasp a work cognitively.

Causal chains are one such pattern, which have become conventionalized and canonized during the development of Western narrative traditions and has become a story schema that is often referred to as the canonical story. Referring to the experimental research of the psychologist Jean Mandler, David Bordwell (1989b, 26ff.) has noticed that "Mandler and her colleagues propose prototypical schemata that are characteristic of narratives. These 'canonical stories' consist of certain elements in a standard order: an initial description of time and place; a delineated episode that undergoes development; a development that consists of either a character's simple reaction that triggers immediate action or a character's complex reactions that cause a 'goal path' to be initiated; and other components. This schema, with a few hierarchical branches, acts as a structured set of expectations into which the data of a given text can be factored. Such a schema can be shown to facilitate understanding and recall of a wide number of stories [...] For example, the classical Hollywood narrative is in many ways similar to Mandler's 'canonical story,' and it delegates to the spectator the task of assembling events into a coherent causal whole."

As early as the tragedies of antiquity, well-known myths served as narrative stereotypes. The playwright Friedrich Dürrenmatt, as quoted above, wrote of them: "The audience knew what it was about, it was less curious about the subject matter than about how it would be treated" (1955, 13).

Archetypes work in a similar way, as Eco (1989b, 296) has proved—in a very amusing way—using a whole network of archetypical situations in Michael Curtiz' *Casablanca* (1942): unhappy love, escape, sacrifice, the love triangle, and the way to the Promised Land. The spectator has standardized expectations, as it were, about the further course of action, when he or she is confronted with this kind of second-hand formal element.

Stable narrative patterns are clearly visible in genre films. Mikhail Bakhtin accurately referred to genre as a "representative of creative memory" (1972, 179) within artistic development, and pointed out the unchanging and barely flexible skeleton of genres and the references to them. Here too, complex cognitive schemata come to exist in the minds of filmmakers and viewers during the course of a long cultural process of learning. These can be re-activated when they are used again within a film narrative. These semantically highly stable cognitive schemata are related to rigid and quite specific patterns of expectations in individuals. The narrative conventions of various genres can evoke very strong hypotheses about the further development of the plot, which most likely will turn out to be true. The viewer can count on a happy ending in a comedy, on a showdown between the opponents at the end of a western, on the capture of the perpetrator in a crime movie, etc. It is not only easy to anticipate the events, but they also automatically cohere into larger complexes of information. Thus the viewers can understand them effortlessly, and they channel or direct the process of reception.

Narrative forms that make significant use of stereotypes are characteristic of the current media culture, particularly the innumerable examples of entertainment movies and television programs that make use of serial forms (cf. Eco 1989b, 301ff.). A second-hand culture has come to shape the audio-visual media over the last two decades.

Filmmaking learned to use stereotypes at an early date, since what early fictional films offered the public was generally patterned on the audience's narrative and genre expectations, which had already been developed in mass culture and particularly in its theatrical forms.

When the cinema developed its own formal possibilities, this did not mean that a theoretical understanding of this aspect of storytelling also developed. And even today there is no generally recognized term to refer to this phenomenon in the language of film and media studies. Following a concept that Jörg Schweinitz, for example, has developed over the last two decades in Germany (1986, 1987, 1990) which concerns itself with the concept of stereotypes within a framework of film aesthetics, I have integrated this concept into the PCS model based on cognitive psychology. In doing so, I have tried to make use of the knowledge gained in various disciplines and areas of research concerned with related phenomena (Wuss 1992, 1993). Alongside information gained from the history of discourses directly about film and media studies (Schweinitz 2006), there also exists a broad range of experience gained in other disciplines. It is related to specific directions of psychology, literary studies or cultural scholarship, so that we have to do with a whole field of related concepts of stereotypes, which all make use of the same term, but in very divergent ways when we arrive at details (cf. Wuss 1993, 158ff.).

Thus psychological conceptions with regard to the idea of stereotypes in film range from Pavlov's psycho-physiological idea of the "dynamic stereotype," which referred to systems of partially reflexive neural connections that develop and reach a certain stability as a response to repeated, analogous stimuli (cf. Pavlov 1972, 212), through social psychological theories about "public opinion" like those of Walter Lippmann (1922) up to cognitive theories of schemata and their attempts to define story grammars, such as Rumelhart (1975), Thorndyke (1977) or J. Mandler (1984) have undertaken.

Following the ideas of Walter Lippmann, who viewed people's ideas about external reality as being shaped to a very large extent by socially mediated opinions, often including inappropriate or false ones, American social psychology has approached stereotypical ideas largely in terms of false judgments and prejudices (cf. Lilli 1982). This seems to have given a pejorative association to the term "stereotype". Even though there have been a number of new approaches to the concept of schemata from the perspective of cognitive psychology in the meantime, which have shown the usefulness of strong "perception-expectation hypotheses from earlier cognitions" (Lilli 1978, 24) in human information processing, the negative connotations of the concept which are anchored in everyday thinking have hindered the use of a neutral model of cinematic or narrative stereotypes such as the one I am trying to apply here to objectively describe formal devices.

Literary studies in the 19th century developed ideas about the construction of dramatic stories that described the basic process of the formation of stereotypes (without calling them that) in a quite different, but equally judgmental way—that is, as a positive norm. The five-level pyramidal structure for the construction of drama in Gustav Freytag's *Technik des Dramas* (1965 [1863]) is particularly well known. This schema has the advantage of describing general rules within causal chains of events and defining phases of action, but even at that time applied only to a very limited number of works (cf. Pfister 1982, 320ff.). Although nowadays it is not applicable to a large number of excellent plays and films, it is undergoing a certain revival in recent scriptwriting guides and schools, apparently because Hollywood favors this kind of plot pattern and it serves as the linchpin for such textbooks. To clarify this issue: the pyramidal formation is valuable as a descriptive model of structural relationships, but causal relationships cannot be made into a universal norm that governs every production, since other basic structures of narration with their own rules and norms also exist. As structural theories of narrative developed out of normative poetics and dramaturgical rules during the 20th century and were applied to film (Wollen 1976; Fell 1977), these proved to be applicable only to a certain group of examples as well. For example, they fit the films of a certain genre, but through combinations with other descriptive models they could be made more flexible. Will Wright (1975) combined descriptive methods from Vladimir Propp's *Morphology of the Folktale* ((1928]1969) with elements taken from Claude Lévi-Strauss's work on mythology in order to investigate narrative conventions in westerns.

Cultural theory and its approaches to phenomena of mass culture and intertextuality have also contributed to knowledge about the construction of narrative stereotypes. Eco's comments about intertextual repetition in contemporary popular literature probably apply to film as well: "If we examine the iterative scheme from a structural point of view, we realize that we are in the presence of a typical high redundancy message. [...] The task for the iterative scheme is presented then as a taste for redundancey. The hunger for entertaining narrative based on these mechanisms is a hunger for redundancy. From this viewpoint, the greater part of popular narrative is a narrative of redundancy." (Eco 1972, 21) According to Eco, the pleasure found in such stories arises when "[...] the public recognizes (with satisfaction) always and ever the same story, under superficial disguises." (Eco 1997, 21) In order for narrative stereotypes to arise, it generally seems important that the audience have already developed an idea on the basis of having seen the same configuration of stimuli before, thus giving it a semiotic quality and storing them in long-term memory. It is even conceivable that they are anchored in the permanent or tertiary memory of the audience and thus can hardly be forgotten. In that case, they are of course highly redundant.

It is interesting and somewhat paradoxical that narrative stereotypes become cultural signs and fixed in the individuals' memory, but can also become habitual and ordinary through constant use. This means that they lose their power to gain attention and often may become hardly even consciously noticeable. Their reception then occurs nonconsciously. The viewer perceives them, but hardly pays attention to them.

Examples of Films with Dominant Narrative Stereotypes

In order to briefly explain what narrative stereotypes look like and how they can function as basic narrative structures, I will make use of examples that are all linked to the special case of genre conventions that stick to certain procedures. As classical, popular, or hybrid genre forms create specific types of possible worlds they also provide for certain types of probability with regard to coming events and their narrative stereotypes set up corresponding patterns, for example with regard to the final resolution of the plot. They often overlay and modify clearly defined causal chains or topic lines and enter into a new synthesis with them. Thus many of the film examples already used to describe these basic structures also reveal how the plot is reshaped through narrative stereotypes of a particular genre, as can often be seen in the film endings.

The events in Wajda's *Ashes and Diamonds* and Chukhrai's *The Forty-First* confront their heroes with unresolvable conflicts and thus lead them to the kind of catastrophe that has defined the ending of tragedies since ancient Greece. The protagonist of Chukhrai's film, who shoots her lover, is portrayed as the victim of a society that demands that individuals sacrifice personal happiness for the sake of politics.

A film like Teshigahara's *Woman in the Dunes* comes close to the structure of a parable, in that the actions and the course of life shown can easily be related to a certain idea. When the protagonist accepts living in the dunes as his life trajectory, this stands for the idea that he finds this way of life, despite its difficulties, to be more meaningful than his previous middle-class existence.

In many ways Zinnemann's *High Noon* adheres to the conventions of the classical Western, which require that the bitter conflict between the protagonist and his opponents end in a showdown, in which the antagonists will finally find their downfall. However, it is also apparent that the plot also resembles a parable with its specific patterns, for instance in that the film portrays the responsible individual, deserted by his fellows. This mixture of different genre elements turns the film into a predecessor of a tendency that became more important in later decades, in which narrative stereotypes from various genres become mixed into poly-genres.

After having radically based his tetralogy of behavioral films at the beginning of the 1960s on topic lines, Michelangelo Antonioni made use of narrative stereotypes from popular genres in his later works such as *Blow up* (1966), *Zabriskie Point* (1970) and *The Passenger* (*Professione: reporter*, 1976). He combined these stereotypes with other elements such as those from parables and thus moved in the direction of hybrid genres, but also integrated extensive topic series that reveal patterns of behavior. These were, however, reshaped by the stereotypes, making the film plots more coherent and straightforward. *Blow up*, for example, employs stereotypes from detective movies, but modifies these to a great degree so that the story of a photographer who believes he has discovered a murder does not end with the murderer being arrested, as the genre conventions would demand, but instead becomes mixed with a parable about someone searching for the truth but constantly being distracted from his goals. Topics then vary this pattern of behavior.

In *The Passenger*, the opening sequence is based on recurring topics, but after that the pace of the film changes abruptly and narrative stereotypes from adventure films come to the forefront. The unfortunate reporter takes advantage of the opportunity when the man next door in an African hotel dies. He takes his passport to switch identities. The other man turns out to have been a weapons dealer, and the new identity brings the reporter into contact with African liberation movements. It is quite revealing, however, that the protagonist's inability to enter into a dialogue with the Africans, which is shown at the beginning, is carried on in different ways throughout the course of the film. The reporter's apparent interest in the cause of the liberation front soon fades away and he even quite intentionally deceives their representatives when he promises them something he cannot deliver. And even though the protagonist dies at the end of the film, this is by no means a conventional adventure movie.

These last examples show that the descriptive models discussed here can make it possible to account for the coexistence of narrative stereotypes from different genres in the same work and also to analyze regularities in the films that derive from other basic structures of narration.

Characteristics of Basic Structures of Narrative Stereotypes

(1) Stereotypes as a basic narrative structure are grounded in the
     use of cinematic structures governed by stereotypes that have
     already proven their value in organizing narratives in
     previous cultural processes. These proven narrative patterns,
     which already have a relatively stable signification, can be
     verified through their intertextual repetition in certain given
     forms, for instance through their recurrence within a particular
     line of tradition or within the current ensemble of a certain
     area of media culture.

(2) Stereotypes are based on the frequent use of certain narrative
     patterns in the past. This leads to a cultural process whereby
     the audience or, more exactly, a particular audience learns
     these narrative structures and they become conventionalized.
     As stereotyped narrative patterns overlay the occurrences
     shown in the film, they build larger units of information,
     which promote the viewers' cognitive access to the film story.

(3) In artistic productions, narrative stereotypes serve not only to
     make the course of action more predictable, but building larger
     units of information also follows an aesthetic strategy of using
     already known elements to make it easier to gain insight into
     new and unknown areas. Therefore the aesthetic learning
     processes that are initiated through narrative stereotypes
     constantly alternate between conscious processes of rational
     reflection and nearly unconscious processes at the level of
     probability learning.

(4) Narrative stereotypes are highly complex systems, which
     generally integrate previously canonized narrative structures
     such as causal chains and topic lines; in the special case of
     genre stories they also incorporate stereotypes of themes,
     characters, conflicts, etc.

(5) Recurring exposure to the same narrative patterns causes these
     structural relationships to become stored in the viewers'
     permanent memory and thus provoke correspondingly strong
     expectations, which is why they can be viewed as semantically
     stable forms. This also applies to those cases where frequent
     use has led to habituation, whereby the stereotypes become

less conspicuous and viewers tend to take them up nonconsciously without noticing them.

(6)   There are innumerable possibilities for the use narrative stereotypes. Particularly intense, systematic, and effective use of this basic structure occurs in genre stories. Since there are various film genres with corresponding stereotypes, no general model that could serve as an ideal type has yet been recognized.

(7)   In an analogous way to more elementary structures governed by stereotypes, narrative stereotypes not only initiate cognitive processes, but also set off whole subroutines of complex psychological activity, including images, emotions, opinions, etc. The use of genre stereotypes in particular tends to generate specific imaginative worlds (possible worlds) and strong emotions, as will be discussed later.

6. Toward the Application of the Model of Narration

6.1 Generalization of the Analytic Approach by Means of Combined Descriptions

The basic narrative structures I have sketched out here are meant to show that there is not just one structural relationship that can be used to describe the narration of a film and to explain its way of functioning, but rather several, maybe even many of them. I have discussed three of them, which can be determined and differentiated empirically. In all three cases we find relationships that correspond to Aristotle's "standards of necessity or probability." But in each case this occurs in a different way and according to different rules, and is based on a different means of functioning. The differences make it clear that one must read a film more closely in order to be able to analyze the coherence of its story. One cannot just follow the inner logic of one structure, but always has to deal with several possible structures that can shape a film according to their various logical relations. The chain of narration can be made up of very different links connected in differing ways.

The model I have suggested here has the advantage of making it possible to collect all the potential narrative structures in a film comprehensively and without bias, since it works on a descriptive rather than ideal-typical basis. Above all, it can be generalized. Thanks to the possibility of freely combining the three basic structures, the model can be used to describe all forms of narration instead of only those that correspond to a particular ideal type. Since the model permits such wide access to different films, it is particularly useful in analyzing artistic films, since these always attempt to create a message based on original experience and at the same time to make use of innovative formal stimuli in aesthetic communication. Distinctiveness of intention and form is particularly important for such films, and analysis must pay special attention to these divergences from known or common forms to make us aware of them, if it is to do justice to new creative developments.

As to the three basic structures, the viewer's process of narrative comprehension is not revealed to us, but it seems that in trying to understand the meaning of a story we begin with the more easily recallable or semantically stronger structures, i.e. the stereotypes of narration or the conceptualised causal chain of events, and then proceed to the semantically weaker and hardly recallable topic lines. Bordwell, drawing on the work of the psychologist Jean Mandler, writes: "Mandler takes the canonical story to be a structured mental representation that is essential to understanding narrative texts. She appears to assume that such schemata function heuristically. The perceiver selects from the schema those features that seem most appropriate to the task at hand (that is, understanding the story). If the case at hand does not fit the canonical, then other strategies must be deployed to make sense of it" (Bordwell 1989b, 27). This leads to the supposition that, in some cases, topic lines are able to substitute for the canonical stereotypes and causal chains in organising the process of storytelling and story comprehension.

6.2 Combination and Interaction of Different Basic Structures

Normally, topic lines, causal chains, and narrative stereotypes work together to determine the structure and function of film narration. The model allows us to describe the basic structures separately, but assumes the possible co-existence of multiple basic structures and aims at examining their interactions. This is important because the basic structures never exist alone or in a "pure form." Their connection to different phases of processes of cognition is one reason for this. Although there may be identifiable relations of dominance among them, their innumerable possible combinations result in a richness of forms of storytelling and must be grasped by analysis. The various forms of interaction lead to different consequences for the contents.

In many cases, the effects of one level directly reinforce the aim of another, so that we may speak of semantic cooperation among the basic structures.

Tony Richardson's *The Loneliness of the Long Distance Runner* (1962) tells of a highly unusual occurrence: a young inmate of a home for juvenile delinquents is a talented long-distance runner and therefore the head of the institution fosters him, so that the institution can win the most important prize in a competition with prominent schools. However, shortly before reaching the finishing line, he intentionally loses the race and thus forsakes the privileges he could have gained. The youth's inner conflicts, which lead him to this act of resistance, are not shown through a linear and causal dramatic story-line, but rather through a series of flashbacks which are edited into the sequences of training and competition and which depict his previous life. Through situations that describe and thematize the boy's social misery, the viewer learns about his motivation to rebel against the rules of society. In terms of content, the series of episodes thus works hand in hand with the dramatic decision, creating a form of narration that corresponds both to causality and to a topic line, thus gaining the advantage of making it possible to experience the inner conflicts of the protagonist more intensely. The resolution of these conflicts, which at once represents the protagonist's overcoming of himself and an affront to the establishment, closely corresponds to the narrative stereotype of a certain genre, the British social drama of that period.

Causal chains and topic series work hand in hand in a different way in Orson Welles's *Citizen Kane* (1941). The film plot, concerning the contradictory personality of an American press

tycoon, begins with Kane's death and is linked to the story of a
team of journalists trying to discover the meaning of the man's
dying word: "Rosebud." The journalists never find out that
"Rosebud" was the brand name painted on a sled that Kane had to
leave behind in his rural childhood home, but through a series of
interviews with various people who were close to Kane the viewers
do experience episodes from his life that illustrate his contradictory
personality, as he degenerated from a vigorous self-made man to
an inhuman despot. The journalists' investigation serves to link the
events causally, while the interviews and flashbacks systematically
build up a series of topics that show the protagonist's character to
be determined by an inner conflict. This is further supported by the
narrative conventions of a genre that was coming into being at the
time, in which the schema of the detective film is carried over onto
the actions of an investigative journalist.

Beginning a biography with the protagonist's death generally
gives the narrator the opportunity to focus on particular episodes
from the character's life as central conflicts that shape his or her
personality and fate. Agnès Varda's *Vagabond* (*Sans toit ni loi*,
1985) begins with a sequence in which a young woman is found
dead in a vineyard, where she has obviously frozen to death in a
weakened condition. An investigation conducted in the style of TV
interviews then allows the film to present various people from the
area who provide information about the life of the deceased
woman and also express their opinions about her way of life. Both
series of topoi reveal similar contradictions. On the one hand, the
viewers are shown various situations from the young woman's life,
showing her as someone searching for individual freedom and
rebelling against society by living the life of a vagabond. On the
other hand, the at times contradictory attitudes of the people she
came into contact with make it clear that they viewed her
endeavors with contempt as well as admiration. In a way similar to
that of *Citizen Kane*, the combination of the structure of an
investigation, as something governed by ideas, and the series of
perceptual motifs creates the possibility of finding a suitable way to
develop the complex dialectic of the character in the narrative.

The examples mentioned here show that the different basic
structures of narrative interact with each other, thus permitting
contents from one level to be developed further at another level;

thus they cooperate in generating meaning.

This is not always the case, however. As was shown with regard to dominant topic lines, semantically weak narrative structures can replace semantically stronger ones, if these are not prominent enough or are not present throughout the entire film. Then we have a case of semantic substitution; elsewhere I have spoken of a "substitutional law of basic narrative structures" (Wuss 1992, 33). The effects of such a law can clearly be seen in films of behavior, in which neither narrative stereotypes nor the causal chain of a traditional plot holds the film together. The viewer has to start with the series of recurring topics to begin to understand the film, since they help provide some guidance about how to put the events into perspective.

A third possible form of interaction between the various basic structures is that of semantic conflict. This usually results in the viewers being confronted with a film ending that is intentionally ambivalent, for instance in that two processes with contradictory meanings are shown. In a film like Fellini's *8½*, such a conflict appears in the final resolution, which is intentionally kept ambivalent. On the one hand, we see how the protagonist, a film director, gives up on his new film project, which is already in production, because he is unable to articulate the meaning of the film. He decides to stop shooting, and this is shown at the level of a quasi-real story organized according to causal relations. On the other hand, a second ending offsets this relentless decision, which amounts to giving up on a work of art. Here we see the protagonist's inner visions, which are lively and euphoric and the exact opposite of giving up. This further develops impulses from a chain of expressive topics systematically established earlier in the film, particularly at the ends of scenes and sequences. In these scenes we see joyful expressions and movements, dances, and other gestures that show that the difficulties of life can be overcome, that individuals can cope with the world. As the narration makes this series of motifs more and more dominant, it also points to the film's meaning in a corresponding direction (as will be shown more closely later).

In this sense, one could further extend the three-step model of narrative structures suggested here in regard to correlations and interactions between these structures and identify three basic variations of such correlations:

(1) semantic cooperation,
(2) semantic substitution,
(3) semantic conflict.

Each of these types of correlation has its own consequences for the narrative strategy of a work.

6.3 Application of the Model to Changes in the Cinema

One advantage of the three-rung model of narrative structures is that it can help to differentiate the various structures that a film offers and to discover various kinds of rule that may lead to the construction of coherent narratives, including those that are consciously received, many of which have been known since antiquity, as well as others that are processed in a relatively unconscious way or that are based on nonconscious structural relationships.

This ability to differentiate is not only useful to characterize individual works or a whole artistic tendency more exactly, but the model can also be of value in that it makes it easier to compare concrete forms of narration, thus allowing us to discern changes in narration more precisely. It makes structural shifts in the works of individual filmmakers, complete stylistic movements, or whole periods of film history visible.

For filmmaking it is always relevant whether a certain film story is predestined to be portrayed as a singular, dynamic incident, based on a hard conflict, or whether it is better suited to being shown as many similarly formed, small, static moments, whose conflicts tend to remain under the surface instead of escalating. In other words, whether the story is closer to a causal chain or a topic line. And it is no less important to recognize when stereotypical sequences of action have to be introduced.

The search for appropriate forms of narration for changing kinds of content has led to conspicuous modifications in narrative forms in the *œuvre* of some filmmakers. As could be seen in the works of Michelangelo Antonioni already discussed, whose *Story of a Love Affair* (*Cronaca di un amore*, 1950) still adhered to the norms of classical closed narration, the director came to renounce the basic structure of a causal chain in his tetralogy of behavioral films during the first half of the 1960s, which unreservedly adopted the direction of establishing open forms of narration in film, based on topic lines. Contemporaries were then astonished to see the same director's apparent return to classical narrative film in 1966 with *Blow Up*. Looked at more closely, however, the film could be recognized as an active step forward towards employing narrative stereotypes from genre films. Similar turning points can be found in the work of Andrei Tarkovsky, who had used an extreme form of open narration in *The Mirror*, but then drew on the science fiction genre in *Stalker* (1979), where he combined its narrative stereotypes with a parable. Like Antonioni, this writer-director also made use of the pre-conscious experiential contents of topic lines, and went on to reshape them into semantically more stable structures, making the course of action easier to comprehend. A similar change with regard to the choice of narrative structures took place in the work of representatives of a younger generation of filmmakers. Jim Jarmusch's early films were clearly based on open narrative structures supported by topic lines; in *Dead Man* (1995) or *Ghost Dog: The Way of the Samurai* (1999) stereotypes, including those of genre stories, became dominant over longer stretches; and in the meantime a tendency to a partial return to episodic forms is discernable in films like *Coffee and Cigarettes* (1986) and *Broken Flowers* (2005). Wong Kar-wai, on the other hand, began his career at a time when the postmodern tendency toward stereotyping converged with the trash culture of popular cinema. He made his own way in the midst of this by beginning with dominant stereotypes but progressively giving topic lines greater weight, which permitted him to observe the complex forms of behavior of his protagonists very precisely in a film like *In the Mood for Love* (*Fa yeung nin wa*, 2000).

This description of changes in the narrative structures in the *œuvres* of outstanding filmmakers applies in similar ways to group styles. Again and again we see certain shifts in narrative structures in entire tendencies, and the model helps grasp these changes more easily. The analogous changes in the form of storytelling do not occur at the same time for different filmmakers and stylistic movements, but if one observes longer historical processes, one sees that certain conspicuous changes do go on within relatively short periods, so that the model can help in breaking the stylistic history of cinema up into periods. The formal criterion of a classical style oriented toward narration according to causal chains dominated European cinema after 1945, but Italian neo-realism, which clearly favored episodic structures, marked a turn toward a cinema of modernism that introduced obviously open forms and topic lines, and in the last decades of the twentieth century narrative stereotypes became highly influential in postmodern cinema, in which films often went without causal chains, combining stereotypes with recurrent motifs. Each of these breaks brought a different quality of aesthetic stimuli with it and also led to a new view on life.

The kind of description developed in this model can also be applied to other types of films, for instance documentary or animated films, since similar basic forms of narration have evolved there. This applies to experimental films of all kinds as well. Furthermore, the existence and generally also the dominance of the basic forms can often be particularly plausibly proven with examples of good advertising commercials. Their extreme brevity forces the filmmakers to make clear decisions as to whether to use dominant topic lines with their repetition of the same elements, a causal chain centered on a particular event, or genre stereotypes to structure the film. In the case of commercials that use genre stereotypes we can see that the viewers only need a second, or rather just a fraction of a second, to recognize a genre and call up its conventions in their mind, since without immediately accessible memories of the basic situations of crime stories, spy stories or comedies, they would not be able to understand the message of the advertisement at all.

If we want to see what value the PCS model can have for the creative process of filmmaking, we must first realize that descriptive models are not a kind of construction blueprint. Therefore it would be wrong to expect that we can use their categories to form patterns for film plots. In the process of working on a film, which always includes phases of analysis in the sense of critical reflection on what has been accomplished thus far, a descriptive model can be of assistance in objectifying the author's individual impressions. In this sense it can help to define the passages that the author finds satisfying within the intuitively-defined structure more clearly in formal terms, in order to use them as a pattern for the narrative organization in developing the rest of the film story. That does not mean that external rules have to be applied, but rather that the model define standards that have been set in successful decisions of the author during the work thus far and they can then be used to monitor the further development and perhaps prevent the writer or director from deviating from his or her own line.

Seen from a theoretical perspective, the model-based approach can provide a number of advantages, the most important of which is that it seeks to be compatible with traditional film studies, but also tries to look for connections to psychology. The three basic structures of film narration can be empirically verified in the case of concrete cinematic works, and the conclusions about their function that I have drawn here could be turned into hypotheses about the effects of films, but testing these hypotheses will of course require further work.

To make progress in this area, it would make sense to pick up on the work of earlier approaches to the narrative effects of causal chains (Trabasso et. al. 1984; Böhm 1990; Ohler 1991; Tan 1996) and to continue more recent investigations of plot points and topic lines (Suckfüll 1997; 2000). The latter have made apparent to what an astonishingly large extent audiences unconsciously react to the repetition of similar structures in films, as changes in the heartbeat and skin resistance of test persons have shown.

Chapter III: Conflict and Problem-solving

In the last chapter, I described specific modes of cinematic narration and developed a model of cognitive psychology to describe these modes in their varying dependence on the dominating basic structures of narration such as topic line, causal chain or narrational stereotype. The following considerations deal with the dynamics of narration linked with the problem of conflict.

Cinematic narration is based on showing. We can see the actions and events depicted on the screen, in a life-like form, which includes their original movement. Thus, the dynamics of the live processes come immediately into the moving image, into the single images, scenes, sequences and also the film's entire story development. Since these dynamics are very important for the narration and the viewer's experience, the theory must look for methods and models to describe and explain this aspect of the cinema.

For these reasons, European filmmakers and theorists use the categorical notion of "conflict", which has its origins and a long tradition in theatrical dramaturgy, as an appropriate analytical instrument. I would like to develop this old idea, and connect it with some newer concepts of psychology.

Therefore, I want to explore the links between the understanding of conflict and the cognitive aspect of problem-solving. The next chapter will be dedicated to the relations between conflict and emotion.

1. The Notion of "Conflict" and Its Philosophical Background

The notion of conflict used in theatrical dramaturgy refers most fundamentally to human agency, or the various interests and intentions that are taken up by the characters and lead to concepts of "collision" and "colliding action" upon which, according to Hegel (1965, II: 521), all dramatic action is based.

Early filmmakers and theorists quickly recognized the profound influence which situations of conflict can exert on the screen. Hugo Munsterberg ([1916] 1970), Urban Gad (1920), Sergei M. Eisenstein ([1929] 1988) and Vsevolod Pudovki ([1929] 1983) all modified this notion of "conflict" for an application to film, usually in connection with storytelling.

In the *Dictionary of Literary Terms* (Shaw 1972, 289) we find the following definition: "Conflict: The oppositions of persons or forces upon which the action depends in drama and fiction is called conflict. Dramatic conflict is the struggle which grows out of the interplay of opposing forces (ideas, interests, wills) in a plot; conflict may be termed the material from which a plot is constructed." The term "conflict" implies a great inner dynamism and a particularly emotional unfolding of events in the portrayal of fictional life. Strangely enough, in more recent texts on filmic narration one rarely encounters the term. During the last decades, the notion of "plot" has been integrated into the understanding of conflict and has displaced the term.

To locate the philosophical background implicit in the term "conflict" as a dramaturgical category, one must look at the dialectical principle of contradiction and the movement it evokes. The formula that all actions occur because of an opposition is to be found as early as Heraclite (cf. Herakleitos of Ephesos 1958, 133). According to Hegel, contradiction is the "principle of all autonomous movement" (1951, 58ff.).

And one can find elaborate explanations of this principle in the writings of the philosophers of dialectical materialism such as Marx and Engels.

Contradictions are significant phenomena that can be easily verified empirically. They have the merit that we can see their opposite tendencies. So it is not without reason that this principle has been used to explain the train of events in the dramatic structures of European theatre and film. In this model, it is contradictions within the segment of life shown in a work that drive the plot forward through collisions between the character's actions. They create a dynamic process, a course of action with changing situations, which we refer to as "mimetic narration."

The moments of conflict in an artwork seem to have their basis in the real contradictions of human life. In the reality of human society, one can find a broad field of oppositions that permanently causes changes. Therefore, philosophy speaks about a "causal field" (cf. Mackie 1980, 39) as the source, or starting point, of all development. The events in a film depict the realities of life as a causal field, as well. They demarcate an entire "conflict field" within the film's story. This field of conflict relies on a diverse range of contradictions and antagonisms that cannot be reduced to one key dramatic conflict, even if such a conflict can be seen as dominating the story.

2. Conflict Situations in "High Noon"

One can begin by finding such conflict moments, embedded in a course of action with changing situations, in a concrete film—in a sequence near the end of Fred Zinnemann's *High Noon* (1952).

The conflict potential of this film is more than obvious. The American marshal Bill Kane has worked in the country-town of Hadleyville for many years and has maintained law and order there. But on the day of his wedding, as he is leaving the town together with his young wife, he learns that Miller, a notorious outlaw, who had been handed a long jail-term with Kane's help, has been discharged from prison. Miller is on the way to town to meet up with his former gang and, presumably, to take his revenge on the marshal as well as to resume his robberies. Although his wife does not support the idea, Kane decides to stay in Hadleyville to fight the Miller gang, in belief that the town's inhabitants are willing to help him. But the marshal soon has to realize that the town's people are cowardly, and that they will leave him to fight this unequal battle on his own. Even his wife forsakes him. Nevertheless, Kane is ready for action when the gang leader arrives at the train station at high noon.

Minutes before the gang leader's arrival, Kane is refused the support of the inhabitants of Hadleyville, who have assembled in the church, and an old friend, his predecessor. Moreover, the marshal is forced to engage in an energy-wasting fist-fight with his young deputy, who sees him as a disturbing rival. As the marshal asks for some water in the barber-shop to clean his wounds, in a back house a carpenter is busily hammering together the coffins for the victims of the imminent struggle. Minutes later, at his office, the marshal is visited by his voluntary deputy Herb, who, though originally willing to take part in the struggle against the Miller gang, now bows out after hearing that he is to be the only helper of the marshal. As a family man he feels compelled to abandon such a suicidal mission. The only offer of assistance comes from a young boy who is turned away because of his age. Thus Kane remains alone in his office, and after loading his gun he begins to write his last will.

While the hands of the big clock are moving unrelentingly forward, we can see the Miller gang getting ready for the fight, the parishioners in the church persisting in their inaction, and the people in the saloon waiting for the crucial events. Each shot becomes a cinematic stereotype, a symbol: The clock, the track, the faces of the town's inhabitants in close-up, the judge's empty seat (see fig. 5). While one can hear the approach of the train from afar, Kane's wife Amy, together with the Mexican woman who once was the marshal's lover, steers her carriage to the train station, leaving her husband behind, speechless. By the time the carriage arrives at the station, the train has already arrived. Miller gets off, welcomed by his gang: Let's begin! After the gang sets off for the village, we see the marshal, alone in the deserted square, while the camera pans away from him, leaving him in his loneliness.

The viewer can realize the culmination point of the dramatic conflict, or, more precisely, he can experience an entire conflict field that includes different contradictions and tendencies to colliding actions.

3. Kinds of Collisions and Conflicts

The human being is an entity of different, and often opposite, forces, tendencies or interests that lead to colliding actions. This "field of conflicts" can vary in different ways, and I would like to show some categories of variation:

3.1 Varying Conflict Types: Inter-personal vs. Intra-personal Conflicts

There are interpersonal conflicts based on outer contradictions, for instance between two persons, or between two groups of persons.

On the opposite end of the scale one can find conflicts based on the inner contradictions of the same person. Our own life includes both kinds of contradiction, and the dominant type is often changing. We can suffer when the outer contradictions are painful for us in a given situation, and we can suffer when the inner conflicts, the collisions in our heart, in our soul, are unbearable. But in many situations we have problems coming from both directions. The heroes of the cinema have similar problems, and thus film stories follow the development of these various contradictions simultaneously.

In *High Noon* we can find both types of conflict. The interpersonal conflicts are the most obvious ones; Kane has to fight against the Miller gang. But the sequence shows another interpersonal conflict, too: Kane is confronted with the situation that he must go into the struggle without any help from the people of the town. And there is yet a third important contradiction: his wife is forsaking him, because her religion forbids all violence. Kane is also confronted with his own inner, intra-personal conflict—struggling under the new conditions of his own life compared to his self-perception from the past. The former marshal remains true to himself. At the moment of danger, he cannot change his convictions, his aims and attitudes. In the beginning, the decision to remain in the town seems bearable to him, but in the phase of the citizens' treachery, he has to pay for his nobility.

The dramatic situation is rooted in the complexity of relations between interpersonal and intrapersonal contradictions, which provide the activities of the protagonists with a system of barbed hooks. The fight between the Miller gang and the forces of civilisation would not take place if the retired marshal had left the town without moral constraints. And on the other hand, the dramatic tension would be considerably weaker if he could find like-minded people as comrades-in-arms, instead of facing combat entirely alone.

Often we find films with a less complicated construction of conflict situation. They are based, for instance, on dominant outer, inter-personal conflicts between human beings and nature, i.e. the natural environment, or between two individuals or two groups of persons following opposite interests. A very important case of interpersonal conflicts is the social contradictions and conflicts, the political or military fights, of which *The Battleship Potemkin* (*Bronenosets Potyomkin*, 1925) is a well-known example. Sergei M. Eisenstein's film shows the colliding action of different groups of Russians, who are pursuing their antagonistic class interests. Although the spectator can see the actions of separate individuals, unmistakable in their faces and shapes, and also the differences in their thinking and political convictions, the conflict of the story is based on the opposition between two entire blocs—the representatives and soldiers of the Tsarists and the rebellious mariners, the most active part of the revolutionary Russian people.

Intrapersonal contradictions can lead to another type of dynamics, connected with individual problems, of psychic conflicts. These inner conflicts are not isolated from the environment, from day-to-day life, or from society. They are, on the contrary, mostly the result of the historically-driven formation of a specific character. The reasons for the inner contradictions are often based on change in societal circumstances or conditions, for instance on a historical change in a society that also requires a shift in individual life.

Maciek, the war-weary protagonist of Andrzej Wajda's above-mentioned film *Ashes and Diamonds* (*Popiół i diament*, 1958), lives with such an inner conflict, which structures the whole story. It consists of Maciek's desire to remain true to himself by following the orders of the National Polish Home Army, even though the historical conditions, defining the context in which he is active, have changed and now this force is fighting against its former ally, the People's Army. In spite of his long, upright service in the Home Army, on the first day of peace, the young soldier can no longer use his weapon without pangs of doubt. Wajda (1964, 357) considers Maciek's conflict unresolvable, in that the hero, at the hour of historical change, can neither follow the rules of war nor those of peace.

Similarly to *High Noon*, the story of *Ashes and Diamonds* contains both types of contradiction. In each case, the interpersonal, as well as the intrapersonal conflicts, are working together in forming the "barbed hooks" for the dramatic situation. Nevertheless, the structure and decision-making of these different conflict types is not the same.

3.2 Varying Ways of Decision : Crossroad vs. Presented Bill

It makes a difference whether or not a conflict situation is structured in such a way that the characters are given a genuine alternative in their courses of action. Where they are, aesthetics speaks of "the crossroad problem" in the life of the person or society (Lukács 1955, 101). In this case, the protagonist or an entire group of characters can choose several possible courses of action. He or she can go one way, or another, can become the winner or the loser. He is, indeed, given a real alternative in his actions.

Altogether different is the sort of conflict situation in which a person or a group of people will be "presented with the bill" for an action or behaviour that was concluded in the past (Lukács 1955, 101). In this case the essential decisions of life are brought to a head and the protagonist cannot make his choice at the present. His conflict is how to carry on and to cope with a situation that he cannot change essentially.

As discussed earlier, in *High Noon* we can find both types of conflict decision. The fight can bring victory to Kane or to his antagonists. But in his decision to remain the marshal, Kane is not altogether free. We know the proverb: "a leopard can't change his spots". The protagonist is not able to change his personal make-up. He has arrived at his convictions and intentions in a long process of personal experience that is connected with the historic postulates of society for an upright Westerner. The crisis in the town leads to a "presentation of the bill"-type conflict with regard to Kane's previously attained identity, and he has to pay. "To pay" means, in this case, he has to cope with the painful disagreement with his young wife, and the nearly unsolvable problem of surviving the unequal fight with the gangsters. Kane does not hesitate in his attitudes, but one can see his inner exertions on his face. The scriptwriter Carl Foreman had planned a shot of the hero holding his—unloaded—revolver against his temple, minutes before high noon, at the moment of doubt (cf. Drummond 1997, 61). This gesture was eliminated by Zinnemann in the later working process, but it bears witness to the fact that the authors saw a serious inner conflict in the hero's person.

3.3 Varying Importance: Relevance vs. Irrelevance

With regard to the story and its development of the events, a conflict can be more or less relevant. In the hierarchy of contradictions establishing the causal field for the dynamics of the whole, a conflict can function on different levels. This depends on various factors: for instance, whether it is connected with the activities of the main or minor characters and whether it is powerful and eye-catching or rather weak and inconspicuous.

The central dramatic conflict of classical narration needs very strong contradictions which are relevant for the dynamics of the events, and which usually are based on essential contradictions in reality.

The varying relevance and strength of contradictions leads to a specific hierarchy of conflicts generating plot and sub-plots. Such sub-plots are based on subordinate and marginal events. The position in the conflict hierarchy can change in the flow of filmic events; a weak contradiction, for example, can become stronger and of increasing importance for the whole story.

The described sequence in Zinnemann's film shows, for instance, that the opposition of the young deputy toward Kane, which is based on the assistant's sense of inferiority, grows into a serious danger for the marshal, who needs to preserve all his strength for the fight with the gangsters. Another sub-plot that becomes more important for the outcome of the story focuses on the contradictory attitudes of Kane and his wife. At first, Amy deserts Kane, but in the end she gives him support in the gun fight against the Miller gang, and it is her active and fearless contribution that decides the battle's outcome. Amy's actions are, in part, prepared for by the arguments of the Mexican woman Helen, Kane's former lover, who convinces Amy that she must not forsake her husband. In Zinnemann's film, all the sub-plot relationships and activities of the minor characters lead to conflict structures on the level of conceptualisation and are molded into the central plot. As I will show later, there are other modes of narration that intentionally do not lead to such conspicuous conflict structures.

3.4 Varying Ability for Solution: Solvable vs. Unsolvable

Conflicts have a varying likelihood of being solved; there is a wide range of possibilities from easily solvable to unsolvable. The conflict between the attitudes of Amy and those of the marshal, for instance, turns out to be solvable. Kane's conflict with the stance of the men of Hadleyville remains until the end, and the contradiction between Kane and the Miller gang is an antagonistic one—that is unsolvable in a peaceful way.

But let us say a few words about some aspects of filmic conflicts in general.

On the one hand, a conflict's capacity for solution depends on the tendencies of the real contradictions which are represented on the screen, for instance on the actual contradictions within a society; but it also depends on the author's view of life and his imaginings concerning possible developments in the future. And finally, it depends on the spectator's own experiences, desires and imaginings.

The world, with its contradictions and conflicts, is ever-changing, and at times our imaginings can be helpful in this process. The solution to conflicts and contradictory situations, in life as well as on the screen, is always connected with the author's interests and imaginings and, at the same time, with its psychological impact on the viewer. This impact functions, in a process of mental regulation, with varying methods to influence the emotions of the viewer; for instance, to compensate his inability to overcome his own problems with a happy ending, or to provoke his self-satisfied attitudes to life by film endings of uncertainty, or to confirm his experience of a difficult world by the film's ending tragically. A film ending is not invariably perceived by the audience as good, because of a happy end, and bad, because of a tragic ending. The differing film endings can be helpful for the mental situation of the audience in each case, because the impact on the viewer does not depend solely on the film's actions and outcomes with good or bad endings, but also on the viewer's cognitions, emotions and imaginings with regard to the contradictions of reality.

Parallel to this, I will now examine some aspects of the cognitive processes during film reception.

4. Conflict on the Screen and Problem-solving in the Audience

Not only the collisions which occur on the screen are relevant to an understanding of the concept of "conflict"; the tension which is created within the audience is equally pertinent. That these two realms are not identical becomes clear when we consider the fact that some films do not touch us, in spite of the most violent clashes, while others are extremely moving, although they suggest the presence of only the most minor complications. Cinematic conflict obviously must be seen within the context of the psychology of viewer response.

The framework of the cognitive theory of problem-solving presents a sensible and practical way to model the experience of watching a film because the characters' colliding actions on the screen, and the viewers' form of response, can both be described as processes of problem-solving. The psychological approach sees problem-solving as necessary when

(1)   an unsatisfactory starting situation

(2)   is to be changed into a satisfactory situation, but

(3)   obstacles hinder this (cf. Klix 1971, 604; Dörner 1979; Hussy 1993).

Dramatic conflicts in a film often provide such starting situations for the characters. They have to try to change an unsatisfactory situation, for example the protagonist of Aki Kaurismäki's *Ariel* (1988), who has to change his position in a society that made him an unemployed loser with poor chances of survival. In other films, the protagonists are confronted with the conflicting interests of personal enemies. Their actions do not always succeed or obstacles may prevent a quick solution.

In general, the plot presents the confrontation of opposing forces: the unchanging situation as a whole and the protagonist's desire for an outcome.

If we consider the plot of a film as a process of problem-solving for the characters that leads to a certain decision, we must look not only at the beginning and the ending in terms of such phases of a goal-oriented process, but also grasp the whole course of action that leads to a decision as an on-going confrontation, in which certain sub-goals are reached. Phases of action that intensify the events also tend to lead to preliminary decisions about the possible outcome. They thus represent turning points in the action or various forms of plot points that function as sub-goals in the goal-oriented process of problem-solving.

These plot points not only intensify the action on the screen, but also psychologically activate the audience. This activation is a cognitive one in that it helps to explain the situation rationally, for example, by making certain decisions seem more likely. We know from experience that as viewers, we will become more strongly emotionally involved in such phases of the plot's development. The affective arousal of the audience always rises when decisions and problem-solving seem to be approaching and the action dramatically comes to a head. The activation of both functions goes hand in hand and the viewer becomes both cognitively and emotionally involved in what is happening. Let us begin with the cognitive function.

How can we understand the fact that the viewer takes part in the problem-solving on the screen, although his own problems are not identical with those of the characters? In my opinion, this involvement is the consequence of a fundamental or, more precisely, a "primary motivation", namely man's "need for control" (Oesterreich 1981, 223). Confronted with a constantly changing environment, humans attempt to retain control and to stay in command of present and future situations as much as possible. This attempting has consequences for fictive situations as well, although in a modified way.

Generally, humans rely on their ability to maintain a degree of "active control" over their surroundings and to shape them according to their needs. If this is not possible, they feel the need for "passive control", meaning control in a cognitive sense, the ability, to a certain extent, to foresee what will happen to them and to their surroundings (cf. Dörner, Reither, Stäudel 1983, 63). The experience of film is defined by this fundamental "need for control", but one can have only passive control—as a way to anticipate the filmic events and to foresee the future decisions in the actions on the screen. The film viewer is inclined to reduce the subjective uncertainties implicit in narrative events as much as possible, optimizing the flow of information.

Cinematic narration itself depends on this inclination, since of all events deemed possible by the viewer, those which are anticipated and are concerned with the solution of the conflict take on particular importance in that they resolve uncertainty. Contradictions in the actions of the characters lead to the focusing of the viewer's attention and to a change in cognitive activity. The obligation to resolve the subjective uncertainty perceived by the viewer transforms the act of viewing the collision of the fictive character's actions into a kind of problem-solving process. The protagonist's collision course of action demarcates the parameters of the problematic situation, within which all of the participants are forced to orient themselves.

The viewer is, however, equally implicated in the situation: the actions depicted take place within a dis-equilibrium which increases the viewer's subjective uncertainty about the outcome. The obstacles preventing the protagonists from achieving their ends also hinder the viewer in his attempt to reduce his subjective uncertainty regarding filmic events.

Feelings of uncertainty are produced in the viewer through various modes of narration, any of which may in turn evoke the problem-solving stance. Certain patterns of expectation arise that allow the viewer to differentiate between potential developments in the narrative which are more or less probable. In this manner cognitive processes interact with the events on the screen and together function as one of the determinants of the narration.

Approximating film experience by means of the problem-solving model can be extended in another direction as well. In real life as in films, problematic situations rarely appear in such a highly developed form that they are rationally solvable in the same way that an arithmetic problem, or a strategy game, is. Before we can solve a problem, we first have to identify and define it as such. Therefore, cognitive psychology has attempted to describe the phases of problem-solving behaviour. A well-known scheme is the IDEAL scheme of Bransford and Stein (1984, 12), which distinguishes five steps:

I = Identify the problem
D = Define and represent the problem
E = Explore possible strategies
A = Act on the strategies
L = Look back and evaluate the effects of your activities

These phases of problem-solving are established for both the characters and the viewers of the film, since they often have to identify and define a conflict before they can come up with a strategy to handle it, or retroactively evaluate it in terms of common patterns such as the plot stereotypes of a genre.

In the first chapter, I spoke about three levels, or stages, in the formation of cognitive invariants, beginning with the level of perception that leads to perception-based filmic structures and topic lines of narration. With regard to the IDEAL scheme of problem-solving, one can bring together the two stages "I=Identify the problem" and "D=Define and represent the problem" with the level of perception-based structures and topic lines. "Identifying", "defining" and "presenting" the problems also means choosing and emphasizing a specific moment of contradiction or conflict in the flow of events.

5. Identifying and Defining Conflict Moments by Topic Lines

The film medium in general, and the camera in particular, are able to identify the problematic moments of life by focusing on, and showing, them on the screen in a repetitive way. The repetition of motifs that show the similar disturbances and interruptions of goal-oriented micro-actions in *Ashes and Diamonds* establishes, for example, such an attempt to identify, define and represent a problem or moment of conflict.

Parallel to this example, we may see the repeating motifs of "definitely being final" in the opening sequence of *Ariel*.

There are films, and entire group styles of cinema, that use narration as a strategy for the identification and definition of problems. The aforementioned "Cinema of Behaviour" practised the repetition of similar behavioural patterns of its characters in order to identify and define their conflicts and problem situations. Certain subtle nuances of opposing moments in the characters, such as insignificant activities during their day-to-day life, become more and more conspicuous to the spectator by their iterative showing.

A stark example of the performance of such topic lines can be found at the opening sequence of Michelangelo Antonioni's *L'Eclisse* (1962). The film begins with the final separation of a well-off young couple who have lived together for more than a half decade; The whole sequence lasts 13 minutes. It starts off in the man's elegant flat, where for nearly three minutes the couple are together without saying a word—only the sound of the ventilator is audible. From his armchair, the man is staring reproachfully at the younger woman, Vittoria, who looks serious as well, while she is walking around the room in a strangely undecided manner. Hearing her first words, we learn that she had already made up her mind to leave her companion the previous night and now has only to reconfirm this decision. His suggestion to try to continue their shaky relationship is once again rejected by her. A short translation she took on for him is returned by her undone. His question as to why she is leaving him remains unanswered, obviously because they have already spoken enough about this matter. She flatly refuses to receive phone calls from him in the future. When she sets off for home, across a field on the outskirts of town, he follows her by car and, since she refuses to get in, he walks alongside her. It appears that the two have seldom been in the open so early in the morning, and for a moment they take one another by the hand like a couple. But Vittoria refuses his suggestion they go to a restaurant for an early breakfast, and, finally, they say goodbye to one another in the hallway of her house. He heads back home, and she arrives silently at her flat, which is of a similar fashionable elegance to the man's.

There are neither striking physical actions in this sequence nor verbal expressions which give further information for the characters or the spectator. The situation seems to be unambiguous and even banal. The spectator is confronted with analogical attitudes and behavioural patterns of the characters that recur. The actions and reactions bear witness to a state of affairs that has existed obviously for a long time. Their love is gone, and all attempts to rekindle it are to no avail. But there is no serious effort on the protagonists' part to find the reasons for this, no apportioning of blame, not even accusations as a token of their pain or passion. Such activities seem to be irrelevant in view of the protagonists' feelings of frustration and alienation. The permanent camera observation of the couple's behaviour in different situations brings to light the overwhelming quality of their feelings and attitudes and helps to identify and define their problem or conflict situation. The problem is not that their love is over, the problem seems to be that the protagonists are not able to realize a close relationship due to a kind of self-alienation.

The further events of Antonioni's film continue this process of problem identification. Although Vittoria soon finds a new partner and begins a relationship that looks, for a while, like love, this connection loses its strength immediately, and the partnership does not last due to the protagonists' "illness of feelings" (Antonioni 1964, 85).

The Documentary Style of fiction film in Eastern Europe, another group style, that occurred in the cinemas of the then still socialist countries from the sixties on (cf. Wuss 2003), also used topic lines based mainly on the repetition of similar inconsistent patterns in the characters' behaviour, which the spectator had to identify and to define during the reception processes.

The best films of this group style create a coherent narrative. This is the case with Otar Iosseliani's *There Once Was a Singing Blackbird* (*Iko shashvi mgalobeli,* 1970), produced in Soviet Georgia.

The film begins by showing how the members of a large orchestra playing in the Georgian capital of Tiflis are anxiously waiting for a young musician, who has to give the kettle drums a couple of beats towards the end of the piece. Gija, the sympathetic hero of the film, manages to show up just in the nick of time. This occurrence is, as it turns out, no exception, but rather characteristic of the young Georgian, whose everyday life we are shown in the film. Gija's work is not very demanding, and he pays thus more attention to the little things of life and is constantly fighting the clock. When, at the end of the film, he is coincidentally killed in a car accident—he had turned around to look at a pretty girl—he seems not to have left behind anything more than the nail that he helpfully and attentively hammered into the wall of a clockmaker's

room so that the man could hang up his cap. Here, too, the
succession of events seems to be coincidental; in any case, there is
no causal chain or plot. However, the film continually varies
situations that show a contradiction: the young man is a good-for-
nothing, since he is not trying to reach any recognizable goal. He
abandons the composition he began just as quickly as the book he
borrowed from the library, but in his friendly and considerate way,
he enriches the lives of others. He uses his connections to get a
friend treated by a well-known and very exclusive doctor, he
organizes a serenade for his aunt's birthday, and he is always
willing to take on little tasks without a fuss. On the one hand, the
film emphasizes how the hero immerses himself in trivialities; on
the other hand, it also becomes evident that his development, as
aimless as it seems, constantly serves one of the most sensible aims
there is, namely, making life friendlier and more pleasant for other
people.

The periodic recurrence of the same contradictory element may
not strengthen the dramatic conflict or involve the viewer in the
process of problem-solving, but it does ensure that a problem is
identified. It marks the beginning of problem-solving and creates a
field of conflict that, in its own way, moves the events forward. A
topic line thus becomes evident in the course of the film, and this
directs the viewer's attention to a certain coherence of meaning and
at the same time links the events, since they activate the viewer's
expectations and point in a certain direction. The repetition makes
the contradictory nature of the protagonist's behaviour more and
more apparent for the spectator. The protagonist's conflict is also a
social one, since it reflects the situation of a generation and its
turning away from the norms of a society that presents itself as
achievement-oriented, but fails to keep the promises made.
Iosseliani (1994) stated that, in constructing his film narrative, he
did not stick to the usual dramatic construction, but rather oriented
himself towards the compositional techniques of musical works
with their recurring motifs.

In a similar way, one can see the spectators' attempts to identify
and define the conflicts and problem situations in the newer films
that are characterised by the above-mentioned parallel lines or
forking-path narratives.

The detailed description of such stories as Wong Kar-wai's

Chunking Express (*Chung Hing sam lam*, 1994) or David Lynch's *Lost Highway* (1997), which both link two big episodes, apparently based on completely unconnected events which, in each case, are realized by different characters, reveals numerous analogical structures, i.e. "ordered relationships articulated as similarity-in-difference" (Staffort 1999, 9). Sometimes these similarities are more or less obvious, but often the film shows them rather allusively, in a kind of insinuation. Thus, Wong Kar-wai's complex story about two Hong Kong policemen, whose paths through life cross only for a moment and without actual consequences, makes us aware that some details in their day-to-day lives are very similar. One episode is mirrored in the other in order to make the analogous details more perceptible. The iteration of similarities leads the spectator to abductions. That is, it appeals to the uniquely human "instinct of guessing" (Peirce 1929, 281) which leads to first hypotheses about facts that are, to a great extent, as yet unknown. The spectator realizes only step by step which moments of the performance he should focus on in order to come closer to the true essence of the story. Bit by bit, his first presentiments regarding the similarities in the characters' behaviour, their analogous conflicts and their motivations of acting, consolidate and lead to the crucial point, the hidden theme of the story. Or, using the terms of criminology, the spectator comes to an "initial suspicion" concerning the meaning of the whole.

Likewise, the narrational strategy of *Lost Highway* establishes such an initial suspicion in the spectators' minds. In this instance, the suspicion is with regard to the question of which kinds of expression of strength are really at work in the mysterious incidents in the film, whose events obviously tend to a criminal case. The story tells how Fred is sent to prison for the murder of his wife Renee, but one morning he has vanished, and another person, Pete, is in the prison cell—all this without any plausible explanation, neither for the characters nor the spectators. Since the prison warder cannot prove Pete's guilt, he is set free. After the discharge, his personality obviously changes. He takes a liking to a woman named Alice, who shows a remarkable resemblance to Renee, and a tendency to psychotic reactions appears which the spectator has already become familiar with through Fred—who is evidently paranoid. The state of mental strain and disease seems to apply to both protagonists, and this may lead to the spectator's initial suspicion, namely that in the protagonists' social sphere there prevail permanently fatal powers which frighten them and drive them insane. They are caught in a mad world where a mysterious metamorphosis of the main character in his prison cell seems possible and where, in the end of the film, Pete, who is copulating with Alice, metamorphoses back into Fred. Even if this muddled and intricate horror film story of the post-modern era doesn't seem to strive for any enlightenment function, it offers a diffuse social criticism because it brings to the surface, by the permanent repetition of similar stimulus material, a certain conflict potential that one can also find in the social milieu of the characters and in their mental dispositions and behaviour. Analogically, some of the films that are structured by parallel lines or forking plots follow the principle of iteration on different levels, and their analysis may use a description of topics for the understanding of their specific way of the construction of meaning. Beyond this model, some authors began, intuitively, to search for similar forms at the level of themes, motifs and actions.

In many cases, the hermeneutic approach to such multi-draft narratives adopts the considerations of literary theory developed, for example, by Jose Luis Borges, whose *Garden of Forking Paths* gave the paradigm for the construction of possible parallel worlds that is established in certain artworks. The acceptance of such decentralised worlds can be seen as a model for the generation of the variables that humans need to adapt to life conditions. Although some of the similarly-constructed film stories mentioned here also encourage the tendency to mystify the world, the playful generating of variables practised by forking-path narratives belongs to the possible means of cognition at the level of perception.

This will suffice in support of the IDEAL scheme for the understanding of those groups of films, where the moments of conflict are not evident and must be found and articulated in the process of storytelling, often by a careful camera observation of the characters' behaviour. Of course, there are other possibilities for dealing with the conflicts, but in my opinion the IDEAL scheme is also helpful for describing them, because it encompasses three additional steps for problem management.

Incidentally, even in the case of *Lost Highway* and some other examples of forking-path narratives, the processes of identifying and defining of problem situations brought about by the repetition of similar structures, or entire topic lines, are accompanied, or complemented, by concept-based filmic structures and stereotype-based structures of genres, which tend to these higher phases of the IDEAL scheme of problem-solving.

6. The More Conscious Steps of Problem-solving and their Structures of Narration

Before dealing with further aspects of the IDEAL structure, I would like to avert a possible misunderstanding that can easily occur in this context. Although the characters on the screen have to solve their problems and the spectator has to try to foresee their decisions, the storytelling of cinema is not identical with the cognitive activity of problem-solving. Thus the heroes on the screen solve their problems practically and not theoretically i.e. cognitively-rationally. There are many cases, particularly in action movies, in which the characters solve their problems without any sort of reasoning. The spectator, who is trying to foresee the decisions of cinematic conflicts, is not primarily interested in a rational method, but is rather steered by his intuition. Nevertheless, the behaviour of the characters, as well as that of the spectators, shows analogies to the proceedings of problem-solving, and therefore it makes sense to use the latter as a model for them and to look for cues issuing from this direction to understand the complexity of the film's aesthetic experience. It is in this process of experience in the spectator's mind that cognitions and imaginings occur resulting from the interactions between the spectator's witnessing of the conflicts on the screen and his involvement in similar contradictions in his own life. These cognitions and imaginings can be valuable for him with respect to the question of how to assess the world, and what kind of changes to wish in it.

In this spirit, the spectator is concerned with the picking-up of information that comes from the more evident conflict moments on the screen. The next two steps of the IDEAL scheme mark corresponding positions named "E = Explore possible strategies" and "A = Act on the strategies". They correspond to concept-based structures and the causal chain of the classical mode of narration. At this level, problem-solving is possible in an appropriate and rational way. The viewer follows the conceptualised relations in the flow of events, i.e. the causal chain of the film's plot, beginning from the unsatisfactory starting situation, via the obstacles that hinder a change for the better, and finally to such a change to a satisfactory situation, in other words, from an evident opening of colliding actions that culminates, and leads to a decision.

The reception process of *High Noon*, including the central sequence earlier mentioned, may serve as a suitable example. It should be stated that in this film the activation of cognitive processes in the spectator's mind that are described here in terms of problem-solving is also not confined to a mental duplication of the chains of causes and effects shown on the screen, but helps the spectator in his processes of creative thinking. Finally, the audience has to conceive of the unheard-of fact which is represented in the shown incident, and that needs creative thought. Like all syuzhet constructions, the story of *High Noon* tells of a particular occurrence requiring of the protagonist an act of borderline crossing, an overstepping of common rules, which can be mastered only by active characters: in this case, that the marshal, as a defender of civilisation, was deserted and betrayed by just that civilisation, yet preserves undisturbed the values of it that he acquired in his past—and this although he could easily have just left the town.

The last position in the IDEAL scheme is termed as "L = look back and evaluate the effects of your activities". For film studies, the ways and methods of problem-solving suggested by a concrete film can refer to cultural experiences gained with specific modes of storytelling in one's past. This, then, leads to the acknowledgement of certain standards and norms concerning specific proven problem-solving techniques. This experience developed into conventions and norms, and corresponds closely with our understanding of the formation of filmic stereotypes, particularly in the realm of narration. The process of stereotyping leads to the formation of canonical stories with certain formal peculiarities, and also to the development of film genres and historic group styles. Following his own concept of cognitive processes in film experience, David Bordwell (1989b, 26ff.) has analysed structures and functions of canonical stories, as well as the most important group style, the Classical Hollywood Cinema (cf. Bordwell / Staiger / Thompson 1985; Bordwell 1986) which includes *High Noon*. Emphasising the conscious components of the cognitive process of film experience, David Bordwell's and Douglas Gomery's (1989) detailed accounts of the properties and criteria of the Hollywood cinema always speak of an entire framework of conditions for the elements of dramaturgy and visual style, which leads to the functioning of the form concept.

Similar considerations may apply to the understanding of genres. The formation of genres has, among other things, to do with the cultural experience of different ways of problem-solving during the telling of a story. The viewer is pre-conditioned by his past experiences with narrational problem-solving. Now the viewer knows the effect of specific ways of storytelling and is able to recognise and to evaluate a concrete strategy of narration because this strategy is based on a well-known stereotype of narration, for instance, one of a specific genre. Genres are, as well, the result of a "looking back" and evaluation of human attempts to find efficient standards and norms for problem-solving.

How important the cultural experience of the different types of conflict and their outcome may be is manifested in the existing spectrum of standardised film endings, which show a wide range between catastrophe and happy ending, and which are always partly based on problem-solving on the screen and in the viewers' mind. In *High Noon*, for example, the culmination of the conflict in the colliding actions of the heroes leads to the show-down.

The Western genre uses a well-known ritual as narrational stereotype, which channels the information processing in the viewer's mind and enables him to foresee the actions and to comprehend easily what has happened. *High Noon* has been classified by André Bazin (1971, II, 150) as a "super-Western" dealing with ideas that reach beyond the common films of this genre. In *Sixguns and Society*, Will Wright (1975, 74) pointed out that this film, and a small group of others, can be interpreted "as transitional occurences of the myth-Western that, while remaining in the classical framework, present a significant reorganization of images and narrative and create new meanings that can only be fully expressed outside of the classical structure. In many respects, this transition theme is almost a direct inversion of the classical plot. The hero is inside society at the start and outside society at the end." In my opinion, the film even follows the rules of two different genres, namely the Western and the parable genre. On the one hand, the protagonist is a Western hero with an interpersonal conflict, fighting a gang of outlaws; on the other hand, he has to suffer under the citizen's treachery, which gives the film an affinity to a parable about the loneliness of man in a world of opportunism and treason. One can find a lot of cues to this genre. Thus, the film begins with the country-song "Do not forsake me, oh my darling…", and the action culminates in situations of social loneliness. When, after the Western's show-down, the victor Kane, who is leaving the town, lets fall to the ground his marshal's star, the parable finds its end.

7. Problem-solving and the Meaning of the Characters' Action Potential

Unfortunately, the possibilities for the construction of hypotheses and inferences concerning the process of narration using the model of problem-solving are at present far from empirical psychological research and should be taken as an encouragement for further thinking into this direction.

Even so, the psychological theory of problem-solving leads to a field which could be helpful for film studies, insofar as it develops an understanding of the so-called problem space in which the solution can be found. "In each case, the searching process determines the problem space. When the solution state is placed in this space, then the transformation to the solution can be found, if the solution is not placed in there, then the problem space must be enlarged" (Klix 1971, 644). On occasion, this searching space might require a retrenchment rather than an enlargement.

In the cinema, the problem space is mainly determined by the action potential of the characters. How the conflict situations will be decided and how they can be foreseen by the spectators, depends on the characters' possibilities of acting, and as well, on the lucidity of their action potential for the audience. Let's take

High Noon as an example: That the inhabitants of Hadleyville keep out of the armed conflict testifies to their poor potential for acting, and gives rise to an outcome where Kane's survival seems all but impossible. Nevertheless, the story provides for an enlargement of the searching space for problem-solving. Bill Kane's wife Amy, who is on the verge of leaving the town, turns back and suddenly yields him support, and, strangely enough, she does it because her husband's former lover has urged her to help him. Thus, the impulse for the story's turnaround comes via a minor character from the periphery of the story's action space.

However, the probability of certain conflict solutions varies not only with the action potential of the characters, which depends on the likelihood of corresponding life processes, but also according to the spectator's experience with certain outcomes in the relevant genre. Genre stereotypes have to do with the last position of the IDEAL scheme:"Look back and evaluate the effects of your activities." They refer back to the spectator's previous experience with a specific type of film whose events follow the rules of a genre. In the case of *High Noon*, Amy's obligation as Kane's wife and confidante is not solely responsible for her turnaround. Also important is the ritual showdown of the Western genre with its high likelihood of a "last minute rescue", an action realised by Amy's unexpected decision to take the gun.

In such films as Antonioni's *L'Eclisse*, Iosseliani's *Once upon a time there was a Singing Blackbird*, or Jarmusch's *Stranger than Paradise*, which seek and articulate their conflict moments through an observation process of lifelike events, this kind of sudden turn seems hardly possible, because their group style and genre established other degrees of likelihood for changes of events and their anticipation by the audience.

Different genres or group styles of films apply different rules of expectation. In normal life, the likelihood that an imprisoned person could be transformed into another approaches zero, and therefore such an event seems improbable for the audience and correspondingly unacceptable for most film stories. For a film such as *Lost Highway*, which tends towards the horror genre of postmodern cinema, this kind of unbelievable action seems rather tolerable and therefore worthy of an experiment for director David Lynch, the more so as the same author-director, in his debut

Eraserhead (1977), had already portrayed a gruesome metamorphosis of his hero, who was stripped of any lifelikeness.

The genre changes not only the probability of possible events, for example, the outcomes of conflicts, but also the profile of the characters, which always has consequences for the spectator's imageries. Recently, cognitive film theory (cf. M. Smith 1995, 2005, 291; Eder 2008) has found a successful approach to analysing film characters by considering their interrelations to the narration and the viewer's imagination. Murray Smith (1995, 74) noticed that "engaging with fiction is a species of imaginative activity"; "...fictions prompt and enrich our 'quasi-experience', that is, our efforts to grasp, through mental hypotheses, situations, persons, and values which are alien to us". In my opinion, it is possible to use this research as a hypothesis about the relations between the characters' action potential and the viewers' imaginings concerning the searching spaces of problem-solving. Assuming that the character seems to be the actual key to an understanding of the film's message, it is not merely because he or she represents a human being existing in a similar way as in our society, but also because his or her genre-determined action potential delineates a suitable searching space for the viewers' problem-solving. Storytelling always becomes more interesting when the events are not limited to representing the processes of life, but the story enables us to overcome problem situations in the fictional and in the real world by the construction of searching spaces, because this "quasi-experience" permits a more creative approach to our conflict situations. The aspect of problem-solving may be helpful, because it connects the intentions of the characters and the spectators with the conflict moment and is constitutive of the dynamics of narration and, at the same time, of the cinematic emotions.

Even the documentary film, which always has more difficulties than the fictional film in showing colliding actions, follows the general trend to conflict situations in its most important phases. This inclination is not new. Due to the ponderous equipment for shooting and sound recording, the documentary had a considerable handicap in observing real conflict moments for a long time. After the shift in the development of film technique on the threshold to the sixties (cf. Salt 1992, 241-268), the documentary's chances of drawing level with the fiction film in respect to conflict performance increased. And already, at the beginning of the 1960s, the first attempts of the American Direct Cinema represented events of life with conflict constellations at their heart coming from election campaigns, police operations, race riots, controversial political decisions, executions and so on. These events represent colliding actions, or dramatic confrontations, in the cinematic documentation following the so-called "crisis structure" (Mamber 1974, 115–140). This approach leads from an exposition of the conflict via its culmination to a kind of solution and, in this way, complies with the spectators' need for closed action (cf. Beyerle / Brinckmann 1991, 35). Up to the present, in documentaries tendencies occur again and again to look for conflict constellations in real-life material, with the result that the crisis structures do not solely evoke cognitive activities which lead to enforced problem-solving in the viewers' mind, but also arousal effects and emotional reactions.

Although the documentaries gained the image of conducting "discourses of sobriety" (cf. Nichols 1991, 3) they are far away from conducting any sobriety (cf. Brinckmann 2005, 33; Naber 2008, 108). The experts in this mode of cinema have noticed, for a long time, that the conflict moments here not only enable the documentaries to create a crisis structure, organising the process of narration more stringently, but can be seen in close connection with the evocation of emotions in the spectators' mind, as well, an aspect which is the subject of the next chapter.

Chapter IV: Conflict and Emotion

1. From Peals of Laughter about Chaplin to Empirical Research on Emotion

Some days after its première in the fall of 1925, Charles Chaplin's *The Gold Rush* served as the point of departure for a bizarre radio experiment. While the audience was reacting to a central sequence of the film in the London Tivoli movie theater, BBC radio recorded the sounds and then broadcast about ten minutes of well-articulated laughter across all its stations. They chose the section of the film where Charlie and his partner Big Jim are getting up in the morning in their gold diggers' hut and are puzzled about why the floor of the little wooden house starts to tilt with their every step. Finally they realize that a snowstorm has moved the house during the night so that it is hanging on the edge a cliff and teetering with every shift of their weight (cf. Robinson 1985, 358ff.).

That film is a privileged place for eliciting emotions had already been recognized in 1916 by the German-American psychologist Hugo Munsterberg, who pointed out: "To picture emotions must be the central aim of the photoplay" ([1916] 1970, 48).

A decade later, the radio project made clear that it is possible to grasp the emotional responses of a film audience, and this gives us reason for optimism in regard to our attempts to move from statements about emotion in films based on individual introspection to statements that can be empirically confirmed by experimental psychology. Furthermore, the film sequence that the BBC chose also points to a sensible starting point for specific studies on effects: namely, elements of conflict in the film plot. The affective responses that they stimulate in the viewers may show most clearly how films evoke emotions. In searching for efficient approaches to research on emotions and film, I would like to follow up on this assumption. Since the concept of conflict plays an important role in both film studies and the psychology of emotions, it makes sense to try to put the allied, but by no means identical, concepts of the two disciplines into relation with each other and to try to use them as the starting point for an interdisciplinary approach to the emotional effects of films. According to my presuppositions, elements of conflict in film plots can be viewed as the source of emotional reactions in the audience.

The film example confirms this in its own way. What takes place in front of the viewers' eyes is a conflict situation *par excellence*, and one that also stands in contradiction to the audience's expectations. In a hair-raising way, the protagonists do not understand what a dangerous situation they are in, and this increases the affective arousal of the audience with every step that the characters on the screen take. But it is not as easy as it might seem to judge which emotions are involved, since the reactions of the film's heroes do not carry over to the audience in a linear way. Instead, the British audience, known for its enjoyment of black humor, responded to the characters' fear and anxiety with incessant laughter. Thus, it is not easy to find reliable information about the real emotional processes that go on during the reception of a film, not even in the case of an ingenious source of emotional effects like Chaplin and a significant reaction on the part of the audience. So it seems that research on the emotional effects of films has a long way to go before it can reach empirical psychological findings.

2. The Concept of Emotion in Psychology

If film studies have only begun to approach cinematic emotions seriously in the last ten years, despite having long ago recognized the necessity of examining this topic, this is at least in part due to the fact that psychology has also only recently re-discovered emotions as a major area of study, after the information-processing model provided a way to focus its divergent concepts.

In 1980, the psychologist Klaus Scherer commented on the situation in this discipline at that time: "Viewing the research work of current psychology, there are pictures from the times of gold rush in the American West that involuntary suggest themselves: gold diggers from all four corners of the earth are hurrying in droves to the Attribution Canyon for pegging out a claim; at the Cognition River, one can see the people suffering from gold fever untiringly riddle sand to find perhaps nuggets yet; Emotion City has nearly dropped down to a ghost town in which only a few inveterate lone wolves are digging among the many given up claims. In psychology, there is a number of such ghost towns that rightly or wrongly were lost. In my opinion, in case of the emotions this was a mistake" (1981, 304ff.).

Since that time, psychological research into emotions has again started up, and this with a vengeance, and now we have a vivid psychology of emotion—with fortunate consequences for media studies.

Nevertheless, to define the essence of emotions and to establish the right strategies for research was by no simple. If the Dutch psychologist Nico Frijda accentuated a specific quality of emotions: "Their passionate nature is their most distinctive feature" (2007, 25), or "Passion: What emotions really are" (2008), then, in the same breath as this assertion, he had to follow up with an entire network of closer definitions to do justice to the complexity of this analysis. Frijda pointed out: "Emotions are probably the most individual and often idiosyncratic of human phenomena. They express what the world means to the individual, as a particular person at a particular crossroads in the world, and they compose his or her individual reaction to that crossroads. Yet, at the same time, emotions are lawful. They emerge and develop according to definite laws that can, at last in principle, be specified" (Frijda 2007, 1). Frijda's early sketch of a series of laws which govern the emotional phenomena was well received and is, in its rewritten version, convincing to this day (Frijda 1988; 2007).

But the inter-subjectively observed reaction pattern to environmental stimuli called emotion is a very complex one, and includes reactions at various levels of human behavior. Carroll Izard (1991, 24ff.) wrote in consequence: "A complex definition of emotion must take into account physiological, expressive, and experiential components. The emotions occur as a result of changes in the nervous system, and these changes may be brought about by either internal or external events. [...] It is a general and fundamental principle of human behavior that emotions energize and organize perception, thought, and action tendencies. Emotion directly influences what is perceived through the senses and thus affects all subsequent information processing and actions."

The problems of definition go hand in hand with the issues of research strategy. Certainly, the well-known cognitive approach had suggested itself to emotion psychology, but its framework also permits different interpretations. According to Keith Oatley, the understanding of the correlation between cognition and emotion is not plain to begin with: "Cognition and emotion—this phrase connects two concepts, but it is ambiguous. For some people it means the cognitive approach to emotion. For others it means the joining of two domains, cognition and affect, that were previously thought disparate" (1999, xvii). Then, Oatley describes an essential advantage of his own concept: "A current cognitive conception, for which there is a broad consensus, is that emotions are central to mental and social life because they are fundamental mediators between inner and outer worlds. They relate what is personally important (goals, concerns, aspirations) to the world (events, people, things). If we humans merely worked from what was important to us, we would be bundles of drives and species-typical action patterns. If we merely responded to events, we would be reflex machines. Instead, because of mediation by emotions, some aspects of our lives are given meaningful urgency, some people we know become uniquely important, and our many goals are prioritized" (Oatley 1999, xviii).

Attempts to model these complicated relationships have shown that it makes sense to attribute to emotion the properties of a system (Strongman 1987, 244). This permits the description of emotions as separate entities which follow their own laws of development and can be seen in numerous relationships to other functional systems of the mind. It also facilitates the understanding of emotions in their functional interactions with other psychic systems, for instance cognition and motivation. In his outline of the "trilogy of mind", Lazarus points out: "I should note too that in the trilogy of mind, there is a real difference between emotion and the two other functions, cognition and motivation. Thought without motivation is emotionless. Motivation without thought is drive or energy, without direction that cognition provides. The three constructs are also not parallel in that emotion is an amalgam of the other two" (1999, 10). Such an integration of the emotion system into the other systems is mainly helpful for the understanding of emotion as adaptive behavior and to place it into a comprehensive relationship with human activities that are dominated by goal-oriented actions, and also by social and cultural factors which in some ways influence the emotive processes (Stein / Trabasso 1992;

G. Smith 2003, 34; Frijda 2007, 80). Moreover, the modeling of dynamic systems can successfully provide closer connections between emotion theory and the discoveries of neurobiology (Lewis 2005).

Undoubtedly, it makes sense to examine the eliciting of emotions in the framework of adaptive behavior. Robert W. Levenson (1994, 123) suggests: "Emotions are short-lived psychological phenomena that represent efficient modes of adaptation to changing environmental demands. Psychologically, emotions alter attention, shift certain behaviour upward in response hierarchies, and activate relevant associative networks in memory. Physiologically, emotions rapidly organize the responses of different biological system activity and endocrine activity to produce a bodily milieu that is optimal for effective response. Emotions serve to establish our position vis-à-vis our environment, pulling us toward certain people, objects, actions, and ideas, and pushing us away from others. Emotions also function as repository for innate and learned influences, possessing certain invariant features along with others that show considerable variation across individuals, groups, and cultures."

Viewed in this way, emotional reactions are motivated by certain kinds of adaptive pressure, as has been expressed in various concepts that can be related to one another through central terms like control, coping, and action readiness. Confronted with a constantly changing environment, humans attempt to retain control and to stay in command of present and future situations as much as possible. Thus a "need for control" is seen as being a "primary human motivation" (Dörner et al. 1983, 63), or coping processes are seen as having the function of modifying an uncertain relationship between the individual and his or her environment, or of maintaining a desirable one (Lazarus 1991, 112). The necessity for action readiness has a similar function, whereby this term includes the capacity, ability, and competence to act. Emotions fulfill the function of creating the proper psycho-physiological climate, which helps ensure effective adaptive behavior and helps to retain control and the ability to act in relation to the environment.

This necessarily involves (1) appraisal, that is, an assessment of the changing situation in relation to its subjective meaning for the individual; which then is set into relation to (2) action readiness, that is, to the real possibilities a person has to react to the changing conditions.

Frijda (1986, 474) explains the existence of emotions by way of changes in action readiness, and his student Ed Tan has used this concept to develop a practical working definition of the concept of emotions: "An emotion may be defined as a change in action readiness as a result of the subject's appraisal of the situation or event" (1996, 46).

It appears that the tension between the evaluation of a situation and the available ability to act in order to deal with it generally leads to an affective stimulation, a complex psychic activation. This results whenever a new situation places the ability to take action in question. This model seems to provide a very reasonable explanation for the standard case of an adaptive reaction to a situation.

What is important about the appraisal process is that it expresses the degree of significance, as well as the subjective relevance, of the stimulus for the individual. Tan and Frijda (1999, 51) suggest: "Emotions occur when a situation is relevant for an individual's concern. They consist of an appraisal of the situation's significance and an action tendency. The emotional experience is the awareness of the situation's particular meaning in terms of a relevance for a concern, reality and difficulty, and the felt-action tendency. The action tendency itself consists of an inclination to act in a particular way. For example, fear is an appraisal of a threat of physical harm that cannot be countered, and the urge to run away, to protect oneself, or to freeze. The action tendency in emotion, moreover, is characterized by its control precedence. That is, it strives toward completion at the cost of other ongoing actions and cognitive processes. This is what lends any emotion its force and relative impenetrability to purely cognitive considerations." Scherer (1999, 637) emphasizes the factor of subjectivity in the appraisal process: "A central tenet of appraisal theory is the claim that emotions are elicited and differentiated on the basis of a person's subjective evaluation or appraisal of the personal significance of a situation, object, or event on a number of dimensions or criteria." One can find similar assertions in the texts of other scholars (Smith and Ellsworth 1985; Oatley and Johnson-Laird 1987).

But what about the reasons or occasions for the emergence of emotions? Frijda suggests a heuristic approach to answering the question of how one can plausibly imagine the concrete cause or immediate source for affective arousal: "Emotion might be defined as action readiness change in response to emergencies or interruptions; and this action readiness change itself might be restricted to activations and deactivations of actual, overt response: activated behavior and physical arousal or upset" (Frijda 1986, 474). This brings us closer to a concept that we can call the conflict approach to the psychology of emotions.

3. The Conflict Approach to the Psychological Theory of Emotions

As early as 1960, Daniel Berlyne noted in his book *Conflict, Arousal and Curiosity* that psychology had often recognized conflict "as the principal source of emotion" (Berlyne 1960, 31). He substantiates this claim with a list of names including Dewey, Lurija, Darrow, Hebb, Brown, and Farber.

Today we can also explain this finding within the framework of the theory of cognitive schemata. Constructing cognitive schemata in our mind is always related to setting up patterns and attitudes of expectation. Expectations are not necessarily made solely to be fulfilled, but rather they can also be destroyed or frustrated by unexpected events or by discrepancies among stimuli, thus upsetting our adaptive behavior. According to George Mandler, a stimulus generally arises when a person registers discrepancies in his or her environment. Emotional experience, then, would arise out of the Gestalt-like connection of the two main components: visceral arousal and cognitive evaluation. Each connection of arousal and evaluation then creates a new state of consciousness, the phenomenal experience of an emotion (cf. G. Mandler 1984b, 129).

According to Mandler's theory of the evaluation of discrepancies, most neural arousal results from discrepancies in perception, action, and thinking. This is true of both positive and negative situations (1992, 106). According to Frijda, even minimal deviations from expectation cause arousal (1993, 381). They provoke appraisal and call for an appropriate psychological attitude in the sense of managing our life processes. Berlyne follows a similar train of thought in regard to fictional experience, which he relates to the existence of "collative variables," variables of comparison, which obviously are connected to moments of conflict or discrepancies in the stimuli. Along with characteristics like "incompatibility," "novelty," "surprisingness," or "uncertainty," he also explicitly mentions "conflict" (Berlyne 1960, 44).

This then leads to the question of the extent to which discrepancies and elements of conflict, which have always been part of what dramatic art on stage or on screen has offered, can evoke genuine emotions or be emotionally effective.

4. Film-elicited Emotions as Witness Emotions

We cannot directly apply the conflict model of emotional psychology that I have sketched out here to the cinema, since the assumption that discrepancies or conflicts in stimuli serve to evoke affective arousal applies to the individual who is confronted with a real-life situation and not with fictional actions on the screen. Watching a film does not directly require any adaptive behavior in regard to our own ability to take action, since in the movie theater the action on the screen has no immediate effects on us and we cannot influence it. However, one of the advantages of the explanatory model is that, in a modified form, it can be applied to the analysis of cinematic emotions.

The conviction that emotions in the cinema are genuine emotions has now become dominant, even if there is a big—and empirically measurable—difference between reacting affectively to an authentic situation in the real world and to a fictional situation portrayed in the medium of film.

Therefore it makes sense to follow Tan and Frijda (1999, 52) and to speak of specific "witness emotions": "Film-elicited emotion [...] consists largely of witness emotions. [...] The viewers of film are led to imagine themselves as invisible witnesses that are physically present in the fictional world." Nevertheless, sometimes the experience of fictional actions can be felt to be extremely moving and to be relevant to one's own life (cf. Scherer 1998, 277).

The approach I am suggesting makes it possible to find a common basis and to recognize the differences between emotions arising from real situations and those evoked by representations in media. In doing so, one can refer to the findings of current studies of film and media psychology, particularly those of Noël Carroll (1990; 1999), Ed Tan (1996; 2000), Torben Grodal (1997), Greg Smith (2003) and the authors of articles printed in the volumes *Passionate Views*, edited by C. Plantinga and G. Smith (1999), *Kinogefühle*, edited by M. Brütsch et al. (2005), *Narration and Spectatorship in Moving Images*, edited by J.D. Anderson and B. Fisher Anderson (2007), and *Emotion—Empathie—Figur: Spielformen der Filmwahrnehmung*, edited by T. Schick and T. Ebbrecht (2008).

It is certainly true both of emotions evoked in the cinema and those evoked in normal life that they are psychic conditions of limited duration, which involve changes in the person caused by stimulation. Furthermore, these processes cannot be seen directly, but can potentially be observed at three levels: (1) the neural level, as shown by neuro-physiological data, (2) the expressive level, as shown by expressive behavior, or (3) the level of experience, where certain feelings become conscious and thus allow us to verbalize emotional effects. It is more difficult to analyze the causes of emotional processes and to differentiate between various origins of affects from film or reality. This should be done employing the conflict approach.

Currently, various attempts are being made to develop research on emotions from different perspectives within cognitive film theory, in particular from three directions: narration, empathy with characters, and the effects of genre. The conflict-oriented approach I am suggesting does not exclude these approaches, but rather attempts to find a common denominator for them, in part in the hope that it will be possible to bring the ways that psychologists and film practitioners think about emotions and cinema closer together.

To improve interdisciplinary understanding, I would first like to shift the perspective and look at how film dramaturgy conceives of conflict by linking my thoughts closely to a concrete film example. This combines the advantages of having a very clear pattern of conflicts and narrative structure, while at the same time inducing strong emotional effects, even if the work differs substantially from *The Gold Rush*.

The work that I have in mind is the eight-minute animated film

Father and Daughter (2000) by the Dutch filmmaker Michael Dudok de Wit. That this film is able to awaken such unusually strong feelings in the audience and to make them sad and deeply touched is certainly one reason it won an Academy Award in its category in 2001. To ask how and why a work like this, which has the emotional qualities of a melodrama, evokes emotions is certainly a question that most of the audience would not ask and that may seem overly rationalistic and uncalled-for, but this cannot be of concern here.

5. Conflict Factors in Film Narration

It is obvious that the film's story is centered on a course of action based on a human conflict: a little girl has lived harmoniously with her father until one day, for reasons we are not told, he leaves her. The child returns again and again to the place on the shore where her father's boat sailed away, apparently hoping that he will return someday. But this does not happen, not even when the girl has become a grown woman. Her longing for her father remains, however, and on one winter day, as the woman, now old, lies down next to a boat frozen in the ice, one that resembles the boat in which her father had rowed away, she finally experiences that he does return and hugs her—she has suddenly been transformed back into a child. But this is obviously a dream.

The conflict situation in which the character is involved is narrated in a terse and systematic way and the events captivate the viewer, who participates emotionally. This shows how closely the dramatic concept of conflict, which Hegel used in his *Aesthetics* to analyze dramatic art in connection with the concepts of "collision" and "colliding action" (1965, 2, 521), is tied to the dialectical principle of contradiction and the movement it evokes.

According to Hegel, contradiction is the "the root of all motion and life" (1951, 59). It is not without reason that this principle has been used to explain the train of events in the dramatic structures of European theater and film. In this model, it is contradictions within the segment of life shown in the work that drive the plot forward through collisions between the characters' actions. They create a dynamic process, a course of action with changing situations, which we understand as mimetic narration.

Two different kinds of contradictory factors are connected in *Father and Daughter*: the external, interpersonal conflict that results from the father's leaving and the inner, intrapersonal conflict, which is intensified as it becomes clear that the daughter cannot reconcile herself with her loss the situation. In general, even very different kinds of contradiction create a field of causality to develop the plot. In a film this becomes effective as a hierarchically organized field of conflicts. In the case of *Father and Daughter*, this field of conflicts is particularly homogenous and centered, so that the events form a causal chain of the kind that has always governed classical narration.

In its narrative macrostructure, the film shows a clear causal chain of events structured by two plot points, which are based on the above-mentioned conflicts: (1) the father's leaving, which is fundamentally at odds with the child's wishes, and (2) the daughter's sorrowful recognition that this loss is final and can only be reversed in the world of fantasy (see fig. 6).

These two first-order plot points form the decisive turning points in the action and build the framework for a series of smaller developments that form the microstructure of the story. Although these appear quite different, in terms of content and structure they prove to be very similar. The viewer notices that it is the same protagonist who appears in all the episodes, even though her appearance and age change, and that she always has the same goal, but that each episode leads to the same disappointing result. This repetition of the same basic situation, which recurs like a leitmotif in each of the second-order plot points, gives the father's departure a further meaning. It has become a permanent problem in the daughter's life and thus represents an essential loss.

These two levels of the film's narrative are overlaid by a third, a plot stereotype that our expectations of the genre bring into the process of reception. In both its outward appearance and its resolution of conflicts, the course of action seems to fit the canon of melodrama. The protagonist seems to be heading into an unavoidable catastrophe, but then suddenly the plot steers toward a happy ending, the desired solution of the conflict, albeit only in the character's fantasy. On the one hand, the utopian ending solves the unhappy situation, but on the other hand, by transposing the solution from the real to a dream world, it also reinforces the sad ending in reality. As analogous examples of feature films like Jane Campion's *The Piano* (1993) or Lars von Trier's *Breaking the Waves* (1996) show, this is a common variant for film endings in this genre.

Related elements of conflict are at work on all three cognitive levels of the narrative structure of the film (mentioned in chapter III). These factors reinforce each other and drive the plot towards its goal. The phases in plot development in which these conflicts appear most clearly in the form of colliding actions are thus not only effective in moving the plot forward, but also make up the source or stimulus for emotional reactions.

According to Ed Tan, the continuity of narrative processes in film is tied to continuous interest, whereby "interest" is seen as a kind of basic emotion. Then the narration is able to continually redefine the meaning of the events within each situation and each change can lead to a new "emotion episode" (cf. Tan 1996, 62), whereby plot points play an important role in setting the borders of narrative segments. This explanation makes sense. I would like, however, to accentuate the importance of elements of conflict. It seems to me that it helps explain the connections between the dynamics of film narration and the affective arousal of the viewer particularly clearly, and it also helps to further elaborate the model of the emotional effects of film, for instance with regard to the questions of control or the ability to act.

Modern theories of narration such as those of Todorov (1972, 57ff.) or Greimas (1983), which do not employ a concept of conflict, explain the dynamics of the narrative process as a series of consequences from a disturbance in a state of equilibrium or as tensions between states of balance and imbalance. In relating the course of action to a model of equilibrium, they define a state of harmony or equilibrium as having what cybernetic theory calls a governing role. This is not new to aesthetics. According to Hegel, a dramatic collision "has its source in an injury, which cannot remain an injury, but must be subsumed; it is a transformation of conditions that would be harmonious without it, and which must itself again be transformed" (1965, 1, 203). What happens in *Father and Daughter* is the injury of a harmonious condition par excellence, since the story is based on the protagonist's suffering an essential loss. Hegel's reference to the disturbance of a harmonious condition, of equilibrium, also shows that such injuries or conflictual elements are not necessarily sudden or abrupt changes in the course of action, but that these discrepancies must also be connected with a threat to the human capability to take action if they are to be of emotional consequence. Furthermore, this relates not just to the characters' situation, but to our own as well. The tension between the conflict situation and human ability to act on it thus proves to be a decisive factor in the behavior of the characters and the audience. In order to be able to make more exact judgments about the stimulus or the high-points of affective arousal, it would now be helpful not only to relate what we know about conflicts to the film plot, but also to see how these kinds of discrepancy appear to have effects on the viewers. A model based on processes of problem-solving will be helpful in examining this function.

6. Problem-solving and the Experience of Conflicts

The framework of the cognitive theory of problem-solving presents a sensible and practical way to model the experience of watching a film, because both the characters' colliding actions on the screen and the viewers' form of reception can be described as processes of problem-solving. The dialectic of the two operations then leads to a clearer view of the emotional processes. The psychological approach sees problem-solving as necessary when (1) an unsatisfactory starting situation is to be changed into (2) a satisfactory situation, but (3) obstacles hinder this (cf. Hussy 1993). Dramatic conflicts in a film often provide such situations for the characters. They have to try to change an unsatisfactory situation, for example when they are confronted with conflicting interests. Their actions do not always succeed or barriers may prevent a quick solution. *Father and Daughter* shows the protagonist in such a problematic situation, in which a satisfactory ending—a harmonious life after the return of the father—is not reached even over the course of decades. Although it is left up to the viewer to think of the possible reasons why this cannot be achieved, the plot presents the confrontation of opposing forces: the unchanging situation as a whole and the protagonist's desire for happiness.

If we look at the plot of a film as a process of problem-solving that leads to a certain decision, then we must look not only at the beginning and the ending for such phases of a goal-oriented process, but also grasp the whole course of action that leads to a decision as an on-going confrontation, in which certain sub-goals are reached. Phases of action that intensify the events also tend to lead to preliminary decisions about the possible outcome. They thus represent turning points in the action or various forms of plot points. In *Father and Daughter* this is the case whenever the protagonist's attempts fail. But these plot points not only intensify the action on the screen, but also psychologically activate the audience in the theater.

This psychological activation is a cognitive one in that it helps to explain the situation rationally, for example by making certain decisions seem more likely. We know from experience that as viewers we will become more strongly involved in such phases of the plot. Our affective arousal always rises when decisions and problem-solving seem to be imminent and the action dramatically comes to a head. Activation at both levels goes hand in hand and the viewer becomes both cognitively and emotionally involved in what is happening.

The emergence of emotions cannot simply be explained by claiming that the viewer shares the characters' concrete problems and situation. The viewer may have conflicts and problems that are similar to those of the protagonist, but they are never identical. When the conflicts portrayed in a film are able to involve the viewers in the problem-solving process, then this is probably more closely related to the fact that they, as humans, constantly follow the primary motive that has been referred to as the need for control of one's environment. Real-life situations require active control in order to change events in the environment practically in line with what the individual wants. In the case of artistic experience, however, nothing of the kind is possible, since the viewer cannot change the course of events in a film, but he or she can at least attempt to gain passive control in the sense of anticipating coming events. This differentiation in terminology, which cognitive psychology did not at first apply to artistic processes (cf. Dörner et al. 1983, 63), offers significant advantages in understanding the cognitive and emotional dimensions of the experience of art. On the one hand, it helps to grasp the noticeable differences between the forms of experience found in real-life situations and in the fictional situations of a film, in that it links the latter to passive control only; on the other hand, through the appraisal function, it also links this cognitive form of passive control quite closely to the system of emotions. The so-called passive control which the viewer seeks in relation to the film's story line is then not all that passive after all. Even if we cannot really affect the outcome of the plot, we are psychologically activated and thus at least intuitively try to make good guesses about how things will develop, since we want to overcome our insecurity about how the conflicts will be solved on the screen. This is then at once a cognitive and emotional matter.

Approximating film experience by means of the problem-solving model can be extended in another direction as well. In real life as in movies, problematic situations rarely appear in such a highly developed form that they are rationally solvable in the same way that an arithmetic problem or a strategy game would be. Before we can solve a problem, we first have to identify and define it as such. Therefore, cognitive psychology has attempted to describe the phases of problem-solving behavior. One well-known way is the IDEAL schema of Bransford and Stein (1984, 12)—mentioned in chapter III—which distinguishes five steps: I = Identify the problem, D = Define and represent the problem, E = Explore possible strategies, A = Act on the strategies, L = Look back and evaluate the effects of your activities.

These phases of the problem are established for both the characters and the viewers, since they often first have to identify and define a conflict in the course of the film before they can come up with a conscious strategy to handle it or evaluate it retroactively in terms of common patterns such as the plot stereotypes of a genre. Even in the condensed and highly stylized plot of *Father and Daughter* there is a certain difference to be seen, since the essential problem of the heroine is not immediately obvious, but rather has to discovered by an attentive and perceptive viewer over several episodes. The external appearance of the situation often hinders perception considerably and becomes quite confusing, since it seems at one point that the protagonist has even overcome the loss of her father. This is when she comes to the shore with the man she loves and in the twilight it is impossible to see whether she looks out to the sea as she usually does. Then, however, the problem is defined all the more clearly and the film makes the viewers aware of the impossibility of a solution. This leads them to fall back on the genre's standard solution for such cases and to accept the dream happy ending.

Normally, each step in the plot brings a re-definition of the situational meaning of the events, and with it a specific emotional impulse. In the case of *Father and Daughter*, this is generally the continuation of the previous sad-emotion episodes. Only at the end does the fictional dream re-orient us to a contrary emotion. The reference to the various stages in the recipient's awareness of the problem is important, however, since it implies they carry out various different cognitive and emotional activities in experiencing the course of action and these require correspondingly variable strategies for empirical research. Since we always work out the situational meaning of events in a film in relation to human actions and these are always bound to the film's characters, the audience builds up a relationship of empathy.

7. Empathy

Currently, there is an increasing amount of research being done on the role of empathy in cinematic experience. In the broadest sense, this always involves the response of one person to experiences of another. The capability of feeling empathy shows that people can be influenced in this way intellectually or emotionally. From the common concepts of empathy it is evident that this covers a broad range of definitions, stretching all the way from empathy as the understanding of strangers (with regard to their point of view or motives) (Lipps 1907) to participation in the emotions of others (Zillmann 1991). This broad range of variations in understanding of empathy is related to the fact that empathy is obviously made up of cognitive as well as emotional components or at least potentially can involve both. In defining empathy, a number of authors (Sachse 1993, 171; Omdahl 1995) have tried to bring cognitive and emotional tendencies together and integrate them. With regard to the cinema, this integrative concept seems to be the most productive one, and therefore it plays a role in various of the newer approaches to film psychology (M. Smith 1997, 1999; Neill 1996; Eder 2005). The viewers' emotions are thus seen as being tied to the film characters, but there are very different interpretations of the causes, the quality, and the differences of these emotions.

In accordance with my model of analysis, which views the characters in a functional relation to fields of conflict and narration and is seen from the cognitive perspective as approximating problem-solving, empathy can be understood as a phenomenon which results primarily from the imaginary reproduction of problem-solving following the two-tracked process of active and passive control of the situation. Recreating the conflict situation of the character and his or her attempts to solve a problem in our imagination means that we, as viewers, are put into an uncertain position in two ways. On the one hand, we take the position or play the role of the character and—in the sense of active control—try to find a solution for the problem, since the characters usually try to be in command of the situation, particularly if we sympathize with the character and approve of his or her actions. On the other hand, we also try to gain passive control of the situation and we feel uncertain when we cannot foresee the course of decisions and actions. The process of empathy mixes these tendencies, since we must successively work out the subjectively relevant evaluations for the characters, and this goes on parallel to our own anticipation of the further course of the plot. In addition, within the "empathic field" (cf. Wulff 2002, 109ff.) there are further influences that can be evoked by "co-emotions" or result from the affective relations between actor and viewer that are induced through motor mimicry (cf. Scherer 1998, 280), but these influences have only partially been taken account of in models.

The viewer's empathy with the characters may change and become stronger or weaker, depending on the discrepancies in the course of action. In any case, however, the connection between conflict and the capacity to act, which is so important for emotional effects, remains central. Therefore, from my point of view, it is possible to develop an empathetic relationship with any character who "strives ceaslessly" (in a broad interpretation of Goethe's *Faust* quotation: "Whoever strives ceaselessly, with mind and will, him we can deliver") (1988, 228). This applies to close-to-life, vital characters, whose goals we can easily share and whose emotional attitudes are induced in us through so-called co-emotions, as well as to strongly stylized characters or even cartoon characters. One must remind oneself that in *Father and Daughter* people do not immediately appear as actors, but only in the mediated form of animated chalk and pencil drawings that have been colored digitally. Strangely enough, we have no difficulty "feeling along" with these characters. As viewers we appear to be related to the "empathetics," those mythical beings that, according to an article by Christine Noll Brinckmann, "possess an extraordinary ability to feel with others" and thus live according to the motto: "touch, taste, feel" (1997, 60). This is probably why it is also possible, as is described in the same article, to feel empathy for animals and in the end even for characters whose personality and actions we do not accept or even despise. Elementary forms of behavior in situations of conflict, which continuously demand that we master them, seem to bring us *per se* close to all these characters as *actants*, whereby we must also note that empathy does not necessarily mean sympathy.

8. Appraisal and Genre

An approach through the concept of genre has often shaped recent research on film effects, since we know from experience that film genres are often coupled with strong emotions and in particular with specific ones that vary from genre to genre. *Father and Daughter*, for example, obeys the rules of melodrama. In my opinion, the conflict approach can help explain these components of cinematic effects as well.

In a different work (cf. Wuss 1993, 313ff.), I have developed a model according to which genres can generally be viewed as a higher order of stereotypical structure, which initiate specific sub-programs of psychological behavior, including emotional strategies, even highly standardized ones. Each genre builds up specific basic expectations with regard to the dominant emotional patterns that it uses. It calls up the corresponding expectations and satisfies them, thus keeping to a narrowly defined path among the great variety of possible affects and emotions. This leads us to the supposition that the standardization of emotional effects relates to an underlying stabilization of a decisive functional nexus within the evocation of emotions itself. The standardization of feelings probably occurs within the framework of the appraisal function, which is responsible for intuitively evaluating stimuli with respect to their subjective meaning for that person. Appraisal is actually a process, but according to Lazarus (1991, 138) there are also established ways of functioning that come together to form an "appraisal style." In the area of film, genres seem to be able to form such appraisal styles by shaping the patterns and standards for central processes of evaluation. Through an ensemble of familiar forms, genres can call up a corresponding emotional reaction in the viewers as soon as they recognize the genre elements in the film they are watching. In this way genres also lead to a relatively stable emotional climate, characterized for example by "tonic emotions" (cf. Tan 1996, 83). Insofar as genres orient themselves to a certain appraisal style that also has to do with a specific form of coming to grips with the conflicts in the film plot, the genre form becomes an instrument to steer emotions. In this way it operationalizes the appraisal function in the sense of making it an efficient form of emotion management for the viewer.

The basic attitudes and patterns of emotion that genres realize—that is, set up and keep constant—have their decisive point of departure in the elements of conflict within the stimuli that force a change in regard to the capacity of taking action. Comedies solve their conflicts differently from tragedies or melodramas. This means that not only do the ways of reaching a solution in *The Gold Rush* or *Father and Daughter* vary, but also the emotional attitudes that seem appropriate during reception. The dramatist Friedrich Dürrenmatt found a formula for these basic attitudes: "Tragedy overcomes distance [...] comedy creates distance" (1955, 45). Aesthetics and the study of art have also brought together a lot of experience from their own perspectives regarding the construction of classical genres and the emotions they evoke. Now, we must try to evolve these insights into a psychological form and apply them to popular genres as well.

9. Film-elicited Emotions as Process

Films elicit states of affect and emotion in a process of experiencing that is generally based on the representation of contradictions and conflicts which demand again and again a new appraisal. This assessment must be permanently updated insofar as the life processes represented on the screen are developing and changing. But it can comply with invariant structures of situations, i.e. similar conflicts, with the result that significant emotive effects are developed that go into a certain direction.

Greg Smith has outlined a process model for the development of film-elicited emotions: the "mood-cue approach". According to Frijda (1993), this approach, which seems compatible with mine, is based on the interactions between two emotion states, "moods" and "episodic emotions": "The primary set of orienting emotion states is mood. A mood is a preparatory state in which one is seeking an opportunity to express a particular emotion or emotion set. Moods are expectancies that we are about to have a particular emotion, that we will encounter cues that will elicit particular emotions" (G. Smith 2003, 38). Further: "A combination of mood (emotional orientation) and external circumstances forms a sequence of emotional moments that Nico Frijda calls an emotion episode. An emotion episode is a series of emotions that are perceived to be a structured coherent unit having a beginning, a middle, and an end" (39).

G. Smith refers to these general assertions about emotions when he points out differences from the film-elicited ones: "Film structures seek to increase the film's chance of evoking emotion by first creating a predisposition toward experiencing emotion: a mood. [...] To sustain a mood, we must experience occasional moments of emotion. Film must therefore provide the viewer with a periodic diet of brief emotional moments if it is to sustain a mood. Therefore, mood and emotion sustain each other. Mood encourages us to experience emotion, and experiencing emotions encourages us to continue in the present mood. [...] Because emotions can be evoked using a wide range of stimuli linked in an associative network, films can use the full range of perceptual cues to evoke emotion ..." (2003, 42). According to G. Smith, these cues, which work on all levels of film form and narration, provide for redundancy. "Redundant cues collaborate to indicate to the viewer which emotional mood is called for. The viewer need not focus conscious attention on each of these elements. Some of these cues activate the associative network of the emotions, and this creates a low-level emotion. If a film provides a viewer with several redundant emotive cues, this increases the likelihood of moving the viewer toward a predispositionary mood state" (2003, 43).

The short film *Father and Daughter* provides redundancy through the frequent iteration of a very similar conflict situation. The cues formed by the topic structure of narration are extraordinarily conspicuous; they serve as "emotion markers" whose primary purpose is "to generate a brief burst of emotion" (G. Smith 2003, 45). However, the functional link to the conflict situations of the story is always obvious. If, as G. Smith states, "Mood is sustained by a succession of cues, some of which are organized into larger structures (narrative obstacles, emotion markers), some of which are not" (47), then this opinion corresponds with the presumptions of the PCS model extended to the conflict theory of emotion. The peculiarity of contradiction specifies the cues.

But *Father and Daughter* is a special case because the same conflict dominates all three levels of the narrative. Normally, the cues are not shaped in such a homogeneous manner, and they do not achieve such a high conspicuousness; correspondingly, the emotions evoked by them are weaker or more ambiguous.

10. Strength and Intensity of Film-elicited Emotions

According to the strength of the conflict situations on the screen, the affects and emotions in the auditorium gain or lose intensity. And presumably, the various density of conflict moments—i.e. cues—in the course of action provides the differing intensity of the spectators' excitement. Significant differentials ensue within films whose narration is based on stereotypes, causal chains or topic lines, because: in each case, their conflict offer is founded on cinematic structures that affect a different mental state.

The weakest cues occur in the case of topic lines. One can demonstrate this by using examples from the Western-European *Cinéma du comportement*, such as Antonioni's aforementioned tetralogy, or most films by Rohmer or Rivette, and also from the Documentary Style of Fiction Film of the former Socialist countries of eastern Europe, which prefer an episodic structure. Furthermore, the complete *œuvre* of Ozu and the earlier works of Cassavetes and

Jarmusch are endowed with low-level cues. It would be totally wrong to maintain that these films do not elicit emotions. However, their conflict situations, which evoke emotive reactions, do not occur in vivid dramatic upheavals but rather in odd behavioral patterns of the characters showing strange discrepancies. Nevertheless, viewers who have become adapted to these phenomena can find the right attitude to the lowered stimulus threshold and are often moved by weak collisions—but the number of these spectators is small.

Films such as Jim Jarmusch's *Stranger than Paradise* (1984) show that not only are the conflict moments very guardedly formulated, as there are hardly any dramatic decisions, but also that the intervals between these cues are very long.

The story comprises three episodes: A girl from Hungary who is visiting the USA for the first time has to stay at her unenthusiastic cousin's apartment for some days since her aunt's illness prevents the girl from accepting her invitation. She cuts the visit at her cousin's home short.

Some months after having moved in with the aunt, the girl has to welcome the cousin and his friend as guests—but in doing so, she gives them a cool reception, and the two frustrated men drive off again.

However, they return and pick her up for a trip to Florida. Having arrived at their destination, the two amateurish criminals leave the girl behind in the motel while they set off to bet at a dog-race. Then the girl—thanks to the mistake of a drug dealer—unexpectedly receives money, shares it with the two friends and buys an airline ticket to Budapest. However, she does not take the flight but rather decides to stay in America while her cousin flies to Hungary to bring her back.

The three episodes follow a similar conflict schema based on the similar behavioural pattern of the three characters. Although these characters, with the profile of underdogs, have no ideals or long-term plans and rather look like persons without any orientation, they refuse to let themselves be taken in, either by American society which gave them housing in decayed suburbs "stranger than paradise", or, even more remarkably, by each other.

They remain adamantly stubborn about their individuality and their separateness from the others, and thereby forgo many chances for harmonious relationships. Thus, the film tells a story of frustrated relations and missed opportunities to overcome the dilemma of loneliness. The starting point for eliciting the viewer's emotions should be, for instance, the cousin's unfriendly reception of the girl and her unobliging introduction to the American way of life, or when the girl, who has just met with her cousin's first approval for successful shop-lifting, throws away a dress given by him into the garbage can because it is not to her liking.

To make the spectator conscious of these small actions and the behavior of the characters and to evoke certain emotions, this film form provides for redundancies which permit specific accentuations. Thus, 67 plan-séquences of different lengths (from 9 seconds to 3 min 31 seconds) ensure that the behavior of the protagonists in their mixture of idleness and rigorous self-assurance will be exposed. There are phases in which nothing happens and the characters simply "hang out". The camera places the protagonists in dull interiors or in front of dirty industrial landscapes and stays—with one exception—totally motionless, and the frequent two-shots allocate each of them in their own half of the image (sometimes with a piece of furniture in the middle) to emphazise their loneliness and isolation. The editing uses neutral black leader with a length of around four seconds and these "buffer zones" permit a kind of after-image of the previous scene and provide a monotonous rhythm to the flow of events. Since the "buffer zones" are placed among situations which occur in quick succession as well as among those with timely intervals of days or months, the spectator feels that life continues to be always the same. Of course, these are cues for emotions, but thanks to the weak conflict moments and the long temporal intervals between them, the arousals are rather slight.

Other film stories which—at least at first glance—diminish conflicts and show a stable state rather than dramatic change can nevertheless lead to an emotional impact of astonishing strength and intensity, for instance Wong Kar-wai's *In the Mood for Love* (*Fa yeung nin wa*, 2000). That this film does without a plot is not quite the case and is more of an optical illusion. It does in fact have a central conflict which is developed as a succession of causal events which the spectator can consciously duplicate: At the same time, two young couples become lodgers of a large flat in the

Shanghai community of Hong-Kong of the 1960s. Mrs. Li-Zhen's husband is often abroad, as is of Mr. Chow. The two remaining spouses discover that their absent partners are having a love-affair, and they attempt to deal with the situation by reconstructing together how the liaison might have begun. Thus, they grow closer to each other. However, they both refuse to do as their spouses have done and they refuse to accept their new-found nearness as love. This, though, compels them to self-denial and to rein in their passions, with the result that the man decides to escape from the unbearable situation by moving to Singapore.

In this story, which also refers to an exceptional case, the protagonists refuse to follow in the footsteps of the others, whereby they also must renounce their love—a tormenting step that demands their utmost effort and means a frontier crossing in the world of their feelings, namely, a violent giving up of their lovers' bliss. However, the conflict does not culminate in the common dramatic way. Thus, the preparations for the protagonists' first secret date in a hotel room are shown only fragmentarily, and this first meeting alone of Mr. Chow and Mrs. Li-Zhen is skipped altogether and the spectator can only see them parting afterwards in the hotel corridor. The plot points of the whole film are handled in a similar way. They are played off and passed over, and a clear decision at the film's finale is also lacking; the clearing-up is drawn out again and again through several situations which could enable a reunion of the protagonists even after the departure of Mr. Chow. That the story still has a strong emotional impact is caused by the evoking of feelings at all levels of the narrative structure through thematically related cues or conflict offers. Here, a remarkable density of emotional cues occurs, with an outstanding intensity of their interactions and a strong overall response.

The variety of topic lines in this film is conspicuous, mostly developed in a parallel manner from the film's beginning through to the end. These series not only provide for latent expectations in the viewers' mind, but also bring about variations of and completions to the central conflict. Bound to the return of similar locations and motives for actions and pictures, they permanently produce emotional cues for specific moods and tonic emotions.

To this group of cues belong the topics of deserted lanes and narrow staircases, where the protagonists occasionally meet during their lonely walks to the cook-shop, hardly glancing at each other and intent on distance in their making way for each other. The are able to continue this trained posture later when they know one another better. Their attitude helps them to maintain a distance from their desire and yearning for love, a state that is by no means without conflict.

Another often-shown location is the narrow corridor of the apartment, a neutral place between public and private spheres where they can stay without having to declare themselves. The frequent pause on this threshold between the rooms reveals the state of disequilibrium that dominates the protagonists' emotional life—a state of suspension between auspiciousness and resignation.

As often as the director leads the protagonists to this threshold, he moves their unfaithful partners out of the frame—i.e. across the threshold of visibleness—into the off, or decreases their visual presence by showing them solely from behind. Although the conflict of expectancy will not be conscious to the viewer, he can nonetheless feel an element of surprise or discrepancy.

As in his earlier works, Wong here often shows the hands of big clocks, but in this case mostly connected with off-dialogs which bring restlessness into the standardized situations and should be considered as another discrepancy.

The film very frequently shows the protagonists having meals; it uses these scenes on the one hand for a subtle description of their getting closer and on the other to emphasize their isolation in their social environment—in other words contradictions in their life situation.

As immigrants from Shanghai, the protagonists are strangers in Hong Kong and they must live under their neighbors' watchful eyes. The camera underlines the viewpoint of their potential observers by looking through window-grates, peering from behind a curtain and spying from underneath the bed on the characters. Thus, the spectator gets the uncomfortable feeling that his heroes are being threatened.

Often the protagonists are shown in a frame with "limits", for instance by the frames of doors or windows or behind the grates, as if they were prisoners. Sometimes the camera presents them via mirrors or introduces them to the scenes via their shadows, silhouettes, backs or parts of body in such a way that the spectator has to guess who and where they are.

Further guessing on the part of the spectator takes place when the protagonists try to imagine critical life situations with their absent partners and play them through together without letting the spectator know immediately that he is dealing with imageries and events simulated by acting. As the protagonists come closer to each other by this acting their behavior sometimes resembles love-play. At the same time, there occurs a dimension in their action with the quality of "conditionality". The mood for love seems to be palpable like a realizing passion, but this creates discrepancies in the viewers' experience as well.

That the gestures of Mrs. Li-Zhen, who always appears in exciting *étui* gowns which emphasize her figure, are sometimes performed in cinematic slow motion functions as a kind of choreography for their emotional state of suspension.

The emotional balance between promise and renunciation is emphasized by the music, which was highly important for the creating of the film. According to Wong (2000) the film was inspired by a particular waltz and brings together a series of similar tunes, mostly tangos, sung by Nat King Cole, among them the impressive song with the finale "Quizás, quizás, quizás!"—"Maybe, maybe, maybe!".

Through the emotional component of this music the sound-track leans on the stereotype of narration and conflict-solving by complementing the genre schema of melodrama (Jousse 2006, 24ff.). A contemporary variant of melodrama is known for its use of strong emotional conflicts as a central motif of the story, especially those which are unsolvable for the protagonists—mainly of female gender—and lead to a final catastrophe. Indeed, the film tells of a struggle of feelings insofar as both protagonists have to emotionally overcome their painful situation. That their developing relationship yields neither to the mood for love and desire and a happy romance, nor ends in a passionate story of despair and abandonment, expresses the contradictory essence of the events. The conventions of melodrama, which usually serve to elicit tears, are undercut here by the genre conventions of the parable, which aim to orient the viewers' experience to an idea or maxim. Striving for an image of themselves which has not been contaminated by the common immoral behavior of their social environment, the protagonists follow the maxim: "We will not become like the others!" Thus, melodrama and parable generate a hybrid genre with changing expectations of the spectator and heart-stirring effects.

At this point, for the sake of completeness and for methodical reasons it would be appropriate to show the impulses for emotive processes by using examples that focus on dramatic conflict, and this, if possible, within a popular genre. One could speak about the viewers' feelings while experiencing the plot points of Fred Zinnemann's *High Noon* (1952), Andrzej Wajda's *Ashes and Diamonds* (*Popiół i diament*, 1958), or Michelangelo Antonioni's *Blow Up* (1966), not to mention numerous suspense and horror films. But it should not be difficult for the reader to arrive at these ideas on the issues by himself, especially as there exist some very successful analyses of the subject—for instance in the books of Carroll (1990, 1999), Tan (1996), Grodal (1997) and G. Smith (2003). Although their authors do not explicitly use the conflict theorem, the construction of "emotional cues" could serve as a bridge here. Since G. Smith (2003, 47) recommends beginning the study of emotive reactions with cues, as "the smallest unit for analyzing a text's emotional appeals", then one should have to specify that there are always intentional discrepancies and contradictions in the film's offer of stimuli, regardless of whether or not there are P, C or S structures.

These stimuli patterns and their inner contradictions cannot always be discerned at once; particularly those that occur at a perceptual level remain rather unconscious in the process of experience, and it requires an effort to find and describe them. The use of hermeneutic methods can help make clear the subtle relations between the contradictions and themes of episodes. Besides, the moments of conflict do not simply function as a kind of orientation or eye-catcher in the flow of events; their understanding also facilitates a better incorporation of the partial information about emotions into an aesthetic analysis of the whole work and serves as a reliable starting point for psychological hypotheses concerning their impact.

11. Qualities and Basic Tendencies of Emotions

Emotions, including the witness emotions of the cinema, differ not only in the strength and density of their impulses but also in their quality. Generally, the so-called differential emotion theory has tried to study various emotions as "distinct experiential/motivational processes that influence cognition and action differentially" (Izard 1991, 40). Izard speaks of ten fundamental emotions, and the chapters of a handbook of cognition and emotion (Dalgleish / Power 1999) are headlined with terms such as: Anger, Disgust, Anxiety, Panic, Sadness, Positive Affect, Shame, Guilt, Embarrassment, Pride, Jealousy and Envy. In my opinion, a taking-over of these taxonomies into the psychology of film does not seem productive for several reasons. It is a point of contention whether or not it makes sense generally to assume a limited number of fundamental emotions and also how to demarcate them from one another, or discover their interactions. These difficult to determine interactions would undergo further modification or breaking where they occur as witness emotions as experienced by the spectators, with the result that their determination will be yet more complicated. Therefore, for the time being—and this period should be long—it would be illusory to analyze the differentiated qualities of film-elicited emotions systematically at the level of empirical research. Each film confronts the spectator with new stories and events, with new specific characters and their colliding actions, often using an innovative visual style. Hoping to master all of these subtle differentiations, one can only turn to the subject-centered hermeneutic approach of the traditional analysis of art; however, we must take into account psychological findings which are impossible to gain without modeling them.

More productive for film studies than the approach of the differential emotion theory should be the approach of the elementary bi-polar model of two basic tendencies of affects or emotions that pits so-called "positive" against "negative" emotions. The distinction between two basic tendencies has the advantage that one can derive them from the most elementary conditions of adaptive human behavior, namely, whether we come to a subjective appraisal that we can cope with the situation and have gained the feeling of action readiness or not.

In the process of film experience, the spectator has to deal with the struggle between analogous positive and negative tendencies. The consequence of this divergence is reducible to the simple formula of Brechtian aesthetics, according to which the artwork has to represent the world in such a way that the spectator has the impression that he can cope with the conflict situation and will not become a plaything of fate. (cf. Brecht 1990, 226ff.). In numerous older and more contemporary ideas of art (cf. Kreitler / Kreitler 1972, 12ff.) one finds the demand for harmony, the processing of external tensions, or mental equilibrium, in other words, a leading of the spectator's experience to positive emotions in the above-mentioned sense. This concept will be elaborated in chapter IX, which is concerned with genre issues. For the present, I would like to stress the fundamental significance of the conflict principle, which also plays a role in understanding the positive and negative basic qualities or tendencies of witness emotions.

12. Challenge for Research on Effects

Focusing on moments of conflict in cinematic action is thus of central importance because it at once steers the narrative through the various orders of plot points to both the changing relations of empathy with the characters and the effective strategies inherent in the use of genre stereotypes. Wherever conflicts and discrepancies appear in a film plot, they will most likely lead to measurable changes in the level of activation in the viewers and thus make it easier to analyze emotional reactions. This applies to:

(1) the experiential level, where emotional effects become conscious as specific feelings and can thus be verbalized.

In this context one, has to consider that the emotive processes are often not fully conscious but include a substantial proportion of unconscious components (Ekman / Davidson 1994, 298ff.; 424ff.; Öhman 1999).

(2) the expressive level, which manifests observable behavior including the extremes of laughing or crying.

According to Izard (1994, 79), facial expressions belong to the integrative components of the emotion system. Numerous studies have shown that fundamental emotions are identifiable in the human face (Cacioppo et al. 1992; Ekman 1999; White 1999; Frijda 2007.)

(3) the neuro-physiological level, which permits inferences about activity in our mind, above all in the nonconscious central nervous system, whose complicated interactions have been impressively described by Damasio (1999) and others.

To master this task, the assessment of the neuro-physiological component should be carried out in a wide-spectrum manner, that is, with regard to many different relevant variables of reaction (Mangold 1999, 121). According to Mangold (1999) and Tinchon (1999), this wide-spectrum approach includes the analyses of electro-dermal activity, cardiovascular activity, breath frequency; furthermore some data from electro-encephalograms and such nuclear-medical procedures as the single-photon-emission, computer-tomography or positron-emission-tomography.

Thus it would be possible to proceed from work-oriented models and experimentally test the hypotheses formed by them about conflict-related effects at various levels of emotional reactions. Of course, models of specific spectators would have to be considered in order to take different audience groups into account.

It is the task of experimental psychology to carry out such studies. What cognitive film theory can at present contribute is hypotheses that are as precise as possible about the connections between the specific kinds of stimuli a work offers and the emotional consequences they have during viewing, for example by continuing the important lines of research set out by Ed Tan (1996), Peter Ohler and Gerhild Nieding (1996, 129ff.), or Monika Suckfüll (1997; 2001; 2003; 2004).

Working from a cognitivist perspective, Suckfüll, for example, has shown that plot points, topics and some other conflict moments and discrepancies in the flow of actions in *Father and Daughter*, among them motifs that are picked up in a relatively unconscious way while watching the film, have a significant effect on heartbeat and electrodermal activities, even though the spectators may not even register these elements consciously and can hardly remember the motifs later. Suckfüll's pilot study provides evidence for the hypothesis that physiological arousal takes place synchronically to pivotal conflict situations on the screen, which can be considered as sources of emotions. Many participants of the study show significant decelerations in heart rate during these scenes of the film (see fig. 7). Although the research offers hope that we should soon arrive at findings on emotions, it still requires differentiation by a network of specifying conditions. Furthermore, the research in question does not yet show the spectators' emotions—but it proves that, in certain accurately definable phases of the film, intersubjective reactions take place in the auditorium.

The above-mentioned effects of the conflict experience should have a varying significance for the aesthetic impact on the viewer. In my opinion, the nearness of the film's conflict situation to the life-problems of the viewer, particularly to relevant issues, is very important for the strength of his emotive reaction, too.

Any new models of the functional connections between conflicts on the screen and the emotional reactions of the viewers will thus have to take the viewer's involvement in real-life conflicts into account. The question of the essence of cinematic emotions loses its indeterminate character to the degree that film plots refer more clearly to real-life processes and their tensions and conflicts.

While general social interest in the emotional effects of *Father and Daughter* or *In the Mood for Love* can hardly be expected, and most viewers would see the issue as superfluous and unnecessary, the question of what emotions a film elicits and with what intention it does so is of social importance.

This is particularly the case when a film deals with a socially relevant subject that also dominates the immediate life-world of the viewers, and all the more if the meaning of the whole film depends on the kinds of emotion it evokes and if it also affects the attitude toward the real conflicts shown.

When Roberto Benigni's *Life Is Beautiful* (*La vita è bella*) appeared in 1997, it immediately became clear that this film's message could not be judged without taking its emotional effects into account, and these emotional effects were not easy to determine. The film, about a Jewish father who pretends to his little son that the Nazi concentration camp in which they are both held captive is just part of a game, immediately provoked controversial discussions as to whether its emotional effects were at all fitting to the topic, and in particular as to whether comedy and popular culture could be considered legitimate ways to portray the Shoah. Many critics even found the film and its effects to be ethically irresponsible and spoke in protest of "holocaust laughter" (cf. Vaiano 1999, 27ff.). Although the film became a success relatively quickly despite these public accusations, it would have been helpful at that time to document the diverging reactions to its emotional effects scientifically, for instance through empirical psychological or sociological studies of the film's effects. But we are still far from having such studies and methods.

In looking for sources and initiatory points for the various emotions that the film plot evokes, we will find that the fields of conflict in the action are a useful starting point. This refers to various orders of plot points and plot lines, which are oriented to the course of action and the strategies that various genres employ to elicit effects.

The plot is largely determined by two major conflicts: the group conflict between the Nazis and the Jews they persecute, and the intra-personal conflict of the main character as to what strategy of behavior to follow to alleviate the threatening situation. Although the protagonist does not outwardly show many doubts as to his plan of action, he—just like the viewer—is constantly confronted by the fundamental question of whether it is right or wrong to hide the horror of the situation from the child. Although the force fields of both these conflicts determine the external events, the narration focuses interest primarily on the latter problem, which leads to the question of under what conditions and with which concept of life can one avoid a fatal outcome. One of the peculiarities of the film is that this does not at once become apparent; in fact, not fully until the second half of the plot, which is a very unusual dramatic device.

In the first half of the film the Nazi terror has not yet developed to the point that it threatens the lives of Guido's family. It is in the offing, however, and even in this phase Guido must undertake drastic measures to repress his horror through his playful escapades. The love story between Guido and the young teacher Dora, which is developed during the first half of the film, also shows how, despite some small letdowns on the way, he is able to triumph as a creative and playful optimist against his conventional and reactionary rival. His unique, individual form of behavior, which is by no means above question, later—in the urgent situation of the concentration camp—leads to his equally ambiguous but successful defensive strategy. The playful and creative side of Guido's personality succeeds against all odds, first in love, then in creating a life-saving fiction. As an over-arching form of behavior, it is responsible for preventing the film's composition from breaking into two parts.

I mention these details in order to keep the whole impression of the film in mind, despite the emphasis on working out conflict schemata. The special quality of the film often results from the way it presents to the spectator multiple and different processes and elements of conflict that alternate and become intertwined, creating a field of conflicts which constantly drives the plot on and periodically presents impulses for affective arousal, but at the same time requires the viewer to react to a constant change of perspective with varying expectations and changing emotion episodes. Critics were right in speaking of the film as plunging the audience into a hot and cold treatment for the emotions. That this occurs is not least a result of the mixing of genres that the film attempts.

Thus, in the case of Benigni's film, an additional difficulty for analysis arises in that it does not adhere to the criteria of a single genre, but rather aims at a hybridization of several genres, including some with contrary emotional tendencies such as comedy and tragedy. More will be said about this in chapter IX, concerning genre issues.

Chapter V: Strategies of Narrative Tension and Suspense

1. Introduction

There is no doubt: Audiences like the feeling of tension and its special case called suspense. For a lot of people, the experience of tension or suspense is an important, or even the most important, reason to go to the movies. And filmmakers think in a similar way; they take the problem seriously. The effect of tension is simply a crucial part of their job. A film has to be exciting, has to bring tension for the viewer or it won't be worth watching.

But there are various degrees and various modes of this aesthetic response, and scriptwriters and directors have to think about the right strategy for its evocation in every film production as well as about the artistic means of how to achieve it. Although the terms "cinematic tension" and "suspense" are often mentioned in connection with the development of popular genres like the detective, crime, and horror film or thriller, which would probably have lost their right to exist in the cinema without these corresponding effects, one can also find specific forms or modes of tension in other types of film. Even the Italian film director Michelangelo Antonioni, who in the 60s became notorious for his giving up of the classical plot and for his use of a dramaturgy that seemed diametrically opposed to the suspense film, said with regard to his famous early films that he aimed for a kind of "inner suspense" (Antonioni 1964, 39). Thus I believe that directors such as Eric Rohmer or Yasujiro Ozu or Wong Kar-wai in *In the Mood For Love* (*Fa yeung nin wa*, 2000) are also interested—or even keen—to organise their film stories in order to give the viewer a feeling of tension—albeit an "inner tension" or "inner suspense". In other words, tension or suspense is a very important thing for the cinema, in particular for the processes of narration.

But all tension is not equal, and suspense cannot be the same thing in all kinds of film. Theory is challenged to not aim solely at locating tension in a narrowly defined understanding of the suspense genre, but to contemplate how a concept of tension can be extended and modified so as to be applicable to those phenomena that, at first glance, appear to be far removed from the suspense genres.

I would like to suggest a general model of cinematic tension based on the ideas of cognitive processes and emotions mentioned and developed previously. This approach allows differentiations which help in the understanding of the various modes and strategies of cinematic tension, as well as its special case termed "suspense". How can we analyse tension and suspense? First of all, what kind of phenomenon is tension?

I believe tension (including its special case "suspense") is related to the process of cinematic experience, to the process of film reception. It is to be studied as a peculiarity of this process, or, more precisely, of the viewer's behaviour in the process of reception.

The most important, dominant kind of tension seems to be narrative tension related to the unfolding of the events over time, resulting in the colliding actions of characters and in the decisions of conflict situations.

In chapter II I spoke about the variety of processes connected with different modes of narration. I would now like to continue my considerations and apply the PCS model to a differentiated description and explanation of the problems of tension. The academic deliberations concerning a comprehensive understanding of tension that would also allow distinctions to be made have just begun.

An important reason for this situation lies in the fact that, on the one hand, tension is prefabricated within the work's structure, but, on the other hand, it is based on psychologically relevant functional forms, that is, it amounts to a specifically aesthetic reaction that necessitates an interdisciplinary approach. The following considerations follow this direction. They attempt to make use of cognitive psychological findings to depict the process of film reception so that a general and yet differentiated model of narrative tension is created, which can mediate between exterior tension with suspense-like qualities, such as Alfred Hitchcock developed in practice and theory, and the inner tension that Antonioni, Ozu, Wong or others have employed.

2. Tension and Suspense: Aspects of Definition

It is well known that discussions of both cinematic and narrative tension have been stimulated by Hitchcock's concept of suspense. The basic principle of suspense, which I interpret as a special case of tension, was once illustrated very vividly by this master of the genre of suspense by a film situation in which a group of people were sitting around a table under which there was a bomb that could explode at any moment. Unlike the viewers, who are have been informed of this, the protagonists do not know of the danger they are in (cf. Truffaut 1967, 52). This prototypical situation allows one to identify some general prerequisites for tension and suspense in a film. Thus, tension is conditional on:

(1)   The probable occurrence of a relevant (often menacing) event in an undefined course of events.

(2)   The possibility of the protagonists being able to bring the course of events under control by certain forms of conduct (i.e. preventing the negative outcome).

Whereas these two conditions may, in general, apply to narrative tension in film, another characteristic is applicable specifically to suspense.

(3)   There is a difference between the information viewers have about the uncertain situation and the kind of information to which the protagonists are privy.

By the way, there are authors quoted here who do not make a clear distinction between tension and suspense, but rather use very extensive notions of suspense, especially as the determination of the difference between the information of the viewers and the protagonists is sometimes very difficult.

Hitchcock once used the final sequence of *Young and Innocent* (1937) to demonstrate in detail how the sequence of events in the film has an influence on tension and especially suspense.

In an interview with the French journalist and filmmaker Truffaut, Hitchcock said about this scene:

"By the way, *Young and Innocent* contains an illustration of that suspense rule by which the audience is provided with information the characters in the picture don't know about. Because of this knowledge, the tension is heightened as the audience tries to figure out what's going to happen next. Toward the end of the picture the young girl is searching for the murderer, and she discovers an old tramp who has seen the killer and can identify him. The only clue is that the man has a nervous twitch of the eyes. So the girl dresses up the old tramp in a good suit of clothes and she takes him to this big hotel where a thé dansant is in progress. There are lots of people there, and the tramp says, 'Isn't it ridiculous to try to spot a pair of twitching eyes in a crowd of this size.'

Just then, right on that line of dialogue, I place the camera in the highest position, above the hotel lounge, next to the ceiling, and we dolly it down, right through the lobby, into the big ballroom, and past the dancers, the bandstand, and the musicians, right up to a close-up of the drummer. The musicians are all in blackface, and we stay on the drummer's face until his eyes fill the screen. And then, the eyes twitch. The whole thing was done in one shot.

[…] Yes. At that moment I cut right back to the old man and the girl, still sitting at the other end of the room. Now, the audience has the information and the question is: How are this girl and this old boy going to spot the man? A policeman outside sees the girl, who is the daughter of his chief. He goes to the phone. Meanwhile, the band has stopped for a break, and the drummer, having a smoke outside in the alley, sees a group of police hurrying toward the rear entrance of the hotel. Since he's guilty, he quickly ducks back inside, to the bandstand, where the music resumes.

Now the jittery drummer sees the policemen talking to the tramp and the girl at the other end of the ballroom. He thinks they're looking for him, and his nervousness is reflected in the drumbeat, which is out of tune with the rest of the band. The rhythm gets worse and worse. Meanwhile, the tramp, the girl, and the police are preparing to leave through an exit near the bandstand. In fact, the drummer is out of danger, but he doesn't know it. All he can see are those uniforms moving in his direction, and his twitching eyes indicate that he's in a panic. Finally, his beat is so far out of rhythm that the band stops playing and the dancers stop their dancing. And just as the little group is making its way out the door, he falls with a loud crash into his drum.

They stop to find out the reason for the commotion, and the girl and the tramp move over to the unconscious man. At the beginning of the story we had established that the heroine is a Girl Scout and an expert on first aid. [...] So now she volunteers to help the unconscious drummer, and as she leans over him, she notices his twitching eyes. Very quickly she says, 'Will someone please get me a wet cloth to wipe his face off', at the same time beckoning the tramp to come over. A waiter hands her the towel; she wipes the man's face clean of its black make-up and looks up at the tramp, who nods and says, 'Yes, that's the man!'" (Truffaut, 1967, 81–82)

The film was shot in 1937, and although nowadays the mentioned sequence seems to move very slowly I'm sure that at the time the audience could find in it cinematic tension, narrative tension and suspense. And I would like to use this sequence to explain some aspects of tension and suspense.

Concerning the method it seems to be clear that:

Cinematic tension (including narrative tension) has to be studied considering two components, the structures of the work and the structures of the viewer's response.

And, of course, it makes sense to study this aesthetic reaction across the entire field of mental functions, i.e. in the whole complex of their connections.

Contemporary psychology often speaks about these connections very cautiously, perhaps in order to avoid a simplification of the difficult processes of interaction. In the last chapter, I quoted the psychologist Lazarus (1999, 10) who writes about the "trilogy of mind" that consists of the systems of (1) motivation, (2) cognition and (3) emotion.

Following this model, one can approximate some important functional interrelations within the experience of film in such a way that cognition and emotion are not isolated but embedded in the fundamental processes of human activities.

3. Hypotheses on Narrative Tension from a Psychological Viewpoint

3.1 The System of Motivation and Tension

The human being in his individual and social existence has to cope with his environment by doing, by permanent activities; therefore I describe the primary motivation for his behaviour as the "need for control", for "coping", for "action readiness". The main question is always: How to cope with a concrete situation? This has consequences for the understanding of tension: cinematic tension may be artificial, but it is based on a specific situation of human life that has to do with coping and the need for control. This need for control has consequences for narrative tension, too.

Narrative tension is always content-driven because it is based on the protagonist's realisation of specific goal-oriented actions that are relevant to his active control of the conflict situation.

The activities of the protagonists mainly depend on the existence of goals and the necessity of reaching them. Often the heroes have to overcome dangers, and mostly it is necessary to solve conflict situations, to come to a relevant decision regarding the colliding actions. That means, for the analysis of a film story, it is necessary to deduce potential tensions from the dominant contradictions, from the central conflict situation or the entire conflict field. Without conflicts there are no goals of action, without goals there is no tension. Nevertheless, the goals of action can be more or less evident—with varying consequences for the viewer's tensions.

In *Young and Innocent*, the goal of the protagonists' action is obvious. It all comes down to a relevant decision: whether the murderer will be successfully unmasked and thus an innocent man saved from a prison sentence.

The efforts of the protagonists also have an influence on the course of events. In the case of a successful criminal investigation, the situation will have been brought under their active control, that is, changed for the benefit of the innocent man. The narrative tension is based on the motivations of the protagonist and is linked with an analogical motivation of the viewer to foresee the solving of the conflict situation. Hans J. Wulff (1996, 16) pointed out: "The experience of suspense does not come from something exciting being shown in a film. Rather, it results from the extrapolation of possible events from a given situation; it is the result, or concomitant, of the anticipating activity. It is not what the film shows, but what it discloses, that is the subject of the analysis of suspense."

3.2 The System of Cognition and Tension

According to Bordwell (1985, 33), narrative film offers structures of information that "encourage the spectator to execute story-constructing activities. The film presents cues, patterns, and gaps that shape the viewer's application of schemata and the testing of hypotheses." If the pattern or cues are not evident the spectator has to search for them in order to comprehend the story. Meir Sternberg (1978, 65) has characterised the viewers' ability to understand the events as "a lack of desired information concerning the outcome of a conflict that is to take place in the narrative futures, a lack that involves a clash of hope and fear".

Narrative tension is always joint to the related cognitive processes; it depends on the resolving of the viewer's uncertainty concerning the course of action as well as the decisions in conflict situations.

A conflict situation is a situation of uncertainty for the protagonist as well as the viewer, and the tension of both is linked by this unclear state of affairs. Considering cognitive psychology, one can see both processes as problem-solving. There is an unwelcome (conflict-loaded) initial situation, a desired final situation, and an obstacle that in a given moment prevents the transformation from initial to final situation (cf. Dörner 1979).

In the sequence discussed, we are shown the girl, who is on the side of the innocent hero, looking for the murderer, who is recognizable by his twitching eye, in a first-class hotel during teatime, using the services of a tramp. The mass of people in the hotel lobby, however, make it difficult to conduct the search. Thus, the uncertainty of the situation can hardly be resolved by the protagonist, as she needs information about where the wanted man is situated.

The viewer is not able to change the conflict situation actively, but he can gain passive control of the changes by a better cognitive evaluation of them, that is, by better prediction, foresight, anticipation.

Thus, from the cognitive perspective, narrative tension depends on the viewer's possibility to overcome or abolish the state of uncertainty, i.e. his ability to anticipate the unfolding of the events.

For this Hitchcock uses the means of suspense. He explains that just at the point where the tramp airs his doubts about whether they can expect to find a man with a small eye-imperfection in such a throng, the camera situated below the ballroom's ceiling begins to gradually travel toward the musicians. When it gets so near to the drummer that his eyes fill the screen, one sees the lids twitch: the aforementioned twitchy eye! When talking about the conditioning of the viewers considering this suspense scene, Hitchcock said: "The audience is provided with information the characters in the picture don't know about. Because of this knowledge, the tension is heightened as the audience tries to figure out what's going to happen next" (Truffaut 1967, 81).

Suddenly, the viewer is able to foresee better the possible course of actions. He knows that the wanted person is sitting in the room and his exposure is highly likely. This ability of the viewer is linked with processes of attentiveness.

The camera has focused on the viewer's field of attention. Through the travelling camera the uncertainty in the clearly-defined problem space, which is given something of a topographic dimension here, will be reduced. The viewer can conceptualise that the murderer is in the room, and this enables him to make a better prognosis of catching the criminal.

Thus narrative tension seems to be in accordance with the viewer's attention and its changes are likely proportional to the degree of attention. Suspense may be the result of focused attention on a fact that is narrowly linked with a conceptualised goal and a corresponding type of action.

If the viewers' uncertainty concerning the decision of conflict, the problem-solving or the achievement of a goal is over, his attention flags and the suspense wanes as well. Carroll (1996b, 72) points out: "Uncertainty is a necessary condition for suspense. When uncertainty is removed from a situation, suspense evaporates. [...] Moreover, if a situation lacks uncertainty altogether, no sense of suspense can intelligibly arise." The same author calls suspense an "emotional state" (Carroll 1990, 137). Indeed, the processes of film experience, which we have been examining till now from a cognitive aspect, have a clear emotive dimension, too.

3.3 Interrelations Among Emotion, Empathy and Narrative Tension

Narrative tension always has an emotive component because it elicits an affective arousal caused by the conflict situation of the characters that leads to "a change in action readiness as a result of the subject's appraisal of the situation", termed "emotion" by Ed Tan (1996, 46).

According to my presuppositions, elements of conflict in film plots can be viewed as the source or stimulus of emotional reactions in the audience because the development of conflict situations has consequences for the state of control—for the active control of the protagonists and for the passive control of the viewer, who is looking for a better way to predict the events and decisions on the screen. "Emotions are, in our opinion, reactions to felt or anticipated loss or reclamation of control" (Dörner et al. 1983, 66). As a rule, the regaining of a state of control and the repression of uncertainty is accompanied by positive emotions, and a loss of control by negative ones. The viewer is emotionally involved in this conflict situation because of his empathy with the protagonists who have to cope with it.

In accordance with my model of analysis, which views the characters in a functional relationship with the fields of conflict and narration, empathy results from the imaginary reproduction of problem-solving and falls in line with the two-tracked process of active and passive control of the situation. The viewer is confronted with a two-fold uncertainty: on the one hand, he has to take the position of the character who is immediately involved in the conflict situation and unsure regarding the desired outcome; on the other hand, he wants to foresee the course of events following his drive to understand similar tendencies in reality. Thus, the viewer's empathy with the characters may change and become either stronger or weaker, depending on the conflicts and discrepancies in the course of action. In any case, however, the connection between conflict and the characters' coping potential, which is important for the eliciting of emotions as well as for the narrative tension, remains central. Insofar as these interrelations are based on the goal-oriented activities of the characters, the experience of narrative tension is closely bound with empathy.

3.4 Imagination and Narrative Tension

Insofar as problem-solving and empathy with the characters are always based on an imaginary reproduction process of human situations in the viewer's mind, narrative tension is deeply connected with the imagination, the imageries of the viewer.

"Imagery is the mental construction of an experience that at least in some respects resembles the experience of perceiving an object or an event, either with or without direct sensory stimulation" (Katz 2000, 187).

According to Currie (2002, 25) the "doings" in the processes of mental construction are termed "imaginings".

"To act I need a picture not only of how the world is, but also of how I want it to be: I need desires. If perceptions and desires represent, there ought to be imaginative substitutes for these as well. In imagination I can desire things I don't actually desire, and perceive things I don't actually perceive. So an account of imaginative projection requires us to give an account of a range of states that are imaginative substitutes for beliefs, desires, and perceptions, and possibly for other things as well." (2002, 8)

Imageries and imaginings can vary. Following Currie, we can differentiate between perception-like, belief-like and desire-like imaginings based on the viewer's different attitudes. And these varying imaginings are very important for the experience of a film's tension because they are concerned not only with the actions and events but also with the evaluation of the characters on the screen. Usually the viewer has his own world-model, his own will, and therefore he or she is seldom neutral, but rather interested in a specific decision or problem-solving on the screen that relates to his own life. And the normal situation is that he or she is keen to see specific outcomes of conflict situations and film endings that follow his or her own desire-like imaginings.

Narrative tension depends on the attitudes of the viewer to tendencies in reality and their analogies on the screen. Stronger attitude-based imaginings with regard to the tendency of actions and developments of the story influence the feeling of tension as well.

And the viewer's interests are always connected to the characters. It makes a difference whether we perceive a character with sympathy or antipathy, following in this our assessment of his para-social behaviour, whether we can identify with his person or not. It makes a difference to the feeling of tension whether we accept a character or reject him morally, or, with regard to our emotions, whether we love or hate him.

Watching the final sequence of *Young and Innocent*, the viewer activates his specific attitudes and interests. He hopes that the two "detectives" can find the murderer, but the chances for the heroes' reaching of their goals fluctuate, and corresponding to the events on the screen the expectations of the viewer are included in a kind of play.

3.5 Tension and Play

In chapter VIII, I will discuss the importance of the human ability of play; here I can only address the problem briefly, presuming the following: Cinematic and narrative tension are connected with the human behaviour of play, particularly with the altering prospects of the protagonists during different phases of the action and the changing feelings of uncertainty in the viewer's anticipation of relevant decisions in the story, which are organised in a kind of play. Thus the film plays with the viewers' expectations and hopes.

In Hitchcock's sequence, this play is guaranteed because the circumstances always ensure that the chances of finding the criminal keep changing: for example, the drummer sees the girl and the tramp speaking with a policeman and becomes so nervous that he infects the whole band with his bad playing, which results in their stopping and the interruption of the dancing. At the same time, the two "detectives" proceed to leave the ballroom. This could be the drummer's salvation, but he is so afraid that he loses consciousness, and the girl, who wants to administer first aid to him, recognises him by his twitching eyelids. Until the moment when the clarifying pragmatic information is provided, the elimination of uncertainty for the protagonists occurs in a successive manner—by a slow and often artificially delayed journey to the plot's outcome. At the same time, the tension that arises shortly before the dénouement may also be experienced by the viewers as a personal feeling of emotion.

Artistic narration is always linked with a process of reception which tends to reduce the uncertainty of the situation. Nevertheless, this process is not steady and monotonous in its continuity, but a fluctuating process that temporarily gives the spectator control of the experienced situation and the feeling of action readiness, but also the opposite—the feeling of having lost control off and on. There is always a change of tension and release, a continuously ongoing play with the viewer's competence for control.

But in general, the viewer is motivated to exercise passive control regarding the course of action and to anticipate the central decisions of the plot. The narrative tension depends on corresponding hypotheses.

3.6 Typology of Narrative Tension

The viewers' hypotheses can be:

(1)   very strong,

(2)   moderately strong, or

(3)   extraordinarily weak.

Their varying strengths depend on the different levels of schema formation, in other words, on the mental status of the filmic structures and the corresponding type of basic narrative structures. In accordance with the PCS model I would like to draw up a typology of narrative tension:

A: Conventionalised tension, following the strong hypotheses of narrative stereotypes (of canonical stories or genres, using logical operations of deduction often leading to suspense)

B: Dramatic exterior tension, following the strong hypotheses of a narrative causal chain (of classical "fabula", plot, intrigue, syuzhet, using logical operations of induction)

C: Latent tension, following the weak hypotheses of topic lines (using logical operations of abduction often leading to "inner suspense").

4. Dramatic Tension

Let's begin with case B, the dramatic tension that corresponds with the most common basic structure of narration, the conceptualised causal chain of the classical plot.

This type of tension requires an evident conflict that leads to clear goals and to a "significant outcome" (Brewer 1996, 115) as well.

The heroes wish to carry out the action and to reach their goal, for instance a decision in a sort of struggle, and in doing so they perform various actions. In a dramatic conflict this striving for a goal is always connected with an obvious process of problem-solving by the protagonist, because there are obstacles that must be overcome; the most important one is created by the antagonist in the conflict. And at the same time the viewer is also in a problem situation; he cannot foresee the course of action and has to subdue a state of uncertainty. Because of the clear goal of the hero's action, the viewer is able to develop clear hypotheses regarding the possible course of action. But the hypothesis is one thing, the reaching of the desired goal is another. Often the obstacles seem insurmountable and the goals out of reach. In other words, the tension can increase—the tension for the acting protagonists, and also for the viewer who wants to anticipate the events.

The construction of strong hypotheses about the possible decisions leads to a kind of inference-making. We suppose some decisions using logical operations of induction.

In the case of more suspenseful films, according to Carroll the viewers become "question-formers" (1996a, 67) who are longing for clear alternative answers concerning the outcomes: "If a scene is suspenseful, then it is composed of a questioning event and an answering event, such that the possible narrative answers are logically opposed" (1996a, 103).

Let us consider film stories based on dominant causal chains of events, i.e. the classical plot or syuzhet mentioned in chapter II. Their conflict construction always confronts the spectator with a possible decision or problem-solving that tends to an alternative significant outcome, to narrative answers which are logically opposed: Will the revolutionary sailors on the Battleship 'Potemkin' overcome or not? Can the old middle-class teacher who fell in love with the show-girl Lola-Lola in the pub "Blue Angel" survive this passionate affair or not? Will the insect-hunting man in Hiroshi Teshigahara's *Woman in the Dunes* (*Suna no onna*, 1964), who came under the influence of the permanently-working woman who attempts to rid her home of sand in the dunes, leave the hollow or not? Will the working-class inmate of the juvenile prison, who gets the chance to live a privileged life as the winner of a long-distance race, realise this compromise with the establishment or not? Will the hesitating agent in Francis Ford Coppola's *Apocalypse Now* (1979), who is hunting in the jungle of Vietnam for the former Colonel over whom the U.S. Army has lost all control, be able to fulfill his mission?

In all these cases, the goals of the protagonists are very clear, and for the audience the alternative outcomes are significant as well. The viewers' expectations can arise despite, or even thanks to, the fact that the film stories artificially create barriers for reaching the goals. In doing so and playing with the tension, the narration temporarily increases it.

Of course, the creating of tension is far from a linear mechanical process, because it depends on numerous factors. Analogously to real-life situations, the performed conflicts on the screen have an uncertain likelihood regarding their outcomes; they seem more or less solvable and their catastrophes are more or less inevitable for the protagonists. Furthermore, the viewers have their own interests and desires concerning the outcome of the actions, and all these relations modify the tendency and the strength of tensions. But here the various "mental states" of the tension-producing narrative structures are mainly at issue, which seemingly give different opportunities for the experiencing of tension and suspense.

5. Conventionalised Tension and Suspense

Let us take the most obvious type of tension, conventionalised tension. Usually, this kind of tension is based on stereotypes of narration, on standardised forms of storytelling that can be found in the canonical stories of popular genres, for instance in specific action films, detective and criminal films, horror films and so on. These stereotype structures allow strong hypotheses about the course of events, and in this way the viewer is equipped with clear expectations. Often, action cinema even calculates the specific impact of tension-feeling on the viewer. Having recognized the genre, the viewer begins automatically to construct hypotheses and to make corresponding inferences. Probably, he uses the logical operation of deduction. According to the rules of the genre, the viewer is able to anticipate the central trends of the plotting, including the valid emotion strategy. There are differences between the genre rules of films of the adventure, the horror or detective genre, but the method of tension-making is similar.

I would like to repeat my definition of tension: Very important for these films is the probable occurrence of a relevant (often menacing) event in an undefined course of events and the possibility of the protagonists bringing the situation under control by reducing its uncertainty, for instance by preventing the negative outcome of specific events.

Films with conventionalised tension have a particular affinity for a special mode of tension, so-called suspense. I have pointed out that there is in this case a difference between the information viewers have about the uncertain situation and the information to which the protagonists are privy.

The "barriers" of the problem situation are somewhat formalised here, due to the existence of certain pieces of pragmatic information which the viewer possesses but the protagonist does not.

In *Young and Innocent* again, the heroine and the viewer are interested in the murderer being caught and the innocent man being saved. Emotions arise from the fact that their goals cannot be achieved straight away because they lack certain pieces of information. The aforementioned relationship between motivating need and the chance of realisation on the part of the subject in the story can also be described within the framework of a comprehensive theoretical concept of information-processing, as being an information deficit. According to Simonov (1975), certain "pieces of pragmatic information" are necessary to satisfy a need, and, as the psychologist says, one can "see emotion as a specialised neural mechanism which serves to compensate for the information deficit which the organism needs to organise its process of adaptation" (1975, 83). The unsatisfied desire for such pragmatic information is always the source of emotional tension. The degree of tension depends, quantitatively, on (1) the intensity of the needs and (2) the difference between those amounts of information that are anticipated as being necessary and those that one actually receives. Thus, in addition to needs or motives, the compensation mechanism also always receives prognostic estimations that indicate whether additional information is necessary or not.

In dramatic films without genre tendency, these factors are often hard to define, but in suspense movies, such as detective films, the abstract concept of information, which amounts to the significance of a news item for viewers, comes very close to the trivial concept of information. A simple piece of information is needed that enables a very rational approach to the stores of knowledge touched on. The protagonists' deficit of pragmatic information is a deficit in its literal sense.

Viewers are then able to appreciate the character's information deficits with corresponding ease. In the case of *Young and Innocent*, it basically comes down to the heroine's need to know where the man with the twitching eye can be found.

The ability to define the characters' information deficits seems to be a precondition for suspense. It in fact puts viewers in the position of being able to compare their own level of knowledge with that of the protagonists and to realise the difference. This clearly raises the underlying emotional tension because the prognosis for the necessary increase in information becomes that much easier. In *Young and Innocent*, the direction ensures— through the camera movement that makes the viewers discover the man with the twitching eye in the room—that there is a considerable restriction to the uncertainty in the clearly defined problem space, which is given something of a topographic dimension here.

One can find a similar device in Jonathan Demmes' *The Silence of the Lambs* (1991). The story of this thriller is based on the conflict between the FBI agent Clarice Starling and the serial killer Buffalo Bill. The goal of the female agent is obvious: she has to catch the murderer of numerous women as he again and again cunningly thwarts the plans of the policemen. Finally, unaware that she is already very near to her goal, Starling meets an unknown man in his home where certain details give evidence of his being the wanted criminal. The man attempts to hide in the empty house and the woman searches for him at pistol-point, but although she is acting very professionally, he gets her activities under control by extinguishing the lamps and monitoring the dark rooms with night vision equipment.

Analogously to Hitchcock's descending camera, which makes it clear to the viewer that the wanted man with the eye-tick is sitting in the room, the night vision equipment allows him to watch the female agent, who is looking for the killer in total darkness. In both cases, thanks to this visual information, the spectator knows more about the situation than the protagonists and can focus his attention under suspense. But in *The Silence of the Lambs,* the pragmatic information given by the camera is very important not only for the result of detection but even for the detective's life. Thus, tension and suspense can increase in an extraordinary way.

The protagonists' deficit of pragmatic information is the obvious source of the viewers' arousal in an entire group of popular film genres commonly termed "suspense genres": thrillers, detectives, Westerns, adventure, war, mystery, and horror films, and so on. The impressive sequences of Henri-Georges Clouzot's suspense film *The Wages of Fear (Le Salaire de la peur,* 1953), where some tough guys take on the job of bringing truckloads of dynamite across the mountains to a distant place, use different devices of suspense produced by repeatedly showing detailed indications of an impending explosion that the protagonists are unaware of, for instance the slowly unravelling rope which holds the imperilled truck.

Also highly suspenseful is the long sequence at the end of David Lean's *The Bridge on the River Kwai* (1957), where a group of British prisoners of war living in a Japanese jungle camp, after having constructed a bridge in a painful process, attempt to blow it up again to interrupt the rail connection of the Japanese army. Having fixed the dynamite at the bridge pier under cover of darkness, the British officers—and ahead of them the spectators— must experience that a sudden drop in the river's water level exposes the efforts of their nocturnal operation to their Japanese antagonists.

Most wild chases in action films organise the spectator's information about the problematical situation that faces the protagonist in a similar way. The latter seems frequently to be incapable of controlling the course of events (i.e. is unable to escape or fails as a pursuer). In these cases, a play with the respective possibilities of the protagonists takes place; for instance, of the policeman's potential to catch the fugitive criminals during the endless pursuits in William Friedkin's *The French Connection* (1971) and John Frankenheimer's *French Connection II* (1975).

In numerous films, the suspense-producing relations between the spectators' and the characters' knowledge about the state of affairs in a problem situation is closely connected with the understanding of real-life situations and the facts on which the story is based; but there are others, particularly in action movies, where the need for pragmatic information is formalised in such a way that a determination of the value of an action becomes entirely irrelevant, and the formal reaching of the goal seems important solely for the creation of tension or suspense. In the famous interview, Hitchcock (1967, 98–100) explained to Truffaut his device of the so-called MacGuffin:

"Most of Kipling's stories, as you know, were set in India [...] Many of them were spy stories, and they were concerned with the efforts to steal the secret plans out of a fortress. The theft of secret documents was the original MacGuffin. So the 'MacGuffin' is the term we use to cover all that sort of thing: to steal plans or documents, or discover a secret, it doesn't matter what it is.[...] The only thing that really matters is that in the picture the plans, documents, or secrets must seem to be of vital importance for the characters. To me, the narrator, they're of no importance whatever. [...] The main thing I've learned over the years is that the MacGuffin is nothing.[...] My best MacGuffin, and by that I mean the emptiest, the most nonexistent, and the most absurd, is the one we used in 'North by Northwest'. The picture is about espionage, and the only question that's raised in the story is to find out what the spies are after. Well, during the scene at the Chicago airport, the Central Intelligence man explains the whole situation to Cary Grant, and Grant, referring to the James Mason character asks, 'What does he do?' The counterintelligence man replies, 'Let's just say that he's an importer and exporter.' 'But what does he sell?'. 'Oh, just government secrets!' is the answer. Here, you see, the MacGuffin has been boiled down to its purest expression: nothing at all!"

In the framework of genre-stereotypes with their formalised goals, it seems to be sufficient for the production of suspense if the action of the character has a goal that the spectator accepts as important without knowing it or considering it to be worthy. The problem-solving can occur in the given searching space without changing the reference field during the play with the pragmatic information. The absence of any commitment to contents only makes the stereotyping of certain cinematic structures easier and helps in the play with the information, the creation of tension or suspense.

6. Latent Tension

Latent tension, called by Antonioni "inner suspense", is based on weaker hypotheses concerning the course of events. This situation often corresponds with unclear goals. The viewer is seeking an elementary orientation in the scene; he has to identify and to define the problem situations.

The opening sequences of Michelangelo Antonioni's *L'Eclisse* (1962) or *The Passenger* (*Professione: reporter*, 1975) show these characteristics. The earlier work, for instance, needs more than a dozen minutes to describe the splitting up of a frustrated couple, since the woman, who is more active in the separation, cannot articulate clearly the reasons for her intentions. Even though her behaviour has a specific tendency, the spectator will not have a feeling of directed tension.

The remarkable thing about the opening sequence of *The Passenger* is that it begins with a situation in which viewers find it very difficult to orient themselves because they can only divine from the reporters' questions to his companion that he wants to make contact with the African Liberation Front. Although the hero's enterprise has a goal and a respective action program—and thus represents a so-called "cyclical unity of action" (Oesterreich 1981, 12) through which viewers can inform themselves and take note—we are nevertheless kept in the dark for a long time about what the protagonist actually intends to do here. However, a certain state of anticipation, as well as a form of more internal emotional tension regarding the course of events, develops. Given the uncertainty of the course of events, viewers may try to orient themselves by using the few regularities that appear in the events.

This occurs according to the principle of probability learning or autocorrelation, which "occurs 'inevitably' according to the law of given probabilities or frequencies" (von Cube 1965, 159). In the case of the film sequence, a certain probability distribution of events is effected by having similar behavoural patterns repeat themselves in all of the actions on the part of the hero: An unsatisfactory result follows from the attempt at communication. In the film, one can see topics in those concentrated constructs that are created as a result of latent expectations about abduction. The spectator undertakes so-called abductions, looks intuitively in the flow of events for invariant moments on the perceptual level.

Charles S. Peirce (1958, 137) pointed out: "Abduction makes its start from the facts, without at the outset, having any particular theory in view, though it is motivated by the feeling that a theory is needed to explain the surprising facts. Induction makes its start from a hypothesis which seems to recommend itself, without at the outset having any particular facts in view, though it feels the need of fact to support the theory. Abduction seeks a theory. Induction seeks for facts. In abduction the consideration of the facts suggests the hypothesis. In induction the study of the hypothesis suggests the experiment which brings to light the very facts to which the hypothesis had pointed. The mode of suggestion by which, in abduction, the facts suggest the hypothesis is by resemblance,—the resemblance of the facts to the consequences of the hypothesis. The mode of suggestion by which, in induction, the hypothesis suggests the facts is by contiguity,—familiar knowledge that the conditions of the hypothesis can be realized in certain experimental ways." According to Peirce (1929, 218), who emphasizes the man's unique instinct for guessing, "abduction is, after all, nothing but guessing" (Peirce 1958, 137).

The concept abduction renders plausible the specific way in which invariant moments of cinema are experienced on the perceptual level. The spectator's abduction starts from the facts, without, at the outset, having any ready-made hypothesis or rule in view; the consideration of the facts suggests the hypothesis—not least thanks to guessing.

With regard to tension, the resulting cognitive activity leads to "inner tension" or, according to Antonioni, to "inner suspense".

Viewers suffer with the protagonists due to a deficit in pragmatic information, especially because uncertainty about the course of events deprives them of the ability to predict and of every kind of passive control. This does not lead to true suspense, as the level of the viewers' knowledge of the situation is still below that of the protagonist.

Wong Kar-wai's *In the Mood for Love* also creates an artificially lowered level of the viewers' knowledge about the situation. In spite of the existence of a strong conflict, the film refrains from a dramatic clash. As Mr. Chow and Mrs. Li-Zhen learn about their spouses' affair, they do not change the pitch of their conversation in the restaurant and they do not show any reaction of fury, revenge, or despair. Maintaining their composure, they merely attempt to reconstruct the first steps of their partners into their disloyalty by a kind of helpless play to get the situation straight in their own minds. Thus, the viewer has to observe their behaviour to find out their real emotions and intentions; he has to look for hidden rules in their acting and to undertake abductions. Sufficient information about their emotional state is found, not in the protagonists' reserved facial expressions, but rather in the language of their hands. Among the topic lines of the film is a very impressive one showing the protagonists' feelings via the gestures of their hands: their reconciliation, their mood for love, their renouncement of it.

I have already mentioned another kind of layering of the dramatic intensity by omitting the protagonists' first secret meeting in the hotel. From the point of view of tension strategy, this scene could be highly important, because it functions as the goal of a cyclic unity of action. But Wong artificially lowers all narrative tension and suspense by levelling the entire sequence, including the phase of its preparation, and the cutting-off of the expected—highly likely—emotional climax. Usually, the most important decisions of the characters of a film are exposed in such a way that the spectator can experience these plot points as palpably as possible, for instance, by seeing the actions and reactions of the protagonists fully. But in the scene where the despairing hero of Wong's film asks the woman he loves whether she would go with him to Singapore at once, the spectator can only hear their dialog without seeing the two persons in a normal way. This extraordinary levelling of conflict performance leads to a kind of latent tension with specific emotional consequences for the viewer.

7. The Combination of Different Modes of Tension

Until this point I have discussed three different modes of tension which are based on three different cinematic structures or basic structures of narration. In order to illustrate these modes, I have used examples in which one of these types of structure dominates. Such cases are possible, and they are not too rare. Nevertheless, as has already been said, the basic forms generally do not appear on their own in a film's narration, but are combined in variable interactions. What one might choose to term the narrative structure in film stories is, thus, not homogeneous, but potentially consists of these three components with varying degrees of awareness and evidence.

At the same time, viewers experience the varying narrational structures as being connected with varying modes or degrees of tension; the spectrum ranges from:

(1) somewhat latent tensions founded on latent expectations or weak hypotheses in the area of perception and topic lines; through

(2) dramatic tension, following the strong hypotheses of conceptualised narrative causal chains; to

(3) conventionalised tensions grounded in stereotypes that have been developed in a long process of cultural communication and socialisation and led, for instance, to a narrational stereotype of a specific genre.

In other words, according to the different narrational structures that work together, we also find varying modes of tension or suspense in the same film.

Alfred Hitchcock's famous film *The Birds* (1963) may serve as an example of such a mixture and, in my opinion, it even follows a schema of shifting domination which starts at the film's opening with concentrated perception-based structures and leads—via conceptualised structures—to dominant stereotype-based cinematic and narrative structures in the final part.

The film shows how birds, mainly seagulls and crows, begin to attack people, initially by individual assaults on single persons, then for a while in flocks that frighten groups of children, and finally in gigantic swarms which invade the houses of the terrified humans.

The animals make their offensive step by step through a series of topics linked with single birds. At the film's opening, there is a young man who is flirting with a woman using a couple of little parrots. As the woman sits in her suitor's boat, a seagull attacks and wounds her. Later, another bird dies after having tried to penetrate a door. A pattern of expectancies forms in the viewer's mind; he undertakes abductions and a latent tension appears. Whenever a bird appears, the spectator expects the occurrence of similar events.

This phase of topics arrives at a shift at the latest when the woman intends to pick up her boyfriend's little sister at school with the intention of protecting her from the birds. The protagonist's action is consciously planned, and the viewer expects possible attacks of the birds as well; a dramatic tension occurs. And indeed, the young woman, who sits down in front of the school listening to the children singing in the classroom, takes her place near a climbing frame on which crows begin to settle, at first one, then two, three, five, and finally an enormous flock. The montage arranges the shots of the waiting woman and the climbing frame with the crows in their rhythmical change, and the viewer experiences the threatening danger more clearly and more emotionally, too. Thanks to his knowledge and the pulsation of dramatic tension, he should feel the horrific situation even more intensely than the protagonists. As everybody knows, the terror of birds will increase yet more. Finally, the birds have entirely occupied the human space, and corresponding genre stereotypes dominate the possible world on the screen.

I have only sketched some structures of narration, and of course, these relationships provide only for one component of the whole impact of tension and suspense. The others are evoked by means of cinematic technology creating the audio-visual style which, unfortunately, I have to pass over here, although such films as *The Birds* should provide good material for plausible analyses of numerous corresponding devices.

Although, with regard to tension and suspense, Antonioni's works seem to be more like the opposite of Hitchcock's movies, a few films by the Italian director offer a combination of the three narrational basic structures which leads to a mixture of latent, dramatic and conventionalised modes of tension, though of a very particular kind. After Antonioni had constantly moved away from narrative cinema and its development of suspense through his unremitting suppression of the classical plot in the films of the famous tetralogy of behaviour during the first half of the 1960s, he later took a step back in that direction with *Blow Up* (1966), *Zabriskie Point* (1970), and *The Passenger* to the extent that he offered stories which correspond, at first glance, fully with Aristotelian dramaturgy. Of course, this impression is illusory. The depicted events aim less for an original plot and, instead, seek to adhere to certain stereotypic schemata, which originate from syuzhet stories by developing plot conventions from popular genres, i.e. narrative patterns from the detective and adventure films. Consequently, the observation of the characters' behaviour, and its establishment through corresponding narrative topics according to the sequence principle, was not abandoned. They continued to be of interest to the director, but were integrated within procedural schemata recognizable by the viewers from popular genres; and this doubtless made it easier to understand the events.

I have already mentioned the opening sequence of *The Passenger*, which seems to be more typical for the topic lines of the tetralogy than for the trend to genre conventions, and could serve, therefore, as a paradigm for dominating topic series. But within the described first sequence, there are instances in which the repeatedly-shown conflict of unrealizable communication is so evident that it begins to be conceived of as a significant structural relationship within the film's action, for instance, when the man in the next room of the protagonist's hotel is unable to communicate because he is dead. By this, the cinematic structures move onto the level of conceptualization that permits the viewer a much simpler understanding of the course of events and also leads to a different quality of narrative tension.

The mental level of the structural offers shifts, because the storytelling obviously tends towards a classical plot. Having discovered that his neighbour is dead, the reporter switches on a tape-recorder, on which there is a recorded conversation with the deceased, and he learns that this man had been in close contact with the African underground movement. Unlike the hapless reporter, he had evidently been able to offer them practical aid—as an arms dealer, as we later find out. The verbal pronouncements help viewers to textually identify and evaluate the previously withheld film events. They also contribute to the formation of dramatic conflict, which confronts the viewer with the question of what will happen if the reporter makes the desired contact, using false identification papers to allow him to appear to be an arms dealer. According to Aristotelian dramaturgy, this should have given rise to tangible exterior tension in the plot that is steered by a specific anticipation, i.e. the resolution of the conflict. Thus, Antonioni seemingly creates dramatic tension, even by following the conventions of a suspenseful popular genre. The forging of the passport brings standardised expectations into play which viewers connect with comparable plots in films belonging to the adventure genre that are well known for the motif of the hero who changes his identity, disguising himself or masquerading as somebody else. But for the later sequences of the film Antonioni decided in a certain way against the classical plot.

Although we are shown how the reporter appropriates the dead man's papers and sticks his own photograph in his passport—i.e., undergoes a change of identity,—the film does not follow this through in an ordinary logical manner, because there is no practical involvement of the journalist in the Africans' cause, and so the dramatic conflict can hardly deepen any further. The reporter does go to several secret meetings around Europe, which have been arranged with representatives of the African liberation front, but, instead of helping, he falls into their debt by accepting money from them as an advance for weapons he does not even possess. Thus, viewers wait in vain for an explanatory event. When the reporter is killed—evidently by opponents of the underground movement who see him as a real enemy—the uncertainty is hardly reduced, and the famous, endlessly wandering pan at the end of the film does not help either. Specific external tension is deliberately avoided. The viewers' attention remains still more involved with the topics of disturbed communication than this action. Their line extends into a subject of disturbed or frustrated human engagement.

As the narrative state of the film's story moves from the level of the topic line to one of narrative stereotypes and passes quickly over the usual conceptualisation, it creates a form of tension that is deliberately heterogeneous by, on the one hand, following a principle of "inner suspense" within the framework of tense behavioural observation, and, on the other, by submitting the artificially dynamized action to the norms and outwardly suspenseful plots of adventure stories. The analytical eye of the observer is transported, to a certain degree, at a faster rate through the events.

Similar mixed strategies of narrative tension are at work in the director's earlier films *Blow Up* and *Zabriskie Point*, and also in Andrei Tarkovsky's *Stalker* (1979) or Jim Jarmusch's *Dead Man* (1995), productions which also combine the observation of behavioural patterns with genre tendencies.

Blow Up (Michelangelo Antonioni 1966)

Fig. 1: After having detected the form of a revolver aiming at the woman's partner the hero can conceptualise the fact and acknowledge the threat. In this way,
the film sequence gives evidence of a dangerous situation in the past, and, at
the same time, of the active, step-by-step perceptive process and the subse-
quence phase in which the conceptualisation of the object takes place in the
hero's mind. A series of photographs shows the different phases in the process
of cognition.

Popiól i diament (Ashes and Diamonds, Andrzej Wajda 1958)

Fig. 2: The events are broken down into shots which express the repeated disruption of purposeful action. Nearly all parts of this scene have on thing in common: goal-oriented actions are hindered, discontinued, or require reorientation.

Ariel (Aki Kaurismäki 1988)

Fig. 3: All these micro-actions follow the same principle. They are marking a situation of 'the game is up!' of 'to be at an end' of 'definitely being out'.

Professione: reporter (The Passenger, Michelangelo Antonioni 1975)

Fig. 4: Although the hero's enterprise has a goal the viewers are nevertheless kept in the dark for a long time about what the protagonist actually intends to do. In spite of this irritation situation the viewer will be confronted again and again with episodes following the same principle: The desired communication will be disturbed, is not accomplished, comes to naught. The semantic gesture of all these episodes express the selfsame: The protagonist's attempts to establish contact with the natives is doomed.

High Noon (Fred Zinnemann 1952)

Fig. 5: Each shot becomes a cinematic stereotype, a symbol: The clock, the track, the faces of the town's inhabitants in close-up, the judge's empty seat.

Father and Daughter (Michael Dudok de Wit 2000)

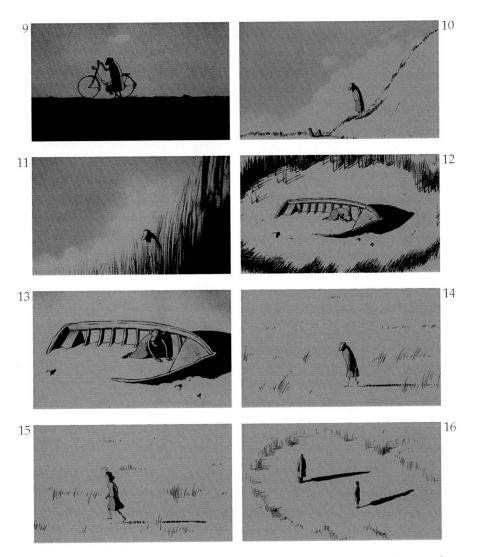

Fig. 6: In its narrative macrostructure, the film shows a clear causal chain of events structured by two plot points, which are based on the above-mentioned conflicts: (1) the father's leaving, which is fundamentally at odds with the child's wishes, and (2) the daughter's sorrowful recognition that this loss is final and can only be reversed in the world of fantasy.

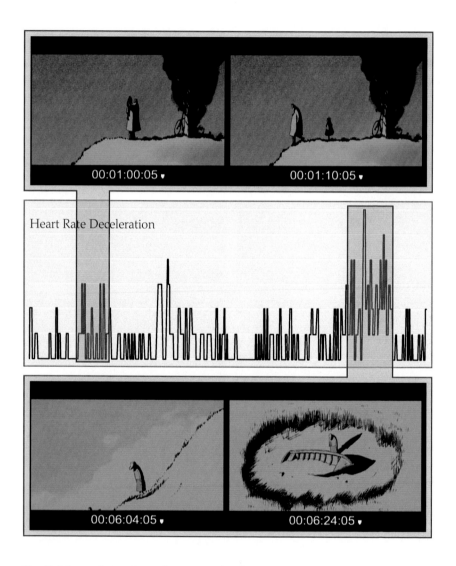

Fig. 7: Mean of significant heart rate decelerations during the reception of the animated short film FATHER AND DAUGHTER (2000). M. Suckfüll's pilot study provides evidence for the hypothesis that physiological arousal takes place synchronically to pivotal conflict situations on the screen, which can be considered as sources of emotions. Many participants of the study show significant decelerations in heart rate during these scenes of the film.

8½ (Federico Fellini 1963)

Fig. 8: These are images of elementary human situations formulated in a nearly symbolic manner. For instance: The situation of the protagonist's terrible imprisonment in the car shown in the first daydream, his liberation that turns into happy flight over the sea, which follows in there, and also the situation of drop and crash, when Guido is yanked back by `the others' with a cord that ties him to the ground.

One Flew Over the Cuckoo's Nest (Milos Forman 1975)

Fig. 9: The scene shows the protagonist involved in activities in which one can clearly recognize the central characteristics of play behaviour.

Down by Law (Jim Jarmusch 1986)

Fig. 10: This temporary `free acting' of play helps them to overcome their dilemma; their attempt to escape from jail succeeds and initiates in the viewer's mind a sensation of action readiness as well. In other words: `Overcoming conflicts by play' seems to be a paradigm for numerous art processes.

La Vita è bella (Life Is Beautiful, Roberto Benigni 1997)

Fig. 11: A possible first step for film research could be the separate psychological analyses of individual cinematic effects, which traditional aesthetics have described and which have noticeable emotional components. Several of the concepts used here, such as `parable-like alienation', `comedy', `tragic catharsis', `dramatic tension', and `pathos', refer clearly to such effects, since they describe genre-specific responses in the form of significant effects in the viewer's mind.

Chapter VI: The Reality Effect in Fiction Films

1. Introduction

The cinema has a specific capacity to give the viewer the impression that the world on the screen, or at least some details of life shown there, is exceptionally true and genuine. Not every film uses this opportunity, but in many cases we can observe this so-called "reality effect" ("effet de réalité", Dominique Château 1983) or "impression of reality" (Richard Allen 1995), or, using a further synonym common in German terminology, "impression of authenticity" ("Authentie-Eindruck").

This effect, which is noticeable to the viewer as a significant impact, seems to be relevant only for the audiovisual media. It can be linked with different objects of cinematic representation, such as inanimate things and landscapes, as well as subtle nuances of human behavior, but, generally, it causes the spectator to consider certain moments or the entire events of a film, as extraordinarily close to life, true or authentic.

The viewers' experience can vary in its intensity. What is shown on the screen may appear extremely authentic, and sometimes the viewer even has the impression that he could never perceive it so clearly in real life. This effect occurs, although the spectator knows very well that he is dealing with the events of a fiction film, and not with an actual situation represented by a documentary film. For documentaries, the issue of authenticity also exists, but documentaries are specific and not the subject of this study.

Since the effect occasionally has considerable consequences for the aesthetic impact of films, it has been the subject of many debates, and there are many opinions regarding its essence and the reasons for its appearance—ideas to which my model-based approach, unfortunately, can refer only in a limited way.

An important problem for our studies consists of the fact that the appearance of the reality effect not only varies from one work to another, but has also changed considerably in the history of film.

2. Some Characteristics of Fiction Films with a Reality Effect

There have often been individual and group styles of film that attempted to capture aspects of life realistically. Interest in the reality effect has been articulated in connection with a concept of realism that seems particularly relevant to cinematic representation, even if it has also been claimed by other art forms.

Siegfried Kracauer's *Theory of Film* (1961), with its concept of the "redemption of physical reality" in film art, seems to confirm the reality effect by stressing five strong affinities of the medium which describe the essential properties of realistic filmic expression. The terms Kracauer uses for these affinities are well-known: "unposed reality", "coincidence", "endlessness", "uncertainty" and "flow of life".

Such characteristics can be identified in the formal aspects of Italian Neorealism, for example, and artistic programs such as those formulated by Roberto Rossellini or Cesare Zavattini clearly prove this.

The fiction films influenced by *cinéma vérité*, for example the Documentary style in Eastern European fiction films of the sixties, also tended toward a similar understanding of the reality effect. These films, though they did not deny their fictionality, developed cinematic forms of the representation of reality that approached documentary film, both in their formal qualities and in the kind of response they elicited. Thus the term "Documentary Style" came to be used to describe this tradition.

I discussed one example of this group style above—Otar Iosseliani's *Once Upon a Time There Was a Singing Blackbird* (*Iko shashvi mgalobeli,* 1970). Another instance, Milos Forman's *Black Peter* (*Černý Petr,* 1964), from the former Czechoslovakia, recounts the everyday life of an adolescent apprentice in a general store in Prague in a relaxed way. The camera follows the boy unobtrusively; it lets the viewer in on his life, which unfolds without any unusual occurrences. The events seem to occur almost randomly. Nonetheless, the film shows an unbroken series of contradictory situations of the same kind: instruction is given. His environment, especially his parents, continually confront the hero with norms and standards. The protagonist endures this, but it soon becomes clear that the guidelines and advice are not sound. The older people's conventions of how one should live continually fail to deliver. What Peter's father says in one sentence, he retracts in the next. Here the spectator can experience a piece of human behavior in the context of day-to-day problems with a strong impression of authenticity, i.e. feeling a reality effect. Forman's colleague Vera Chytilová (quoted in Gehler 1987, 57) stated that the film might help the spectators to "separate what is authentic from what is not", since "lies in art should be legally banned." Whatever the filmmakers showed on screen about everyday life was supposed to correspond to the truth, no more and no less. The audience should be able to test the film's authenticity against their own personal experience, regarding both the whole and all its details.

That was in the sixties. Thirty years later a tendency has evolved among filmmakers, critics, and film theorists to connect the reality effect with a certain canon of film forms, which are linked with the concept of realism and show stylistic similarities to documentaries. But this is sometimes done in a specific way. The fascination with recent Scandinavian film production, especially the works of the Danish filmmakers associated with the *Dogma 95* manifesto, cannot be explained simply by the contents of the films, which show contradictory and often emotional forms of spontaneous behavior. Instead, their particular appeal, as difficult as it is to define, emanates from the discovery or renewal of specific cinematic forms that are used to portray fine nuances in human emotions and actions. What at first glance seems to be just an unconventional form of filmmaking, characterized by the forced use of handheld cameras, proves, on closer inspection, to have important consequences for film in general. The camera does not just tell a story, but rather the actions it captures visually gain a value of their own, without which it is difficult to understand the story. These cinematic methods undoubtedly cause the viewers to be moved emotionally, to experience the particular excitement elicited by the films. These methods also cause certain moments and details of life, as they are shown in the films, to appear exceptionally true and genuine. An intense impression of authenticity is created, which—even if often fleeting and transient—does cause the viewer to believe the most unlikely things about the characters on the screen and to willingly follow them in situations he or she would find unacceptable in everyday life.

Indeed, the Dogma manifesto, which was signed on March 13, 1995 and which, despite its humor, does outline professional intentions, shows a strange resemblance to the procedures of earlier documentary styles. The document, with the signatures of Lars von Trier, Kristian Levering, Thomas Vinterberg and Sören Kragh Jacobsen, states the following rules:

1) All shooting must take place on location.
2) The sound may not be produced independently of the image.
3) Only handheld cameras are to be used.
4) Special lighting for color sets is forbidden.
5) Optical gimmicks must be refused.
6) Any gratuitous action is to be rejected.
7) The films must take place in the here and now.
8) Genre films should be avoided.

However, the Dogma films are conceived differently to previous film styles. The reality effect appeared in a relatively dominant and pure form in discussions around the middle of the century. It was fused with other stylistic components into a homogenous, inseparable unity and motivated the films of the movements I mentioned to try to approximate the form and effects of documentary films quite closely. In the current films, however, there is little to be seen of this earlier documentary impulse. Instead, the Danish films highlight their fictionality and artificiality. Von Trier's works, *Breaking the Waves* (1996) (a kind of predecessor to the Dogma films) and *The Idiots* (*Idioterne*, 1998), as well as Vinterberg's *The Celebration* (*Festen*, 1998), which I use here to represent the whole movement, do offer exact observations of life that are astonishing in their verisimilitude, but these are combined with obviously fictional worlds of an equally astonishing irreality. Thus the impression of authenticity is modified. Instead of trying to create an attitude of distanced observation in the audience, the camera now provokes a permanent inner agitation. Instead of leading to the observation of life and a kind of contemplation, the films stimulate hectic attempts to achieve some degree of orientation.

Can a reality effect come into being under such conditions?

Christian Metz responded unequivocally in a similar context: "The impression of reality is a factor common to both the realistic and fantastic film content" (1974, 256).

Even if one might be glad to agree with this opinion, it is difficult to prove scientifically, since even identifying the phenomenon empirically is problematic. Methodically, it is difficult to isolate the reality effect from the rest of the cinematic effects, but this would be necessary in order to objectify it and evaluate it psychologically. There are, however, productive approaches that work in this direction, which I can use as a basis for my thoughts here. In this chapter I will be applying a cognitive psychological approach to help explain how the impression of authenticity functions in general, and to identify the innovative contribution of the Dogma films to the development of the reality effect.

3. Preconditions for the Occurrence of the Reality Effect

What is the essence of the reality effect? And how can its fundamental functions be described? My hypothesis is as follows: The effect is a particular quality of film experience that concerns, on the one hand, the object-perception of the represented situation, and on the other, the viewers' self-perception in the process of film experience. Looking at the represented object, we notice that we can perceive it more intensely and consciously than we could before. In other words, the viewers' information processing shifts to a new quality, to a turn.

Following the PCS model we can say: regarding the object on the screen in our cognitive activities, we experience a remarkable shift from the phase of perception to that of conceptualization. Thus the film helps us to reach a new level of awareness of a specific part of our environment.

But what are the conditions and preconditions for the occurrence of this effect?

3.1 Cognitive Conditions

The cinema provides temporally correct representations of life events which can substitute for reality in the perception process and gain a cognitive function; watching a film, the spectator may discover unknown aspects of reality.

The French director Robert Bresson points out (1980, 21): "What no man's eye is able to capture, no crayon-, paintbrush- or penholder is able to record, your camera does catch, without knowing what's the matter, and records it with the conscientious indifference of a machine."

The most fundamental precondition for the occurrence of this phenomenon is the use of the cinematographic apparatus for perception, which leads to a specific kind of mechanical representation of the world and serves as a substitute for reality.

Technically, film's particular quality of representation is based upon the fact that moving pictures capture a particular part of the optical stimuli of physical nature and retain them on the film strip so that they can be reproduced and experienced again—and this in real time.

André Bazin (1971, Vol. I, 96-97) already noted: "The photograph proceeds by means of the lens to the taking of a veritable luminous impression in light—to a mold.[...] The cinema does something strangely paradoxical. It makes a molding of the object as it exists in time and, furthermore, makes an imprint of the duration of the object."

The Russian director Andrei Tarkovsky picked up Bazin's idea in noting the "sealed time" or "imprinted time" of the film. He found that this new aesthetic device provided people with "a matrix for actual time" (1986, 62). "Time, printed in its factual forms and manifestations: such is the supreme idea of cinema as an art, leading us to think about the wealth of untapped resources in film, about its colossal future." (1986, 63) He writes: "The cinema image, then, is basically an observation of life's facts within time, organised according to the pattern of life itself, and observing its time laws." (1986, 68)

The represented facts of life, or more precisely, some stimulus configurations of our physical reality that are reproduced in their original duration, lead to the vicarious function of film; they allow the cinema, in a limited way, to substitute for the world. Thus, in the processes of perception and cognition, the film works as a medium, an external storage of information, or modelling system.

Its representations contribute to the construction of dynamic situation models in the viewers' mind. They activate cognitive processes and enable people to discover the world indirectly through the means of film. In this, film takes over a vicarious function for reality. To a large degree we can experience the world in its beauty and contradictions via its modelling.

Human beings need information about their environment in order to survive and to cope with their life situations. The world must permanently offer new invariants of stimuli, new aspects and innovative moments. This applies to the perception of film, too. With respect to the reality effect, the audience wants new moments of life, nowadays especially unknown moments of human behavior.

The technical apparatus of audiovisual media, particularly the camera, supports this process in a specific way. It fixes invariants and selects certain portions of the stimulus spectrum which reality provides. The technology of cinema has been able to capture these visual and auditory parts of reality and the life world in minute detail.

The psychologist Henri Wallon pointed out: "An essential of the film is that it is working in the viewer's place. It establishes its discoveries in the place of ours" (quoted in Morin 1958, 226.)

What is thereby produced is, however, analogous to the original stimuli, rather than a complete copy of life. Because their technology works in a selective way, in reproducing reality the cinematic apparatuses reduce the portrayal to certain sections and thus change the processing of information as a whole. This reduction causes some configurations of stimuli to be perceived particularly intensely, probably because the perceptual learning initiated by new invariants also activates the sensory apparatus.

In the thirties, Walter Benjamin (1969, 235) wrote: "The film has enriched our field of perception with methods which can be illustrated by those of Freudian theory. Fifty years ago, a slip of the tongue passed more or less unnoticed. Only exceptionally may such a slip have revealed dimensions of depth in a conversation which had seemed to be taking its course on the surface. Since the 'Psycho-pathology of Everyday Life' things have changed. This book isolated and made analysable things which had heretofore floated along unnoticed in the broad stream of perception. For the entire spectrum of optical, and now also acoustical, perception the film has brought about a similar deepening of apperception gone unnoticed until then to be extracted from the stream of perception."

Film has delved ever deeper into the possibilities of extending perception through the technical capacity of the medium to isolate invariants. For contemporaries of the Lumière brothers, it appeared to be an attraction because it could show the "quivering of leaves in the wind" (Kracauer 1985, 11). Later on, it was "unintended gestures and other fleeting impressions" (11) of which film suddenly made the viewer aware.

It is the connection between the observed details of life and the time frame in which they are shown that filmmakers see as crucial to film comprehension. This also plays a central role in the work of the psychologist James J. Gibson. In his book *The Ecological Approach to Visual Perception* (1979), which includes a short chapter on film, Gibson links the principles of the perception of actions to the discovery of invariance in reality, and applies them to the interpretation of film reception.

Gibson views perception as an extraction or "pick-up" of information. This is conceived in terms of a continuous process, as a form of human activity that continues life-long. The perceiving person picks structural invariants out of the flow of stimuli in reality. In this way, Gibson's theory of visual perception becomes something of a "theory of invariance detection" (1979, 249), whereby the observation of reality is tied to the matrix of time.

According to Gibson, images, including the images of film, open up a kind of second-hand knowledge. Here, too, invariant structures are extracted from the flow of visual information. In fact, Gibson views the moving images of film and the perception of events as a primary form of pictorial representation, whereas the static, still images of photography or painting are to be seen as special cases.

In 1966, Gunnar Johansson had already turned his attention to the important difference between "static perceptions" and "event perceptions" and pointed out that visual event perceptions are the most frequent ones in everyday life. In the development of vertebrates, event perceptions are the most elementary and also fundamental. Thus, for humans needing to orient themselves in a world which is in motion, the experience of event perceptions is the "normal case" of perception. The cinema takes up this normal case and models it through its technological medium, and thereby realizes specific invariance detection.

If perception reacts in this way to invariance, it reacts to change with perceptual learning. The balance of change and constancy is of fundamental importance to cinematic perception, since each shot records and conserves certain amounts of information that contain moments of both variation and constancy. Thus whole complexes of relations remain constant during perceptual interactions. They are perceived along with everything else, but require no new learning. Attention is directed to what is new and tends to concentrate on changes and divergencies. "The essence of perceiving is discriminating" (1979, 249). At these points, perceptual learning begins, what Gibson refers to as a "continuous practice" that "purposefully directs attention to the information contained in the stimuli" (1973, 329).

A "difference-quality" of the represented phenomenon compared to other experiences seems to be necessary; it must have an innovation for the viewer and offer him a certain potential for changing his internal model of the environment. The spectator's "difference-sensation" should mainly work at the level of perception to discover new information. But despite its tendency to a conceptualization, the information processing should more or less remain on the threshold to a higher consciousness of the stimuli. The fascination of the reality effect seems to be linked with its oscillating existence on the border of thought. We have the feeling of discovering new things, but we do not have the right terms for them yet.

Many filmmakers use the fact that films are able to present attentive viewers with partially unchanged, though second-hand, sensory impressions of reality, as the point of departure for their creative endeavors. This is the case for many documentary filmmakers, but also for those who make use of the reality effect in fiction. Because elements of real life, as Tarkovsky emphasizes, remain in their proper temporal relations within individual shots, the medium of film allows viewers to observe or discover aspects of reality that would be difficult to notice without such representation. Furthermore, the perceptual effort required leads to a stronger involvement.

Precise observation of such apparently unintended gestures and spontaneous expressions also plays a major role in the new Scandinavian films. However, these are presented to the viewers in the context of conflicting behavior, as an act of intentional extraction of invariants.

In order to have an innovative character for the viewers, cinematic observations of life must bring new insights which revise, extend or differentiate the pre-existing view of the world. If such observations relate to behavioral patterns of the characters that are already familiar from other films, perceptual learning is unnecessary. The phenomena are already conceptualized, often even stereotyped, since the stimuli have lost their edge through overuse. Thus, much depends on pointing the camera at phenomena that are new or can be seen in a new, perhaps more differentiated or complex way. Furthermore, the circumstances shown must also be relevant to the understanding of the story and characters.

In *Breaking the Waves*, for example, we observe the protagonist as she tries to live her life in an emotionally honest way and remain open to love, despite the bigoted environment around her. The same pattern of behavior is repeated again and again with slight variations: the desire to do good and the readiness to make sacrifices for love. When, in the course of the story, her naive unconditionality turns into blind surrender, into an obsession, and turns her into a borderline case, this reveals a contradictory aspect of behavior to be an invariant, in a way that had never before been shown on screen or made publicly conscious. Here, the camera discovers a perceptual invariant in Gibson's sense, and it does so by employing unusual formal devices. I will come back to the problem later.

Lars von Trier describes the paradox on which the behaviour of the protagonists in *Breaking the Waves* is founded: "For a long time I have been wanting to conceive a film in which all driving forces are 'good'. In the film there should only be 'good', but since the 'good' is misunderstood or confused with something else, because it is such a rare thing for us to meet, tensions arise....Bess is fooled; she is doing 'good' for him. He is doing 'good' for her. Nobody is forcing anybody. They both act from their will to do 'good'....By trying to save her, he loses her. By doing 'good'! By trying to save him, by doing 'good', the world that she loved turned against her." (1996, 20ff.)

Thomas Vinterberg's *The Celebration* shows a strange form of group behavior: at a patriarchal hotel owner's birthday party, the toast that his son proposes to him reveals to the guests that he used to molest his children sexually. Although this fact is revealed several times, the guests ignore it. Here again, the film turns an invariant of behavior into a perceptual invariant.

Vinterberg (1999) describes the conflict situation in the behaviour of his characters: "When something terrible happens in my film and the evil comes at last to light, the people's only reaction is: 'Let's have a coffee!' That is cynical. The 'cosiness' often serves to hindering social explosions or for suppressing truth. Even the son in *The Celebration* uses the means of cosiness. When the father is finally expelled from the family, the others, smiling, continue having their breakfast. So they kill him definitely." Antonioni produced an impression of authenticity in the 60's when he disclosed certain emotional deficiencies in his characters and, through repetition, turned them into noticeable invariants. The Danish films present new, more pronounced forms of such disorders. These films do not just present critical observations of human behavior, but rather show a borderline disease of the entire society.

Finally, in von Trier's *The Idiots*, young people from a good background imitate the behavior of the mentally handicapped, thus provoking confrontations both with society and their own way of life. Here once again, a specific form of contradictory behavior becomes evident through the extraction of invariants.

In each case, perceptual learning occurs in the viewers, even if it involves much more complicated patterns of stimuli than those Gibson describes. Still, it works in an analogous way.

If I draw on Gibson's ideas here, I should mention that in fact this is an approach that has been elaborated by Joseph D. Anderson (1996). With its integrative conception, Anderson's approach has addressed some of the facets of Gibson's thought that have been variously criticized (cf. J.D. Anderson 1996, 19ff. and P. Ohler 1990, 1991). Perception is not seen as limited to an immediate interaction between the environment and the perceptual system, but is also embedded within hierarchical cognitive, processes as well as biological evolution and its phylogenetic and ontogenetic dimensions. Gibson chose an ecological strategy that assumed that psychologically relevant phenomena could better be described using ecological concepts borrowed from biology, rather than those of traditional physics, since organisms and environment are inseparable. This meant that perception was to be understood as a form of interaction. However, for Gibson, perception remained an immediate form of interaction, which required neither mediation nor interpretation. Therefore, concepts such as mental representation play no role in his theory. Memory is also not explicitly mentioned, even though his understanding of the reception of information through changes in stimuli does involve a relationship of change and constancy, which seems to imply some form of internal representation or memory. And as Anderson has shown, Gibson's understanding of the extractions of invariants is not inconsistent with Ulric Neisser's Perceptual Cycle or with David Marr's Computational Theory. Perhaps we should re-evaluate Gibson's theory with its paradoxical gaps and view him as a transitional figure between traditional theory and a form of mid-range model-building. Gibson was able to view many things with inexorable exactitude because, just as inexorably, he pushed other things to the periphery of his attention. In the context of traditional psychological theories, which aimed at closure and processes which are always limited, such abstraction need not necessarily be seen as one-sided, but can be viewed in terms of usefulness as a model, a tool to gain information.

3.2 Narrational Conditions

Film can make us aware of new nuances of life by repeating observations of similar structures. It is important to view the preconscious processes of perception as closely connected to conscious processes of thought. This is necessary in order to grasp the dynamics of the reality effect.

The reality effect has to do with the way viewers experience how a certain appearance of reality, cast on the screen by a film, becomes intensely conscious. What is shown then appears extremely authentic and close to life. And it must be the transition from sensory apprehension to consciousness that gives the viewer the opportunity to see such appearances at once more analytically and more emotionally. In order to examine these inner dynamics, it makes sense to understand information processing in the film experience as a phasic process, i.e., not as homogenous and even, but rather as an adaptive learning process developing on different levels.

A film does not merely depict concrete events: the events are also a product of an artistic abstraction deployed upon the material, which transforms and focuses them in a particular manner and is a product of cognitive schema formation which has taken place in the filmmakers mind. It is along these lines of differentiation that three types of filmic structures may be distinguished, each corresponding to a different phase in the formation of schemata and leading to the aforementioned PCS model.

This model helps, not only to describe structural relationships, but also to represent the dynamic transitions between the levels of schema formation and the corresponding effects. The transition from perceptual to conceptual structures is probably most relevant for the reality effect.

Ulric Neisser, whose theory of perception is fully compatible with Gibson's, points out that perceptive schemata are subjected to dynamic developments within a cycle of perception:

"Schemata develop with experience. Information pick-up is crude and inefficient at first, as are the perceptual explorations by which the cycle is continued. Only through perceptual learning do we become able to perceive progressively more subtle aspects of the environment. The schemata that exist at any given moment are the product of a particular history as well as the ongoing cycle itself" (Neisser 1976, 64ff.).

The realization that perceptually guided structures can be made noticeable through cyclical repetition, and in this way become consciously received and conceptualized when applied to the reality effect of film, leads to the hypothesis that the same thing also happens with invariant structures in film that are at first hardly noticeable. The reality effect probably characterizes phases in which one level of abstraction turns into another, for example the transition from perceptual to conceptual structures—or the conscious re-discovery of stereotype structures that had fallen into nonconsciousness.

Such turning points arise from the interaction between what is currently being shown and what the viewer has previously stored in his or her memory. Psychological activity or cognitive work is necessary for this to occur. This may explain why reality effects are felt to be significant, to be an attractive stimulus that can be at once meaningful and emotional.

The reality effect is thus never simply a cinematic structure *per se*, but is always the result of psychological activity on the part of the viewer, for instance the effort of perception necessitated by the interaction of the film form with the viewer's internalized models. According to Dziga Vertov (1960, 54), the "camera eye" demands a certain amount of effort. The reality effect "is not a point of departure, but rather the result of the viewer's confrontation with reality; thus it is the consequence of active perception. A creative process of appropriation takes place. We go behind the outward nature of things. The film reveals certain structures, it generalizes, hence it can not be identical with reality." In this way "the authenticity is the result of our work in the experience of art, i.e., we formulate our own relationship to the world represented on the screen as—we think—a relationship to the real world" (Richter 1964, 1003).

The creative work of the spectator is to a large degree a cognitive one, which is accomplished largely by means of the construction of perceptual invariants. It makes certain aspects of occurrences more conscious and helps to conceptualize them. This leads to the impression that only the medium of film can let one see, for the first time, certain parts of reality with new clarity and certainty. Active participation on the part of the viewer is therefore a necessary prerequisite for the effect to occur. This means, even if the cinematic techniques create representations of the world that help the viewer to select and retain patterns of stimuli, these techniques do not automatically lead to a reality effect. Particular objects of representation or their characteristics, such as moments of reality that seem unposed and coincidental, also do not necessarily constitute a reality effect.

A crucial point for the occurrence of the effect is the narrative structure and the form of editing. The moments of life that are to be made conspicuous and conscious must be presented tersely, but at the same time must be presented to the viewers through multiple repetitions. Terseness can often be achieved when the film images capture contradictory moments of what is shown—a subtle field of conflicts, such as minimal actions or character behavior. The principle of repetition, which keeps the perceptual cycle active, is often an episodic, open form of narration, which repeats the important invariant structures at certain intervals. This can be reinforced by the principles of montage, such as appear in the so-called distance montage (cf. Peleshian 1989). The required perceptual learning does not occur unless there is such an organization of the invariants being shown.

The three Danish films discussed all utilize the intratextual repetition of recurrent forms, or, to be more exact, of certain invariant behavior patterns. Along with the conflict-oriented behavior already mentioned, which is planned into the script and becomes an effective part of the narrative in the form of topic lines, the actors must show similar spontaneous reactions, which result from their improvisation and which vary the semantic gestures of the film as a whole.

3.3 Cultural Conditions

In order to create the necessary stimuli for the reality effect, the individual film must neither remain behind the general development of cinematic technologies, nor ignore the expectations of the audience regarding the current standards for a true representation of the reality.

It is not enough that certain invariants be separated from reality and composed into a narrative structure. The authenticity effect is not an isolated phenomenon of perception, but instead becomes effective within a feedback process that links the individual work and its innovative observations to the entire media culture, i.e. its technical development as well as the spectators' attitudes and expectancies for the trueness of cinematic representations.

Spectators watch many films and TV shows, and in doing so come to accumulate knowledge about how the media deal with reality. In the early years of the movies, to reproduce basic physical processes of motion in a film, for instance the rhythm of a train journey, was sufficient. Now, to appear authentic, the cinema must reveal the smallest psychological changes in the protagonists' behavior. It is therefore no wonder that film delves ever deeper into the private sphere of people, as the Scandinavian film examples show.

Since the audience is involved in what seems to be a permanent cultural process of learning, its demands on technical standards grow continuously. Thus it is often necessary for a filmmaker to make use of the newest recording and reproduction technology to capture the details of real life effectively.

The new technical capacities of *cinéma vérité* and Direct Cinema provided important impulses for the creation of a new culture of observation in the European fiction film of the 1960s and also in some of the American independent films of that time, which showed portrayals of seemingly authentic and spontaneous human reactions and behavior.

The deliberate use of handheld cameras has a similar function for the Dogma films, which I will describe more closely later.

The occurrence of the impression of authenticity does not solely depend on film structure, but also on the viewer's attitudes and expectations with regard to the truth of the cinematic representation. The spectator's view of the film can make the accomplishment of the effect more or less difficult.

Over time, the reality effect developed from characteristics of the documentary film to a peculiarity of a realistic or documentary style in the fiction film. This led to specific expectations regarding the shape and context of this effect. The viewer was looking for the films' tendency to specific formal qualities and a type of reception they elicited; when finding these characteristics he was ready to believe in the film as an authentic document of life.

Thus some filmmakers began to manage or manipulate the attitudes and expectations of the audience by imitating the established form for creating the reality effect. They did so using varied means. We can find different kinds of mixtures between fiction films and documentaries whose makers are seeking to use the aesthetic power of the reality effect.

There are outstanding efforts that continue the line of the Documentary Style of Fiction Film, as one can see in *Gummo* (1997), Harmony Korine's detailed description of the day-to-day problems of a boy in the American suburbs, or in Jean-Pierre and Luc Dardenne's *Rosetta* (1999), about the humiliating situation of an unemployed young woman.

And there are attempts to draw the action near to a historical event, carried out, for instance, in Oliver Stone's *JFK* (1991), or to fake authenticity in order to play with the viewers' feelings in a shocking artificial reality using supplementary means of communication like the Internet, as in the case of Daniel Myrick and Eduardo Sánchez's *The Blair Witch Project* (1999).

Recently, a specific genre based on these preconditions emerged, the Docu-soap. Today, the most common way that films lead to an impression of authenticity is by a sort of random-shooting with a shaky handheld camera accompanied by a dramaturgy of randomness.

Regardless of such machinations, the production of fiction films seems to be dependent on consideration of the reality effect. Even if, in the concrete case, it would be unclear whether a significant reaction occurs or not, the specific aesthetic functions of the cinema must always include the potential for an impact that is based on the impression of reality. This remains the case when the film story is obviously a fictional one. The hard conditions of modern filmmaking dictate that the performance of the characters must maintain a certain level of accuracy in the observation of behavioral subtleties to which the spectator has already become adapted in a cultural process of learning, by watching documentaries and live transmissions on television. The conscious effort to provide for the possibility of reality effects may also help the filmmakers in cases where there is no compelling demand to lean toward a documentary style or similar trends.

4. Relationships of the Reality Effect to Play, Possible Worlds and Genres

The reality effect is incorporated into an active process of film experience that confronts the spectator, on the one hand, with a surrogate for the physical world (i.e. an actual substitute for something else), and on the other hand with his voluntarily undertaken entrance into the diegetic world of fiction by means of a genetically-endowed capacity for play (cf. Anderson 1996, 161).

The connection between the surrogate character and the diegetic world of a film, which is based on play, places the reality effect under very variable functional conditions. Play is an important part of life. Without a kind of mental play we would have no forethought, and without the anticipation and evaluation of coming events we would have no chance of mastering the future.

Art is useful here, since the viewers not only remember their experiences, but are also able to vary the schema they have learned. Art activates and trains the capacity to grasp new cognitive structures as a pattern in an emotional or intuitive, playful way. As I will argue later, art plays with different systems of preferences and evaluates phenomena according to different values. In this way, various systems of values can prove their usefulness for possible future worlds.

The possible worlds of film can be constructed in different ways. They can be very similar to the world we inhabit in everyday life, or they can be an obvious fiction or fantasy very far removed from it. As the history of cinema shows, extremely different forms have developed, including many that worked only during a short period as well as others that functioned for a long time. Both the similarity to real life and the difference from it can produce meaning and aesthetic effects equally well.

Bazin wrote: "The guiding myth, then, inspiring the invention of cinema [...] is a re-creation of the world in its own image" (quoted in Currie 1995, 79). Film is able to link its fictions and fantasies—its possible worlds—to the processes of sensory perception so well because it does not just produce representations of reality, but also simulates the natural processes of perception by utilizing many of the functions of our perceptual mechanisms.

If the new rules of probability in the possible world of the film, which may well be totally improbable in the real world, are set up and proved to function in the story, then it is easy for the viewer to accept further steps in the same direction. He or she accepts the possible world as a playful variant of the real.

Of course, in each individual case this acceptance depends on the extent to which the viewers are able to follow the narration and genre of these films, since the possible worlds of the films are largely legitimized and stabilized by narrative and genre structures.

Narration and genre mold the possible worlds of films particularly in that they shape their macrostructures. Genres rest on very complex relationships and create stereotypes of a second or higher order, which often incorporate elementary forms. Arising out of a cultural and historical process, they serve to standardize and diversify aesthetic devices and their effects.

But what about the reality effect in stereotype-based films?

Within the macrostructures dominated by genres, reality effects, in so far as they exist at all, are given the status of microstructures. They are often hardly noticeable and become negligible in the whole experience. But they do exist and have an important function.

Just as Antonioni could portray the "illness of emotions" of his protagonists, the Documentary Style in Eastern Europe exhibited subtle moments of conflict and contradiction in the behaviour of characters influenced by the social problems of Eastern Socialist society, and the above-mentioned Scandinavian films show a specific kind of conflict situation: a borderline-syndrome of their society.

Von Trier's *Breaking the Waves* must be viewed as a genre mix, a hybrid form made up of fairy tale, parable, and melodrama and structured in blocks according to epic form. Rumour has it that the film was originally modeled on an early fairy tale experiment by the director. In *Gold Heart*, a little girl gives away all she possesses, but is finally rewarded for her compassion with stars falling from the heavens as golden coins. The film treats the well-known fairy tale motif as the ancient Greek dramaturgists treated their myths; this motif becomes a narrational stereotype. At the end of the film a miracle is needed. The central event has the function of a parable, i.e. it can be transformed into a sentence or maxim. Indeed, in an early phase of scriptwriting the story was titled: *Amor omnia*— "Love is everything". The paradigm of the melodramatic approach originates from the Romantic literature of the 19th century, particularly the emotional dramas of the Brontë sisters, and from Douglas Sirk's lofty film melodramas of the fifties (cf. Björkman 1996, 4). The flow of the melodramatic action is interrupted by panorama-like Turneresque landscapes, which—although cinematic shots—have a postcard-like effect. They are underlaid by popular music from the early 1970s (from David Bowie to Elton John). Per Kirkeby (1996, 12), who created these sequences, said about their function: "...fundamentally it was perfectly obvious that they were intended as the antithesis of the palpitating intrusion of the other images into the tropistic intimacy of the film."

Corresponding plot stereotypes are used to organize the story. They build up expectations that, from the beginning, go in divergent directions and lead to a certain activation of the viewer, who searches for fitting genre patterns and tries to discover perceptual invariants in certain forms of behavior that suddenly become conscious through the reality effect. This creates a certain feeling of unrest, which is reinforced by the cinematic images.

The Celebration also tends toward a genre mix. Strangely enough, initially the film's video aesthetics awaken genre expectations well known from family soaps on TV. However, it soon becomes clear that the film is rooted more in the tradition of the Scandinavian social drama, which rarely paid much attention to Aristotle's three unities, but was generally a family drama, and often also approached melodrama quite closely. In the background, a parable also seems to take shape in the theme of socially-accepted mechanisms of psychological repression, since child molestation is not really the theme of the film, even if it does play a central role in the plot.

The characters appear, at first, to be standardized types, but at times they break out of their stereotypical behavior and exhibit spontaneous behavior that seems remarkably authentic.

The borderline syndrome of society becomes most clearly evident in *The Idiots*. The action takes place on two separate levels. Karen, a young, working-class woman, watches how a group of middle-class intellectuals pretend to be mentally handicapped. This behavior at once fascinates and repulses her. She decides to remain with the group, but stays in the background until, in the end, she adopts a stance of protest against her rigid and conventional family.

Parallel to this story, the film confronts the viewer with six supposedly "documentary" interviews, in which the members of the group look back on this strange experiment and explain their personal attitudes to it.

The film's macrostructure thus does not seem to offer a real plot or a clear use of multiple genres. Yet it is based on a recycling of previous forms, and thus on a process of cinematic and cultural stereotyping.

A parable seems to form the center of the film, insofar as the characters not only dissociate themselves from the normal way of life in their scandalous experiment, but also recognize that their provocations are just as flawed as the conventional attitudes in society. Inasmuch as it paints a group portrait, the film follows the tradition of the Scandinavian social drama.

In a certain way, the film also shows a resemblance to comedy or farce, since it keeps as fiction what one could just as well interpret as morally perverse or as a carnivalesque act of violence. The ambivalent forms, individually and in their interaction, make the story appear to be artificial and intentionally alienating, but also hinder attempts to grasp it intellectually, since the action remains too enigmatic to be understood rationally or judged morally.

Despite the postmodern denial of responsibility in the film as a whole, there are exact observations of human behavior that appear to be highly authentic, particularly where subtle spontaneous reactions are captured in the cycle of perception. Perhaps it is characteristic of all three films, and the Dogma style as a whole, that they create a semantic conflict between the familiar course of events in the macrostructure and the fine nuances of behavior shown in minimal character actions.

The contradiction between stereotypes in the filmic macrostructures and the perceptual invariants in the microstructure of the *Dogma 95* films comes to a head in their extraordinary visual form, which provokes orienting reactions that intensify the impression of authenticity.

5. Camera Work and Orienting Reactions

The immediate and individual expressions that involve the viewer in the characters of *Breaking the Waves* are created, not only by the acting and a specific form of dramaturgy, but also by a specific form of camera work. The constantly moving handheld camera in CinemaScope format follows the protagonist in a setting that gives it complete freedom to operate in a 360° radius. Frequently using close-ups, the camera attentively follows the action and adjusts its rhythms to it. It follows the action in a way that the cinematographer Robby Müller (1996, 5, 23) referred to as "a search for a naive way of seeing, for an uninhibited way of filming." Certain conditions were created to achieve this attitude. After the actors had rehearsed for weeks in advance of filming and the cinematographer and camera operators had become very familiar with the script and the setting, the scenes were often filmed in such a way that the camera team did not know the exact arrangement in advance (von Trier had already worked this way in filming *Kingdom*). They walked onto the set without final instructions as to what exactly would happen during the scene and attempted to orient themselves to the action as it unfolded. They received no further instructions from the director and had to just "shoot away" (ibid.). The camera team spoke of "random shooting" (Oppenheimer / Williams 1996, 19). Surprised by the course of events, the crew often was not able to frame their shots "properly" or compose the images. There were even a number of unfocused shots. The spontaneous camera action gave the images a documentary quality and made many of them quite rough. Von Trier was very interested in producing this effect and is supposed to have put up a cardboard sign on the video monitor with the instruction, "Make Faults!".

The actors had to play through whole scenes without interruption, and without knowing exactly when the camera was shooting. The long rehearsal processes, followed by the uncertainties of the actual shooting, generated spontaneous reactions.

This way of shooting visually transmits to the viewer the camera team's search for orientation. When the film is shown in the cinema, this effect is amplified into an orienting reaction.

The orienting reaction, which Pavlov called the 'what-is-that reflex,' is in psychological terms the organism's reaction to new or unfamiliar stimuli or to data that is insufficient to allow the recognition of an object. It is independent of the stimulus and can thus be induced by varying sensory impulses. Following the studies of Sokolov (1960, 1963), we know that primarily low- to mid-intensity stimuli induce such reactions and that they increase the organism's receptiveness to stimuli. Therefore, they can be viewed as a specific component of the activation of the organism (cf. Clauss 1976, 377).

That orientation reactions lead to increased psychological activation applies to film reception, too. While the camera work in *Breaking the Waves* attempts to present recognizable objects and to present the decisive events of the psychologically complex story in close-ups, the spectator finds him or herself confronted with the unfamiliar stimuli of a story filmed in a way that—quite unlike mainstream cinema—seems quite uncertain and rarely allows reliable prognoses about the coming plot development. *Breaking the Waves* brings together the emotional unrest of the protagonist and the agitation consequently produced in the viewer with the authenticity effect, and the moments of insight it leads to, as well as the visual turbulence, are produced by the camera's attempts to find an orientation, provoking renewed orienting reactions in the viewer.

For the other two films, different technical conditions apply, but similar orientation reactions are produced in the audience. Furthermore, a similar interaction can be found among the conflict-laden story events, vibrant reality effects, and orientation reactions caused by the camera-work in these films.

The Celebration and *The Idiots* are shot with handheld cameras on video (Sony VX 1000) for projection in Academy 35 format. The action radius of the camera also allows it to move in a 360° range; real locations that give the impression of natural lighting are used, and spontaneous reactions in the affective situations of the protagonists are taken over from the set as immediately as possible.

They thus lead to an exact observation of conflict-laden patterns of behavior, which are at once highly relevant to the story and charged with reality effects. They are also accompanied by orienting reactions and psycho-physiological activity. The protagonists' search for functioning forms of behavior are thus linked to uncertainty at the perceptual level, induced by disturbances in the ordinary perception of events and the orienting reactions this leads to.

The reality effect of the fiction film can be seen as a significant response of the spectator which only occurs through experiencing films and audiovisual media. Via their representation on the screen, certain phenomena of his life-world become more consciously known to the spectator and thus a discovery of reality takes place through the camera observation. These discoveries can be integrated very variously in the artistic form and have varying influences on the aesthetic impact by creating an impression of authenticity, or reality effect. The historic development of the cinema shows that there exist, besides clear tendencies to a documentary style, also opposite tendencies which use the reality effect, in a modified version, within obviously fictional stories or genres.

From the position of cognitive psychology, one can describe the effect as a successive transition from the threshold of pre-conscious perceptual filmic structures to more consciously experienced conceptualized ones. Presumably, this transition could be demonstrated empirically by psychological experiments.

Although the utilization of cinematic technologies for the recording and reproduction of stimuli from the real world is the basic condition for the occurrence of the reality effect, this reaction does not appear automatically through the use of these means but only under the observance of certain cognitive, narrational and cultural preconditions which modern film directing must take into consideration.

Chapter VII: Imagination and the Formation of Dream-like Sequences in the Cinema

1. Imagination and the Cinema: Imageries and Imaginings on the Screen and in the Viewer's Experience

This chapter deals with some small aspects of a huge and complicated problem, the interrelations between the imagination and the cinema. Imagination is "the ability of human beings to generate mental representations of objects, persons, or physical and social events not immediately presented to the senses" (Singer 2000, 227).

Imagination plays a central role in all thinking, understanding, and reasoning. "Without imagination, nothing in the world could be meaningful. Without imagination, we could never make sense of our experience. Without imagination, we could never reason toward knowledge of reality." (Johnson 1987, IX). In other words: Without imagination we are neither able to understand the world around us nor the "possible worlds" of cinema, because we can sense that film is not solely an emotion machine, it is also an imagery machine that uses various imageries in constructing its fictions and possible worlds and at the same time evokes different imaginings in the viewers' mind.

I have used two terms: "imagery" and "imagining". What do they mean? "Imagery is the mental construction of an experience that, at least in some respects, resembles the experience of perceiving an object or an event, either with or without direct sensory stimulation.

The recognition that one can call up a mental 'copy' of experiences (such as memory images of specific episodes) or create novel images of events that never happened has long played a central role in notions of thought, memory and knowledge representation" (Katz 2000, 187).

"Imaginings are doings" (Currie 2002, 25): because the ability to construct imageries is connected with mental activities that lead to doings, to mental processes with a specific result in our mind.

"The imaginative dimension of human experience is generally linked to four kinds of specific processes. These are (1) consciousness and the stream of thought, (2) daydreaming, (3) night-dreaming and (4) creativity"(Singer 2000, 229). These processes have been the subject of considerations for a long time. 5000 years ago we find the first evidence concerning human thinking about dreaming on the hieroglyphic tablets of Mesopotamia/Sumer. And a textbook on psychology notices: "Investigations of mental imagery can be traced back over more than 2500 years, they were an important part of the earliest attempts to devise a scientific psychology in the 19th century, and they were at the forefront of the initial development of cognitive psychology in the 1960s. Since then, research on mental imagery has presented a challenge for mainstream cognitive psychology by generating new kinds of theory concerning potential mental representations and new methods for investigating those representations" (J. Richardson 1999, 1).

But we also know that the varied imageries, called by Kosslyn (1983) "ghosts in the mind's machine", are not so easy to observe. And, unfortunately, concerning the cinema the study of these ghosts is still at its very beginning.

Every film requires a mental construction of our experience that leads to various activities, but we are still far away from being able to analyze these processes at the level of experimental psychology. Nevertheless, we can divide some kinds of imageries and imaginings from others in a more philosophical manner, using categories such as perception-like, belief-like or desire-like imaginings (cf. Currie 2002, 2ff.), and also dream-like imaginings.

It makes sense to start a study of the central problems of cinematic imageries with a look at more obvious phenomena, such as dream-like sequences on the screen. Later, we can consider these types of imaginings in the viewer's experience. Of course, there are huge differences between the two dimensions of this problem, but it is better to begin with the simpler question. I hope that analyses of some outstanding films can lead to a deeper understanding of the specific possibilities in the cinematic depiction of dreams and other types of mental imagery. Therefore I would like to begin with an analysis of Federico Fellini's *8½* (1963), whose story is based on different kinds of imaginings, particularly dream-like and desire-like imaginings.

In the history of film, Fellini's work is not an isolated phenomenon. At the beginning of the 1960s, a particular form of film composition became increasingly important; besides depicting "actual" occurrences or "real events", these films also included "mental events" by showing subjective memories, imaginary scenes, fantasies, and dreams. This body of work, which now almost seems to follow a group style, includes not only Alain Resnais' *Hiroshima mon amour* (1959), *Last Year in Marienbad* (*L'Année dernière à Marienbad*, 1961), and *Muriel ou Le temps d'un retour* (1963), Federico Fellini's *8½* and *Juliet of the Spirits* (*Giulietta degli spiriti*, 1965), Ingmar Bergman's *Persona* (1966) and Luis Buñuel's *Beauty of the Day* (*Belle de jour*, 1967), but also Nagisa Oshima's *Violence at Noon* (*Hakuchu no torima*, 1966) and Andrei Tarkovsky's *The Mirror* (*Zerkalo*, 1975).

Not only did these films include dreams or related mental states, but important characteristics of these sequences seem to be transmitted to the composition and narrative forms of the films as wholes, giving the overall film compositions dreamlike characteristics. 'Dreamlike' is here understood in the sense of psychologist Carl Gustav Jung (1996, 134), who saw dreams as "involuntary psychic activity" that "is just conscious enough to be reproducible in the woken state." Like actual dreams in Jung's characterization, the films present many "irrational states" and are "less transparent and comprehensible."

Spectators and critics alike have often been fascinated by these devices of film composition, but they pose an extraordinary challenge for film analysis. It is often difficult to grasp relationships within their composition, and in some cases regularities in terms of narration can hardly be found; as a result, the interpretation of such works becomes increasingly arbitrary or itself takes on the blurred aspect of dreams. The more unconscious elements of experience communicated by the films seem in this way to be moved towards the foreground. My cognitive model of description will make it easier to represent structural relations within these films that are perhaps difficult to apprehend, but nonetheless present: in particular, perception- and stereotype-based filmic structures. In addition, I would like to combine this description with an exploration of Carl Gustav Jung's ideas about problems related to dreams and the so-called archetypes, because one can use the research done by the famous Swiss psychologist nearly 100 years ago to complete and improve the cognitive model of stereotyping. In my understanding, Jung's archetype can be considered as a special case of a cognitive stereotype.

2. Fellini's *8½* as an "Open Work"

The film's story is based on an elaborated conflict situation: Its hero, the film director Guido Anselmi, is starting the production process of a film. But although the crew has already assembled, famous actors have been engaged and even expensive sets have been built, a scenario does not exist, and the author-director feels incapable of coming up with a suitable story. According to the common attitudes of late-bourgeois society towards the artist, his environment has obviously created a mystique about the film director and given him freedom for his creative intentions, but now it puts pressure on him. The producer and the members of the crew unswervingly ask him for further details regarding the progress of the project, although the protagonist is seeking on his own—unsuccessfully—for authorities who are able to give him spiritual orientation. The Catholic church, which has been influencing Guido's education from his early childhood, has no advice that could conduct him to a productive world-outlook which seems necessary for creative work. Thus, at the finale of the film, he is willing to accept the blame for his failure and seems ready to give up the film project, which probably would mean the end of his artistic career; an attitude that has, by the way, analogies to those of other heroes of late-bourgeois art and literature.

Already this short sketch of the conflict situation, whose philosophical essence is described more fully elsewhere (cf. Wuss 1986, pp 81ff.), provides for the conditions of the basic narrative structure of a causal chain. But the traditional fabula of narrative cinema, in which the cognitive structure ensures that the spectator is easily aware of events in the film, is demolished to a considerable degree or is entirely absent in Fellini's film. This presents a problem for analysis, since filmic events escape the grasp of thought.

Fellini (1974b, 157) gave the following synopsis of his film: "The story of a director who is supposed to make a film, which he then forgets, and which then progresses in two directions, that of fantasy and that of reality."

This apparently clear structure, which results from an obvious dramatic conflict and the inevitable self-questioning of the protagonist, by no means possessed this easy clarity for spectators at the time, since the course of actual events in the film is disrupted and overgrown in a quite baroque way, dominated by memories of childhood, imaginary notions, fantasies, night-dreams, and daydreams.

What was new about these representations of memories and dreams was not only that they were not clearly distinguished from real events, but also that they followed in the succession of real events, often making orientation very difficult.

The film *8½* can be considered an "open work" in Eco's sense: it strives towards an aesthetic effect that transmits the "fundamental ambiguity of the artistic message," and does so "based not merely on the nature of the aesthetic object and its composition but on the very elements that are combined in it" (Eco 1989a, 39f.). On the one hand, the spectator is left in the dark about the tendency of the film's message, which mainly depends on the issue of whether the central conflict of the story can be solved or not, i.e. whether the hero, who feels himself unable to make the film, will capitulate in this situation and give up the project, and even abandon all his creative intentions, or, on the contrary, find a way out of this highly difficult state of affairs. On the other hand, the viewer can scarcely recognize the meaning or tendency of some elements of the story striving toward the aesthetic result, particularly those which show dreams and other "mental events," including unconscious moments.

But the ambiguity of the artistic messages does not equal arbitrariness. Commonly, the open artworks of this period made an appeal to an active spectator who was willing to search out, from the field of possible meanings of a work, those that could be considered as dominant and representing the idea of the whole.

Analogous to the film experience, the PCS model can help a similar process of semiotic sifting through its description of contradictory stimulus patterns. It can help to relate them to different basic structures of narration and to define their specific semantic tendency. In the case of *8½*, it should be clear that causal chains, topic lines and stereotypes of narration do not semantically cooperate, i.e. strengthen one another, but, on the contrary, produce a semantic conflict, leading to the ambiguity of the artistic message.

Simply stated, the causal chain of the real events mainly expresses that the protagonist runs deeper into a conflict which is unsolvable for him, with the result that his project seems to be doomed to failure.

Nevertheless, topic lines based on his real actions, as well as his imageries, show that he is trying to cope with the situation, often succeeding in a playful manner. And the stereotypes of narration, which, on the one hand, are based on archetypal situations of dreams and imageries and, on the other, simulate actions of comic genres, mainly strengthen those impulses of the topic level which encourage Guido's will to overcome his dilemma.

Of course, this elementary model of basic narrative structures provides only a rough approximation to Fellini's highly complicated mode of storytelling.

Faced with a lack of conceptualization on the level of narration, the spectator is forced to orient himself in a way that places him or her in a position like that of a searching protagonist struggling to articulate himself. In terms of film history, this results in a transformation comparable to what Ricardou noted for the narration of the *nouveau roman*, the shift from the traditional "narrative of an adventure" (le récit d'une aventure) to the "adventure of a narrative" (l'aventure d'un récit) (cf. Jean Ricardou, quoted in Schober 1979, p. 38). To describe analogous forms of representation in the work of Alain Resnais, film critics of the time coined the term "mise en conscience" (cf. Lenz 1990, 12), in my translation: "arranged in the mind".

Another important way to arrange cognitive processes in the mind is the method of reflection of the actual situation. Fellini found a specific form, the so-called (in French) "construction en abyme". The term originates from heraldry. In a shield of a coat of arms one can find a little version of the same (identical) heraldic figure, and so on. Although Fellini did not invent this principle of film construction, he was the first to build an entire film in this way, subjecting all individual elements to the principle. "For *8½*, one should be careful to realize, is a film that is *doubly doubled*— and, when one speaks of it as having a mirror construction, it is really a double mirror construction one should be talking about. It is not only a film about the cinema; it is a film about a film that is presumably itself about the cinema; it is not only a film about a director, but a film about a director who is reflecting himself onto his film" (Metz 1974, 230; emphasis in original). The starting point for this specific methodology of reflection was formed by dream representations, too.

In addition to this, there was a strange doubling between the situation of the film protagonist and the personal situation of the author-director, since Fellini came up with the central idea of the film—a protagonist searching in his own mind for a way out of the dilemma, and who is also a director by profession—only after beginning his own project, which had been in progress at this time. For the audience, the contours of the two film projects began to blur; this not only further complicated understanding the events in the film, but also caused the spectator to find him or herself placed in a kind of "work in movement" (cf. Eco 1989a, pp. 12ff.; Wuss 1986, p. 104)

3. Topics in *8½*

With regard to modelling of narrative structure, I do not intend here to draw a detailed plot line developing the above ideas about the conflict situation, because such descriptions already exist (see Wuss 1986, 73–110). The film's rejection of the classical form seems to be more important. Even if the loss of the traditional fabula in the sense of a predominant causal chain results in the disappearance of the usual reference system for the comprehension and interpretation of the film plot, this does not necessarily entail a categorical refusal of coherent filmic narrative or overall meaning.

The representation of dreams, with this effect of limitlessness, does not legitimate an arbitrariness of composition—a chaotic film—, or a refusal of meaning. A connection between individual events, like episodes of a film plot, is established by forming similar complex stimulus patterns, although such a structural invariant can only be received on the level of perception and only minimally become consciously recognised in the spectator's actual experience of the film. On the basis of the multiple repetition of the same stimulus pattern, a corresponding attitude of expectation is formed on the part of the spectator in his or her internal model. In the perceptual cycle, this pattern is increasingly stabilized and, as a cognitive schema, provides hypotheses for the subsequent process of reception. In this way, the invariant structure becomes increasingly apparent and ever more effective in art-semantic terms. On the perceptual level, a concentration in terms of relations of meaning already begins to emerge, a topic. Developed to a whole topic line, it can become a basic structure of filmic narration.

On the "real" level of the story, Guido, the protagonist, abandons his film project and all further artistic strivings. But over the course of the film, Fellini forms a dense topic line that expresses anything but capitulation; on the contrary, it expresses the feeling that the protagonist will overcome his main problems. The director Guido is repeatedly shown in positions that testify that he can cope with life and face situations in a playful, euphoric, dream-like or desire-like way. Almost every scene ends on a light note, with playful, dancing movement. The series of similar semantic gestures that thus emerges saturates both real and imaginary worlds.

The film begins with a dream-like opening sequence which shows the protagonist, who seems to be locked up in his car, breathing hard as if suffocating from gas that is filling-up the cabin. The car is stuck in the midst of the traffic jam but the occupants of the other vehicles callously look at his panic without helping. Finally, the hero frees himself from the nightmare and begins a high-altitude flight over the sea. For a moment, this flight also animates the spectators to euphoric feelings, as do the protagonist's motions in front of the mirror after the doctor's visit—curious motions partly resembling knee bends and partly dancing steps.

Later, one can see the hero friskily quickening his steps to escape the irksome questions of the crew members about the progress of the slackened development of the film project.

As his crisis begins and he decides to ask the cardinal's advice, on the nocturnal hotel corridor, Guido is executing a strange kind of steps which look like a stenographic shortening of an exquisite dance.

And when, at the end of the story, the producers are leading the protagonist to the press conference, the whole arrangement resembles a condemned man's way to his execution—with the peculiarity that the protagonist's motions look rather like those of an infant who is pretending to swing from the hands of his parents while on a family walk.

The other characters show similar unserious gestures. An older nun looks into the camera like a teenager flirting with the imagined audience of a live transmission on TV. In Guido's memory, the children are dancing and jumping for joy, and the monstrous Saragina dances for the exited pupils on the beach.

All these euphoric gestures, which often conclude the scenes, have the function of topics. In the first chapters I have mentioned topic lines that emphasize the existence of unsolvable problem situations by stressing a disappointing outcome. But this most important topic line of Fellini's film has the opposite function. It emphasizes the possibility of solvable situations, of a happy outcome of the scenes and the whole story and, in this way, draws the protagonists away from the catastrophe.

The semantic gestures which underline the euphoric outcomes continue to the end, when a dream-like sequence, a great celebration of creativity, is held: the carnivalesque reversal of the protagonist's dilemma and at the same time the incarnation of all euphoria.

The constant recurrence of playful-optimistic resolutions to difficult situations leads to a process of the viewer's probability learning, and through this a happy ending becomes plausible; it seems to be plausible that sad situations can change for the better. In a semantic conflict against the fatalistic tendency of actual events, the topics in the end win the upper hand. They help to constitute worlds of possibility following the desire-like imaginings of the hero and, at the same time, the desire-like imaginings of the spectator. Thus these small scenes and gestures are highly important in communicating the director's point of view. Fellini wanted to say that the human being is able to overcome all conflict situations. I think that today this message remains of immediate interest.

But one of the central problems was: how could the spectator see these subtle signals, how could he understand this message?

The director was aware of this problem, and sought for more clarity by using the means of comedy. The above-mentioned light and euphoric gesture of play or desire-like imagining is a typical means of comedy; it makes obvious the conflicts and the chances of the protagonists. And at the time of shooting, Fellini fastened to the camera a small poster with the inscription FILM COMICO, in order to emphasize this genre tendency.

I wish to argue that the dream-like images, gestures and scenes can help the viewer in his process of becoming aware, in that they reactivate his knowledge, values and emotions through their partial status as cinematic stereotypes or, following Jung, so-called "archetypes."

4. Dreams as Specific Stereotypes or Archetypes

The dream-based modes of representation in *8½* not only contain preconscious structural relationships on the perceptive level, but also structures on the level of stereotypes that are also received more or less unconsciously, even if under different conditions. Perception-based structures rely on stimulus patterns where schema formation has only just begun, thus allowing the forms to go almost unnoticed and be maintained on a preconscious level. In contrast, stereotypes are forms in a late stage of cognitive appropriation; long ago conceptualized, due to their multiple communicative use they have surpassed their maximum conspicuousness and are only received accidentally by the spectator and often non-consciously due to habit. When the spectator is confronted with such stimulus configurations, their cognitive patterns, emotions and values are stored in the long-term memory of an individual, or often an entire social group, yet their informational content has in the meantime nevertheless become quite low. Many stereotypes fade, and their form dissolves like that of a dream that escapes our reconstruction.

Since potentially all structural relations of a film composition can reach this stage, filmic stereotypes can appear in various forms: as myths, canonical stories, or conventionalized plot patterns, standardized conflicts or typified figures, but also as elementary situations and images that I would like to term filmic archetypes. These are images of elementary human situations formulated in a nearly symbolic manner. For instance: the situation of the protagonist's terrible imprisonment in the car shown in the first daydream, his liberation that turns into the happy flight over the sea, which is also an example, and also the situation of drop and crash, when Guido is yanked back by "the others" with a cord that ties him to the ground (see fig. 8).

Jung, who saw dreams as the "spontaneous self-representation of the current state of the unconscious in a symbolic form of expression" (1996, 115), emphasized the important role of archetypes in dream material. According to his definition, archetypes are "to be understood as specific forms and image-like configurations that are found not only in the same form in all times and places, but also in individual dreams, fantasies, visions, and mad notions. Their repeated occurrence in individual cases as well as their ethnic ubiquity show that the human soul is not only individual and subjective or personal, but also collective and objective. We thus speak on the one hand of a personal unconscious, on the other of a collective unconscious, a layer deeper that that of the personal unconscious, which is closer to consciousness" (Jung 1996, pp. 142ff.).

The collective unconscious is made up of "preexistent forms, archetypes that can become conscious only in a secondary manner and grant the conscious experience clear contours." (Jung 1990, 46)

"The archetype represents an unconscious matter that changes in its becoming conscious and being perceived in the sense of each individual consciousness in which it emerges". (ibid., 9)

Jung calls this "integration of the unconscious into consciousness" a "process of individuation." (ibid., 42) Art, in my view, is always tied to the integration of the unconscious into consciousness, and thus returns to such a process. Analogously, filmic archetypes can be understood as form relations that are initially received by the unconscious, but are familiar because they are produced through prior cultural communication with its semantics, emotions, and values. These are perceived and activated in a specific work and the concrete act of reception; in this way, they are returned to consciousness, but the degree of consciousness can only be considered relative. The emergence of such preexistent forms is to be explained as the result of two different relationships of invariance that cross in all cultural stereotypes (cf. Schweinitz

1987, 121). On the one hand, a cognitive invariant lies behind the filmic archetype, which the individual grasps through the mental appropriation of an object; on the other hand, this operation of invariance becomes intersubjectively effective in a sociocultural process of appropriation, resulting in cognitive invariants specific to a particular group. On closer inspection we can also find in Jung an attempt to connect the archetype to experience and cognitive strategies. He writes:

"There are as many archetypes as there are typical situations in life. Endless repetition has left the imprint of these experiences on psychic constitution, not in the form of images that are filled with one content, but rather initially with 'forms without content,' which represent merely the possibility of a certain type of worldview and behavior" (Jung 1990, 51).

Archetypes are thus not inherited concrete "imageries", but inherited "'possibilities' of imagining." (ibid., 69) Jung compares the "a priori given possibility of the imaginary form" [Vorstellungsform] with the axis system of a crystal, which in a certain sense predetermines crystal formation in the mother liquid, but without having material existence. The archetypes also have an "invariable core of meaning that only appears in principle, but never concretely determines its mode of appearance" (ibid, 79). Jung supports this claim by providing a whole range of various concrete variants of the mother archetype.

As we know, Jung also developed fields of concrete variants for other archetypes: for the Anima, the child archetype, the Kore and trickster figures.

Fellini, incidentally, had been directed to some of Jung's books by the German psychotherapy professor Bernhard, and called the reading "a pleasant revelation; an exciting, unsuspected, unique confirmation of something that I had only to a small part already suspected" (see Fellini 1984, 132). As a film director who used symbolic images in his work, he was particularly impressed by the different ways in which Jung and Freud saw the phenomenon of symbolism:

"For Jung, the symbol is a means to express an intuition, for which no better form of expression can be found.

For Freud, the symbol is used as a replacement for something subject to repression, and thus cannot be expressed, but must be forgotten.

For Jung, the symbol is thus a means to repeat something that can be expressed, if not in an unequivocal way.

For Freud, it is a way to repress what is not allowed to be expressed." (ibid.)

To represent what cannot be expressed, and this in a way that is not completely unequivocal, was completely part of Fellini's project. Jung's view of archetypes thus quite clearly coincided with Fellini's own creative program. Jung writes that whatever an archetypal content might say initially seems like a linguistic simile, but on closer inspection a still unknown third lies behind the two compared phenomena, something unknown and resistant to formulation. (Jung 1990, 112ff.)

The ambivalence of *8½* thus results to a large extent from its use of archetypes, which never allow for similes with a rational precision (like those of the Brechtian parable), but instead always include an unknown third factor, giving the film a puzzling and opaque quality. Many fleeting images from night- and daydreams in *8½* are archetypal in their sense of a "basic pattern of instinctual behavior." (ibid., 46) When, at one point in the film an intellectual criticizes the protagonist, the next shot shows the protagonist hanging from a noose; when the journalists want to know what the film the protagonist is beginning to make is supposed to look like, we see how Guido hides under a table and shoots himself in the head. However, these abrupt turns are always subject to a subtle reversal; this also often takes place with the help of archetypes. The bright figure of the "girl from the wellspring," played by Claudia Cardinale, that idealistic "offering of genuineness that the protagonist no longer knows what to do with," (Fellini 1974b, 12) is a variation of the archetypal Kore figure Jung sees in the "unknown young girl" of the "Gretchen type" (Jung 1990, 139). Aspects of the "earth mother," described by Jung as "having a primitive or animalistic facial expression—the figure not seldom like the Neolithic ideal of the Venus de Brassempuoy, or that of Willendorf," (ibid., 140) are clearly visible in Saragina.

Numerous times in the film, visual motifs appear that show water: not only Guido's flight over the sea at the start of the film, but also as the background of the dancing Saragina or in the scenes showing the protagonist sitting in a bath tub, first as a child, later as a successful filmmaker. From this early experience of bathing derives a strange phonetic series that sounds like a magic formula: ASA NISI MASA. The beginning letters of these three words, which the hypnotist reads from Guido's thoughts, spell "Anima." This is the term for the archetype that stands for the inexhaustible life power, symbolized by water and recurring to the myth of creativity. Anima also lies behind the intentions of the main figure, and thus the entire story line of the film. No matter how much the film director Guido might seem like a fraud, or at any event someone not too concerned about truth and morality, behind all his feeling, thought, and action lie the unshakeable drive and compulsion to create—a characterization that clearly distinguishes him from most intellectual figures in Italian film of this period. This creativity myth is simply a variant of the anima archetype. If the protagonist of *8½* was not so determined by the anima, the film narrative with its confusing multiple layers would lack a decisive main plot line. The archetype is given in the composition the "ordering influence on the consciousness content" (Jung, quoted in Wilhelm Laiblin 1991, 14) that Jung attributes to it in psychological life. The spectator thus has a solid expectation, a very "strong" hypothesis about the course of action Guido will ultimately take: he will remain faithful to his basic position! In the conflict between his creative drive and reality, Fellini shifts from the Anima stereotype to the child archetype. Jung writes:

"An essential aspect of the child motif is its character of futurity. The child is potential futurity. Thus, the appearance of the child motif in the psychology of an individual is as a rule an anticipation of later development, even if it seems at first to appear like a retrospective figure" (Jung 1990, 120ff.).

In moments of distress and self-doubt, Guido summons up scenes from his childhood, and the film's conclusion, which takes place after Guido's final cancellation of the film project, and thus more or less in his imagination, ends with his friends and acquaintances emerging as figures dressed in white, grasping his hand and, as Fellini puts it, dancing "a happy ring-a-round on a kind of stage. Guido steps together with Luisa into her circle. Slowly the lights go out, leaving Guido alone as a child in the middle of the meadow, one final image of the lost and perhaps regained purity." (Fellini 1974b, 159)

The memory, then, leads into the future, and this takes place through a series of challenges and hardships in which Guido in a way becomes the lost child to whom mythical powers are attributed "that far surpass human measure, representing the strongest and most ineluctable drive, the drive to realize oneself." (Jung 1990, 126) In this sense, Christian Metz (1974, 234) termed *8½* a "powerfully creative meditation on the inability to create." The archetype of the child allows each of these moments in *8½* to be clearly recognized.

I hope that I have been able to show that in this film, governed by a dream logic, a great deal of what might seem confused in fact exhibits certain regularities—even those of narration—that can perhaps be better understood using a model of topics and stereotypes. As I have been able to demonstrate elsewhere (cf. Wuss 1998b), Tarkovsky's *The Mirror* can be analyzed in a similar way.

Comparable problems of form and analysis continue into the present. In this way, many postmodern film compositions are analogous to the aforementioned films from the 1960s and 1970s; here as well, while causal chains within storytelling are increasingly lacking, the films often abound with stereotypes that, together with the topic series, often carry the cinematic narration. Relationships of meaning still result, and these must be searched for, regardless of how hidden they might be and how difficult it is to distill them. Jung (1996, 60) writes: "Our conscious thoughts are often concerned with the future and its possibilities; the unconscious and its dreams are no less concerned with the future. There is even a view spread across the entire world that the main function of dreams is to tell the future."

Representations of dreams in film are thus particularly illuminating for the formation of relations of significance, since they fundamentally refer to possible worlds, the construction of which relies on the value of a view towards future possibilities. In this way, they create various imageries in the viewer's mind; they evoke belief-like imaginings that confirm the viewer's will and desire-like imaginings that develop his hopes to cope with his conflicts.

Chapter VIII: Play Behaviour on the Screen and in the Viewer's Mind

1. Starting Point: Play Behaviour in a Film Sequence

Film is interwoven with play or play behaviour in various ways: the actions on the screen often include moments of play, the creative process of film-making makes use of various kinds of play behaviour, and the experience of watching a film appears to be based on a kind of internalised play behaviour or mental play.

Interestingly, play activities show similarities and even close connections to essential psychological functions and systems such as motivation, cognition, emotion, and imagination. Thus, analysing them may help us to understand some interrelations between these areas, which seems to be very useful.

But what is play? Since no consensus has yet been reached about the general significance and function of play in human life (Sutton-Smith 2000, 218), it makes sense to approach the phenomenon through an inventory of relevant characteristics, as some psychologists have also done, and to attempt to discover functional relationships between them.

Starting from a sequence from Milos Forman's 1975 film *One Flew Over the Cuckoo's Nest*, which includes salient portrayals of play behaviour of the characters, I would like to sketch out such a list. In the following stage I shall then try to show how elements of play modify the experience of film, paying particular attention to connections between play and emotions.

Forman's film tells the story of Randle McMurphy, who is transferred from prison to a mental hospital for observation. He refuses to submit to the authoritarian methods used there, and thus becomes increasingly involved in conflicts with the head nurse. These conflicts escalate when the protagonist tries to get permission for the patients to watch the baseball championships on TV and come to a head when the nurse manages to manipulate the results of a vote among the patients to change the rules, thus turning Randle's victory into a defeat. However, the protagonist finds a way to escape his plight through a strange form of play. In front of the turned-off TV, he simulates being an enthusiastic spectator following the baseball game that the hospital authorities had strictly forbidden him to watch. He is even able to get the other patients to follow his example and take part in this play of make-believe.

The scene shows the protagonist involved in activities in which one can clearly recognize the central characteristics of play behaviour (see fig. 9). Seven of them are listed here in the form of hypotheses:

2. Hypotheses on the Role of Play in Human Life

2.1 "As-if" Behaviour

Play enables a specific kind of "as-if" behaviour by combining practical and fictitious behaviour.

When the characters in *Cuckoo's Nest* simulate viewing the TV broadcast and act like spectators watching a baseball game, they are carrying out a specific form of play behaviour that is clearly different from everyday life. They temporarily step outside the real world and enter a fictive world. This does not just happen in their heads or merely theoretically; instead, they act it out immediately and physically, and thus make it visible and tangible for themselves and others.

Thus, play is based on being able to carry out a double-layered form of behaviour that combines practical and fictional actions and makes them effective simultaneously, not serially (Lotman 1981, 72). This then creates a third term, a sphere with special rules that permit an independent system of actions, captivating the actors within this sphere for a certain period of time.

2.2 Adaptive Capability

Play furthers adaptation, since by inducing more flexible forms of behaviour, it helps people to cope with potential conflicts and to deal with uncertainties.

The sequence shows characters in a difficult conflict situation.

The idea of playing comes to the protagonist just when it becomes clear that he will be imprisoned for a long time. The transition to "as-if" behaviour then seems to be a possible way to escape this situation of constraint through more flexible actions, even if it means turning it into a fiction.

Here we can discern a motive for action that psychologists refer to as the "need for control" of one's own life and that is rightly considered to be a "primary motive for human behaviour" (Oesterreich 1981, 223; Dörner et. al. 1983, 63). In order to survive, one cannot lose control over one's situation; one must attempt to cope with circumstances. For Randle and the other patients, who are at that time completely controlled by the institution, play appears to be an almost compulsory reaction to a basic situation of uncertainty that becomes even more virulent in the course of increasing conflicts and is diametrically opposed to the human "drive for certainty" (Dörner 1999, 352). The ability to play proves to be an adaptive capability (Sutton-Smith 1978); Peter Ohler (2000, 39) writes: "Play is adaptive since it represents a system that makes variability possible in a systematic way."

The ability to develop variants of behaviour, which play involves, is not only useful in immediate situations, but also represents both phylogenetically and ontogenetically an evolutionary advantage for individuals and species that possess the ability to play (Ohler 2000, 135).

In the course of long-term processes, play developed into an "adaptive emergent system of acting" (Ohler 2000, 48), in which the functional mechanism of behavioural flexibility was detached from the original conflict motivation and became independent, so that it no longer relies on conflicts as a starting point. Play thus appears to be an intrinsically motivated and non-instrumental form of acting.

2.3 Change of Emotions

Play behaviour changes emotional structures.

In the film scene, the emotions of the protagonist and the other patients change during the course of their play behaviour. Their dejection turns into a mood of euphoric happiness.

This shift from negative to positive feelings can perhaps be explained in that both emotions and play have their origins in adaptive behaviour. This means that positive emotions result when subjects view a situation as possible to cope with (Lazarus 1991, 112) and see themselves as in control (Oesterreich 1981), or—to use another term—feel themselves to be in a state of action readiness. The concept of "action readiness change" is to be found in the theories of emotions developed by Nico Frijda (1986, 474) and Ed Tan, who writes: "An emotion may be defined as a change in action readiness as a result of the subject's appraisal of the situation or event" (1996, 46).

A change in emotions depends on a gain or loss of "action readiness." Basically negative moods can be turned into positive ones and vice versa.

When processes of play help determine situations in life, they change the subject's degree and ability of control, thus also changing the quality and strength of emotions. This means that play can channel emotions.

2.4 Functional Pleasure

Play creates functional pleasure and thus has hedonistic value.

In the film scene, the characters become increasingly "high" as they enter into play and carry on with it, and by the end of the scene they are completely wild. It was not without reason that Karl Bühler called play "an activity that is endowed with functional pleasure and that is sustained because of or directly by this functional pleasure" (Bühler 1929, 457).

This concerns the organized use of freedom, and its dynamics are described by the psychological theory of activation (Berlyne 1960, Hutt 1980) in terms of achieving a moderate level of activation, which ensures optimal information processing in the central nervous system. *Hedone*, the sensation of pleasure, is achieved in this way, and it appears to be the central motivation for play, which creates a specific drive to play.

This sensation of pleasure and the motives connected to it can have effects at various levels. These comprise an unconscious sensory level of a "play instinct" as well as a level where surplus energy works back on mental processes, including aesthetic and ethical impulses. Schiller (1937, 233) wrote: "Man only plays where he is human in the full meaning of the word, and he is only fully human where he plays."

2.5 Generation of Variables
By generating variants of behaviour, play makes it easier to create new ideas.

At first, the film protagonists do something that one could certainly describe as just nonsense. But in the course of this nonsense, the players suddenly discover a new possibility of acting, and one that they find more favourable and preferable to their normal situation. Along the way, notions arise that do not just represent the given circumstances, but rather as counterfactual representations of desires divergent from them.

Differing from imageries that never leave the level of mental acts, in play situations these "ghosts in the mind's machine" (Kosslyn 1983) take on external physical appearance in the form of practical, experimental acts of trial and error. In this way, ideas are not just created and thought through, but also practically tested in real life. By generating and testing variables of behaviour, play makes it possible for ideas and the imagination to find a way into the practice of the life-world.

While not an immediate form of knowledge, play is connected to rational behaviour. Following Johan Huizinga (1938), who coined the term 'homo ludens', Georg Klaus wrote: "As *homo ludens*, humans play in that, in the form of play, they anticipate future situations through inner models of the exterior world, i.e., they use the models to play through possible forms of confrontation with the environment. The activity of *homo ludens* is in so much a form of foresight" (1968, 9). In our lives, this means that *homo ludens* supports the *homo sapiens* and the *homo faber* in us, by playing through possible alternative actions. In this way, our schematic experience is made more flexible and thus adapted to new circumstances, corresponding to a constantly changing world. For this reason, play is a very sensible and useful element in human life. These forms of psychic activity begin in early childhood, permeate the whole of culture, and take on an important role in imagination and thinking processes, inspiring fantasy. "It is no coincidence that we are both the most playful and the most intelligent of animals" (Taylor 1984, 273).

The scene of play in the film shows the connection between play and imagination particularly clearly, since it resembles children's so-called early pretence play, that is, the phase in which children at about age one and a half replace certain things with others to simulate using imagined objects, for example when they telephone with a banana. In this phase, humans acquire the ability to develop "detached representations" (Gärdenfors 1995), that is, mental representations that are separate from immediate perception and that take on aims of their own. This occurs as part of a process in which the various psychological functions are hardly differentiated from one another. Vygotsky noted, "When a child desires, it also acts, in thinking it acts. Interior and exterior actions cannot be separated from one another" (1980, 437).

The main characters in *One Flew Over the Cuckoo's Nest* may not be children, but they, too, separate their imagined ideas from the perception of their real misery, and they do this in a naive, childlike, and innocent way. That makes them at once believable and emotionally touching.

2.6 Regularities

Play tends to be governed by rules and because of its repeatability becomes established as a cultural subsystem with a social function.

Even if this film scene does not show a form of play with rules, but rather the transition from early try-out play to pretence play, it does reveal a number of forms of inner organization that determine the "as-if" behaviour for a certain time and space and that the group can adopt, for instance in rhythmic repetitions of actions. Of course, the play action only goes on for a limited time; the euphoric scene is followed by a cut to a phase of calmness or even depression.

In relation to time and place, play is a limited phenomenon, within which a certain order is maintained, which limits the possibilities of making use of freedom. In general, play is shaped by principles of order and it is because it is rule-driven that it can be reproduced. In itself, it exhibits many moments of repetition, just as it invites imitation and repetition. Because play follows rules, it comes to be standardized and takes on symbolic value within a cultural process of learning, thus turning into a ritual that, as a relatively stable part of human culture, can take on a special function that then can be called up by the ritual of play or game as its elaborate form.

Regarding the film sequence, functional pleasure becomes inter-subjective in the creation of a group identity among the players and thus, as the scene rapidly makes evident, takes on a social function.

It is interesting to see that the players, despite their individual and idiosyncratic personalities, all submit to the rules without protest. Huizinga pointed out: "Paul Valéry once casually said, and it is an exceptionally far-going thought: 'No scepticism is possible in regard to the rules of a play.' [...] A player who disobeys the rules or ignores them is a spoil-sport. [...] He robs the play of its illusion, the inlusio, literally: the entering into play—a meaningful word! Therefore he has to be destroyed, since he threatens the very existence of the community of players" (1938, 18ff.).

2.7 Possible Worlds

Play leads to the construction of possible worlds, which enable people to fundamentally re-evaluate reality.

When the characters behave in a playful manner, it is as though everything were transformed at this specific place for a certain period; the usual order of life is suspended, the usual models of how the world works are temporarily disabled. Only the game and its rules are in effect. This leads to the construction of possible worlds, to use a term developed in modal logic that has since been applied to works of art (Eco 1990, Ronen 1994).

This involves counterfactuals that have a certain credibility, which permit and facilitate a comparison with reality (Doležel 1989). In this case, a world without prohibitions and repression temporarily comes into being for the protagonists, a different kind of life, which cannot entirely be revoked in their future actions.

Possible worlds are an incarnation of our capacity to play. They can be created through play or even, it seems, only through play. They produce complex cultural entities, systems that develop a power of their own because they—although they are not complete copies of reality—address all the important human psychological functions and thus draft an alternative or opposite to real life. This, then, makes it possible to re-evaluate the given at all these levels and thus fundamentally alter one's relation to existing reality.

This list of general characteristics of play behaviour shows that play is located at the intersection of systems of motivation, cognition, emotion, and imagination. As a phenomenon situated at the threshold of such factors, it takes on the role of mediator by channelling and facilitating relationships among them.

3. Play in the Regulatory Process of Art

Cinema, like art and mass culture in general, creates such possible worlds *par excellence*, which is why theory has found the notion of play to be useful in explaining the effects of the medium and especially its diegesis (cf. Anderson 1998, 113ff.). In fact, film—like other forms of art—makes use of structures of play in the form of play-models with a semiotic function (cf. Lotman 1981). These structures are variables of the stimuli, including conflict situations, with which humans are confronted in their real life.

Hans and Shulamith Kreitler (1972, 19) have formulated this idea in the following way: "It is our contention that a *major motivation for art is tensions which exist in the spectator of art prior to his exposure to the work of art. The work of art mediates the relief of these preexisting tensions by generating new tensions which are specific.*" (emphasis in original)

This leads to the hypothesis that the experience of art (and of film, as well) serves as a mechanism of psychic regulation. Therefore, the experience of watching a film could be roughly described as a regulatory function of artistic or cultural systems of signs.

This, too, is achieved through play, but through a form of play that is based on the internalisation of the functions described above and that becomes effective as internalised or mental play. It is connected to the entire imaginative world of the spectator and is certainly very closely linked to the activities of fantasy. It expands and modifies the spectator's ways of dealing with real tensions with which he or she is confronted in real life. How exactly this process occurs remains a mystery, but it can perhaps be helpful to look at some connections among individual effects during the reception process.

In the experience of art, a specific "play effect" comes into being, which Lotman describes: "The mechanism of play effects is not based on the rigid and simultaneous co-existence of different meanings, but rather on the ever-present consciousness that other meanings could be possible than those one has realized. Thus, the playful effect comes into being in that the various meanings of an element do not exist rigidly alongside each other, but rather 'oscillate'" (1981, 82).

Variants of this oscillation can be found in many aspects of the experience of viewing a film, but here I can only briefly mention those that are relevant to conflict management, play behaviour, and the spectators' emotions.

4. Hypotheses Regarding Play Behaviour in the Process of Experiencing a Film

By modifying the list of theses about play behaviour in general, we can come to the following hypotheses with regard to play behaviour as a form of aesthetic experience:

4.1 "As-if" Behaviour and Aesthetic Reaction

In the cinema, the "as-if" behaviour of play becomes the standard form of aesthetic reaction.

While watching a film, the viewers are involved in play behaviour insofar as the darkness of the theatre always represents a form of stepping out of their own practical life and entering into another sphere of experience or a possible world. As film viewers, we are generally involved in a "game of make-believe" (Pavel 1986, 55), which we understand as "involvement" or "aesthetic film experience."

The play effects of art undergo a further modification because the effects of audio-visual media are grounded in the specific oscillation of meanings given by various stimuli from reality and from the cinematic fiction.

4.2 Dealing with Conflicts

Moments of play in films help in dealing cognitively with situations of conflict and uncertainty.

Film's proximity to dramatic art means that its plots are based on locating the characters within situations of conflict, which themselves often correspond to tensions in the audience's life. Play behaviour in the process of reception creates an "as-if" situation in the viewers' minds, which then trains and develops their cognition and imagination, in order to enable them to manage conflicts more successfully in their own lives.

Although the spectator is never in the same situation as the characters in the films, the desire for control over the situations shown remains active as a primary motivation in reception, too. Even the playful versions of life, which are part of the possible worlds of works of art, require people to have a certain degree of control. To analyse the experience of films, however, it is important that the concept of control used here must permit an important differentiation, namely that between "active" and "passive" control. Active control means being practically able to change the situation to one's benefit. In films, this is possible for the characters, but not for the viewers, who have no immediate influence on the action. However, the viewers can exert passive control over the situation, in that they are in command of it cognitively. That is, they can foresee the possible course of future events and thus anticipate decisions to be made about a conflict in the plot.

From a cognitive perspective, then, efforts at passive control take the form of a problem-solving process that engages the viewers, who are always interested in knowing how things will go on or end. The film experience thus involves both decisions about actions on screen and their predictability for the audience. A playful interchange seems to go on between these two areas, by which meanings oscillate on both levels.

The film plot and its specific narrative structure are built up through conflict situations and their developments. The decision-making process in the colliding actions of the characters leads to the turning-points of the story, the so-called plot points, which mark the individual stages and partial goals in the course of problem-solving as a cognitive process that also shows the spectators step-by-step how and in what way the conflicts will be solved (Wuss 2005; 2006).

In this way, the plot in *Cuckoo's Nest* repeatedly creates new possibilities and obstacles for the protagonist to come to grips with his direct opponents. Furthermore, the behaviour of the other patients in relation to Randle's conflicts with the nurse and the authoritarian power structures in general also plays an important role. Still, up until the final scenes, the viewers find it very difficult to anticipate how the story will end. This is a form of mental training for the audience, teaching them how to deal with conflicts in reality and developing their potential for adaptability.

4.3 Emotive Functions

Films create, modify, and regulate emotions in the spectators by generating fictional events in play.

4.3.1   Narration

The moments of conflict in the film plot not only provide starting points for the development of the chain of events, thus structuring the narration, but also a source and motivation for the affective stimulation of the viewers and thus a starting point for the inducement of emotions (Wuss 2005). The intensification of emotional stimulation is clearly evident in the cinema, particularly at the plot points in a film.

The paradox of cinematic emotions can be explained through the functional connection between stimuli that are related to conflicts and the viewer's interest in passive control of the situation on the screen, which require them to anticipate future events. As spectators we are emotionally involved in conflicts that are not our own and that we know do not even exist in reality. However, we simply try to retain control competence, just as we have to do in real life in order to retain action readiness. This situation leads to affective stimulation and various kinds and intensities of emotions.

Control competence can be altered in various ways through the form or the fictional course of film plots. However, the way these stories relate to the conflicts and tensions in the audience's real life-world is no less important. Real conflicts can have a stimulating or a paralysing effect on the viewers and thus influence the basic quality of their cinematic experience as well. Because it takes the form of playing with variations on reality, and thus causes fields of meaning to oscillate, the process of aesthetic reception can fulfil a function of psychological regulation.

4.3.2   Empathy

Emotional effects on viewers are achieved chiefly through empathy with characters. Empathy is connected to a kind of internalised role-playing. The viewer achieves a "feeling-as-if" comprehension of characters in order to imaginarily understand their conflicts and how they try to solve their problems. Empathy with fictional characters is thus linked both to cognitive processes and to the adoption of affects and emotions in regard to unsolved conflicts that the characters face. The experience of a character trying to solve a problem puts us as viewers in a doubly uncertain position. On the one hand, we take on the imagined position or role of the character and search with him or her for a solution in the sense of active control. On the other hand, we ourselves are searching for passive or cognitive control of the situation, and we are unsettled if we cannot foresee the future course of events. Empathy is most likely also an oscillating effect that constantly mediates among different areas of meaning and thereby shifts among modes of "feeling with," "feeling for," and "feeling as-if."

There appears to be a fundamental form of behaviour in conflict situations, which we always try to cope using and which forces us to attempt to improve our cognitive ability to foresee what might happen, and this behaviour brings us close to all the characters as actants in the plot. The prerequisite is a play-related "as-if" situation that allows a certain distance and a moral evaluation, thus permitting antipathy as well as empathy with the characters.

4.3.3   Genre

One important approach to emotion in cinema involves the functional analysis of genres, since their effects are often related to strong, but differing emotions. Genres can be described in terms of standardised or stereotypical structures and stimuli linked to relatively invariable strategies of effects (Wuss 1993, 311ff.; 2002). That is, they build groups that correspond to certain rules of form and function. However, it is also useful to probe behind these rules to find the laws that govern how specific types of possible worlds are constructed, laws that embody forms of play behaviour. In fact, filmmakers deal with genre rules as though they were the rules of a game. They use them to enter an artificial world that is relatively stable because it rests on certain standardised forms and relations of emotional effects; this causes certain emotional tendencies to gain an a priori dominance.

Through an ensemble of well-known forms, genres can almost immediately elicit a corresponding emotional reaction in the viewers, as soon as they recognize the genre elements in the film they are watching. In this way genres also lead to a relatively stable emotional climate, characterized for example by tonic emotions.

The rules of a genre, then, bring the viewers ad hoc to evaluate the situations that are shown in certain ways. Furthermore, they make it easier to predict possible solutions for particular conflicts, such as the protagonist's triumph in drama or the catastrophe in tragedy. Predictability of plot developments also has to do with the viewer's passive control. And if a catastrophe is easy to foresee, since it conforms to genre rules, then this may help explain why the audience can react to a tragedy's unhappy ending with positive emotions (Wuss 1993, 337ff.; 2005; 2006).

In the case of Forman's film it is particularly interesting that the genre tends toward a hybridity, in which elements of the prison escape drama are combined with those of the parable and the tragedy. This is particularly apparent in the ending of the film, which tries to find an appropriate solution for all these patterns and thus counterbalances Randle's death with the successful escape of the chief, who carries on the protagonist's intentions. This gives the film an emotional turn that had already been prepared in the play scene described above.

4.4 Functional Pleasure and Hedonistic Function

Functional pleasure induced by play becomes an integrative constituent of the film spectator's aesthetic response.

Even though we are not discussing the general aesthetic factors that are responsible for art's hedonistic function and film's specific uplifting effects, play behaviour in the reception process does at least partially point to how functional pleasure can arise if the spectator shares a character's positive emotions. If one accepts the assumption that humans generally gain positive feelings from managing situations in their lives, then this must apply even more to play situations in films, when the viewers are able to experience the triumphs of characters they identify with.

A motor component also makes up part of the continuation of the desire-like imaginings of the characters in the consciousness of the viewer. It becomes possible to experience not just *that*, but also *how* and with what dynamics the characters' negative emotions turn around. The communicable motor impulse to overcome their misery is transferred from the screen to the audience, both through motor mimicry and through so-called co-emotions (Scherer 1998, 280). These ensure that the viewers—like the characters—not only momentarily grasp the situation as it is, but also see it as it could or should be.

The play situation mentioned in *Cuckoo's Nest* brings a short triumph, but no real change in the situation. Still, it is more than a pyrrhic victory. The patient's new playful attitude is extremely alarming for the head nurse, since this kind of thing could put the existing power relations in question. In fact, Randle McMurphey soon joyfully experiments with the situation when he takes the inmates on a fishing trip on the open sea. The mere announcement of this adventure makes even the most timid patients suddenly self-assured enough to play the role of doctors, and even to do this believably.

Such kinds of scene show that the characters are suddenly able to cope with their difficult situations, thus giving the on-screen action a playful quality of functional pleasure that invokes an irresistible uplifting feeling in the audience.

What the protagonists do seems to exert a magical effect on the spectators.

As mentioned before, the protagonist's triumph or a happy ending on the screen are not necessary preconditions for the spectator's positive emotions—no more than for his feeling of functional pleasure; the problem is more complicated.

4.5 Innovative Function

Through elements of play, the experience of a film can potentially enable new ideas about the world and thus often leads the viewer to develop new intentions.

As the "as-if" behaviour of play leads the viewers to work through conflicts that the film takes from real life, it brings them to confront their own ideas and images of the world with the conflicts shown more or less realistically on the screen. They must then question their own patterns of thinking and behaving, come up with new ideas, and play these out in fantasy. In this way, they may develop new variations of acting or even new models of the world.

In the film sequence, a conflict leads to a form of play that simulates a new variation of behaving in life. This form of play resembles the symbolic play of early childhood, which is a predecessor of cognitive experimental behaviour. During the experience of viewing the film, this is intensified, since not only the protagonist, but also the viewer, has developed or comes to develop ideas of a better world, a world without the kind of conflict shown in the film. Desire-like imaginings overlap at both levels. Play thus again generates counterfactual variables. These have similar consequences for the transformation of emotions, the prediction of the probability of possible solutions, and the influence of decision-making processes that psychology has discovered in regard to counterfactual thinking (Roese / Olson 2003, 859ff.; Mandel 2005). A conditional world is brought into being alongside the familiar world, and it may well include ideas about the possible future. Along with images of new models of reality and new plans for life, new attitudes and motivations for action in relation to real-world conflicts may develop in the viewer's mind, including the will to change things or to act socially. It is no coincidence that the theorem of control I have drawn upon here was originally developed in research on helplessness (Seligman 1975), and in particular in regard to learned social helplessness, which is exactly what Forman's film tries to combat.

Even if the heroes of *Cuckoo's Nest* are not able to articulate a concept of a different social world, their—and our—rejection of the given one is shaped through the pleasurable action of play and the way it tries out different behaviour. The play shown on screen reveals the intentions of the protagonists through their practical actions.

4.6 Rules of the Artistic Form

Film experience makes use of the rules of the artistic form and their breaching.

Like all kinds of communication the aesthetic experience of the cinema is only possible in compliance with numerous principles and rules. Because of their strictness sometimes these principles remind one of rules of a game. However, according to Lotman: "Art is not play" (1981, 83). Despite many similarities between play and art, there are considerable differences between the two phenomena. According to Lotman, play is important for the acquisition of a human proficiency by providing behavioural training in a fictive situation, where the aim of the playing action is the observance of rules. The aim of art should be, however, the acquiring of new insights about the world expressed in a language of conditional rules (1981, 84). Insofar as aesthetic communication is trying to lead the spectator to new insights regarding the world it creates a contradictory situation: "The text should be regular and irregular, predictable and unpredictable" (Lotman 1977, 76). The communication of the cinema is based on stimulus patterns that must deal creatively with the dialectic tension between the expected and the unexpected, provide for adherence to rules and, at the same time, for a permanent break with them as well.

The dramaturgy and visual style of Forman's film takes into account diverse conventions of the Hollywood cinema of that time, but also breaks them. Thus, for instance, having cast some true inmates of an psychatric asylum, Forman could integrate very innovative camera observations of their authentic behaviour in his film.

At the time, another unexpected peculiarity of the film was its tendency to a genre-hybridisation by using in a parallel fashion the genre structures and the modes of operation of the prison-escape drama, the tragicomedy and the parable and also by its willingness to temporarily break their specific "rules of the game." Genre-hybridisation, which became possible in the historic context of *New Hollywood*, led to the concept of the open artwork. Following such a concept, Forman gave the film an ending which actually comprises three different final tendencies. The first shows the physical catastrophe of its protagonist Randle, the second the successful escape of the "Chief" and the triumph of Randle's ideas, and this lucky escape is met by the last, an aggressive laughter of one of the inmates, a particularly primitive one. Each of these endings is contrasted with the others and thus the ambiguity of the ending demands a changing assessment of the whole story from the viewer—for Hollywood cinema an uncommon thing until this point.

4.7 Play-Effect and Genre

In experiencing the possible worlds of the cinema, a play-effect is realised which enables the spectator to deal more flexibly with the oscillating significance both of reality and of the imageries; film genres thus differentiate and stabilise this field of play-effects.

The possible worlds of the cinema are constructed in such a way that they always—even in their highly fictionalized and fantastic versions—are comparable and by this, compatible with the spectators' life world. The viewer is invited to use the experience of one world for the understanding of the other, i.e. to a learning of meaning. According to Vygotsky (1980, 460) play is the dynamization of a movement in the field of meanings. Just as play helps the player to find a flexible attitude to a change of meaning, art mediates in semantic border-crossing and thus encourages the dealing with polysemy. Therefore, as Lotman (1981, 79) points out, within the framework of art "the principle of play becomes the basis of semantic organisation", because it provides for the oscillation of the different semantic tendencies that are established in the artwork's structure. In this way, art educates the recipients in creative and flexible dealing with the meaning offers that come from the real world as well as from the world of fantasy. Its oscillation of meanings helps with the evaluation of tendencies from both directions with regard to their productivity and suitability for the present and for the future and to confirm or throw into question the world-models of a society and thereby to develop new and progressive ones.

The development of the arts has led to a differentiation and standardization of their form and function. The possible worlds of the cinema, for instance, are organised in a differentiated morphological system of modes, genres and styles. In the practice of film, the possible worlds of the various genres form the most conspicuous field of different play-effects. Indeed, the filmmaker uses the rules of genres like the rules of a game. Genre theories and taxonomies sketch entire maps of these embodiments of play-effects.

5. Film Sequences and Stories Based on Play Behaviour

Insofar as play behaviour is a part of human life, the history of film includes numerous sequences or entire film stories which are based on various kinds of real or mental play that often give to the events on the screen a specific touch of "as-if".

In many cases, the playing on the screen is based on the represented life processes, which are a natural part of human behaviour; in many others it is based on a ritual activity, for instance the carnival, or dancing or singing together, or also on a kind of imagery, fantasy or dream. But mainly it is involved with the possible world of a genre, or, conversely, it has overwhelmed and integrated these fictional worlds. Sometimes, however, the activities of play change successively from one of the levels to another, particularly in more contemporary cinema.

Thus, as a pendant to the described sequence in Forman's film, where a serious conflict situation develops into a simulation of a common action and a theatre-like performance, there is a scene in Jim Jarmusch's *Down by Law* (1986) which shows how three underdogs from New Orleans, who were imprisoned more or less while innocent, become more and more depressive. While playing cards, however, one of the cell-inmates, the Italian Roberto, who is always keen on learning English idioms, gets very excited about a silly rhyming couplet: "I scream, you scream, we all scream—for ice-cream!" Strangely enough, Roberto succeeds in animating the two others to say the rhyme together, and soon they yell louder and louder until all the inmates of the jail are roused to enthusiasm.

Similarly to the patients in the aforementioned film, the prisoners get swept along by the outsider's improvised play and indulge in their desire-like imaginings about a happy life in freedom. And although their happiness will soon revert to their former depression, this temporary "free acting" of play helps them to overcome their dilemma; their attempt to escape from jail succeeds and initiates in the viewers' mind a sensation of action readiness as well. In other words, "overcoming conflicts by play" seems to be a paradigm for numerous artistic processes (see fig. 10).

For this reason, some film stories systematically use a kind of play behaviour to structure their action tendency.

In the next chapter I will describe in more detail how Roberto Benigni's *Life Is Beautiful* (*La vita è bella*, 1997) constructs its story in this manner. The film's hero, an Italian Jew, who together with his little son is being held in a Nazi concentration camp, tells the boy that this activity is only a game that will afford those players who play by the rules the chance to win. Indeed, thanks to his playful efforts the child is able to overcome all the dangers and in the end survive the camp's hell.

The protagonists of Wong Kar-wai's *In the Mood For Love* (*Fa yeung nin wa*, 2000) are able to cope with their humiliating situation mainly through a kind of analytic play where they carefully try to reconstruct how their partners could have become unfaithful to them. Their rehearsals and the acting-out of their spouses' actions also leads them to an understanding of their own attitudes and moral positions and gives them a little play therapy.

There are several very different modes of play which they make use of. When Chow and Li-Zhen realise for the first time that they are both victims of their partners' infidelity, they cover up their shock. Then they attempt to reconstruct the first steps in the affair through improvised scenes which are very hurtful for the woman. Later, during a dinner, they commit themselves to a role play where they adopt their partners' fondness for certain dishes—presumably in order to better understand their aims. But sometimes they even rehearse the upcoming meeting with the expected spouses, and do this much like experienced actors at a theatre rehearsal. Even their own leave-taking is rehearsed—in the hope of overcoming the conflict through play.

Interestingly, the play on the screen sometimes follows the principle of "going through" the situations of life in order to test their potential for further development in certain directions, mainly such those of a dubious nature. The French cinema at the turn of the 1970s, for instance, produced works like Marco Ferreri's *Dillinger Is Dead* (*Dillinger è morto*, 1969) or Claude Faraldo's *Themroc* (1973), exploring how far one can practically get with extreme behaviour. They are playing a principle to excess. Well-known in this group is Ferreri's *The Big Feast* (*La grande bouffe*, 1973) where a group of older middle-class men test a central aim of the pleasure society and surrender themselves to gluttony and sensual pleasure, and thereby successfully arrive at death. The story of Bernardo Bertolucci's *Last Tango in Paris* (*Ultimo tango a Parigi*, 1972) likewise tests the idea of a sexual relationship which seeks total isolation from the social environment and all other human interests—also with a deadly outcome.

Play on the screen often has a more obvious function to render strange a phenomenon of life, and this sometimes leads to a new quality in the viewers' emotions. Alain Resnais' *On connaît la chanson* (1997) begins with a scene where the commander of the Nazi Army in Paris receives by phone Hitler's order to destroy the French capital before it is invaded by the troops of the allied forces. But, having heard this disgraceful order, the German general suddenly starts to sing into the receiver a famous French chanson about Paris. Later, the astonished spectator finds out that the scene only illustrates the account of a modern-day female tour guide who is informing a group of tourists about this mythical historic event. Nevertheless, he is able to experience that the same woman and other inhabitants of present-day Paris sometimes react to everyday conflict situations by singing a *chanson*. With this, the events on the screen change their character, and the spectators' emotions change as well.

A similar effect can be found in Lars von Trier's *Dancer in the Dark* (2000). This melodramatic story, about a young mother from the working class, who is not only suffering from the progression of her own blindness but also from the threatened illness of her son and the greed for money of an evil neighbour, is repeatedly interrupted by inserts showing groups of dancing and singing people moving in the style of the early American musical. These sequences have a certain natural basis insofar as the protagonist is a member of an amateur theatre, but the musical inserts are not fully identical with the amateurs' rehearsals. In incorporating the genre tendency of the musical, on the one hand, the scenes make strange the destiny of the innocent woman, who is facing the death penalty, and on the other hand, they help to change the viewers' feelings by inviting them into a possible world which seems more friendly and easier to cope with than the real one.

The return to the possible worlds of the "light genres" seems to be the most striking device in using play behaviour on the screen. Often the characters' playful activities appear to get support from a ritual that has its roots in the culture of a society. Famous works, such as Federico Fellini's *8½* (1963), Michelangelo Antonioni's *Blow Up* (1966) or Bernardo Bertolucci's *1900* (*Novecento*, 1976), take this play-support from the cultural traditions of the carnival, which has led, in countries dominated by Catholicism, to a specific tendency in the arts called "carnivalisation". Bakhtin (1969, 47-60) has shown that the integration of the carnival's "rules of the game" into literature created an entire stock of artistic devices.

I have elsewhere (Wuss 1986) shown in detail that the three films mentioned not only represent rituals of the carnival in several relevant scenes but also use a central approach of the carnival for their final part: the principle of a temporary reversal of the existing order of the world, which offers hope for its change. The final sequences of the films celebrate such a feeling and thinking in the protagonists' life and—at the same time—provoke other emotions and a new world view from the spectator.

Typical for play tendencies in postmodern storytelling is the practice of using the generation of variables in a pure way, i.e. the repetition of similar courses of events. Films like Wong Kar-wai's *Chungking Express* (*Chung Hing sam lam*, 1994) or David Lynch's *Lost Highway* (1997) link together two separate events without causal connections, but which are nevertheless akin because of the striking analogies in their protagonists' behavioural patterns. An extreme version of the pure generating of variables is offered in Tom Tykwer's *Run, Lola, Run* (*Lola rennt*, 1998) which repeats an analogous action three times as if there were no real actions of the heroes at all, but only different strategies of a computer game. Instead of the rules of a genre or a cultural ritual, the new trends of the computer age should here give support to the viewers' mental play.

Chapter IX: Narration and Genre

1. Film Genre as Aesthetic Experience and Cultural Instance

Cinematic narration takes place within a communicative framework that always demands that the individual work formulates an original aesthetic message; but at the same time, every work is strongly shaped by collective forms of experience that the filmmakers and the audience have gained through previous storytelling. Cinema as a cultural form preserves these common experiential values. It has standardized and conventionalized them, meaning that it has created stable sets of forms that have become norms for filmmaking as well as crystallizing the audience's expectations, which again work as a stabilizing factor in production. This means that we experience a particular film not only as a unique phenomenon, but also within the framework of a particular genre whose characteristics apply to a whole group of works. This can mean that an individual film is subject to, at times, quite rigorous genre-specific modifications of forms and effects. Filmmakers are aware that the choice of a genre not only shapes the viewer's attitude toward the events that are shown, but also changes the aesthetic criteria that he or she applies to the film as a whole and to all its parts. A plot development that might work perfectly in a social drama can be completely out of place in a comedy or a melodrama—and vice versa.

The traditional arts have always involved a similar kind of differentiation into subsystems and this has had comparable consequences. However, since the cinema arose in the epoch of mass culture and has the character of a genuine commodity, genres have taken on quite different characteristics within it. They not only served to stabilize the aesthetic experience of storytelling, but were also oriented from the start to commercial considerations. Thus their classifications, always linked to audience expectations, helped the audience choose among the media products on offer, and they helped producers to manage the market efficiently by systematizing the kinds of audience demand and anticipations they would encounter. In contrast to the older arts, the development of film genres did not take place in a long-term historical process of evolution of increasingly subtle aesthetic distinctions. Instead, genres developed ad hoc from the audience expectations already formed within existing mass culture, which were immediately applied to the cinema. Genres has already existed as cultural norms when the movies began, and these norms shaped the cinema, strongly influencing its development. They defined a particular type of attraction and responded to already existing expectations in regard to the repertoire of mass culture. For example, the earliest films had to fit as smoothly as possible into the typical program of numbers in the vaudeville theaters, adding particular kinds of sensations at predetermined places in the show, bringing in comedy, exoticism, eroticism, etc.

The economic aspects of genres played a role prior to film distribution, since even early film productions often made use of particular genre elements because they helped reduce the cost of sets, locations, costumes, and actors. The standardization of film forms went hand in hand with the economics of cinema—each affected the other and together they formed an economically-based cultural instance. The explicitly genre-based mode of production in leading film-producing countries—for example the studio system in Hollywood—led to an increasingly perfect development in this direction.

2. Theoretical Problems in Dealing with Film Genres

Although genre plays a powerful role as a cultural instance in media practice, theoretical approaches to it have remained difficult. Much of our knowledge and definitions are incomplete or controversial. There have been attempts to set devise morphological systems that define particular characteristics of genres as well as other artistic forms (cf. Kagan 1972). This does not automatically lead to a usable basis for film analysis. And though the relevant literature has come up with many meaningful and colorful descriptions of individual genres, it is still difficult to find a general definition of genre, and that has also rarely been attempted.

Media practitioners may not miss it, but this lack makes interdisciplinary research on genres and their effects more difficult. Such research requires, for example, cooperation with psychology, since without appropriate theoretical concepts it is impossible to form hypotheses about connections between genre-related film structures and their psychological effects.

The easiest analytic approach to the phenomenon of genre seems to me to be that of using the everyday understanding of the kind of commercial films known as "genre movies." Thomas and Vivian Sobchak (1987, 223) write: "What, precisely is a genre film? It is a film which belongs to a particular group of films that are extremely similar in their subject matter, thematic concerns, characterizations, plot formulas, and visual settings." And Barry Keith Grant (1993, xi) introduces his genre reader with these words: "Stated simply, genre movies are those commercial feature films which, through repetition and variation, tell familiar stories with familiar characters in familiar situations. They also encourage expectations and experience similar to those of similar films we have already seen." Such definitions generally rely on several forms of invariants, namely on invariant formal characteristics (i.e. conventionalized forms), which lead to invariant moments of effects in reception (standardized effects) and create a complex interrelation between form and psychological effects, which remain relatively stable over a long period, i.e. are temporally invariant, and which apply to a whole group of films, thus forming intertextual invariants.

Although these relations of invariance certainly form a necessary condition for the existence and function of genres, they are not adequate to clearly define them, since there are various other morphological systems of cinema, such as sub-groups or modes and stylistic movements, which also form stable systems of expectation with regard to the form and effects of individual works. Nonetheless, invariance does represent a sensible starting point for a general understanding of genres, since it refers to two relatively unchanging phenomena that have tangible consequences for cultural processes. Thus it is not without reason that Mikhail Bakhtin (1972, 179) refers to literary genres as "representations of creative memory" of literary development. Each genre exists within a fixed and relatively inflexible skeleton and has a canon that exercises real historical power on the further development of the art (cf. Bakhtin 1975, 449). In the area of film, genre norms also influence the working concepts of filmmakers, and thus shape film production as well as the expectations and the selective interests of the audience, which again contribute to solidifying the filmmakers' formal concepts for future productions.

The criterion of invariance or stability must not, however, be simplified or thought about in a mechanical way. Neither can the temporal stability of genres be seen as absolute, nor do the various characteristics of forms and effects apply equally to individual works. As far as the stability of genres goes, which is seen for instance in unchanging formal qualities and strategies of effects, practical experience shows that genres change over the course of time and can transform themselves according to various parameters. Anyone who has examined differentiated descriptions of the evolution of the Western (cf. Bazin [1955] 1994; Wright 1975) or developments in melodramas (cf. Neale 1993; 2000) and film musicals (Altman 1986) will undoubtedly recognize how large the structural transformations during the development of individual genres can be.

As Tynianov ([1925 and 1927] 1982, 9, 37ff.) mentioned with regard to literary genres, they do not exist for eternity, but rather changes in their characteristics become evident during their evolution, and the lines of development may sometimes break. Some film genres retain their structure and function only over the course of a few decades before they fall apart, change into new forms, or simply disappear. This characteristic is something they share with other cultural phenomena, and even with biological organisms, and it makes sense to look at these processes of development and decline—which take place despite occasional phases of astonishing stability—with reference to models taken from system theory, for example in terms of the kinds of understanding of cybernetic self-organization or autopoiesis (Varela 1987; Maturana 1987) that biologists have developed. Stephen Heath (1981, 16) aptly called genres "instances of balance".

Analogies to what economists have named ergodic processes and systems (O. Lange 1969, 62ff.) also seem fitting. These correspond to a particular law of development for a certain time period, meaning that they are resistant to disturbances from inside and outside. Before and after this period, however, they are open to disruptions to varying degrees and are correspondingly unstable, even to the point of breaking up. A modern understanding of genres must consider these dynamics, criticism concerning genres would otherwise be open to the danger of failure by being unable to resolve a principal dualism between a theoretical and a historical concept (cf. Todorov 1990, 17), as has correctly been criticized (cf. Schweinitz 1994, 113; 2006, 85ff.).

In order to understand genres it is also important to view them—like other morphological systems of art—in terms of systems of probability. At the level of describing their appearance, which always includes very complex and diverse relationships among the elements, this means that their various characteristics are never all to be found in an individual work or in a unified way. Film studies have for the most part still not been able to find out how to analyze such systems systematically. In view of such indeterminacies, Bordwell (1989a, 110) correctly speaks of genres as "fuzzy," i.e. diffuse, categories, which are defined neither by necessary and adequate conditions nor by fixed boundaries.

It may well be helpful for future analytic and methodological attempts to try to learn from other disciplines, for example medical research. In the functional analysis of systems of probability, such as those applied to diagnosis of the cardiovascular system, which requires attention to a large number of variable symptoms, methods such as that which epistemology has generalized as the Wischnewski model of cognition (cf. Klaus 1966, 157ff.) are useful. In a nutshell, Wischnewski sees diagnosis as based on the assessment of the multi-dimensional space of a syndrome, in which various probabilities can be mapped out for each syndrome, which then refers to a particular ailment. Applied to the definition of genres, this would mean that one could define them depending on the appearance and correlation of particular characteristics of a film, for example depending on certain specific formal elements that can be described according to rules of narrative or film form. In fact, people's ordinary genre definitions work the same way. One orients oneself to commonly occurring combinations of particular elements and intuitively sticks to their dominant patterns.

According to my model, these combinations take on the character of stereotypes, since they are based on the combination of elements that are grounded in collective cultural experience, are used repeatedly, and can be empirically determined as an intertextual phenomenon. In another work (Wuss 1993, 318), I have defined genres as a higher order of film stereotype, since they are based on first order stereotypical stimuli in the areas of narration, conflicts, characters, mise-en-scène, images, sound, or editing. Among these, certain combinations prove to be particularly probable and thus serve to define genres. Referring to Varela (1990), Schweinitz (2006, 84) speaks of "emergent networks" in people's memories and continues, "Genres are based […] on whole *networks of stereotypes* of the most diverse sort within intertextual space" (2006, 84; emphasis in original).

Film genres can only function if the audience has internalized them mentally. Thus for genres to fulfill a real cultural function, the subjective disposition of the viewer is always important, along with the objectively given level of formal elements, in order for the individual to recognize and understand a genre. Various factors play a role here. It makes a difference whether or not a viewer has been able to gain genre competence by viewing a large number of films. Individual genre knowledge will probably depend on how much help in conceptualizing particular genres the person has gained from cultural instances, for example genre categories in film advertising or the kind of pragmatic categories provided in video rental stores. Individual genre knowledge probably develops both through diffuse networks of stochastic experience of formal characteristics and through the reactivation of stereotypical structures that are linked to concrete film examples in the form of genre prototypes. Therefore, the paths along which individual genre knowledge develops depend on access to prominent works that can take on the function of prototypes in the sense of experimental realism as described by Lakoff (1987; cf. Grodal 1997, 163).

The identification of genre structures and effects is further complicated in that certain groups of film genres have different historical origins, which lead to differing structural and functional conditions. Thus there are classical film genres that draw on the genres of the theater, such as tragedy, comedy, and parable, whose traditions go back as far as antiquity. Others are related to phenomena of modern popular and mass culture and will be referred to as popular genres here. These include Westerns, historical epics, crime or detective films, melodramas, musicals, etc. And, particularly in recent decades, new hybrid forms have come into being, which combine the new genres with more traditional forms. This hybridization can even lead to the fusion of several genres into polygenres.

Various national cultures have also judged the aesthetic value of genres differently, thus causing popular genres to be viewed as inferior in some countries during the early days of cinema, or to be deprecated as trivial later on. More recently, forms taken from autonomous art and those of popular culture have come to be viewed more equally. Nevertheless, there are essential differences between the two groups of genres in relation to their artistic form and psychological effects. Before looking at these, however, it seems more fruitful to investigate common structures and functions and to look for more precise characteristics than was possible in our first look at invariant moments.

We still have far to go to find satisfactory definitions of film genres. The work of authors like Noël Carroll (1990, 1999), Torban Grodal (1997, 1999, 2001), and Greg Smith (1999, 2003), who have successfully used cognitive approaches to look at questions of film genre, have left no doubt about that. The tight network of arguments they have worked out gives reason to hope for further progress, and I will attempt here to solidify and expand it somewhat.

3. The Regulatory Function of Genres

It seems to me that in defining genres it is important to begin with general functional interrelations, which can be conceived in terms of models and further differentiated in the course of research. One such model can be found in the psychological-semiological hypothesis (Ivanov 1965a, 79; Ivanov 1965b, 352; Vygotsky 1965, 352), according to which signs, including works of art and mass culture, fulfill a regulatory function in human psychology. According to my hypothesis, film genres can be seen as organizational forms of specific constellations of signs, which set up particular kinds of artificial possible worlds in relation to the human life world that is felt to be real. Thanks to their specific forms and strategies of effects, these semiotic constellations are able to optimize these regulatory processes in various ways.

The possible worlds of genres constitute standardized situational models for processes of human life, thereby making it easier for people to adapt to strong changes in situational relationships. On the one hand, this happens when the fictional worlds share certain characteristics with the real world, in that like other possible worlds they appear not to be empty worlds, but rather furnished with individual characteristics (cf. Hintikka 1973, 1; Eco 1989, 54ff.; Doležel 1998, 15 and 22ff.), thus making them appear accessible to people. On the other hand, the genre worlds also present deviations and shifts from the familiar real world.

These modifications apply, not just to the concrete physical furnishings or accoutrements of the possible worlds, but above all to the relations of probability among events within the cinematic fiction. Genre seems generally to take on the function of making these shifts plausible to the viewer through immediate perceptions. The various forms of a genre make sure that quite different types of deviation from the real world appear as legitimate possibilities and are authenticated for the viewer through reference to specific conventions of the genre. Thus they prepare the way for human experience to find an orientation in situations in which different rules of probability apply. In this way courses of events that would be impossible or unimaginable in real life can be accepted as possible on the screen and can, despite their divergence from reality, provide a gain in knowledge by steering the viewer's imagination in new directions.

The achievement of adaptation is probably easiest for the spectator to notice in popular film genres, which portray both accessible and deviating worlds. The furnishing of the possible world seems to follow rules that are more concerned with concrete phenomena of physical reality than those of the classical genres. Westerns, historical films, and detective or horror movies require particular locations, types of characters, and their actions. Such patterns, supported by specific elements of film form, make it easier for the viewer to enter into fictional genre worlds.

Edward Buscombe mentions particular visual elements of film form characteristic for the American Western, with its "stories about the opposition between man and nature and about the establishment of civilisation" (1986, 16):

"There is, first of all, the setting, the chief glory of many of the films. Often it is outdoors, in very particular kinds of country: deserts, mountains, plains, woods. Or it is indoors—but again, special kinds of indoors: saloons, jails, courtrooms, ranch houses, hotels, riverboats, brothels [...] Then there are clothes: wide-brimmed hats, open-neck shirts with scarves, tight jeans [...] or, alternatively, army uniforms or the wide but carefully distinguished variety of Indian costume [...] Third, there are various tools of trade, principally weapons, and of these, principally guns. They are usually specifically identified: Colt 45's, Winchester and Springfield rifles, shotguns for certain situations (such as robbing banks or facing a numerically superior enemy), and, in westerns of an earlier period, single-shot, muzzle-loading muskets.[...] Next in importance come horses, also used in formally differentiated ways [...] Fourth, there are large groups of miscellaneous physical objects that recur and thereby take on a formal function. Trains are invariably of the same kind, with cowcatchers in front of the engine, carriages with a railed open platform at the back (useful for fights), and seats either side of a central aisle [...] All these elements operate as formal elements" (1986, 14ff.).

In contrast, classical genres such as tragedy, comedy, or drama hardly make any requirements with regard to locations or other details of scenery. However, it seems that the complex of relations between narrative structures and constellations of conflicts must adhere to much stricter rules, even though these only become apparent at a more abstract level.

The representation of fictional possible worlds with standardized relations of probability that diverge from those of the real world is not a goal in itself, but serves to help the viewer cope with reality mentally through his or her most powerful psychological functions. Along with a better understanding of the situations that are evoked and that often provide analogies to the condition of the world, the spectator is particularly interested in approaching this situation through productive imagination—for instance in relation to future changes in reality—and in being in command of the represented world emotionally, that is, finding positive basic emotions instead of capitulating in face of the conflicts and contradictions that the film portrays. The connection between the cinematic fiction and the emotions it evokes seems to be particularly important.

In working out a general definition of film genre, Grodal (1997, 163) notes: "Genre [...] is merely a set of dominant features of a given fiction, which shapes the overall viewer-expectations and the correlated emotional reaction." This short formula seems accurate and productive since it emphasizes the organization of expectations in relation to emotions as a central function of genre.

We can go on from this to provisionally conclude that, by means of their specific, complex formal qualities, genres create various types of possible worlds, which, through standardized transformations of the rules of probability in real life, fulfill a psychological function for the viewers by conditioning their cognition, imagination, and affects so that they can better control reality.

The most common and obvious case of psychological regulation results from a constellation that probably played a role in the hunting magic of our ancestors, when they portrayed the combat between hunter and game, showing the hunter, with whom one identified, emerging as the lucky winner. This constellation shows the most important psychological functions involved developing together and reinforcing each other: there is a naturalistic conflict situation, but the viewers' cognition can grasp the problem adequately, the outcome corresponds to their wishes, and their emotions can relate to the situation as one in control and are thus positive. Innumerable popular genres follow a similar pattern and thus perform a kind of hunting magic for modern civilization, presenting the individual with a play situation that prepares him or her mentally for real conflicts. Within a setting that is basically familiar to the viewer from other films, characters with whom he or she sympathizes act straightforwardly to deal with comprehensible conflict situations and their goal-oriented actions solve these problems in spite of obstacles, thus reaching a satisfactory ending. The Western hero overcomes his opponent in the showdown, the historical hero wins a famous battle, the detective catches the criminal, the captured dolphin escapes to the open sea. And the concept of the happy ending has long served to define the conflict resolution of another group of genres including romantic drama, comedy, and musical.

The regulatory functions of classical and popular genres seem to differ greatly in qualitative terms. Popular genres are generally concerned with very elementary sorts of behavior, in order to achieve as direct and immediate a sense of psychological balance as possible. This can be used in a short-term way, tends not to have any great consequences, and thus can be seen as belonging to the category of mental hygiene through entertainment (cf. Wuss 1993, 407ff.). The spectators' minds are given something that at least temporarily serves as compensation for everyday reality, but in no way represents optimal experience. The film experience can make up for deficits that individual and social practice, including cultural communication, has left in real experience. The spectrum of these compensations is very broad, corresponding to the range of possible deficits. Thus popular genres seek to offer the audience carefree entertainment in a way that serious daily life cannot. They present action where immobility and sameness often lame normal life and they present exoticism to break the monotony of an all too familiar and boring milieu (Wuss 1993, 407ff.). Genres form these strange and colorful possible worlds, which in reality are impossible to reach, and satisfy basic needs, as was already noticed in the early days of cinema. As early as 1913, Kurt Pinthus (1913/1983, 21) wrote: "People are driven into the movie theaters by their yearning to expand their radius of knowledge in the easiest and quickest way. The schoolboy wants to see the prairie of his Indian books, strange people doing strange things, or the luxuriant, undiscovered banks of Asian rivers. The modest office worker, the busy housewife yearns for the glimmering parties of elegant high society, for distant, gleaming shores and mountains that they never will reach. And the educated and rich are thrilled to learn about the development of the silk worm or to experience a real battle."

These fantasies of wish fulfillment can easily be thought of as continuing up to today. And in addition to the popular genres, whose function for mental hygiene is generally that of supporting or bolstering the individual's psychological balance, others such as thrillers, horror and disaster films tend to cause temporary discomposure and psychological destabilization, letting fictional stimuli serve to break through their sense of indifference or satiety for a while. A number of theoreticians are now paying attention to the paradoxical effects of these genres (Carroll 1990; Grodal 1997; Bartsch 2007).

The psychology of art (cf. Vygotsky [1925] 1976; Kreitler / Kreitler 1972) has come to the conclusion that a more subtle kind of adjustment of tensions and affects is involved in the aesthetic reception of autonomous art, which is based on a much more strongly mediated and complicated organization of changes effected by artistic compositions and which requires more initiative and effort on the part of the audience. It also leads to a correspondingly higher intensity and to longer-term effects of psychological regulation, which then has consequences for the structure and function of genres.

It is not just the interrelations between the film structure and the viewer's consciousness that are concerned in the processes of psychological regulation we are considering. The way the viewer's own psychological disposition motivates him or her to be open to psychological changes through the film experience is just as important. Kreitler and Kreitler (1972, 19; emphasis in original) stress: "It is our contention that a *major motivation for art is tensions which exist in the spectator of art prior to his exposure to the work of art. The work of art mediates the relief of these preexisting tensions by generating new tensions which are specific."*

There is apparently a functional connection between the tensions and moments of conflict with which the viewer is confronted in his or her life and those that are played out on screen. While the conflicts on the screen are not identical to those in real life, they do gain their emotional impulses and general motivation from them, so that they can influence the spectator's mind in such a way as to promise psychological rewards.

In order to build a psychological model of such a functional connection in the case of a concrete work and its reception, one would have to be able to determine more closely the various individual psychological situations of the viewers that result, for instance, from conflicts in their social life. This is difficult, however, since it would require working out differentiated models of film recipients (cf. Suckfüll 2004). Nevertheless, it seems to make sense to approach the overall functional connections, whose variables obviously lead to different genre effects, through more general assumptions. For example, the psychological regulation of the viewers by the work of art is not only of central importance for its aesthetic function per se, but also in that it has a certain basic quality that has to do with conditions of the viewer's ability to act, to be in control, to manage life, and to be able to adapt to new situations, as well as with achieving a balance among these contradictory affects (cf. Vygotsky 1976, Kreitler / Kreitler 1980).

According to a hypothesis of the Russian psychologist Pavel Simonov (1982, 140), it is characteristic of artistic processes that they evoke so-called "positive" emotive states in the viewers while they are experiencing the work of art. As I understand it, this means that the spectator views life and its moments of conflict as shown in the film to be fundamentally controllable, and thus feels him or herself to be able to act appropriately. This hypothesis will be applied in the following attempt to model psychological regulation through films and genres, since the so-called positive emotion takes on the function of a reference variable in a cybernetic control process. In this way, it creates a clear frame of reference by which to judge all deviations and modifications.

The polar concepts of "positive" and "negative" emotions should not be applied in an unspecific manner to all emotional processes, but only to those that provide stimuli of an artificial sort and are used in human communication, and thus require a further level of information processing in relation to the real stimuli, for example that of the filmmaker, who manipulates the real life material in various ways before it appears on the screen. Drawing on Oatley (1992, 107–109, 174–177), I would like to make use of the concepts "euphoric" and "dysphoric emotions" (discomforting) for an analogous distinction of types of stimuli in reality. The differentiation in terminology may help to separate those emotions that are caused by real life situations from those that arise in experiencing art works and other representations of reality.

The assumption that successful aesthetic response can be associated with the creation of positive emotions must not be thought of as meaning one can use "positive emotive states" as a reference variable for a simple fixed set-point control such as a thermostat carries out in controlling the temperature of a heating system. Humans are simply not built to constantly and undisputedly predict environmental events and constantly control information processing in that way. This would hamstring our psychological activity, dull our mental capabilities, and bore us. Instead, an optimum in the normal processing of stimuli seems to be reached when a free-floating balance between certainty and uncertainty is held (cf. Dörner et al. 1983, 64). This applies even more where the effects of art and media are concerned, since the stimuli they supply always tend to aim at a dynamic alternation between certainty and uncertainty, predictability and surprise, which can be reached in various very different ways through the processes of play and imagination whose different aspects we are exploring. They are not necessary for the understanding of subsequent sections.

Even in the simplification of a model, the experiential quality of "positive emotions" should not be prematurely abstracted from impartial judgments of objective processes, for example the ending of a film, according to the creed that if the plot arrives at a good ending for the protagonist, with whom the viewers sympathize, then they will automatically have good emotions—or the inverse, since that would seem to justify only movies with a happy ending for the main characters, while films showing problems that are impossible to solve would have to be seen as per se counterproductive in terms of psychological regulation. If it is to be used as a criterion, the "positive emotive state" must instead be understood as the result of a complex aesthetic experience that is based on interactions among cognition, imagination, emotions, and other mental processes, whose mechanisms of control can easily lead to paradoxical phenomena such as tragic catastrophes for the protagonist at the end of a film story.
In connection with the evocation of emotions in the cinema, it has already been mentioned that their basic quality is not dependent on the objective character of a changing range of stimuli alone—for example a worsening conflict—but rather on the appraisal of what meaning this change has for the subject, particularly in regard to a gain or loss of control competence in relation to the phenomenon that provides the stimulus. If the stimulus is not the result of a situation in real life, which requires active control through real intervention, but rather results from its representation on screen, then cognitively based passive control plays the decisive role in gaining control competence. This so-called passive control is achieved, however, by improved anticipation of events. If the viewer is able to optimize his or her foresight about courses of events, then this brings an improvement in control competence, which leads to positive emotions—despite events that objectively would be judged as negative. The subjective predictability of conflict resolutions changes the control competence of the viewer and thus the basic quality of emotive effects. Building up cognitive schemata can thus even lead to a reversal of the subjective quality of experiences.
When cognitive schemata are built on the level of genre stereotypes, they undoubtedly further increase the predictability of certain plot

developments and outcomes. The film endings of tragedies and some melodramas tend to lead to the protagonists' catastrophe, but the viewer, who recognizes this as a specific norm of the genre, is mentally prepared for it. He or she does not react to the course of action with naive amazement, but rather expects it from a new emotional perspective. By conforming to the genre pattern, the negative ending loses its negative valency. What in real life would lead to "dysphoric (discomforting) emotions," does not automatically cause negative emotions when it happens on screen. The mechanisms of effect such genres have are based on this kind of emotional reevaluation and reversal of real life situations. Art experts noticed this very early on. Their astonishment at the peculiar pleasure that theater audiences take in tragedy has a long tradition.

Along with cognition, emotions and imagination also play a role in the aesthetic revaluation of phenomena of life, although it is still difficult to ascertain exactly how they take effect. A possible direction for future research might be found in investigating the consequences that the cognitive components of affective processes have for the development of genres and the way specific genre emotions function. Here I would like to suggest that the stabilization of appraisal effects is not only a prerequisite for enduring emotions in real life, but also for the establishment of particular emotional tendencies in individual genres.

As already mentioned in connection with the formation of emotions, subjective evaluation of stimuli does principally occur spontaneously. However, in relation to a recurring stimulus of a similar kind, people develop a stable or categorized version of their evaluation, or a constant appraisal style (cf. Lazarus 1991). The recurrence of similar stimuli among films of one genre thus probably leads the viewers to develop a kind of genre-specific appraisal style.

In connection with his considerations on genre theory, Carrol (1999, 309) explains this process of stabilization in a similar way when he writes: "But just as emotions must meet certain criteria of appropriateness in everyday life, so must emotions in response to fictions be governed by criteria of appropriateness. Thus, a film text can be emotively prefocused by being criterially prefocused—that is, by being so structured that the descriptions and depictions of the object of our attention in the text will activate our subsumption of the relevant characters and events under the categories that are criterially apposite to the emotional state in question." He goes on to say: "On our account so far, a criterially prefocused film text is a standard condition for securing emotive focus" of the audience (31). I use the term "appraisal style" here because the connection between appraisal, emotion anticipations, and belief, as Fridja has conceived it, allows us to construct a tighter connection with the imagination and perception of the film audience, which will be essential for research in the future.

Frijda and Mesquita (2000, 52) have described the products of cognitive appraisal processes as separable beliefs and have thereby been able to point out that they have certain characteristics, in that (1) "they tend to involve generalizations. They are about stable and intrinsic properties of the object...", (2) they "make a claim to temporal persistence", and (3) "for the time they are held, they are strong beliefs, in the sense of appearing to have a high likelihood of being true, or they are felt to be true, period" (2000, 54ff.). These authors also describe how beliefs lead to emotional attitudes or sentiments: "Temporary beliefs entailed in emotions may, however, turn into generalized long-term beliefs. When this happens, an emotion turns into a sentiment. [...] Sentiments thus are dispositional emotions. They are schemas ('affective schemas', Fiske, 1982) with the same structure as emotions. [...] Sentiments turn into actual emotions when their objects are encountered with sufficient urgency or proximity" (2000, 55). In addition, the sentiments that have emerged can be considered as emotion anticipations or virtual emotions: "Emotion anticipations are the anticipations, foresights, and imaginings of actual emotions that might emerge under certain envisaged circumstances. Elsewhere, they are called 'virtual emotions'" (2000, 58). Furthermore, the stabilization processes already mentioned lead to a formation and reinforcement of what is defined as a belief. A belief "refers to a proposition considered to be true. Truth judgements are largely based upon probability, credibility and plausibility estimates" (68).

In very similar ways, genres ensure that the viewers' expectations lead to a noticeable tendency towards the generalization of dominant procedures. If, while watching a film, spectators refresh their genre expectations about comedies, then they try to interpret all the actions that the film presents on this basis. Genres also lead to the audience's retaining an attitude over a certain historical period. Within the framework of a genre, occurrences will then be viewed as probable and even as true, even if no one would accept them in real life. Genre-specific emotion anticipations or virtual emotions thus lead to this kind of judgment in regard to probability, credibility, and plausibility. This also explains the connection between emotion and the persuasiveness of genres.

This leads to an extension of the above hypothesis on emotive regulation, according to which different genres come to have specific and different, but still quite standardized, ways of evoking the required positive basic emotions, in that thanks to the fixed appraisal style and the creation of particular beliefs, sentiments, and emotion anticipations, they carry out a genre-specific process of emotional regulation in each case, in which different criteria for probability, credibility, and plausibility apply for the phenomena that are shown.

The viewers' imaginations, along with their cognitions and emotions, also play an important role in aesthetic revaluation. The spectators' imaginative ideas are to a certain extent attached to stochastic kinds of expectation, which are based on their previous perceptions of reality and thus draw corresponding conclusions about future courses of events. But moviegoers rarely view these occurrences neutrally; they usually see them in connection with their own intentions with regard to what they want to happen. They are influenced by their own interests, hopes, and will, and ideologies and prejudices as well as diverse forms of belief also play a role. Unfortunately, psychologists have to date rarely tried to clarify the interactions among cognition, imagination, and emotion. Fridja, Manstead, and Bem have introduced some important thoughts in this direction in their collection entitled *Emotions and Beliefs* (2000), in which an attempt is made to deal with these two mental states as distinct and separate phenomena and to relate them to each other. The editors note in their preface: "Emotion can be defined as states that comprise feelings, physiological changes, expressive behavior, and inclinations to act. Beliefs can be defined as states that link a person or group or object or concept with one or more attributes, and this is held by the believer to be true. The general proposal thus is that emotions can awaken, intrude into, and shape beliefs, by creating them, by amplifying or altering them, and by making them resistant to change" (2000, 5). The central essay by Fridja and Mesquita, for instance, "is based on the premise that emotions can lead to new beliefs and strengthen existing beliefs. The idea that emotions can create new beliefs arises from the notion that an emotion entails an appraisal based on currently salient concerns. This 'temporary' appraisal entailed in an emotion can turn into a long-term belief when an emotion turns into what the authors call a 'sentiment'. By this they mean a latent representation of someone or something that is of personal concern" (2000, 6). These ideas can for the most part be applied directly to film experience; however, it may prove difficult to work out the various specific modalities of "beliefs" as they apply to the characters and the viewers in each individual case.

The most productive approaches to giving a differentiated picture of the imaginative activity involved in viewing a film have been developed by Gregory Currie (1999, 2002). It makes sense to schematically differentiate several forms of imagination by employing Currie's taxonomy of perception-like, desire-like, and belief-like imaginings. These different kinds of imaginative act are not only found in real life; every form of cinematic action is accompanied by these and other imaginative activities on the part of the spectator, meaning that they are also modified accordingly in the process of experiencing it. Thus the triumph or defeat of a film character can conform to the belief-like or desire-like imaginings of the viewers, or not. In this way, the so-called negative film ending can again be modified, and the various types of imaginative ideas and activities are probably given a different radius of action in each of the various genres.

4. Modelling the Ways Classical Genres Achieve Effects

Beginning with the hypotheses that (1) the semiotic processes of art and culture generally fulfill a function of psychological regulation, (2) tension and conflicts in the real lives of people are to be seen as the starting point for artistic regulation of emotions, and (3) the goal of such regulation is the achievement of positive basic emotive states, we can construct some models for the ways individual films aim to produce effects.

Film genres, then, have the function of fulfilling variable forms of psychological regulation, in that they make use of differing, genre-specific strategies of achieving effects.

Knowledge about the kinds of aesthetic response that film has borrowed from classical stage genres could provide a starting point for modeling such strategies. These reactions culminate in effects such as estrangement, pathos, and catharsis, as the dominant forms in comedy, drama, and tragedy respectively. They are suited to serve as models of psychological effects since they encompass significant kinds of psychological effect that can even allow for empirical, experimental investigation.

In the following sections, an attempt will be made to approximate these effects through models, that is to formulate psychological propositions about how comic estrangement, dramatic pathos, and tragic catharsis may function.

4.1 Estrangement and Comedy

The classical genre of comedy is based on a form of response that I am generally referring to here as estrangement and which includes the effect of comic or humorous estrangement only as a special case, albeit the most important one.

It may seem counterproductive that my thoughts on this important genre make use of a concept which most readers think of primarily or even solely in relation to Bertolt Brecht's theory and practice of theater. There are good reasons for this choice, however. The first is a methodological one, based on the fact that the aesthetic concept of "estrangement" ("Verfremdung")— synonymous with "alienation" or "alienation effect"—and the psychological one of "cognitive schema" both arose in the same epoch of thought. This makes it easier to describe the significant effect of estrangement or alienation that Brechtian theater tries to achieve in the audience's mind through a model of cognition as a shift in schemata.

The concept of "estrangement", which is to be seen as the center of Brecht's theory, has gone through a historical development that has in the mean time been comprehensively described and interpreted by cognitive film theory (cf. Wuss 1968; 1979, 1993; M. Smith 1995).

For example, in 1938 Brecht propounded the idea that "to estrange a character or action means simply to rob it of its matter of course, well-known, self-evident quality and to arouse astonishment and curiosity about it". (Brecht 1964, III, 109). And in 1956 he noted: "The changeability of the world is based on its contradictoriness. There is something within things, people, and events that makes them the way they are, and at the same time there is something that makes them different." (VII, 317) Therefore, an estranging portrayal must direct its interest toward "the contradictions in the state of things that have a tendency to change into new conditions" (VII, 314). The methods used to achieve this aim refer to the whole spectrum of artistic representation and have been characterized more closely by Brecht's interpreters. With regard to narration this means "that the spectator is called upon to take his or her place outside the portrayed action of the play. Let us add, in the cases of the plays that the theory applies to primarily, the composition does not make it possible for the author to express adequately the standpoint that is clear to him" (Kaufmann 1962, 127). This statement refers particularly to representations of social conflicts that are unsolvable for the characters but would generally be considered as solvable by today's viewers.

With regard to characterization and acting this means: "Estrangement should prevent the spectators' empathy, it should bring him to take a critical stance toward the characters"

(Mittenzwei 1969, 247). And a very successful disciple of Brecht pronounced: "Estrangement is *making things truly known*" (Wekwerth 1960, 166; emphasis in original). The various attempts at a definition all mention a moment that plays a decisive role in the alienation effect: a qualitative leap in the spectator's mind that changes his or her relationship to the phenomena that are portrayed.

From the point of view of cognitive model-making, this means that the effect of alienation becomes evident in a noticeable and sudden change in information processing, an abrupt transition from one level of the cognitive formation of invariants or schemata to another. The point is always that certain aspects become more consciously recognised by the spectators, in other words that conceptual structures become evident in the material. These may be organized in two different ways, namely that of a clear deviation and contrast from well-known stimuli that have become stereotypical, or that of making certain contradictory elements become noticeable and conscious at the level of perception through repetition and escalation. Thus one could even speak of top-down and bottom-up strategies of estrangement.

Brecht did not view the achievement of alienation effects as a goal in itself. Instead, they were intended to serve as a process of psychological regulation for the audience that emphasized cognitive components but was conceived in much broader terms. The starting point of such regulation was to be constellations of conflicts in the audience's life-world which appeared difficult or impossible to solve within the framework of the bourgeois model of the world, but which were repeated in a similar way in the representation of this world on stage in so far as these generally also refused to offer a solution that would satisfy the protagonists.

While other authors in the GDR, such as Friedrich Wolf, favored portraying politically-desired changes in individuals and society on stage, even if they did not take place in reality, Brecht (1990, 226-229) was not willing to "correct" the course of events he showed in his plays in a voluntaristic way to fit the Marxist ideology. He did not, for example, give characters like Mother Courage or Galileo any insights, inner transformations, or intentions toward social change that they could not have historically had. He did not falsify the modal values of real character attitudes that tend to suggest a low degree of active control of the problem on the part of the protagonists. However, this could lead to the danger of negative emotions being doubled—on stage and in the audience's experience. Thus negative emotions might initiate aesthetic effects, but at the same time they tended to prevent the audience from coming up with productive ideas about social problems.

The effect of estrangement was intended to block such possible effects. On the one hand, it was to strengthen the viewers' cognitive activity through sudden conceptualizations of the actions, thus leading to a more rational view of why things happen. On the other hand, it was to stimulate imagination to produce ideas about changing the existing world which formed the starting point for the artistic representation. Even if the protagonists are not given a new model of the world that could show a possible solution of conflicts in reality, estrangement was to make it easier for the audience to come up with corresponding desire-like and belief-like imaginings and thus to develop new intentions for social change. In particular, the kind of psychological attitude that social psychology refers to as "learned helplessness" (Seligman 1975) was to be prevented. Brecht's concept of estrangement is particularly motivated by the desire to deter the viewers from adopting an attitude of learned social helplessness.

Thus, in 1955 Brecht answered the question of whether the present-day world could be reproduced by the means of theatre with the words: "the present-day world can only be described to present-day people if it is described as capable of transformation.[...] In an age whose science is in a position to change nature to such an extent as to make the world seem almost habitable, man can no longer describe man as a victim, the object of a fixed but unknown environment. It is scarcely possible to conceive of the laws of motion if one looks at them from a tennis ball's point of view" (Brecht 1990, 274ff.). Through the use of certain cognitive strategies, the spectator was to be made able to see the problems of the characters as manageable for people and this was to form the basis for a positive emotional attitude that would be open to new ideas about social reality.

The abrupt and at times even violent forms of conceptualization involved in the effect of estrangement demanded a high level of mental activity from the audience. They thus proved in many cases to be counterproductive in the theater, but were nonetheless sometimes applied to film. This is true of standard procedures of estrangement including epic forms of plot development such as fragmentation, literary stylization through commenting intertitles and songs, historicization, ostentatious or self-reflexive use of dramatization, stylization, and repetition (cf. Wuss 1993), which I will explain in more depth later.

Abrupt transitions to alienating conceptualizations do not necessarily have to be achieved through forced shifts in cognitive structures. They can often also be created almost as a matter of course when they are oriented towards traditional aesthetic reactions that have been categorized as elements of comedy since antiquity. The awareness of contradictory situations, which makes the audience react with laughter, is obviously based on processes of conceptualization that develop spontaneously within the framework of a culture by means of complex, intersubjective, experiential values until they reach a critical level. In order to make the absurdity of a situation apparent, an author then does not need didactic abilities as much as a so-called comic idea or gag, which makes contradictions immediately and effortlessly apparent to thought; for instance, by showing conflicts in an inadequate, spectacular way, thus making them noticeable. There is a whole range of possible forms of representation, from slight inappropriateness to complete absurdity. Thus, comic effects are not based on uniform kinds of situations and emotional reactions, and this may have led to the evolution of a multitude of sub-genres within film culture such as satire, parody, farce, screwball comedy, sophisticated comedy, sitcom, etc.

Within the framework of what has been defined as estrangement, these forms of comedy can be interpreted as variants or special cases. Brecht, too, confirmed the close relationship between comic effects and estrangement. Thus Brecht wrote in his journal in 1940: "The alienation effect is an old artistic technique, known from comedy, certain traditions of folk art, and in the practice of Asian theater" (Brecht 1977, 91). In discussions with the Italian director Giorgio Strehler about the epic-alienating form of his *Threepenny Opera*, Brecht expressed the opinion that this kind of presentation could most easily be achieved in comedies, "because there is alienation there anyway" (Brecht 1960, 134).

Using the suggested model of strategies of effects, it may be possible to combine different psychological concepts in order to further our understanding in analyzing individual films. If in 1905 Freud used a number of mechanisms of jokes, which can be seen as a special case of the comic, to gain the insight that "in each of them something familiar is rediscovered, where we might instead have expected something new. This rediscovery of what is familiar is pleasurable, and once more it is not difficult for us to recognize this pleasure as a pleasure in economy and to relate it to economy in psychical expenditure" (Freud [1905] 1960, 120). This effect can now be interpreted in terms of estrangement as a reduction of cognitive efforts in human information processing. The same thing can happen when viewers condense separate bits of information out of their past experience into larger information clusters or chunks. If a film presents stimuli that include well-known things, which the viewers recognize as such, then this relieves the strain on the receiving channel to their consciousness, so to speak. George Mandler writes that it takes less effort to acquire new structures of understanding if they have first been consolidated into chunks that draw on less of the capacity of our consciousness (cf. 1984a, 124). If a well-known formal element shows up in a film—for example a popular character like the vagabond Charlie in Chaplin's films or a common, immediately graspable situation—then the flow of information is highly reduced at this point and the viewer can enjoy a moment of psychological relaxation.

Rudolf Arnheim impressively described such a sudden recognition of a pattern from the perspective of gestalt psychology in his 1932 book *Film as Art*, in the way that a viewer of Charles Chaplin's *The Gold Rush* (1925) might have experienced it:

"There is the scene where Charlie as a starving prospector cooks and eats his dirty oiled boots. Elegantly and with perfect table manners he carves his unusual dish—he lifts off the upper so that the sole with the nails sticking up in it is left like the backbone of a fish from which the meat has been removed; he carefully sucks the nails as if they were chicken bones, and winds the laces round the fork like spaghetti. [...] If the scene in *The Gold Rush* showed nothing but a starving man wolfing a cooked boot, it would be no more than a grotesque caricature of poverty. The excellence and forcibleness of the scene consists in the fact that in depicting misery

the contrast of riches is given simultaneously by the most original
an visually striking similarity of the meal to that of a rich man.

Carcass of the boot = carcass of a fish
Nails   = chicken bones
Bootlaces = spaghetti

Chaplin makes the contrast painfully clear to the eyes of the
spectator by demonstrating the similarity of form of such objectively
different things. And the great artistry of the invention lies in that
such an elemental, profoundly human theme as 'hunger versus
good living' is presented pictorially by objective means that are so
truly filmic. Nothing more purely visual can be conceived than
such association of the shapes of things" (Arnheim 1969, 144ff.).

This text reads like an illustration of the thoughts cited above,
according to which the sudden discovery of well-known things,
where the viewer had not expected them, creates a moment of
pleasant psychological relaxation, since the discovery of familiar
structural elements eases the uptake of information. One discovers
chicken bones in the nails or spaghetti in the bootlaces, because
Charlie treats them as such.

Arnheim's text not only includes remarks that emphasize the
importance of individual recognitions, but also some that refer to
multiple, similar recognitions of the same kind of basic attitude and
that form a comprehensive aesthetic system. In the scene described,
this system is formed by the general antagonism "hunger versus
good living." The genre of comedy, like other genres as well, lives
by such coherent systems of meaning. They create a mechanism
that can force such sudden recognitions, and beneath the level of
individual understanding they set up a more comprehensive
formal principle, a specific aesthetic code of the genre, which
permeates the whole work and even extends beyond it. This code is
not directed only by cognition, but also by emotions, imaginings,
and opinions that are often socially shaped.

The overall theme is what sensitizes the viewers to see the
individual things they recognize as variations of a general problem
and to use the comic genre as a way to reflect on a certain model of
the world. In the case mentioned above, the general theme of
hunger remains meaningful in the following scenes as well, for
example when Big Jim suddenly imagines that his buddy Charlie is
a chicken. Everything Charlie does seems well-known to Jim—well-

known as the typical behavior of a chicken, seen from the point of view of someone starving, for whom a chicken would be the greatest luxury imaginable. Just in time, Charlie is able to hide Big Jim's gun, but the system of values in the world of starvation is so strong that Charlie himself begins to act like a chicken, scratching with his feet to make a hole in the snow and cover the gun. It makes the fatality of the whole situation evident, in which Charlie has already come to see himself as a chicken and thus has put himself in the place of the victim and internalized this role. But this is made conscious not through a didactic defamiliarization, but in an at once playful and obvious way—through a so-called transposition gag, which is based on the actor's ability to perceive one object as constantly also having the characteristics of another object and to play with this perception.

Similar approaches to comic effects occur in other Chaplin films. In works like *The Great Dictator* (1940) it is possible to discover how Chaplin seeks a transition from the openly comical form to a more didactic and enlightening kind of alienation effect. The first sequence of the film takes the viewers to a battlefield in the First World War, but it is able to evoke peals of laughter in the cinema. As a uniformed soldier, Charlie is part of the squad working the "Big Bertha," a giant cannon that is supposed to bring victory over France for the ominous empire of Tomania. But instead of firing, the cannon makes a rasping noise and slowly ejects a projectile that falls down right in front of its muzzle, like a freshly laid egg. A peculiar situation has been created: the mechanism fails, the perfect war no longer functions, but the line of command in the army is still intact and its mechanisms keep on working smoothly, in that it is always the subalterns who are sent out to do the dangerous work. And it is Charlie, the little soldier at the end of the line of command, who gets the worst lot, having to go and inspect the shell. The playful repetition of passing the command on up to the breathtaking final point discloses the social mechanism of the whole scene, but in a way that the spectator can still see as amusing. When Charlie cautiously approaches the shell, it suddenly begins to move, constantly turning to aim at the little soldier. This, too, is estrangement—it points out that the war has taken on an existence of its own and above all it shows against whom it is directed.

The short sequence is of similarly alienating elements that make sure the audience is abruptly brought to develop concepts of what is happening, i.e. becomes conscious of it. At the same time, this alienation is so humorous that the inappropriateness of the actions provokes laughter.

The reaction of laughter is generally supported by the fact that the beginning of the film directly aims to connect with pre-existing expectations of age-old traditions of comedy by means of the film's formal qualities and mise-en-scène. Even expectations based on the Charlie character, who stands for a continuation of the genre tradition, are part of this strategy. The Charlie character may have changed his outfit and a steel helmet has replaced the tramp's well-known bowler hat, but the comic character has retained his style of gestures and movement even in uniform. This ranges from stumbling and other mishaps through slapstick to various running gags. When the viewer re-discovers them, he or she immediately remembers the comic experiences of earlier films and is thus shown not to take things too seriously and to watch the film in a playful-unserious way from a somewhat distanced mental perspective.

However, the comic stance of *The Great Dictator* changes toward the end of the story and makes way for another technique of alienation. The plot shows that Charlie, who after the end of the war has gone back to working as a barber in the Jewish ghetto, exactly resembles the dictator Hynkel, whose Fascist subordinates are brutally repressing the ghetto inhabitants. When Hynkel invades the neighboring country Charlie has just escaped, the physical resemblance makes it possible for the little barber to take the dictator's place and hold a big public speech. And he uses this opportunity to present a lofty appeal for freedom and equality for all people.

The film story, which at first contains many elements of slapstick, turns into a dramatic story with tendencies toward a parable, a kind of story structure in which the plot is oriented more towards an idea than a real course of action and in which it points toward an aphorism or maxim, such as is found in Charlie's speech.

If Chaplin moved away from the genre of comedy in *The Great Dictator*, even though he was a master in applying its rules, then this may have been the result of the exigencies of the psychological regulatory function that he was intuitively aiming at. The real historical conditions had changed during the work on the film project. Shooting had been planned before the outbreak of the war, but was only carried out after combat had begun, and the première in London in December 1940 took place at the high point of the German air raids on the city. In light of the increasingly threatening political situation, the humorously stylized portrayal of world affairs unintentionally lost its light touch. Therefore it is no coincidence that Chaplin instinctively reacted to situation and abandoned the light genre in the finale. The result was that many of the crew members and colleagues rejected the break from genre conventions, while most viewers accepted the plain language of the humanistic appeal at the end as a message to the world. The speech, which exactly fitted the feeling of the times, was re-printed in thousands of newspapers.

Various strategies of estrangement, which aim at abrupt conceptualization but not at making the audience laugh, can be found in works of the European *cinéma d'auteur*. Thus in *My Life to Live* (*Vivre sa vie*, 1962), Jean-Luc Godard ensures that the viewers experience various situations and episodes in the story of the young woman Nana, who becomes involved in prostitution and in the end dies in this milieu, from a certain intellectual distance. The protagonist's life story is divided into twelve episodes, which are given titles that serve as a Brechtian technique of literary stylization and are also often accompanied by voice-over commentary. Furthermore, the film includes a passage in which the protagonist carries on a conversation with a real-life philosopher, giving it something of the stylistic quality of an intellectual essay.

Agnès Varda's *Le Bonheur* (1965) tells the story of a young couple who live happily together with their two children in a nice house until the man falls in love with a woman who works at the post office. When he tells his wife that he has a lover but still loves her just as much as before, so that it is as though his happiness has doubled, she commits suicide and the nice post office employee takes her place. The film experiments with and estranges the concepts of happiness that the characters have. To do so it makes use of clichés wherever possible and interrupts and comments on the plot again and again with moments of literary stylization such as formulaic phrases (like "je t'aime," "tentation") that are generally taken from billboards or advertising. These stereotypes and conceptualizations cause the viewer to think critically about the protagonist's ideals and ways of thought and to recognize to what extent his notions of happiness have been shaped by consumerism.

Bernardo Bertolucci's major film epic *1900* (*Novecento*, 1976) uses alienation effects to make the social behavior patterns of two friends become apparent and thus open to judgment. They grow up in the same vicinity, but as the sons of a big landowner and of one of his poor workers. Many different episodes repeat the same basic patterns of behavior, making them become conspicuous and thus open to conceptualization. The rich man's son again and again claims to be the other's friend, but abandons him when he is beaten up by Fascists and desperately needs help. The poor man's son, however, denies being the other's friend, but protects him when partisans are going to call him to account after the war. The film ends with a big, carnivalesque altercation, in which an open-air people's tribunal accuses the *padrone* until the other shows how unnecessary a conviction would be, because he is to all intents and purposes already "dead," i.e. powerless. Despite this sophisticated nonsense, the audience is not moved to laughter because immediately after this scene the peasants are disarmed and the *padrone* is returned to his position.

Laughter is not the audience reaction that Lars von Trier's *Dogville* (2003) was aiming at, either. Inspired by Kurt Weill's "Pirate Jenny" song in Brecht's *Threepenny Opera*, in which a dishwasher fantasizes about how a band of marauding pirates will give her bloody revenge for the way the townspeople have mistreated her, the film tells the story of a young woman who carries out a similar act of revenge. The protagonist Grace, who claims to have come to the American town of Dogville to seek protection from a group of gangsters, is allowed to hide out there, but only on the condition that she help out the villagers. She does so, but the more willingly she seems to serve them, the more they lose their respect for her, even to the point of acting out their sadistic fantasies on her. After a supposed friend has betrayed her to the gangsters it turns out that she is in fact the daughter of the boss of the gangsters. Led by the conviction that people are basically good, she had turned away from the gangsters out of moral considerations and fled, but now she decides to destroy the town and its inhabitants. The film uses formal techniques that are very close to Brechtian alienation. It presents the action in ways that require the viewers to take a distanced stance toward what is shown, in that the scenery of the town is just barely indicated by theatrical sets and the characters act in a pantomime-like way, accompanied by conspicuous light and sound effects. Although the story of the film reminds one of Brecht's *Saint Joan of the Stockyards* and techniques of segmentation, literary stylization, and historicization are used to transmit the story to the audience, which normally would lead to alienation effects, thus making the world seem understandable and reducing social helplessness, these artifices here tend to have the opposite effect. Instead of disclosing contradictions and leading to productive attitudes, the world here seems to be deconstructed in such a way that one tends to look at it with cynicism. Thus the use of techniques of alienation does not automatically lead to constructive forms of psychological regulation in the audience.

Other film *auteurs* do not forego using gags. Aki Kaurismäki's *I Hired a Contract Killer* (1990) shows an employee of a water works who loses his job and is in such despair that he wants to kill himself. Since his half-hearted and clumsy attempts to commit suicide fail, he hires a contract killer to murder him. When he falls in love with a woman, however, he wants to revoke the contract, but the killer's company is no longer to be found. So he has to try to keep out of the killer's grasp, which leads to highly exacerbated conflict situations that certainly do not hide their comic quality, at least in the sense of black humor.

Pedro Almodóvar's *High Heels* (*Tacones lejanos*, 1991) uses exaggeration to give an alienated view of familiar discrepancies in mother-daughter relationships, thus making them into a source of laughter. Because of her singing career abroad, the mother had abandoned her daughter, but upon returning home she finds out that the now grown-up daughter has married one of her former lovers. Meanwhile, the film confronts the viewers with the violent death of the man, making both mother and daughter suspects for the murder. The case is handed over to the prosecution, but the prosecuting attorney who is supposed to solve the crime turns out to lead a double life. A friend of the daughter, he has for some time been appearing on stage as a transvestite and successfully imitating the mother's singing performances, and apparently has also gained considerable knowledge about both their lives. When the daughter finds out that the transvestite is identical with the prosecutor, the murder case seems to be solved: The daughter seems to have killed her husband out of injured pride, because he had renewed his affair with her mother. However, the mother, in the mean time terminally ill and thus no longer liable for trial, takes the blame herself, thus making up for the wrong she had done her daughter, while the transvestite uses his position to cover up everything. Thanks to this bizarre character, who repeatedly brings unexpected turns into the story in the form of unexpected gags, many conflicts in the "normal" lives of the others become more apparent.

4.2 Pathos and Drama

The Russian director Sergei M. Eisenstein used the term "pathos" to describe a different strategy that leads to significant effects, which appear to be particularly relevant to the genres of drama and social drama. Using the example of his film, *The Battleship Potemkin* (*Bronenosets Potyomkin*, 1925), he clarified that an audience reaction of this kind occurs when the director is able to coordinate the course of action of the protagonist and the development of consciousness in the audience as much as possible, so that the two processes resonate with each other. This then leads to increased emotional intensity, causing the spectators to experience a kind of ecstasy.

One can analytically approach the effect of pathos more closely if one hypothesizes that it is not based on emotions alone, but rather on a mutual reinforcement of cognitive, imaginative, and emotional activities. The viewer is then confronted with a type of conflict on screen that is relevant to his or her own life and which remains unsolved and ambivalent in the film as well as in reality, but in both cases seems to have a chance of being resolved.

In Eisenstein's film, the characters' situation is determined by the grim conflict between the social interests of two groups or classes of people, the mutinous crew on the ship and their superiors and oppressors. The power relationship between the conflicting parties is at first dominated by the officers, but in the course of the story it shifts more and more to the side of the rebellious sailors until they eventually win the fight. The situation for the spectators and their understanding of the problems shifts in an analogous way: at first it is difficult for them to control the situation cognitively, since the outcome is difficult to predict, but this later proves to be possible.

Certain steps are built into the narrative structure in order to steer this cognitive process. Eisenstein commented on them in relation to the effect of pathos. They can also be described within the framework of the PCS model, that is, in terms of similar formal elements within the macro and micro dimensions of narration as well as in intertextual phenomena in the cultural context, such as those provided by genre stereotypes. In this way the filmmaker is able to direct attention to the fact that qualitative shifts repeatedly occur in many small incidents of the plot and these thus pre-figure the shift of power between the two groups of characters, helping to make it predictable by means of repetition. These shifts become similarly noticeable at the level of causal chains, through breaks within the five acts of the film plot. In each case, the direction of actions reverses, taking a new and opposite course. In regard to the individual episodes of each act, Eisenstein stated:

"In the actions of its episodes each part of the drama is totally unlike the others, but piercing and, as it were, cementing them, there is a repeat.

"In 'Drama on the Quarterdeck', a tiny group of rebelling sailors (a small particle of the battleship) cries 'Brothers!' as they face the guns of the firing squad. And the guns are lowered. The whole organism of the battleship joins them.

"In 'Meeting the Squadron', the whole rebellious battleship (a small particle of the fleet) throws the same cry of 'Brothers!' towards the guns of the flagship, pointed towards the *Potemkin.* And the guns are lowered: the whole organism of the fleet has joined them.

"From a tiny cellular organism of the battleship to the organism of the entire battleship; from a tiny cellular organism of the fleet to the organism of the whole fleet—thus flies through the theme the revolutionary feeling of brotherhood. And this is repeated in the structure of the work containing this theme—brotherhood and revolution. [...]

"Look intently into the structure of the work.

"In its five acts, tied with the general thematic line of

revolutionary brotherhood, there is otherwise little that is similar externally. But in one respect they are absolutely alike: each part is distinctly broken into two almost equal halves. This can be seen with particular clarity from the second act on:

"II. Scene with the tarpaulin—mutiny
"III. Mouring for Vakulinchuk—angry demonstration
"IV. Lyrical fraternization—shooting
"V.   Anxiously awaiting the fleet—triumph.

"Moreover, at the 'transition' point of each part, the halt has its own peculiar kind of caesura" (Eisenstein 1949, 163-164). The director interprets the character of this *caesura*: "And it should be further noted that the transition within each part is not merely a transition to a merely *different* mood, to a merely *different* rhythm, to a merely *different* event, but each time the transition is to a sharply opposite quality. Not merely contrasting, but *opposite*, for each time it *images exactly that theme from the opposite point of view*, along with the theme that *inevitably grows from it*" (Eisenstein 1949, 165; emphases in original)

This mode of narration makes the rebels' victory at the end appear foreseeable because it constructs cognitive schemata. That the plot development also follows a genre stereotype, the long-standing convention of having the protagonist win in the end, makes it even easier for the viewer to anticipate this turnaround. Since the same structural schema pervades all three levels of perception, conceptualization, and stereotypes, the various starting points for constructing cognitive schemata are fused together and thus lead to successive transitions among the various phases of information processing. It is very probable that a similar kind of successive fusion and coordination goes on within the imaginative and emotional activities of the viewers as well.

With regard to imagination, *The Battleship Potemkin*, like most social dramas, clearly shows that the viewers develop strong sympathies for the protagonists at the beginning of the action, and with them ideas about plot developments and desirable solutions for the conflicts. A favorable solution to the protagonists' conflicts simultaneously represents a new model of the world for the audience, in this case one including a social dimension. They must be able to recognize something that had not or was not allowed to exist in social life before and to view it as possible. In general, drama as a genre is suited to evoking perception-like imaginings, which attest to changes and which lead to belief-like and desire-like imaginings, in order to help the audience overcome the borders of everyday ways of thinking that are in the broadest sense moral ones. The imaginings that social dramas initiate are generally closely linked to ideologies and the effects of political forces. In this way, the ending of *The Battleship Potemkin* certainly must have had a propagandistic function in its time, in that it was intended to make it seem plausible to the audience that revolutionary acts of this type were not only possible, but also could be successful. They were to be seen as analogies to successful social change, in this case the historical forerunners of the October Revolution. Eisenstein thus intended the pathos in his film to fulfill a particular ideological function: to ensure that the viewers would at once consciously and emotionally experience the real historical changes. This form of effect, however, hardly seems to be a necessary or generalizable one.

A necessary condition for the effects of pathos can, however, be found in the duplication and affirmation of the positive emotions that are evoked. At the beginning of the *Potemkin* film, the feelings of the protagonists are first characterized by an alternation between anger and despair. These dysphoric emotions arise because the officers ride roughshod over the sailors' most elementary needs and threaten them with execution in case of protest. This emotional state then becomes transformed into its opposite, which might be characterized as a euphoric emotion, when the rebels are able to succeed against the officers, then in the port of Odessa, and finally in the face of the Czarist fleet. The audience was invited to participate in this emotional turnaround at the same time as the sailors. A successful outcome for the protagonists appears more and more probable and foreseeable as the insurgents become more successful, which provides the possibility of a positive basic emotional attitude according to the cognitive point of view. It seemed necessary to reassure the audience that the act of liberation of the sailors would have a happy ending, however, since a victory of the social utopia still seemed far away, making the reinforcement of such ideas anything but superfluous when the film was made. The duplication of the euphoric-positive emotions through a positive ending for the protagonists most likely belonged to the

prerequisites for the pathos effects of the film, which had to be
experienced—perception-like—immediately and sensuously as part
of the mutual reinforcement of cognitions, emotions, and
imaginings in order for the spectators to "lose themselves" in these
feelings.

Robert Bresson's *A Man Escaped* (*Un condamné à mort s'est
échappé*, 1956) adheres to a similar principle of structure and
effects. Here again, the basic situation conveys the impression of a
real conflict with an open outcome. The protagonist, a French
resistance fighter, is waiting to be executed in a German occupation
prison, but he fights against the feeling of powerlessness in the face
of his fate and carefully plans an escape, which succeeds in the end.
Here, too, the film aims at creating consonance between the
protagonist's actions and the audience's cognitive, emotional, and
imaginative activities. The viewers feel with the hero and hope for a
good solution to this conflict and for the corresponding positive
emotional consequences. The cognitive structure of the story is
based on innumerable small actions at the level of topics, which
show the hero's diverse efforts to prepare for his escape. They are
accompanied by mental efforts that boil down to the maxim, "help
yourself", i.e. "Aide-toi", the original title of the film. This maxim
also forms the topic of the film, the resolutely executed escape from
the death cell, which helps other prisoners to keep themselves from
capitulating in the face of their circumstances as well. And with its
finale, which shows the protagonist's triumph, the story sticks to
the conventions of social drama in its prison escape variety. All
three levels of the narrative structure are built according to the
same semantic tendency and they are meant to harmonize the
wishes and emotions of protagonist and audience. Although the
characters and their liberating actions are quite different from
Eisenstein's, the concept of pathos still seems fitting. Since the
music and voice-over text, along with the micro and macro
structures of narration, serve to create an atmosphere that is
conducive to the resonance between the on-screen action and the
audience's experience, pathos seems to be the correct way to
characterize the film's effect.

In Sidney Lumet's *Twelve Angry Men* (1957), a youth from the
slums is being tried in court, accused of having murdered his
father, and is facing the death sentence. Cloistered in a hot room,

twelve jury members, men of different ages, education, and backgrounds, have to reach a unanimous verdict on whether or not the young man is guilty. Since the arguments of the prosecution seem conclusive and a quick decision is expected, the jurors react very angrily as one of them begins to express doubts about the court's argumentation, since this seems to be an unnecessary delay. However, when they are forced to look at the case more closely, one after another adopts a different attitude, making it possible for them to overcome their routine ways of thinking, to look at the evidence with an open mind, and in the end to reach the verdict of not guilty. In describing how a criminal case is solved, the film shows the moral efforts that are required of the jurors if they are to search sincerely and actively for the truth. Here again, the protagonists and the audience are faced with an intense and undecided conflict, and here again a solution is reached that represents the correct moral decision, which is associated with the effect of pathos. The cognitive effects work in this direction, too, being based on series of topics of the jurors' moral decisions, the causal chain of the court trial, and the plot stereotypes of the courtroom drama and its typical ending in an acquittal—basic narrative structures that all follow the same schema. They successively build up belief-like and desire-like imaginings in the viewer, which then lead to the victory of the moral decision and to resonance between the positive final emotions of protagonists and audience.

4.3 Catharsis and Tragedy

The concept of catharsis concerns a strategy of effects that dominated the Attic theater. The reaction of the spectators was linked to their witnessing conflict situations that the protagonists could not solve and that led to their downfall. This outcome was not coincidental, but was grounded in essential oppositions within the constellation of conflicts, often ones that were fundamentally social in nature, which made them principally impossible to solve individually. The cinema later adopted corresponding, but modified, narrative modes for its film tragedies, which involved an inexorable dramatic crisis as part of a plot development, which Hegel characterized as "the constant advance toward the final catastrophe" ("die stete Fortbewegung zur Endkatastrophe" 1965,

II, 523). As the dominant effect of the genre, catharsis is obviously also based on a particular form of psychological regulation. The starting point for this kind of effect is to be found in the fact that the conflicts shown on the screen are not only relevant to the protagonists, but have or have had effects in the world of the audience. Since the experience of the individuals' helplessness in the face of unsolvable problems demands that they come to grips with them mentally, art is called on to make use of its means to contribute to this. Here, too, the basic principle is that of helping the spectators arrive at a positive emotional state, despite the undeniable fact that the outcome of the conflicts will be disastrous for the protagonists and will take an extremely undesirable course for the audience, as well.

In the more than two thousand years of the history of aesthetics and performing arts, attempts have again and again been undertaken to explain why the audience finds pleasure in tragic subjects. Aristotle's *Poetics* already describes the effects of tragedies: "Tragedy, then, is a representation of an action which is serious, complete, and of a certain magnitude [...] in the mode of dramatic enactment, not narrative—and through the arousal of pity and fear affecting the katharsis of such emotions" (Aristotle 1987, 37). Another translation: "A tragedy arouses pity and fear and thereby effects a purgation of these and similar emotions" (Aristotle 2001, 17). In his *Hamburgische Dramaturgie*, Lessing explains the effects of catharsis more closely by defining the character of fear as being fear for ourselves, which results from our similarity to the suffering person: "[...] this fear is pity that is applied to ourselves" ("[...] diese Furcht ist das auf uns selbst bezogene Mitleid" [1954, 381]).

In his study *Aeschylus and Athens*, George Thomson looks into the paradox that is built into the psychological process of purification: "Aristotle's conception of purgation or purification (kátharsis) is closely allied to the use of this term in medicine. In the doctrine of the Hippocratic school, disease is a disturbance of the bodily humours, leading to a crisis, in which, in the event of recovery, the morbid matter is evacuated or expelled, and the physician's aim is to induce the crisis in conditions which will have that result. But Aristotle's statement goes further than that, implying that, before the morbid affections can be expelled, they must first be artificially stimulated" (1966, 350).

According to Thomson, both the tragedy and other cultural forms such as important religious rites in ancient Greece fulfilled a common function of "...kátharsis or purification, which renewed the vitality of the participants by relieving emotional stress due to the contradictions generated in the course of social change. And this purpose was achieved by the expression of what had been suppressed" (358).

Catharsis is able to "heal" the spectators of certain psychological cramps, damaging imaginations, or unproductive attitudes, which generally have to do with unresolved social conflicts, in a sense by using homeopathic means. That is, they again confront the viewer with the stimulus from which he or she is already suffering. Instead of soothing or blocking the painful experiences, it exacerbates them. And it does so in a highly concentrated way, but in a way that leads to a functional interplay among cognitive, imaginative, and emotional activities, so that the method is like fighting fire with fire.

The impossibility of solving certain problems, which is hard to accept in real life, is made sensuously perceptible through its radical expression in the final catastrophe, thus being freed of taboos and authenticated as a part of life. This addresses the cognitive activities of the viewers, in that a really existing and painful part of life is objectified and made perceptible in a clearly structured way. Furthermore, the certainty with which things take the worst possible direction works to change the viewers' ways of thinking about the world. In this way, imagination is also activated. The experience of the catastrophe generates perception-like imaginings, as well as belief-like and desire-like imaginings. Thus, tragedies organize the human use of models of the world, in that the failure of certain kinds of idea-driven actions gives one reason to re-think the values that shape or have shaped the thinking of a society. The catastrophe can act as a polemical argument for or against a certain system of values. Like any radical decision, the catastrophe also causes wish-fulfillment fantasies to be activated in the viewers, who do not want to accept an individual's doom. Hence they also prepare the way for new models of the world.

The tragic catastrophe can also be a way to carry out an evaluation of characters, their actions, and their ideas. In the German literary theory of the 19th century, this led Herrmann

Hettner to set up ideal types of tragedies, contrasting the "tragedy of circumstances" (Tragödie der Verhältnisse) with the "tragedy of character" or the "tragedy of the idea" (1959, 212ff.). Somewhat simplified, the downfall of the protagonist can serve to polemicize against social conditions that deny the individual's fundamental life-needs, as well as against a certain kind of basic human attitude or personality structure which is entangled in fruitless principles.

Thus "tragedies of circumstances" end with the catastrophe of their protagonists because they cannot assert their legitimate interests against the resistance of a hostile environment, as can be exemplified by the fate of the lovers in Shakespeare's *Romeo and Juliet*, which has often been adapted to the screen. The motif of the lovers whose values stand in contrast to inhuman social conditions has been varied in innumerable film stories that take place in the midst of combat, war, or revolutions or under dictatorships or other repressive social forms. Kurt Maetzig's *Ehe im Schatten* (1947) can serve as one example of the many films that were directed against the tragic circumstances of the Holocaust. It tells the story of a married couple, a German actor and actress, who choose to commit suicide together because the Jewish woman is being threatened with deportation to a Nazi concentration camp.

In comparison to the tragedy of circumstances, in which the catastrophe of the individual is used as the starting point to put the blame unequivocally on the social environment, the processes of judgment involved in the tragedy of character are less linear. Even if the spectator views characters like Shakespeare's Coriolanus with "tragic sympathy" (Hegel 1965, II, 551) and can identify with him to a high degree, he or she still feels that the catastrophe is the result of a certain basic attitude, which he or she does not share, or at most to a limited degree, and may look at critically or even condemn. The viewer may suffer together with the hero, who cannot avoid his downfall, because he or she discovers elements of this attitude, which is open to criticism, in him or herself, thus making it easier to develop empathy with the character on his way toward his ensnarement in tragic conflicts from which he will not be able to escape.

The Polish director Andrzej Wajda (1964, 357) spoke in a similar sense about the hero of his film *Ashes and Diamonds* (*Popiòl i diament*, 1958), who follows the orders of the Home Army High

Command and kills a high-ranking functionary of the Polish Workers Party: "Maciek found himself in a hopeless situation: if he carries out the order, he will be acting against the laws of peace; if he does not carry it out, he is disobeying the brutal laws of war. The two laws come into conflict within this character. It is not a coincidence that the action takes place on the last day of the war and the first day of peace."

The spectator views the protagonist very sympathetically, and for a Polish audience toward the end of the fifties it was probably the first opportunity to experience a young resistance fighter in the London-directed nationalist Home Army not being automatically portrayed as a political opponent and enemy of the new People's Republic, as the official political perspective had demanded until 1956. Instead he is depicted as a sincere patriot who participated in the war against Hitler's troops and survived the bloody Warsaw uprising. Maciek's personality structure was formed during these war years, with the consequence that soldierly values like loyalty and a naive kind of daredevilness dominate, as well as a tendency to avoid thinking about whether or not orders make sense. When, with the change in the times at the end of the war, a new situation and new conditions redefine what kind of actions are appropriate, the hero tries to remain true to himself, but now the character traits he has gained put him into danger of acting against his own beliefs and interests if he blindly follows the orders of the Home Army and acts against the new laws of peacetime. Upset by his own violent act, which could be a step towards a looming civil war, he panics when he runs into a routine check of the People's Army, which probably was not aimed at him, runs away and is fatally shot. The heap of ashes where he then dies is a location with ambivalent symbolism, since it reminds one of the questioning verses of the romantic poet Norwid which gave the film, and the novel by Andrzejewski on which it is based, their title: "…Whether only ashes remain / And dust that blows away in the wind / Or if in the bed of ashes / A lustrous diamond appears, / The morn of eternal victory…" (C. Norwid, quoted in Andrzejewski 1964, 17).

Hegel had already emphasized that in character tragedies it is not an epic totality of relationships that is presented for examination, but rather a particular trait in the character's behavior. In the film story this is the way of acting that Maciek has learned in the war and which makes him incapable of adapting to the new circumstances. In contrast to the novel, which takes place over a two-week period, the film condenses the protagonist's inner conflicts into a few hours, thus increasing their dramatic power, as Wajda mentions: "Since the action takes place in this exceptional night that ended the war and introduced peace and its hopes, I had the feeling that everything that might destroy these hopes would cause a shock for the audience" (1987, 12). The hero reacts in a correspondingly insecure way and often loses control of himself; for the first time in the introductory sequence, in which he kills a victim of the assassination attempt with an unending machine gun volley, which also destroys the door latch of the chapel and thus makes the act seem sacrilegious.

Later on, Wajda uses the rhetorical possibilities of Christian iconography several times to comment on the action (cf. Wuss 1993, 386), and in doing so he appeals to belief-like imaginings in the Catholic audience in Poland. If the director was able to evoke a positive basic emotion in the audience of this character tragedy despite the catastrophe of the hero, then this probably resulted from the mobilization of their imagination and fantasy and particularly from an intensification of cognitive and emotional processes.

The already-mentioned opening scene is typical of the way cognitive structures are built up according to the same schema on all three levels of invariants and thus serve to cause an unusually intense level of analogous cognitive activities. Again and again, the actions that are shown are interrupted; they do not reach their intended goal. This applies to minimal actions as well as larger-scale events. Nothing happens the way it was planned. Characteristically, the assassination kills different people to the intended targets of the bullets. The following actions in the film are characterized by a similar unease. Almost every action on the part of the characters is marked by disruptions. When Maciek lets his later lover fill his glass, he constantly pushes it around on the bar, and when they meet in their first romantic encounter in the room, Maciek is continually looking for parts of his pistol on the floor while he greets the girl. In the course of the film, one repeatedly sees how everyday objects fail to function. The locations seem to be strangely porous, since an alien outside world again and again intrudes into the main action, altering its character (Wuss 1986, 205ff.). That none of the major characters succeed with their schemes of life corresponds exactly to this pattern of development. Even the successful assassination at the end does not correspond to the intentions of the perpetrators, who wanted it to be a sign of irreconcilable hate. In the light of the fireworks celebrating victory, the murdered Communist falls into the arms of his adversary, making them appear less as natural enemies than as close relations of different generations, as father and son who come together in the face of tragedy.

What has been described here in terms of analogous structures, which can be grasped cognitively at the level of perception, conceptualization or stereotyping, also has an emotional function in this particular case. The courses of action are not organized arbitrarily, but rather center on particularly intense, unresolved moments of conflict, which put the viewer in a situation of necessary appraisal of stimuli, thus provoking arousal and affects, that is, introducing potential episodic emotions. The similarity in kind of the affects leads to emotional saturation that increases constantly until it leads to the final catastrophe. Genre helps strengthen this process of emotional saturation, which here is also closely connected to the intensity of cognitive processes. Perhaps similar cases can help further the study of catharsis in an interdisciplinary framework.

These paradoxes within the course of events, which can be described in terms of cognition and emotion, are easier to predict due to their frequent repetition during the film. The catastrophe of Maciek, who only wanted to be a good Pole, but ends his life on the heaps of ashes on the outskirts of the city, is—despite all its absurdity in light of the whole picture—not as improbable as it appears and does follow a logic of its own. Probability learning, which enables the viewer to adapt cognitively to all the ruptures in the plot, also contributes to submitting the events to the spectator's passive control, thus making it possible to reappraise their emotional quality, conforming to or being supported by the process of emotional saturation.

5. Applications of the Model

5.1 Summarized Hypotheses on Classical Genres

If we compare the hypothetical statements about the dominant strategies of effects in the three most important classical genres, we arrive at a schematic comparison of comic estrangement, dramatic pathos, and tragic catharsis. Although all these effectual strategies lead to psychological regulation through positive basic emotions in the end, the kinds of conflict situation involving the protagonists and the spectators, the course of action, and the results are different in each case.

(1) The device of estrangement, including the special case of comedy, seems to be appropriate when the protagonists are not or are only partially in control of the conflicts and when analogous situations in the audience's real world also seem difficult to control because their models of the world are inadequate. In this case, the regulatory function of the genre seems to be that of changing the viewer's way of processing information by exposing him or her to abrupt and unexpected conceptualizations, thus enabling him or her to reflect on these events more effectively and to better combat possible tendencies of learned social helplessness.

(2) Pathos is to be understood as an aesthetic response that is valuable when both the protagonists and the audience are lacking control over their situations, but have hopes of a solution. The successive creation of cognitions as well as resonances for imagination and emotions helps promote the search for solutions on both levels, so that the spectator can even lose him or herself emotionally in these developments.

(3) Catharsis is to be seen as an aesthetic reaction that is appropriate when the spectators are confronted with the protagonist's unresolvable problems and they themselves also face real problems which they cannot solve on the basis of their previous understanding of the world. Thanks to the intensification of cognitive and imaginative processes, which helps them give up an inadequate world model, the films create mental conditions that allow for a positive emotional state despite the protagonist's catastrophe.

These hypotheses simplify and schematize the above-mentioned structures and functions, with the goal of making the various strategies for achieving effects more easily comparable and observable for an empirical investigation of psychological effects.

Here, as in the case of the analysis of narrative structures, we have descriptive models that help make it possible to approximate the existing genre models for films, if we find empirical evidence for significant aspects that indicate whether a certain effective strategy that has evolved historically for a particular genre is present or not. These are by no means constructive models that can or should be used to produce classical genre films, and they do not provide standardized blueprints for movies.

Of course, there are other ways to arrive at descriptive models of genres, and some of them are less schematic and more flexible. However, there too, a similar basic principle has proved to be useful, which Carroll (1999, 33) calls "to pith the emotive structure of the film." This means, "finding the aspects of the depictions or descriptions of the object of the emotion that satisfy the necessary criteria for being whatever emotional state the audience is in. This is what explaining the emotional state of the audience generally amounts to (along with identifying the depictions or descriptions that give rise to the concerns and preferences the audience is meant to bear to developments in the narrative)." Carroll has applied this method to various kinds of popular genres: "Suspense, horror, and melodrama, then, are three genres where films count as instances of the relevant genre only if they are dedicated to eliciting certain specifiable kinds of emotions from spectators." (1999, 35) In my opinion, the descriptive models with their varying degrees of schematization are not mutually exclusive and they can be combined whenever this is expedient in analyzing a film, for instance in the case of hybrid genres. It will be one of the primary tasks for future genre theories of the cinema to discover how to conceptualize the shared qualities and differences in these groups of genres systematically so that we will be able to better understand the individual genres and their historical development, as well as the various transitional forms and combinations among them.

5.2 Applications Regarding Weak Genre Tendencies

"Hard" descriptive models of the sort I have suggested here are valuable with regard to media practice in particular because it rarely involves phenomena that directly fit the categories of pure classical genres, but includes innumerable ones that have something to do with estrangement, pathos, or catharsis. That is, media practice partially employs certain strategies to reach specific effects, by making use of particular narrative conventions. The strongly schematized conventions can be used to describe concrete film examples, even in cases where not one but two, or more, strategies are at work simultaneously and in cooperation with each other. This interaction can then be described through a combination of several narrative patterns. This also makes it easier to do justice to various shifts and transitions in the use of genre forms.

Thus there are a number of film plots that end with the catastrophe of the protagonist, but without being tragedies or melodramas, and others that end euphorically, but without having the other characteristics that would correspond to a drama or a comedy. Nevertheless, in analyzing them it may be helpful to consider whether certain strategies of achieving effects may be being used and can be discerned through the use of narrative conventions, even if they only appear in a diminished or highly modified form.

Films like Andrzej Wajda's *Kanal* (1957), Michelangelo Antonioni's *The Cry* (*Il Grido*, 1957), Jean-Luc Godard's *Breathless* (*À bout de souffle*, 1960) and *My Life to Live* (*Vivre sa vie*, 1962), Dennis Hopper's *Easy Rider* (1969), Bernardo Bertolucci's *Last Tango in Paris* (*Ultimo tango a Parigi*, 1972), Theodoros Angelopoulos's *The Beekeeper* (*O Melissokomos*, 1986), and Jim Jarmusch's *Dead Man* (1995) and *Ghost Dog: The way of the Samurai* (1999) end with unequivocal catastrophes for the protagonists, but their very diverse forms of narration do not otherwise correspond to the schema of tragedy. The resolutions of their conflicts also evoke very different insights, ideas, and feelings in the audience, and do not correspond to the pattern of causing fear and pity. Nevertheless, the catastrophes do lead to intensified emotions in the viewers and can help transform their ideas.

Wajda's *Kanal*, which shows the last skirmishes of a company of the Polish Home Army (AK) during the Warsaw uprising in 1944, ends when the Polish troop, broken up into small groups, tries to get out through the sewers to escape the German army. A young woman, who has dragged her sick lover to one of the manholes, is forced to see that the way to freedom is barred, another group falls into the hands of the waiting SS when they climb out in the dark, and when in a third group the company leader and his adjutant have finally managed to get out in the open after almost having been killed by hand grenades that booby-trapped the exit, the lieutenant colonel recognizes that his helper has tricked him, since he had not told him that they had long lost the men that the officer thought were right behind them. He then shoots the adjutant and returns to the sewers to search for his troops. The film, which otherwise is a broad epic group portrait of the insurgents, here makes use of the multiply repeated catastrophe to appeal to the audience's emotions and to attempt to achieve a revaluation of the Warsaw uprising. The anonymous AK fighters are honored as patriots who lost their lives in a heroic mission, which the Polish leaders had officially ignored up to 1956 for political reasons. The fate of the main characters thus provoked public opinion and helped to correct ideological misrepresentations of national history.

The protagonist of *Breathless*, a small-time crook who has killed a policeman almost by accident, at first seems to be a macho with a lust for life, but does not even attempt to flee or save his life after his girlfriend betrays him, letting himself be hunted down and in the end be shot by the police. The audience does not feel that this catastrophe is tragic. Nonetheless, the demise of the antihero, who was viewed with sympathy, particularly by the younger generation, must have been seen as a strong provocation for the bourgeois values of French society, which at the time was on its way toward a restoration of conservative social structures.

The catastrophe of the protagonists in *Easy Rider* was also definitely not aimed at evoking tragic catharsis. The heroes appear—in the Brechtian sense—to be asocial, but in an asocial society. The film shows that they are shot down by American rednecks who do not accept their unconventional way of life and thus attempts in a way similar to Godard's film to create sympathy for the antiheroes, using the catastrophe as an emotional provocation to question the dominant social system of values.

The protagonist in *The Beekeeper*, a frustrated elderly retired teacher whose family life is ruined and whose aged friends are on the verge of death, still sets out with his bees to start another season in the spring. He is accompanied by a young woman hitchhiker, and after a short phase of affection and love for her he falls back into his agony and commits suicide by letting himself be stung by the aggravated swarms of bees. His parting from life corresponds on the one hand to the myth of natural decay, but on the other hand implies an unmistakable criticism of the lethargic attitude that seeks its confirmation in the catastrophe.

The story of the young bookkeeper in Jarmusch's *Dead Man*, who breaks out of bourgeois society to take a job in the Wild West, but immediately is turned into a doomed man by a pistol bullet, also moves along a straight path toward the catastrophe. He does, however, fight vehemently and even courageously against his fate, and finds an ally in a representative of the real America, an Indian, who for a long time is able to protect him through his supernatural powers. In the end, weakened by his wound and marked by death, he faces an old adversary again and the exchange of shots is fatal for both of them. Throughout the film it is never questioned that the conflict is unsolvable, but the efforts of the individual still appear to be promising and desirable.

The aesthetic effects and meanings that result from the protagonists' catastrophes are as different as the film plots mentioned here. All the same, the unsolved conflicts all present a major challenge to the audience's cognitive abilities, imagination, and emotional world. Perhaps it will be important for future research to begin with these kinds of significant stimuli and their potential effects when looking into more specific effects of films.

An approach to film effects through a diametrically opposed constellation, the positive ending, seems equally promising. This, too, has an enormously wide range of variations, which depend in part on the probabilities of certain conflict resolutions in the concrete stories and in the life world of the audience, whose psychological situation is to be regulated by the film experience. The development of wishful social fantasies may also play a role. Here we will be looking less at the standardized kind of positive endings of classical dramas that mainstream Hollywood cinema has adopted and occupied as its own—the modern kind of hunting magic—and will instead concentrate on examples from European art cinema that developed skilfully made fictions: films by Federico Fellini such as *Nights of Cabiria* (*Le Notti di Cabiria*, 1957) or *8½* (1963), Michelangelo Antonioni's *Zabriskie Point* (1970), Bernardo Bertolucci's *1900* (*Novecento*, 1976), Theodoros Angelopoulos's *The*

Suspended Step of the Stork (*To Meteoro vima tou pelargou*, 1991), as well as works from Aki Kaurismäki's trilogy of losers like *The Match Factory Girl* (*Tulitikkutehtaan tyttö*, 1990) or *Ariel* (1988).

At the beginning of Fellini's *Nights of Cabiria*, the protagonist, a poor prostitute, is almost killed by one of her customers, and at the end of the film such an attack by a man is repeated. Her precarious situation has not changed and the filmmaker has not shown her struggle for life as a drama that could lead to triumph. In a conversation about the ending, he stated that he did not wish to give his protagonist advice, where he himself could not see any way out of the dilemma. Nonetheless, he did try to find an emotional impulse that might better correspond to the wishes of both protagonist and audience. Thus he provides for a reinforcement of an optimistic feeling about the world through the arrangement of the actions. He comments on this: "That was why the only thing that I could offer my characters, who always suffer so much misfortune, was solidarity, that is, I could say to them, 'Listen, I can't explain why everything always goes wrong, but I'm on your side and I'll play a serenade for you'" (Fellini 1964, 77). Therefore the idea occurred to him for the ending to let the heroine "meet a small group of merrymakers, very young people, that is, people who still have their future before them and who make fun of them in a nice, but totally innocent, way and who sing them a song as a sign of their gratefulness" (1964, 78). Even if little is to be found here of a strategy aiming at the effect of pathos, the arrangement of this serenade does change the attitude of the protagonist and the emotions of the viewers considerably, since it feeds the hope that thanks to solidarity it is possible to master individual life.

It is revealing that Fellini draws certain parallels in regard to dealing with unsolved conflicts between the ending of *Cabiria* and that of *8½*. "At the end of *8½* Marcello smiles just like Cabiria: in reality they have gone through different processes, different developments to arrive at this result. Cabiria's optimism was of a physiological kind: that of a little animal that is trusting like a child. Although it is expressed as a premonition, Marcello's inner emancipation is only successful after close scrutiny of the situation. Poor Cabiria does not understand anything about what happens to her; Marcello, however, performs an autopsy on himself all alone.

This ending represents a clear-sighted, precise, and conscious acceptance of himself and of the ideals of a liberated reality, which are unreachable from the catastrophic present. It is an active acceptance, with a very clearly defined sense of responsibility, and is not passive resignation" (1968, 169).

The viewer witnesses the shift in the basic attitude of the director Guido, played by Marcello Mastroianni, even if this only takes place in his fantasy, in such a way that the character's wishes resonate with his or her own in a relationship that is highly intensified in a carnivalesque way. The processes of enlightenment, wish fantasies, and emotions of character and viewer run parallel to one another in a way that appears to have led some contemporary audience members to a kind of ecstatic reaction. Fellini had already given up offering a solution to real-life conflicts in *Nights of Cabiria*, and the ending of *8½* even more obviously transforms the story into a fictional world that is largely borne by fantasy and play.

In Antonioni's *Zabriskie Point*, the viewer experiences how a young man who is suspected of having shot and killed a policeman during student unrests first flees in a stolen airplane, then enjoys a few hours of freedom and love in the desert at Zabriskie Point, only to be shot without warning after he returns to the airfield. When his lover, who works as a secretary for an established construction firm in the desert, hears about his death, we see how she struggles against this dismal fate: we see the company headquarters, which dominated the landscape like a symbol of the establishment, blow up in an immense explosion. The young woman's wishes are made visible and are linked up to those of the viewers in a vision that is intended to cause an emotional upheaval in the audience by reinforcing the impression that an individual can fight back instead of being at the mercy of fate. Here again, it is not the wished-for change in reality that is shown, but a fiction that is clearly characterized as such.

To a lesser degree this also applies to Aki Kaurismäki's loser trilogy, *Shadows in Paradise* (*Varoja paratiisissa*, 1986), *Ariel* and *The Match Factory Girl*. The films appear to observe and document reality, but then diverge strongly from this attitude in their endings, becoming playful fictions.

In *Ariel* the unemployed miner Taisto leaves the provinces for Helsinki, where he hopes to find a job. On arriving, he is immediately robbed, is only barely able to get by with various odd jobs, and lands in jail although innocent. However, he meets a woman who sticks to him and an honest cell-mate who is willing to try to break out with him, so that Taisto and his friends can escape to a distant land. The ship on which he escapes is named "Ariel," which might seem a promising allusion to the mythical spirit, but is not to be seen without irony, since as a coaster it is simply not capable of the kind of journey that would promise salvation. The mental distance that the viewer achieves with regard to this final phase of the story is already prefigured by comic estrangement effects earlier in the film. What started as social drama increasingly turns into a hybrid genre that also includes narrative conventions of the road movie and tragicomedy.

The Match Factory Girl similarly moves away from the genre of the social drama and its intended effect of pathos toward the end. The story of a young factory worker who leads a life of poverty, is exploited by her parents, abandoned by a man after the first meeting, and then pressured to abort her child, would clearly seem to lead to a dilemma, particularly since the she pours rat poison into the man's glass. However, the filmmaker has tacked on an ending that is extremely paradoxical and ambivalent, going in a different direction entirely. In an interview, he commented: "The end of *Tulitikkutehtaan tyttö* is, as I see it, not a sad ending. At least, the girl is able to free herself from society—at least in her head, not physically—, and that is good. I am amused to see how the viewers react: when I ask someone who has seen the movie to tell me the story, they all tell me: the girl killed four people and the police take her to jail. But that is not what I said; I never said that they die, I never said that they are police. I could say those are her uncle and his son, who are taking her out for a picnic in the countryside. I never showed anyone dead. That is in their heads. And such a small amount of rat poison does not kill anyone, anyway. But I do think they die. I hope that they die" (1991, 104).

The representation of real-life occurrences is transformed on the sly into fiction, which neutralizes the sad emotions that arose from observing reality and turns them into a game in which wish-fulfilment fantasies can be realized, but in a form that would be more likely to be found in a black comedy. The narrative conventions of social drama are transformed into those of comedy.

5.3 The Application of Combined Models to Hybrid Genres

These kinds of "impure" genres are not new. The genre of tragicomedy was able to establish itself as a relatively stable hybrid form in the theater long ago. It was of course adapted to film, too, and individual works have often combined drama and comedy in various ways in theater and film. There was a general tendency toward pure genre forms during the first fifty years of cinema history, resulting in a quasi-theoretical understanding of genre effects, according to which there was a kind of contract with the audience which filmmakers would have to adhere to. However, after having become popular with a particular genre on screen, even during the silent period filmmakers like Chaplin began to mix comedy and melodrama without any fear of the consequences. It is interesting that hybrid forms were then not only to be found in the separate areas of classical and popular genres, but also allowed for combinations between the two.

Following a tendency to draw on popular genres within the framework of the arthouse films that had become rampant in Europe in the 1970s, although this had been rejected before, there were a number of artistic attempts to create hybrid forms mixing highly diverse genres or even combining several genres into polygenres. As I see it, these hybrid forms can no longer be described by means of the traditional systems of classification. An approach through a combination of standardized strategies of effects or narrative conventions seems more promising.

In the 1966 film *Blow Up*, Antonioni re-shaped the episodic narrative structure which he had just carried to extremes in his tetralogy of behavioral films by combining it with genre stereotypes, making use of at least two genre forms, the detective movie and the parable. The film shows how a fashion photographer develops shots he had taken by chance of a couple of lovers in a park, and then comes to believe that he can see the image of someone in the bushes aiming a pistol at the man, apparently with the woman's knowledge. When the protagonist's suspicions that he was witness to a planned crime seem to become substantiated, the film takes on the character of a detective story, particularly when the photographer returns to the park and finds the corpse of the man. The film continues to employ conventions of the detective film when the incriminatory photographs are stolen from the photographer's studio.

As in his previous works, Antonioni records the hero's behavior precisely, revealing patterns that show the investigative photographer to be a seeker of truth, who continuously lets himself be distracted from his aim. Close observation of the hero shows that he often pursues something quite energetically and with great commitment but then quickly drops it again. Shortly before the end of the film there is a scene that reveals this contradictory behavior particularly clearly. After the hero has fought with other guests in a disco and managed to grab the remains of a guitar that the musician has just smashed on stage, he throws his trophy away, no longer interested in it. When none of his friends seem interested in the results of his investigations and the corpse in the park is no longer to be found, he seems to drop his attempts to solve the case in a similar way. The detective story turns into a parable about the distractability of the searcher for truth, in a way that might be typical of the emerging hippy generation. More precisely, the film develops the detective story and the parable parallel to one another and begins to repeatedly switch from one genre to the other earlier on. The varying genre expectations impinge on each other, having the advantage of letting the detective story make the observations on behavior, which belong to the parable, become more suspenseful, and at the same time give the detective story a more transcendental quality. The ending fits more with the parable, but involves a strange ambiguity: the protagonist, who has unsuccessfully been looking for the *corpus delicti* in the park and seems to have given up his search for the truth, meets up with a carnivalesque group of young people, who are playing tennis with an invisible ball that only exists in their imagination. When the virtual ball is hit out of bounds, the protagonist picks it up from the lawn and throws it back to the players.

Milos Forman's *One Flew Over the Cuckoo's Nest* is a film which presents basic kinds of occurrences familiar from action movies, especially from the sub-genre of the prison escape drama, but also refuses to stay within the limits of this popular genre. The protagonist, Randle, who constantly provokes the people in charge of the mental institution where he is being held, is at the same time the hero of a tragicomedy. And because he also leads other inmates to question the legitimacy of the psychiatric institution, the viewers also come to be watching a parable about nonconformism in an alienated world as well as about the self-incurred immaturity of people, since only a very few of the inmates are willing to follow Randle's lead, no matter how attractive it may seem to them. The ending is also instructive with regard to the organization of this genre hybrid. In fact, the film presents several possible solutions at the end, each of which is closely related to a particular genre. One direction is found in the psychiatric destruction of Randle's personality through the electro-shock treatment the doctors impose on him. This is intended to finally quiet the rebel and is only overridden by the mercy killing given him by his fellow patient and friend, the Indian chief. The protagonist's tragic catastrophe is contrasted with the chief's violent breakout. The prison escape drama culminates here, fusing with the parable when the step into freedom abolishes the individual's self-incurred immaturity. However, before the Indian disappears into the dark woods, the spectator is shown the twisted face of another patient who reacts to the escape with laughter that sounds at once derisive and incredulous and reminds the viewer of techniques of comic farce. The so strongly emotionally differing endings, which evoke quite different concepts of possible solutions to the conflicts, offer the viewers a kind of psychological regulation that juggles various genre effects to correspond to the complicated dialectic of the subject matter.

Andrei Tarkovsky's *Stalker* (1979) also uses a mixture of genres in that it combines narrative conventions of science fiction with those of the parable. The main character, referred to as "Stalker", has taken on the job of guiding two intellectuals, a writer and a scientist, into a mysterious and closely guarded zone, in the center of which there is a room that is supposed to have the power of fulfilling its visitors' most secret wishes. The zone, which physically resembles a radioactively devastated, uninhabited area, combines characteristics of untouched nature with those of a war-ravaged landscape, and proves to be a place in which the normal rules of life no longer apply. Instead, there are other, unknown laws, and it can be fatal for the visitors if they disobey them. Stalker, who is a professional guide with charismatic qualities, turns out to be strangely upset by the unpredictability of the zone, and thus can serve as a representative of the open-minded Russian intellectuals of the film's period, who on the basis of their social position should have been able to lead the way, but in view of the new conditions in the international situation before the collapse of the Soviet Union were deeply perplexed. The film supports this interpretation. When in the end the intellectuals decide to forsake entering the room they have reached after such hardships and tribulations, because they apparently—and rightly—are afraid to have their secret wishes become true, the film is looking for a parable and anticipates the idea of "new thinking" of the Gorbachev era, which unexpectedly departed from previous ways of thinking and even from central doctrines of the political struggle for power. When at the end of the film Stalker's daughter, who is crippled because of genetic damage by radioactivity, is able to move a glass around on the table in her dingy home just by the power of her thoughts, this is to be seen in the sense of a parable. The final sequence shows that Stalker's world is not powerless, despite or perhaps because of the doubts and insecurities it involves. The genre of science fiction joins up with the parable to direct the audience's imagination to view the individual as being capable of acting despite everything.

Since sketching out the genre conventions used in each case is already laborious, it is impossible to go into them in more detail, particularly since systematic elaborations of individual genre forms are lacking. In view of the current state of research, however, it seems important to recognize that genre hybrids employ diverse narrative stereotypes which can be identified in them. It is not yet possible to say much about the ways in which they are linked together, but in certain phases of plot development in hybrid-form films we can distinguish peculiar pauses during which the action seems to be free of genre characteristics, as if the film shifts into a different kind of regulation at these points. Consider the prolonged sequences shortly before the endings of *Breathless, Blow Up, 8½, Zabriskie Point, One Flew Over the Cuckoo's Nest, Stalker, Ariel,* or *Life is Beautiful,* in which the action seems suspended, as though the film needs some time to concentrate on what is essential and to decide on the most fitting of the possible genre patterns for the final resolution. The audience may in fact need these "waiting times," in view of the various options, before arriving at a conclusive perspective on the course of events and thus at an emotional stance that best corresponds to the intention of the film.

The mixture of genres in *Life is Beautiful,* to which there are many parallels in postmodern film of the last few years, is achieved in as much as the form and effects of the individual phases of action accord to different genre criteria. Although these genre patterns appear only temporarily and change often, their periodic repetition makes them effective throughout the film. Particularly significant in this instance are genre elements of the parable, comedy, tragedy, drama, and fairy tale.

A particularly impressive and characteristic situation is a scene in the final sequence. Guido has been captured by the guards and is led in front of the circuit box in which his son is hiding and looking through a slit. Although Guido himself is in danger of losing his life, he tries to keep on pretending to his son that the camp is just a game and winks and makes faces. This foregrounds Guido's unusual mental experiment, which is to simply ignore the power of terror at times. In this way the film comes close to a parable. This genre does not keep to the laws of probability of real life, instead creating a possible world in which events refer to an abstract idea or maxim. In this sense Benigni remarked about his film: "you should not expect anything realistic. Edgar Allen Poe said that one should not look down over the verge of an abyss, because real horror is immeasurable. If one shows it, then it is only what one shows" (1998, 22). This is why a parable-like story is told, in which a child survives the terror because the power of love and imagination can overcome the paralyzing power of evil. Up to this scene, the father's fictions had mobilized the boy's will to endure, and with it his own, and in the end it proves to be a higher truth, since the child does survive. Although the historical conflict situation is impossible for an individual to solve in reality, its estrangement in the form of the unique experiment of the film plot creates the feeling that it could possibly be coped with. However, the positive emotion that arises is closely linked to mental reflection, and at the same time uncontrolled affective arousal is limited. Brechtian theater, which often makes use of the parable form, always attempts to point out the specifics of such controlled emotions, since alienation effects were held suspect of cold rationality. Benigni's film is unlikely to elicit such suspicion, which certainly has to do with the abrupt change from parable to comedy.

After Guido has winked at his son he parodies marching. Dressed in women's clothes, in parading in front of his son's hiding-place he carries out highly exaggerated movements, thus the genre changes from parable to comic farce. Contradictory elements of the situation become quite evident as incongruities that the viewer can easily conceptualize. Normally the reaction would be laughter, but in the given moment of extreme danger it sticks in our throats. The film makes its general tendency toward the comic genre and its many variants evident from the first sequence on. The actor Benigni hardly ever lets a chance for artificial gestures or exaggerated expressions go by. The use of elements from *commedia dell'arte* is obvious, while slapstick passages and running gags increase the light tendency. The comic effects dominate the beginning of the film to such an extent that some critics claimed that it falls into two parts: the first is comedy and the second tragedy. This judgment is mistaken, however. Closer examination shows that comic alienation is also to be found in the second half of the film, although less often and appearing only in separate moments. It is important, however, that the audience's genre disposition, once it has been set up, leads the viewers to perceive the situation through basic emotional perspectives that allow them a certain mental distance, thus giving them greater foresight and more passive control of the conflict situations. This then makes it possible to achieve a more positive emotional state.

In the final sequence, immediately after Guido's parodied marching, an action follows in which the guard takes the safety device off his machine pistol. He leads Guido around the corner of a wall and we hear shots. The catastrophe has been reached and the film now clearly redefines itself in terms of the tragic genre. With regard to this, Benigni stated: "I have not made a comedy about the holocaust—I am a comedian who has made a tragedy. That is a big difference" (1998). The author Imre Kertész, himself a survivor of a Nazi concentration camp, assures us that the film's "idea is not comical, but tragic" (1998, 55). In fact, it is about unsolvable contradictions in reality upon which the protagonists must physically perish, and their portrayal corresponds to the genre rule of tragic catharsis. But this, too, does not become evident only in the second half of the film; from the beginning there are discrepancies and elements of conflict which point to the increasingly dangerous Fascist threat. They not only remind the viewer of the brutality of the historical situation, but also evoke emotional reactions that correspond to the effective strategy of tragedy or tragicomedy.

A basic tendency in the opposite direction is furthered by the film's temporary reference to the genre of the drama. In the drama, conflicts of interest that are difficult to solve are dealt with in a way that leads to a favorable outcome for the protagonist in the end, often against our general expectations. Benigni's film also keeps this possibility open. Immediately after Guido's death, the guards flee the camp and the prisoners are free. When Guido's little boy leaves his hiding place, he finds himself suddenly in front of an American tank, whose commander kindly asks him to climb in. Curiously enough, it was a tank that Guido had promised the child as the prize for winning the game of hide and seek in the concentration camp. Therefore, the boy can feel that he is the winner when his mother, whom he meets again among the liberated concentration camp inmates, happily says, "We won." The dramatic conflict classically ends here in pathos: the complete congruence of the viewers' desire and the historical triumph of the protagonist.

The low degree of probability that the story could have such an ending in real life is artistically magnified in that the conventions of the fairy tale are evoked. In an early stage of development the film was to have been titled "Good Morning, Princess", and in many ways Guido's principle of life is that of a fairy tale character who relies on magic powers and tricks that again and again lead to carnevalistic twists and favorable turns in the plot. The ending includes references to legends and the genre of fairy tales as well; for instance when, after the guards have fled, the prisoners go out into the courtyard as though they were being pulled by a magic wand and then set out in groups through the open gate, or when in a similarly unreal way the tank that Guido had promised suddenly pops up like some magical creature in the courtyard. In each of these phases of the plot the various genre relations help create a certain emotional tendency that thus comes into dominance. Incidentally, quite lengthy pauses between the phases help the viewers to recognize the genre stereotypes and make it easier for them to re-orient themselves emotionally.

How the various factors that evoke emotional effects interact and interplay is still a great mystery and will most likely remain so for empirical research for a long time. As I see it, a possible first step for film research could be separate psychological analyses of individual cinematic effects, which traditional aesthetics has described and which have noticeable emotional components. Several of the concepts used here, such as "parable-like alienation," "comedy," "tragic catharsis," "dramatic tension," and "pathos," refer clearly to such effects, since they describe genre-specific responses in the form of significant effects in the viewer's mind (see fig. 11). This conceptualization of specific aesthetic reactions may well make emotional relationships more accessible than more general expressions such as joy, fear, anger, etc. do, and there have been some attempts to model them in terms of cognitive psychology (cf. Wuss 1993, 318ff.). This separate modeling of effects could orient itself to genre-related elements of conflict, since we are clearly dealing here with reactions of the recipient that relate to significant changes in stimuli, that is, to discrepancies in Mandler's sense or what Berlyne described as collative stimulus variables.

Of course, models of specific spectators would have to be considered in order to take differing audience groups into account. It appears to be important that the model of the spectator used to analyze emotions in classic genres must also take into account his or her involvement in real-life situations that are similar to those in the film. The viewers' real experience of conflicts often exerts a considerable influence on the degree of emotionality of their experience in a film. The real needs and motives that concrete audiences have can be so strong and long-lasting that they enormously strengthen or totally block the emotions a film potentially aims at. Convincing examples of the latter can be found among the reactions to Benigni's film (cf. Viano 1999). Some viewers, for example, have stated that they needed the distance of half a century from the Holocaust in order to be inwardly able to go along with the film's narration and its tendency toward comedy. Others are still unable to accept an attitude that can allow distance or even laughter in the face of the terrors of the extermination of the Jews, so that the film title *Life is Beautiful* can only appear cynical to them.

The genre's way of functioning is unsuccessful not because of social taboos or the strict limitations of the "eternal values" of an abstract ethic, but rather because it has to rely on very specific, historically developed psychological dispositions in the audience, and these have to do with the primary human motivation of control over our life, that is, with our desire to be able to take action in life. Even if it is necessary to approach emotions in the cinema in terms of psycho-physiological reactions, we must not forget that emotions are more than just affects in the sense of reactions to a stimulus. They always have to do with the subjective evaluation of a conflictual situation, and because of its relation to reality this may retain its horror over a whole human lifespan. That means it does not allow the feeling of being in command of the situation or of being capable of dealing with it to arise, but this feeling is necessary if the experience is to be put into aesthetic form. Recognition of the conflict—that no individual or social group can resolve it—does not mean that it is unfit for art and its positive emotions. However, it does raise the question of which mechanisms of psychological regulation the work can offer in order to give the viewers the feeling of being able to cope and through creative effort to repress the emotional threat that the real conflicts represent. This always involves shifting borders, which Rilke described as „Beauty is nothing but the beginning, which we can just barely endure, of horror..." ("Denn das Schöne ist nichts als des Schrecklichen Anfang, den wir noch grade ertragen." [1959, 1, 233]). *Life is Beautiful* is important beyond its meaning as an instance of art because the events it shows are paradigmatic for an appropriate emotional way of dealing with horror, which is revalued through creative play and thus robbed of its paralyzing force.

The postmodern cinema that makes up the context for Benigni's film in terms of the history of film style has not just led to the formation of first-order film stereotypes. The escalation in the development of stereotypes, which has provided for the mass proliferation of well-known forms as well as for their diversity and omnipresence, has also accelerated and intensified the development of genre hybrids or polygenres in a hitherto unheard-of way. Correspondingly complicated formal approaches, which were extremely rare before, have now become almost standard, making it necessary for analysis to find appropriate ways to register the accompanying increase in unconscious experiential contents. The extended PCS model, which can be applied to the description of certain genre conventions, may be helpful here. It could be of value in that it makes it possible to find rational ways to approximate a description of narrative structures that have relatively unconscious effects. Thus one would not have to relinquish investigating artistic structures and semantic processes, nor judging the effectiveness or failure of the communication of meaning in individual works or whole stylistic movements.

Conclusions

At the beginning of my considerations, there was the desire for a deeper understanding of the interrelations between the form and the impact of a film than is possible within the scope of traditional studies of cinema. This interest was, in part, a consequence of the constraints of the practice of the audiovisual media. Particularly in the last half-century, filmmakers, critics and theorists have been increasingly confronted with theoretical problems that are unsolvable without a differentiated knowledge of film's influence on the viewer's mind. They were obliged, for instance, to evaluate and consider very different modes of storytelling for the screen. Among them are those which obviously deviate from the standards of classical narration of mainstream cinema, including many examples of art films but also numerous other films even beyond art-house productions.

To come closer to a scientific analysis of this phenomenon, it is necessary to create a bridge from film studies to psychology. And in doing so, it also made sense for me to join in the work of the Cognitive Film Theory which has successfully practiced such an effort for some decades, particularly in its research into the cognitive and emotive functions of cinematic narration.

The present treatise outlines a three-rung-model which uses ideas from cognitive psychology to describe various filmic structures, those that are conspicuous and will be very consciously received by the viewer as well as others which are less evident and lead to an experience by the audience that is nearly unconscious. This so-called PCS model, which distinguishes perception-based, conception-based and stereotype-based filmic structures, can be used to describe the different kinds of psychological impact that play a role in our experience.

Even in this elementary form, the modelling of the film's stimulus configurations leads to a differentiated description of the various modes of storytelling. Besides the common recurrence of the causal chain of events which may be consciously experienced by the spectator of films used to classical narration, this method also enables the realisation and consideration of those structures of cinematic narration that the viewer often experiences in a nearly unconscious manner. They are preconscious where they work rather on the level of perception, or they can be sometimes nonconscious where they have become habitual under the conditions of cultural stereotyping. Analogous to the three filmic structures, the model differentiates three basic structures of narration, topic lines, causal chains and stereotypes of narration, which do not exclude one another but interact during the process of storytelling in different ways—though often one of these basic structures dominates.

This analytical approach does justice to the dramatic plot story, based on the causal chain, as well as to its opposite forms termed episodic, epic, or open modes of storytelling, which are characterized by a dominant topic line, and also others that are organised by genres founded on stereotypes of narration. Thus, each extreme mode of storytelling can find a place in its wide scope; likewise their various transition forms and the hybrid results of historic changes which can generally be approximated by differing combinations of the basic structures. In this way, the flexible model enables us to understand the individual modes of storytelling in all their richness.

In order to grasp the inner dynamics of storytelling, the films' conflict situations and colliding actions have been highlighted. In addition to central dramatic conflicts, opposing forces in the films were considered as well, which are based on contradictions of peripheral significance and collisions of weaker intensity. These contradictions can be relevant for the development of on-screen events, too. They form an entire field of conflict which functions in the development of the story as a differentiated causal field.

The repeated reference back to the category of conflict has the advantage that one can link the heroes' conflict situations with the viewers' cognitive processes of problem-solving and especially with the affective arousals and emotions elicited by the film. These connections turn out to be of particular value for further considerations connecting the conflict situations on the screen with the emotional reactions of the spectator. According to these hypotheses, the conflict moments on the screen can be seen as a source of the film's emotional impact. They also provide the foundation for the emotional effects of genres, such as tension and suspense, comic estrangement, tragic catharsis or dramatic pathos, and the model allows the description and functional explanation of hybrid-genres and poly-genres.

Furthermore, the process of coping with conflict situations on the screen seems to be a productive starting point for research into the imageries the viewer's mind constructs thanks to his film experience. Since this area of psychological functions has hardly been analyzed at all until now, my treatise simply seeks cues on how one could conduct research in this direction; for instance, starting from the performances of the hero's dreams and reflections on the screen, his play behaviour for overcoming conflict situations, with its consequences for the development of desire-like imaginings in the audience, or the specific strategies used by different genres for eliciting positive emotions and imageries in the viewers' mind.

Setting out from relevant problems of cinematic storytelling, the book attempts to sketch the outline of an elementary model which brings us closer to the functional relationships between structures of narration and their aesthetic impact on the audience. Although the treatise generally subjects itself to the hermeneutic approach, it tries to support the hermeneutic presentation with model-aided assertions, which are compatible with psychological theories as well. Highlighting such elements of films' influence that lead to significant effects on the viewer should pave the way for empirical psychological research which can verify the assertions concerning the films' impact with corresponding "hard" data, for instance, psycho-physiological measurements.

The modelling of these effects and the construction of hypotheses concerning their evocation within the process of film experience can only be seen as a first step on a long road to empirical analysis of the impacts, and it is by no means identical to a ready-made design for a concrete approach of data-processing. It merely allows the construction of (film-)work-models which are based on various "proposals for reception" given by films to an idealised model-spectator. There remain extensive efforts to enable research which takes into account that the audience comprises different individuals living under varying ethno-cultural and historical conditions, and that each process of art experience is very dynamic and deviates from the ideal-typus of reception. The realisation of these steps, however, lies within the competence of media psychology and sociology.

In my opinion, the present task of film theorists is to set in motion a fertile cooperation with other disciplines by clearly formulated points of attachment for concrete analyses, and I hope that the elaboration, practised here, of aesthetic effects with their good openings for proof by psychological experiments, can be useful in this process. My book has only formulated presumptions and rough hypotheses about certain impacts of film. That is a modest result, but according to Charles Sanders Peirce (Ms. 692), "we must conquer the truth by guessing, or not at all."

Bibliography

Allen, Richard (1995), *Projecting Illusion. Film Spectatorship and the Impression of Reality* (Cambridge: Cambridge University Press).

Altman, Rick (1996), *The American Film Musical* (Bloomington and Indianapolis: Indiana University Press).

Anderson, Joseph D. (1996), *The Reality of Illusion: An Ecological Approach to Cognitive Film Theory* (Carbondale and Edwardsville: Southern Illinois University Press).

Anderson, Joseph D. and Fisher Anderson, Barbara (1996), "The Case for an Ecological Metatheory" in Bordwell, David and Carroll, Noël, (eds.), *Post-Theory: Reconstructing Film Studies* (Madison: University of Wisconsin Press), pp. 347-367.

— (eds.) (2005), *Moving Image Theory: Ecological Considerations.* With a Foreword by David Bordwell (Carbondale: Southern Illinois University Press).

— (eds.) (2007), *Narration and Spectatorship in Moving Images* (Newcastle: Cambridge Scholars Publishing).

Antonioni, Michelangelo (1964), "Die Krankheit der Gefühle" in Kotulla, Theodor, (ed.), *Der Film. Manifeste—Gespräche—Dokumente,* Vol. II (München: Piper), pp. 83–110.

Andrzejewski, Jerzy (1964,) *Asche und Diamant,* Novel (Berlin and Weimar: Aufbau).

Anochin, Peter (1963), "Physiologie und Kybernetik" in *Kybernetik und Praxis.* Mit einem Vorwort von Gerda Schnauss (Berlin: Deutscher Verlag der Wissenschaften), pp. 148–188.

Aristotle (1987), *The 'Poetics' of Aristotle,* transl. and commentary by Stephen Halliwell (London: Ducksworth & Co.).

—. (2001), *Poetics,* translated by Nicholas Geoffrey Lemprière

Hammond (Copenhagen: Museum Tusculanum Press).

Arnheim, Rudolf (1969), *Film as Art* [1932] (Berkeley and Los Angeles: University of California Press).

Baars, B. J. (1988), *A Cognitive Theory of Consciousness* (New York: Cambridge University Press,).

Baddeley, A. D. (1986), *Working Memory* (Oxford, UK: Clarendon Press).

—. (2003a), "New Data. Old Pitfalls" in *Behavioral Brain Sciences*, 26, pp. 729–730.

—. (2003b), Working Memory: Looking Back and Forward" in *Nature Reviews Neuroscience*, 4, pp. 829–839.

Bakhtin, Michail (1969), *Literaturtheorie und Karneval: Zur Romantheorie und Lachkultur* (München: Carl Hanser).

—. (1972), *Problemy poetiki Dostojevskogo,* Izd. tret'e (Moskva: Chudožestvennaja literatura).

—. (1975), *Voprosy literatury i estetiki* (Moskva: Chudožestvennaja literatura).

Bartsch, Anne (2007), "Meta-Emotion and Genre Preference: What Makes Horror Films and Tear-Jerkers Enjoyable?" in Anderson, J. and Fisher Anderson, B. (eds.), *Narration and Spectatorship in Moving Images* (Newcastle: Cambridge Scholars Publishing), pp. 124–135.

Barthes, Roland (1994), *The Semiotic Challenge*, translated by Richard Howard (Berkeley, Los Angeles and London: University of California Press).

Bazin, André (1971), *What is Cinema? Essays selected and translated by Hugh Gray*, Vols. I & II (Berkeley and Los Angeles: University of California Press; London: Cambridge University Press).

Beilenhoff, Wolfgang (ed.) (2005), *Poetika Kino. Theorie und Praxis des Films im russischen Formalismus* (Frankfurt a.M: Suhrkamp).

Benigni, Roberto (1998), "Fünf Fragen an Roberto Benigni: Interview mit Tobias Kniebe" in *Süddeutsche Zeitung* (München), 12.11.1998, p. 22.

Benjamin, Walter (1969), "The Work of Art in the Age of Mechanical Reproduction" in *Illuminations*, ed. Hannah Arendt, trans. Harry Zohn (New York: Schocken Books).

Bense, Max (1954-1960), *Aesthetica*, I [1954], II [1956], III [1958], IV [1960]. (Stuttgart: Deutsche Verlagsanstalt; Krefeld and Baden-Baden: Agis-Verlag).

Berlyne, Daniel E. (1960), *Conflict, Arousal, and Curiosity* (New York, Toronto and London: McGrawHill Book Company).

Beyerle, Monika and Brinckmann, Christine N. (eds.) (1991), *Der amerikanische Dokumentarfilm der 60er Jahre: Direct Cinema und Radical Cinema*. (Frankfurt am Main: Campus Verlag).

Bischof, Norbert (1998), *Struktur und Bedeutung: eine Einführung in die Systemtheorie für Psychologen*, 2, korr. Aufl. (Göttingen, Toronto and Seattle: Huber).

Böhm, Christian (1990), "Die psychologische Realität der Tiefenstruktur filmischer Narrationen: Inferenzbildung und Protagonistenrepräsentation" in Schumm, Gerhard and Wulff, Hans J., (eds.) *Film und Psychologie I: Kognition— Rezeption—Perzeption* (Münster: MakS Publikationen), pp. 143–178.

Bordwell, David (1985), *Narration in the Fiction Film* (London: Methuen).

—. (1986), "Classical Hollywood Cinema: Narrational Principles and Procedures" in Rosen, Philip, (ed.) *Narrative, Apparatus, Ideology: A Film Theory Reader* (New York: Columbia University Press), pp. 17–34.

—. (1989a), *Making Meaning: Inference and Rhetoric in the Interpretation of Cinema* (Cambridge, Mass. and London: Harvard University Press).

—. (1989b), "A Case for Cognitivism" in *Iris* 5 , 2, pp. 11–40.

—. (2002), "Film Futures" in: *SubStance* 31, 1 , pp. 105–114.

—. (2006), *The Way Hollywood Tells it: Story and Style in Modern Movies* (Berkeley, Los Angeles and London: University of California Press).

Bordwell, David, Staiger, Janet, and Thompson, Kristin (1985), *The Classical Hollywood Cinema: Film Style and Mode of Production to 1960* (London: Routledge & Kegan Paul).

Branigan, Edward (1992), *Narrative Comprehension and Film* (London and New York: Routledge).

—. (2002), "Nearly True: Forking Plots, Forking Interpretations. A Response to David Bordwell's 'Film Future'" in *SubStance* 31, 1 (no. 97), pp. 105–114.

Bransford, J.D. and Stein, B.S. (1984), *The Ideal Problem Solver: A Guide for Improving Thinking, Learning, and Creativity* (New York: Freeman).

Brecht, Bertolt (1960), *Bertolt Brechts Dreigroschenbuch* (Frankfurt am Main: Suhrkamp).

—. (1964), *Schriften zum Theater,* Vols. I–VII (Berlin and Weimar: Aufbau-Verlag).

—. (1977), *Arbeitsjournal 1938–1955 (*Berlin: Aufbau-Verlag).

—. (1990), *Brecht on Theatre—the Development of an Aesthetic;* ed. and transl. by John Willett (London: Methuen Drama).

Bresson, Robert (1980), *Noten zum Kinematographen* (München: Carl Hanser).

Brewer, William F. (1996), "The Nature of Narrative Suspense and the Problem of Rereading" in Vorderer, P., Wulff, H. J., and Friedrichsen, M., (eds.) *Suspense: Conceptualizations, Theoretical Analyses, and Empirical Exlorations*, pp. 101–127.

Brinckmann, Christine N. (1997), "Empathie mit dem Tier" in

Cinema (CineZoo), 42, pp. 60–69.

—. (2005), "Die Rolle der Empathie oder Furcht und Schrecken im Dokumentarfilm" in Brütsch, Matthias et al., (eds.) *Kinogefühle: Emotionalität und Film* (Marburg: Schüren), pp. 333–360.

Brütsch, Matthias, Hediger, Vinzenz, von Keitz, Ursula, Schneider, Alexandra, and Tröhler, Margrit (eds.) (2005), *Kinogefühle: Emotionalität und Film,* Zürcher Filmstudien 12, ed. by Christine N. Brinckmann (Marburg: Schüren).

Buckland, Warren (2002), "Cognitive Theories of Narration (*Lost Highway*)" in Elsaesser, Thomas and Buckland, Warren, (eds.) *Studying Contemporary American Film: A Guide to Movie Analysis* (London: Arnold), pp. 168–194.

Buscombe, Edward (1986), "The Idea of Genre in the American Cinema" in Grant, Barry K., (ed.) *Film Genre Reader*), pp. 11–25.

Bühler, Karl (1929), *Die geistige Entwicklung des Kindes* (Jena: Fischer).

Cacioppo, J.T., Uchino, B.N., Crites, S.L., Snydermith, M.A., Smith. G., Berntson, G.G., and Lang, P. J. (1992), "Relationship Between Facial Expressiveness and Sympathetic Activation in Emotion: A Critical Review, with Emphasis on Modeling Underlying Mechanisms and Individual Differences" in *Journal of Personality and Social Psychology,* 62 , pp. 110–128.

Cameron, Allan (2006), "Contingency, Order, and the Modular Narrative: '21 Grams' and 'Irreversible'" in *The Velvet Light Trap,* 58 , pp. 65–78.

Carroll, Noël (1990), *The Philosophy of Horror, or Paradoxes of the Heart* (New York: Routledge).

—. (1996a), *Theorizing the Moving Image* (New York: Cambridge University Press).

—. (1996b), "The Paradox of Suspense" in Vorderer, P., Wulff, H. J., and Friedrichsen, Mike, (eds.) *Suspense: Conzeptualizations, Theoretical Analyses, and Empirical Explorations* (Mahwah, N.J.: Lawrence Erlbaum), pp. 71–91.

—. (1999), "Film, Emotion, and Genre" in Plantinga, Carl and Smith, Greg, (eds.) *Passionate Views: Film, Cognition, and Emotion* (Baltimore: Johns Hopkins University Press), pp. 21–47.

Château, Dominique (1983), "Film et réalité: Pour rajeunir un vieux problème" in *Iris* 1, 1 , pp. 51–65.

Christiansen, Broder (1909), *Philosophie der Kunst* (Hanau: Clauss & Feddersen).

Clauss, Günter et al. (eds.) (1976), *Wörterbuch der Psychologie.* (Leipzig: Bibliographisches Institut).

Cowan, Nelson (1995), *Attention and Memory: An Integrated Framework* (New York: Oxford University Press).

Cube, Felix von (1965), *Kybernetische Grundlagen des Lernens und Lehrens* (Stuttgart: Klett).

Currie, Gregory (1995), *Image and Mind: Film, Philosophy and Cognitive Science* (Cambridge: University Press).

—. (1999), "Narrative Desire" in Plantinga, Carl and Smith, Greg M., (eds.) *Passionate Views: Film, Cognition, and Emotion* (Baltimore and London: The Johns Hopkins University Press) pp. 183–199.

—. (2002), *Recreative Minds: Imagination in Philosophy and Psychology* (Oxford: Clarendon Press).

Damasio, Antonio R. (1994), *Descartes' Error: Emotion, Reason and the Human Brain* (New York: G.P. Putnam's Son).

Dörner, Dietrich (1979), *Problemlösung als Informationsverarbeitung* (Stuttgart: Kohlhammer).

—. (1999), *Bauplan für eine Seele* (Reinbek bei Hamburg: Rowohlt)

Dörner, Dietrich, Reither, Franz, and Stäudel, Thea, "Emotion und problemlösendes Denken" (1983), in Mandl, Heinz and

Huber, Günter, (eds.) *Emotion und Kognition* (München, Wien and Balitmore: Urban & Schwarzenberg), pp. 61–84.

Dogma '95 manifesto, The (1999), in Binoto, T., "Unbändige Lust auf Dogmen" in *Zoom,* 2, 7 .

Doležel, Lubomir (1989), "Possible Worlds and Literary Fiction" in Sture, Allén, (ed.) *Possible Worlds in Humanities, Arts and Sciences* (Berlin: de Gruyter), pp. 221–242.

—. (1998), *Heterocosmica, Fiction and Possible Worlds* (Baltimore and London).

Drummond, Phillip (1997), *High Noon* (London: BFI Publishing)

Dürrenmatt, Friedrich (1955), *Theaterprobleme* (Zürich: Arche).

Eagleton, Terry (1983), *Literary Theory: An Introduction* (Minneapolis: University of Minnesota Press).

Eco, Umberto (1972), "The Myth of Superman" in *diacritics: a review of contemporary criticism* (Ithaca, N.Y.: Cornell University) 2, 1, pp. 14–22.

—. (1979), *The Role of the Reader: Explorations in the Semiotics of Texts* (Bloomington and London: Indiana University Press).

—. (1987), *Lector in fabula: Die Mitarbeit der Interpretation in erzählenden Texten* (München and Wien: Carl Hanser).

—. (1989a), *The Open Work* (Cambridge, Mass.: Harvard University Press)

—. (1989b), *Im Labyrinth der Vernunft: Texte über Kunst und Zeichen* (Leipzig: Reclam).

—. (1992), *Die Grenzen der Interpretation* (München: Hanser).

—. (1997), "Innovation and Repetition: Between Modern and Post-Modern Aesthetics" in *Reading Eco: An Anthology* ed. Rocco Capozzi (Bloomington and Indianapolis), pp. 14–33.

Eder, Jens (2005), "Die Wege der Gefühle: Ein integratives Modell der Anteilnahme an Filmfiguren" in Brütsch et al., (eds.) *Kinogefühle: Emotionalität und Film* (Marburg: Schüren), pp. 225–242.

Eisenstein, Sergei (1988), "The Dramaturgy of Film Form" [1929] in *Writings (1922-34)*, ed. and trans. Richard Taylor (Bloomington: Indiana University Press), pp. 161–180.

—. (1949), *Film Form: Essays in Film Theory*, ed. and trans. Jay Leyda (New York: Harcourt, Brace and Company).

Ekman, Paul and Davidson, Richard J. (eds.) (1994), *The Nature of Emotion: Fundamental Questions* (New York and Oxford: Oxford University Press).

Ellis, Michael J. (1973), *Why People Play* (Englewood Cliffs, New Jersey: Prentice-Hall).

Engle, R. W. (2002), "Working memory capacity as executive attention" in *Current Directions in Psychological Science*, 11, pp. 19–23.

Farthing, G. William (1992), *The Psychology of Consciousness* (Englewood Cliffs, NJ: Prentice Hall).

—. (2000), "Consciousness and Unconsciousness: An Overview" in Kazdin, Alan E., (ed.) *Encyclopedia of Psychology* (Washington DC: American Psych. Ass.), Vol. 2, pp. 268–272.

Fell, John (1977), "Propp in Hollywood" in *Film Quarterly*, 3, pp. 19–28.

Fellini, Federico (1964), "Über meinen Beruf als Regisseur" in Kotulla, Theodor, (ed.) *Der Film: Manifeste—Gespräche—Dokumente*, Vol. 2 (München: Piper & Co.), pp. 73–82.

—. (1968), *Stat'i, interv'ju , recenzii, vospominanija* (Moskva: Iskusstvo).

—. (1974a), *Aufsätze und Notizen* (Zürich: Arche).

—. (1974b), *8½* (Zürich: Diogenes).

—. (1984), *Fellini über Fellini: Ein intimes Gespräch mit Giovanni Grazzini* (Zürich: Diogenes).

Fiske, S. T. (1982), "Schema-Triggered Affect: Applications to a

Social Perception" in Clark, M. S. and Fiske, S. T., (eds.) *Affect and cognition: the 17th Annual Carnegie Symposium on Cognition* (Hillsdale, N.J.: Erlbaum), pp. 55–78.

Frank, Helmar (1959), *Grundlagenprobleme der Informationsästhetik und erste Anwendung auf die mime pure* (Waiblingen: Verlagsbuchhandlung Hess).

—. (1964), *Kybernetische Analysen subjektiver Sachverhalte* (Quickborn: Schnelle).

—. (1965), "Eine informationstheoretische Deutung psychologischer Komponenten innerhalb eines statistischen Rückkopplungs-systems" in *Zeitschrift für Psychologie,* 171, pp. 343–358.

Freud, Sigmund (1953), *The Interpretation of Dreams. The Standard Edition of the Complete Psychological Works of Sigmund Freud,* Vol. IV [1900] (London: The Hogarth Press and the Institute of Psycho-Analysis).

—. (1960), *Jokes and their Relation to the Unconscious. The Standard Edition of the Complete Psychological Works of Sigmund Freud,* Vol. VIII [1905] (London: The Hogarth Press and the Institute of Psycho-Analysis).

Freytag, Gustav (1965). *Die Technik des Dramas* [1863] (Darmstadt: Wissenschaftliche Buchgesellschaft).

Frijda, Nico H. (1986), *The Emotions* (Cambridge: Cambridge University Press).

—. (1988), "The Laws of Emotion" in *American Psychologist,* 43, pp. 349–358.

—. (1989), "Aesthetic Emotions and Reality" in *American Psychologist,* 44 , pp. 1546–1547.

—. (1993), "Moods, Emotion Episodes, and Emotions" in Lewis, M. and Haviland, J. M., (eds.) *Handbook of Emotions* (New York: Guilford, pp. 381–403.

—. (2007), *The Laws of Emotion* (Mahwah, N.J. and London: Erlbaum).

—. (2008), "Passion: What Emotions Really Are", Lecture, XXIX. International Congress of Psychology, July 20–25, Berlin.

Frijda, Nico H. and Mesquita, Batja, "Beliefs Through Emotions" in Frijda, Nico H., Manstead, Anthony S. and Bem, Sacha, (eds.) (2000), *Emotions and Beliefs: How Feelings Influence Thoughts* (Cambridge: Cambridge University Press), pp. 45–77.

Gad, Urban (1920), *Der Film: Seine Mittel—seine Ziele* (Berlin: Schuster und Löffler).

Gärdenfors, P. (1995), "Cued and Detached Representations in Animal Cognition" in *Lund University Cognitive Studies (LUCS)*, 38.

Gaut, Berys (1999), "Identification and Emotion in Narrative Film" in Plantinga, Carl and Smith, Greg M., (eds.) *Passionate Views: Film, Cognition, and Emotion* (Baltimore and London: The Johns Hopkins University Press), pp. 239–255.

Gehler, Fred (ed.) (1987, *Regiestühle international* (Berlin: Henschel).

Gellert, Walter, Kästner, Herbert, and Neuber, Siegfried, (eds.) (1977), *Lexikon der Mathematik* (Leipzig: Bibliographisches Institut).

Gibson, James J. (1973), *The Senses Considered as Perceptual Systems* (Boston: Houghton Mifflin Company).

—. (1979), *The Ecological Approach to Visual Perception* (Boston: Houghton Mifflin Company).

Goethe, Johann Wolfgang (1988), *Faust. A tragedy. Parts One and Two*, translated in a performing version by Robert David MacDonnald (Birmingham /England: Oberon Books)

Gomery, Douglas (1989), "Structuring the Moving Picture Image: The Classic Hollywood Narrative" in Michelson, Annette, Gomery, Douglas, and Loughney, Patrick, (eds.) *The Art of Moving Shadows* (Washington: National Gallery of Art), pp. 49–61.

Grant, Barry Keith (ed.) (1993), *Film Genre Reader* (Austin: University of Texas Press).

Greimas, Algirdas J. (1983), *Structural Semantics: An Attempt at a Method* (Lincoln: University of Nebraska Press).

Grodal, Torben (1997), *Moving Pictures: A New Theory of Film Genres, Feelings, and Cognition* (Oxford: Clarendon Press).

—. (1999),"Emotions, Cognitions, and Narrative Patterns in Film" in Plantinga, C. and Smith, G. M., (eds.) *Passionate Views: Film, Cognition, and Emotion* (Baltimore and London: The Johns Hopkins University Press), pp. 127–145.

—. (2001),"Film, Character Simulation, and Emotion" in Friess, Jörg, Hartmann, Britta and Müller, Eggo, (eds.) *Nicht allein das Laufbild auf der Leinwand... Strukturen des Films als Erlebnispotenziale,* Beiträge zur Film- und Fernsehwissenschaft (BFF) 60 , pp. 115–128.

Hagendorf, Herbert (2006), "Arbeitsgedächtnis" in Funke, Joachim and Frensch, Peter A., (eds.) *Handbuch der Allgemeinen Psychologie—Kognition* (Göttingen et al.: Hogrefe), pp. 340–345.

Hartmann, Britta (2008), *Spuren auslegen, Rahmen errichten: Textpragmatik und kognitive Dramaturgie des Filmanfangs* (Laying Out Tracks, Setting up Frames: Textual Pragmatics and Cognitive Dramaturgy of Film Beginnings) With a summary in English (Proefschrift, Universiteit Utrecht); *Aller Anfang. Zur Initialphase des Spielfilms* (Marburg: Schüren (Zürcher Filmstudien Bd. 22), forthcoming (2009)).

Heath, Stephen (1981), *Questions of Cinema* (Bloomington: Indiana University Press).

Hegel, Georg Friedrich Wilhelm (1951), *Wissenschaft der Logik.* Vol. 2 (Leipzig: Philosophische Bibliothek).

—. (1965), *Ästhetik,* Vol. II (Berlin and Weimar: Aufbau).

Hettner, Hermann (1959), *Schriften zur Literatur* (Berlin and Weimar: Aufbau).

Herakleitos von Ephesos (1958), in Capelle, Wilhelm, *Die Vorsokratiker* (Berlin: Akademie-Verlag), pp. 126–157.

Hintikka, Jaakko (1973), *Logic, Language Games, and Information* (London: Oxford University Press).

Huizinga, Johan (1938), *Homo ludens. Vom Ursprung der Kultur im Spiel* (Amsterdam: Pantheon Akademische Verlags-Anstalt).

Hussy, Walter (1993), *Denken und Problemlösen* (Stuttgart and Berlin: Kohlhammer).

Hutt, Corinne (1981), "Toward a Taxonomy and Conceptual Model of Play" in Day, H., (ed.) *Advances in Intrinsic Motivation and Aesthetics* (New York: Plenum Press), pp. 251–298.

Iser, Wolfgang (1972), "The Reading Process: A Phenomenological Approach" in *New Literary History* 3, pp. 279–299.

Iosseliani, Otar (1994), TV Interview by Marcel Bluwal, *arte*: 27.04.1994

Ivanov, Vyacheslav V. (1965a) "Rol' semiotiki v kibernetičeskom issledovanii čeloveka i kollektiva" in *Logičeskaja struktura naučnogo znanija* (Moskva: Nauka), pp. 75–90.

—. (1965b)"Kommentarij" in Vygotsky, Lev, *Psichologija iskusstva* (Moskva: Iskusstvo).

Izard, Carroll E. (1991), *The Psychology of Emotions* (New York and London: Plenum Press).

James, William (1950), *The Principles of Psychology*, Vol. 1 (New York: Dover).

Jarrold, Chris, Carruthers, Peter, Smith, Peter and Boucher, Jill (1994), "Pretend Play: Is it Metarepresentational?" in *Mind & Language* 9, pp. 445–468.

Jauss, Hans Robert (1970), *Literaturgeschichte als Provokation der Literaturwissenschaft* (Frankfurt am Main: Suhrkamp).

Johansson, Gunnar (1966), "Geschehenswahrnehmung" in Metzger, Wolfgang and Erke, Heiner, (eds.) *Handbuch der*

Cinematic Narration and its Psychological Impact 323

Psychologie, Bd. I, 1: Wahrnehmung und Bewusstsein (Göttingen: Hogrefe), pp. 745–775.

Johnson, Mark (1987), The Body in the Mind: The Bodily Basis of Meaning, Imagination, and Reason (Chicago and London: The University of Chicago Press).

Jousse, Thierry (2006), Wong Kar-wai (Paris: Cahiers du Cinéma. SCÉRÉN).

Jung, Carl Gustav (1990), Archetypen (München: Deutscher Taschenbuch Verlag).

—. (1996), Vom Wesen der Träume. Traum und Traumdeutung (München: Deutscher Taschenbuch Verlag).

Kagan, Moisej S. (1972), Morfologija iskusstva (Leningrad: Iskusstvo).

Katz, Albert M. (2000), "Mental Imagery" in Kazdin, Alan E., (ed.) Encyclopedia of Psychology (Washington DC: American Psych. Ass., Vol. 5, pp. 187–191.

Kaufmann, Hans (1962), Bertolt Brecht—Geschichtsdrama und Parabelstück (Berlin: Rütten & Loening).

Kaurismäki, Aki (1991), "'Jetzt habe ich zuviel geredet...und zuviel geraucht.' Ein Gespräch mit Aki Kaurismäki. Geführt von Bruno Fornara und Francesco" in Kaurismäki, Aki: I Hired a Contract Killer Drehbuch (Zürich: Haffmanns Verlag), pp. 71–105.

Kertész, Imre (1998), "Wem gehört Auschwitz?" in Die Zeit, 48 (19.11.1998), pp. 55–56.

Kirkeby, Per (1996), "The Pictures Between the Chapters in Breaking the Waves" in Björkman, Stig, Lars von Trier: Breaking the Waves (London: Faber & Faber), pp. 12–14.

Klaus, Georg (1966), Kybernetik und Erkenntnistheorie (Berlin: Deutscher Verlag der Wissenschaften).

—. (1968), Spieltheorie in kybernetischer Sicht (Berlin: Deutscher Verlag der Wissenschaften).

Klix, Friedhart (1971), *Information und Verhalten* (Berlin: Deutscher Verlag der Wissenschaften).

Kolmogorov, Alexej N. (1965), "Tri podkhoda k opredeleniju ponjatija 'količestvo informacii'" in *Problemy peredači informacii*, I, 1 , pp. 3–11.

Kosslyn, Stephen M. (1983), *Ghosts in the Mind's Machine* (New York and London: Norton & Company).

Kracauer, Siegfried (1961), *Nature of Film: The Redemption of Physical Reality* (London: Dennis Dobson).

Kreitler, Hans and Kreitler, Shulamith (1972), *Psychology of the Arts* (Durham, N.C.: Duke University Press).

Laiblin, Wilhelm, (ed.)(1991), *Märchenforschung und Tiefenpsychologie* (Darmstadt: Wissenschaftliche Buchgesellschaft).

Lakoff, George (1987), *Woman, Fire and Dangerous Things: What Categories Reveal About the Mind* (Chicago: Chicago University Press).

Lange, Oskar (1969), *Ganzheit und Entwicklung in kybernetischer Sicht* (Berlin: Akademie-Verlag).

Langer, Dieter (1962), *Informationstheorie und Psychologie* (Göttingen: Verlag für Psychologie).

Lazarus, Richard S. (1991), *Emotion and Adaptation* (New York: Oxford University Press).

—. (1999), "The Cognition-Emotion Debate: A Bit History" in Dalgleish, T. and Power, M., (eds.) *Handbook of Cognition and Emotion* (Chichester, New York et. al.: John Wiley & Sons), pp. 3–9.

Leprohon, Pierre, (ed.) (1964), *Michelangelo Antonioni: Der Regisseur und seine Filme* (Frankfurt am Main: Fischer).

Lenz, Benjamin (1990), "Vom Terrorismus des Schönen" in Jansen, Peter W. and Schütte, Wolfram, (eds.) *Alain Resnais,* Reihe Film 38 (München: Carl Hanser), pp. 7–26.

Levenson, Robert W. (1994), "Human Emotions: A Functional View" in Ekman, Paul and Davidson, Richard J., (eds.) *The Nature of Emotion: Fundamental Questions* (New York and Oxford: Oxford University Press), pp. 123–126.

Lewis, M. D. (2005), "Bridging Emotion Theory and Neurobiology Through Dynamic System Modeling" in *Behavioral and Brain Sciences,* 28, pp. 105–131.

Lessing, Gotthold Ephraim (1954), *Gesammelte Werke,* Bd. VI (Berlin and Weimar: Aufbau).

Lilli, Waldemar (1978), "Die Hypothesentheorie der sozialen Wahrnehmung" in Frey, Dieter, (ed.) *Kognitive Theorien der Sozialpsychologie* (Bern, Stuttgart and Wien), pp. 19–46.

—. (1982), *Grundlagen der Stereotypisierung* (Göttingen, Toronto and Zürich: Hogrefe).

Lippmann, Walter (1949), *Public Opinion* [1922] (New York: Harcourt & Brace).

Lipps, Theodor (1907), *Zur Einfühlung: Psychologische Untersuchungen* Vol. II).

Lotman, Jurij (1976), *Semiotics of Cinema,* trans. with foreword by Mark E. Suino (Ann Arbor: University of Michigan).

—. (1977), *The Structure of the Artistic Text,* trans. Gail Lenhoff and Ronald Vroon, Michigan Slavic Contributions, No 7 (Michigan: Dept. of Slavic Languages and Literatures, The Univerity of Michigan).

—. (1981), "Die Kunst als modellbildendes System (Thesen)" in Lotman, Jurij M., (ed.) *Kunst als Sprache: Untersuchungen zum Zeichencharakter von Literatur und Kunst* (Leipzig: Philipp Reclam jun.), pp. 67–88.

Loukides, Paul and Fuller, Linda (1990), *Beyond the Stars (1): Stock Characters in American Popular Film* (Bowling Green, Ohio: Bowling Green University Popular Press).

Lukács, Georg (1955), *Der Historische Roman* (Berlin and Weimar: Aufbau).

Mackie, John L. (1980), *The Cement of the Universe: A Study of Causation* (London and New York: Oxford University Press).

Mamber, Stephen (1974), *Cinéma vérité in America: Studies in Uncontrolled Documentary* (Cambridge, Mass. and London: MIT Press).

Mandel, David R. (2005), "Counterfactual and Causal Explanation: From Early Theoretical Views to New Frontiers" in Mandel, D.R., Hilton, D.J., and Catellani, P., (eds.) *The Psychology of Counterfactual Thinking* (London and New York: Routledge), pp. 11–27.

Mandler, George (1984a), "The Construction and Limitation of Consciousness" in Sarris, Victor and Parducci, Allen, (eds.) *Perspectives in Psychological Experimentation: Toward the Year 2000* (Hillsdale, N.J.: Erlbaum), pp. 109–126.

—. (1984b), *Mind and Body: Psychology of Emotion and Stress* (New York).

—. (1992), "Emotions, Evolution and Aggression: Myths and Conjectures" in Strongman, K.T., (ed.) *International Review of Studies on Emotion*, 2 .

Mandler, Jean M. (1984), *Stories, Scripts, and Scenes: Aspects of Schema Theory* (Hillsdale, N.J.: Erlbaum).

Mangold, Roland (1999), "Zum Einsatz hirndiagnostischer Verfahren bei der Untersuchung kognitiver und insbesondere emotionaler Medienwirkungen" in *Medienpsychologie*, 11, 2, pp. 121–142.

Maturana, Humberto R. (1978), "Cognition" in Hejl, Peter M. Köck, Wolfram, K. and Roth, Gerhard, (eds.) *Wahrnehmung und Kommunikation* (Frankfurt am Main and New York), pp. 29–49.

Metz, Christian (1974), *Film Language: A Semiotics of the Cinema,* trans. Michael Taylor (New York: Oxford University Press)

Mejlach, Boris S. (1977), *Künstlerisches Schaffen und Rezeptionsprozess: Zur Methodologie der komplexen*

Erforschung von Kunst und Literatur (Berlin and Weimar: Aufbau).

Mittenzwei, Werner (1965), *Gestaltung und Gestalten im modernen Drama* (Berlin and Weimar: Aufbau).

Montagu, Ivor (1964), *Film World—A Guide To Cinema* (Bungay, UK: Penguin Books).

Moles, Abraham (1958), *Théorie de l'information et perception esthétique* (Paris: Flammarion).

Morin, Edgar (1958), *Der Mensch und das Kino* (Stuttgart: Klett).

Mukařovský, Jan (1974), "Beabsichtigtes und Unbeabsichtigtes in der Kunst" in Mukařovský, (ed.) *Studien zur strukturalistischen Ästhetik und Poetik* (München: Hanser), pp. 31–65.

Müller, Robby (1996), "Auf der Suche nach dem naiven Sehen, dem unbefangenen Filmen: Gespräch mit dem Kameramann Robby Müller" in *Filmbulletin,* 5, pp. 23–24.

Munsterberg, Hugo (1970), *The Film: A Psychological Study* [1916] (New York: Dover Publications).

Naber, Christina (2008), "Alles andere als nüchtern: Der aktuelle Dokumentarfilm und sein emotionales Wirkungspotenzial" in *Beiträge zur Film- und Fernsehwissenschaft (BFF)* 62, pp. 107–130.

Naumann, Manfred (ed.) (1976), *Gesellschaft, Literatur, Lesen. Literaturrezeption in theoretischer Sicht* (Berlin and Weimar: Aufbau).

Neale, Steve (1993), "Melo talk: on the meaning and use of the term 'melodrama' in the American trade press" in *Velvet Light Trap,* pp. 66–89.

—. (2000) *Genre and Hollywood* (London and New York: Routledge)

Neill, Alex (1996), "Empathy and (Film) Fiction" in Bordwell, David and Carroll, Noël (eds.) *Post-Theory: Reconstructing*

Film Studies (Madison: University of Wisconsin Press), pp. 175–193.

Neisser, Ulric (1976), *Cognition and Reality: Principles and Implications of Cognitive Psychology* (San Francisco: W.H. Freeman and Co.).

Nichols, Bill (1991), *Representing Reality: Issues and Concepts in Documentary* (Bloomington: Indiana University Press).

—. (2002), "Film Theory and the Revolt against Master Narratives" in Williams, Linda and Gledhill, Christine, (eds.) *Reinventing Film Studies* (London: Arnold), pp. 34–52.

Oatley, Keith (1992), *Best Laid Schemes: The Psychology of Emotions* (Cambridge: Cambridge University Press).

—. (1999), "Foreword" to Dalgleish, Tim and Power, Mick J., (eds.) *Handbook of Cognition and Emotion* (Chichester, New York et al.: John Wiley & Sons), pp. xvii–xviii.

Oatley, Keith and Johnson-Laird, Philip N. (1987), "Towards a Cognitive Theory of Emotion" in *Cognition and Emotion,* 1 , pp. 51–58.

Öhman, Arne (1999), "Distinguishing Unconscious from Conscious Emotional Processes: Methodical Considerations and Theoretical Implications" in Dalgleish, T. and Power, M., (eds.) *Handbook of Cognition and Emotion* (Chichester, New York et al.: John Wiley), pp. 301–320.

Oesterreich, Rainer (1981), *Handlungsregulation und Kontrolle* (München, Wien and Baltimore: Urban & Schwarzenberg).

Ohler, Peter (1990), "Zur Begründung einer schematheoretisch orientierten kognitiven Filmpsychologie in Auseinandersetzung mit der ökologischen Wahrnehmungspsychologie von James Jerome Gibson" in Schumm, Gerhard and Wulff, Hans J., (eds.) *Film und Psychologie* I (Münster: MakS Publikationen), pp. 79–107.

—. (1991:1994), *Kognitive Filmpsychologie: Verarbeitung und mentale Repräsentation narrativer Filme,* Phil. Dissertation

(Berlin: Technische Universität and Münster: MakS Publikationen).

—. (2000), *Spiel, Evolution, Kognition: Von den Ursprüngen des Spiels bis zu den Computerspielen,* Habilitationsschrift (Berlin: Technische Universität).

Ohler, Peter and Nieding, Gerhild (2001), "Antizipation und Spieltätigkeit bei der Rezeption narrativer Filme" in Friess, Jörg, Hartmann, Britta and Müller, Eggo, (eds.) *Nicht allein das Laufbild auf der Leinwand...Strukturen des Films als Erlebnispotentiale,* Beiträge zur Film- und Fernsehwissenschaft, 60, pp. 13–30.

Ohler, Peter and Nieding, Gerhild (2002), "Kognitive Filmpsychologie zwischen 1990 und 2000" in Sellmer, Jan and Wulff, Hans. J,. (eds.) *Film und Psychologie—nach der kognitiven Phase?* (Marburg: Schüren), pp. 9–40.

Omdahl, Becky L. (1995), *Cognitive Appraisal, Emotion and Empathy* (Mahwah, N.J.: Erlbaum).

Oppenheimer, Jean and Williams, David E. (1996), "Von Trier and Müller's Ascetic Aesthetics" in *American Cinematographer,* Dec. 1996, pp. 18–22.

Pavel, Thomas G. (1986), *Fictional Worlds* (Cambridge, Mass. and London: Harvard University Press).

Pavlov, Ivan P. (1972), *Die bedingten Reflexe. Eine Auswahl aus dem Gesamtwerk,* ed. Gerhard Baader and Ursula Schnapper (München: Kindler).

Peirce, Charles S. (1929), "Guessing" in *Hound and Horn* 2, 3, pp. 267–282.

—. (1958), *Collected Papers of Charles Sanders Peirce,* Vol. VII: Science and Philosophy, ed. Arthur W. Burks (Cambridge, Mass.: Harvard University Press).

Peleshian, Artavazd (1989), "Distance Montage, or The Theory of Distance" in *Documentary Films of the Armenian Soviet Republic: A Retrospective Programme of the 21st Nyon*

International Documentary Film Festival, Switzerland (Nyon and Berlin: Co-produced with the Panorama Section of the 40th Berlin International Film Festival), pp. 79–102.

Perrig, Walter, Wippich, Werner and Perrig-Chiello, Pasqualina (1993), *Unbewusste Informationsverarbeitung* (Bern, Göttingen, Toronto and Seattle: Verlag Hans Huber).

Pfister, Manfred (1982), *Das Drama: Theorie und Analyse* (München: Fink).

Pinthus, Kurt (ed.) (1983), *Das Kinobuch* [1913–14] (Frankfurt am Main: Fischer Taschenbuch Verlag).

Plantinga, Carl (1999), "The Scene of Empathy and the Human Face on Film" in Plantinga, C. and Smith, G. M., (eds.) *Passionate Views: Film, Cognition, and Emotion* (Baltimore and London: The Johns Hopkins University Press), pp. 239–255.

Plantinga, Carl and Smith, Greg M. (eds.) (1999), *Passionate Views: Film, Cognition, and Emotion* (Baltimore and London: The Johns Hopkins University Press).

—. "Introduction" to Plantinga, C. and Smith, G. M. (eds.) (1999), *Passionate Views: Film, Cognition, and Emotion* (Baltimore and London: The Johns Hopkins University Press), pp. 1–17.

Postle, B. R. (2006), "Working Memory as an Emergent Property of the Mind and Brain" in *Neuroscience* 139 , pp. 23–38.

Propp, Vladimir (1969), *Morfologija skazki* [1928] (Moskva: Izd. Nauka).

Pudovkin, Vsevolod (1983), "Die schöpferische Arbeit des Filmregisseurs" [1929] in Pudowkin, W. (ed.) *Die Zeit in Großaufnahme: Erinnerungen, Aufsätze, Werkstattnotizen* (Berlin: Henschel), pp. 289–304.

Richardson, John T. E. (1999), *Imagery* (East Sussex, UK: Psychology Press Ltd. Publ.).

Richter, Rolf (1964), "Zur dramaturgischen Struktur des tschechoslowakischen Films 'Der schwarze Peter'" in *Filmwissenschaftliche Mitteilungen*, 4 , pp. 988–1006.

Rilke, Rainer Maria (1959), "Duineser Elegien" in *Werke,* Auswahl in zwei Bänden, (Leipzig: Insel), Vol. I , pp. 231-266.

Robinson, David (1985), *Chaplin: His Life and Art* (London: Collins)

Roese, Neal J. and Olson, James M. (2003), "Counterfactual Thinking" in *Encyclopedia of Cognitive Science* (London, New York and Tokyo: Nature Publishing Group), Vol.1, pp. 858–861.

Ronen, Ruth (1994), *Possible Worlds in Literature Theory* (Cambridge: Cambridge University Press).

Rumelhart, David E. (1975), "Notes on a Schema for Stories" in Bobrow, Daniel and Collin, Allan, (eds.) *Representation and Understanding: Studies in Cognitive Science* (New York, San Francisco and London: Academic Press), pp. 211–236.

—. (1980), "Schemata: The Building Blocks of Cognition" in Spiro, Rand J., Bruce, Bertram C., and Brewer, William F., (eds.) *Theoretical Issues in Reading Comprehension: Perspectives from Cognitive Psychology, Linguistics, Artificial Intelligence, and Educations* (Hillsdale, N.J.: Erlbaum), pp. 33–58.

Rumelhart, David E. and Ortony, Andrew (1977), "The Representation of Knowledge in Memory" in Anderson, Richard C., Spiro, Rand J., and Montague, William, (eds.) *Schooling and the Acquisition of Knowledge* (Hillsdale, N.J.: Erlbaum), pp. 99–135.

Salt, Barry (1992), *Film Style and Technology: History and Analysis,* 2nd edition (London: Starword).

Sachse, Rainer (1993), "Empathie" in Schorr, Angela, (ed.) *Handbuch der Angewandten Psychologie* (Bonn), pp. 170–173.

Seligman, Martin E. P. (1975), *Helplessness: On Depression, Development, and Death* (San Francisco: Freeman).

Schacter, Daniel L. (1996), *Searching for Memory: The Brain, the*

Mind, and the Past (New York: Basic Books).

Schacter, Daniel L., Dobbins, Ian G., and Schnyer, David M. (2004), "Specificity of Priming: A Cognitive Neuroscience Perspective" in *Nature Reviews Neuroscience*, 5 , pp. 853–862.

Schacter, Daniel L., Wig, Gagan S., and Stevens, W. Dale (2007), "Reductions in Cortical Activity During Priming" in *Current Opinion in Neurobiology*, 17, pp. 171–176.

Scherer, Klaus R. (1981), "Wider die Vernachlässigung der Emotion in der Psychologie" in W. Michaelis (ed.) *Bericht über den 32. Kongress der Deutschen Gesellschaft für Psychologie in Zürich 1980*, vol. 1 (Göttingen: Hogrefe), pp. 304–317.

—. (1998), "Emotionsprozesse im Medienkontext: Forschungsillustrationen und Zukunftsperspektiven", *Medienpsychologie* 10, 4 , pp. 276–293.

—. (1999), "Appraisal Theory" in Dalgleish, T. and Power, M., (eds.) *Handbook of Cognition and Emotion* (Chichester, New York et al.: John Wiley), pp. 637–664.

Schick, Thomas and Ebbrecht, Tobias, (eds.) (2008), *Emotion—Empathie—Figur: Spielformen der Filmwahrnehmung*, Beiträge zur Film- und Fernsehwissenschaft (BFF) 62 .

Schiller, Friedrich von (1937), "Über die ästhetische Erziehung des Menschen" in *Sämtliche Werke* (Sanssouci-Ausgabe) (Berlin: Büchergilde Gutenberg), vol. 7, pp. 181–289.

Schmidt, Robert F. and Thews, Gerhard (1985), *Physiologie des Menschen* (Berlin et al.: Springer).

Schober, Rita (1979), "Für einen neuen Realismus" in *Weimarer Beiträge*, 7 .

Schweinitz, Jörg (1987), "Stereotyp: Vorschlag und Definition eines filmästhetischen Begriffs" in *Beiträge zur Film- und Fernsehwissenschaft*, 29 , pp. 110-125.

—. (1991), "Stereotypen der populären Filmkultur: Aspekte zur theoretischen Fundierung" in *Weimarer Beiträge* 37, 5, pp.

645–655.

——. (1994), "'Genre' und lebendiges Genrebewusstsein" in *montage/av.* 3, 2, pp. 99–218.

——. (2002), "Von Filmgenres, Hybridformen und goldenen Nägeln"in Sellmer, Jan and Wulff, Hans J., (eds.) *Psychologie und Film—nach der kognitiven Phase?,* GFM-Schriften 10 (Marburg: Schüren), pp. 79–92.

——. (2006), *Film und Stereotyp: Eine Herausforderung für das Kino und die Filmtheorie: Zur Geschichte eines Mediendiskurses* (Berlin: Akademie Verlag, 2006).

Shannon, Claude E. and Weaver, Warren (1949), *The Mathematical Theory of Communication* (Urbana, Illinois: University of Illinois Press).

Shaw, Harry (1972), *Dictionary of Literary Terms* (New York, Toronto and London: McGraw-Hill, Inc.).

Shklovsky, Victor (Sklovskij, Viktor) (1965), "Art as Technique" [1916] in *Russian Formalist Criticism: Four Essays,* trans. and ed. Lee T. Lemon and Marion J. Reis (Lincoln: University of Nebraska Press), pp. 11–12.

Simonov, Pavel V. (1975), *Widerspiegelungstheorie und Psychologie der Emotionen* (Berlin: Volk und Gesundheit).

——. (1982), *Höhere Nerventätigkeit des Menschen: Motivationelle und emotionelle Aspekte* (Berlin: Volk und Gesundheit).

Singer, Jerome L., "Imagination" in Kazdin, A. E., (ed.) (2000), *Encyclopedia of Psychology* (Washington DC: American Psych. Ass.) Vol. 4, pp. 227–230.

Smith, Greg (1999), "Local Emotions, Global Moods, and Filmic Structure" in: Plantinga, C. and Smith, G., (eds.) *Passionate Views: Film, Cognition, and Emotion* (Baltimore and London: The Johns Hopkins University Press), pp. 103–126.

——. (2003), *Film Structure and the Emotion System* (Cambridge: Cambridge University Press).

Smith, Murray (1995), *Engaging Characters: Fiction, Emotion, and the Cinema* (Oxford: Clarendon Press).

—. (1999), "Gangsters, Cannibals, Aesthetes, or Apparently Perverse Allegiances" in Plantinga, C. and Smith, G. M., (eds.) *Passionate Views: Film, Cognition, and Emotion* (Baltimore and London: The Johns Hopkins University Press).

—. (2001), "Parallel Lines" in Hillier, Jim, (ed.) *American Independent Cinema* (London: BFI), pp. 155–161.

Smith, C. A. and Ellsworth, Phoebe C. (1985), "Patterns of Cognitive Appraisal in Emotion" in *Journal of Personality and Social Psychology*, 48, pp. 813–838.

Sobchak, Thomas and Sobchak, Vivian C. (1987), *An Introduction to Film,* 2nd edition (Boston and Toronto: Little, Brown and Co.).

Sokolov, E. N. (1960), "Neuronal Models and the Orienting Reflex" in Brazier, M. A., (ed.) *The Central Nervous System and Behaviour* (New York).

—. (1963), *Perception and the Conditioned Reflex* (Oxford: Pergamon Press).

Stafford, Barbara M. (1999), *Visual Analogy: Consciousness as the Art of Connecting* (Cambridge, Mass. and London: Harvard University Press).

Stein, Nancy and Trabasso, Tom (1992), "The Organization of Emotional Experience: Creating Links Between Emotion, Thinking, and Intentional Action" in *Cognition and Emotion,* 6, pp. 225–244.

Striedter, Jurij, (ed.) (1988), *Russischer Formalismus* (München: Fink).

Strongman, K. T. (1987), *The Psychology of Emotions,* 3rd ed. (Chichester, New York et. al.: John Wiley & Sons).

Suckfüll, Monika (1997), *Film erleben: Narrative Strukturen und physiologische Prozesse—"Das Piano" von Jane Campion*

(Berlin: Edition Sigma).

—.   (1998), "Aktivierungswirkungen narrativer Strukturen" in *Medienpsychologie* 2 , pp. 87–109.

—.   (2000), "Filmanalysis and Psychophysiology" in *Media Psychology* 2, 2, pp. 269–301.

—.   (2001),"Das PKS-Modell in der medienpsychologischen Forschung" in Friess, Jörg, Hartmann, Britta and Müller, Eggo, (eds.) *Nicht allein das Laufbild auf der Leinwand...Strukturen des Films als Erlebnispotentiale,* Beiträge zur Film- und Fernsehwissenschaft (BFF) 60 (2001).

—.   (2003), "Ansätze zur Analyse von Wirkverläufen" in Vorderer, Peter, Mangold, Roland and Bente, Gary, (eds.) *Lehrbuch der Medienpsychologie* (Göttingen: Hogrefe).

—.   (2004), *Rezeptionsmodalitäten: Ein integratives Konstrukt für die Medienwirkungsforschung* (München: Reinhard Fischer)

Sutton-Smith, Brian (1978), *Die Dialektik des Spielens: Eine Theorie des Spielens, der Spiele und des Sports* (Schorndorf: Verlag Karl Hofmann).

—.   (2000), "Play" in Kazdin, Alan E. (ed.) *Encyclopedia of Psychology* (Washington DC: American Psych. Ass., Vol. 6, pp. 213–219.

Sternberg, Meir (1978), *Expositional Modes and Temporal Ordering in Fiction* (Baltimore: The Johns Hopkins University Press).

Tan, Ed (1994), "Film-Induced Affect as a Witness Emotion" in *Poetics,* 23, pp. 7–32.

—.   (1996), *Emotion and the Structure of Narrative Film: Film as an Emotion Machine* (Mahwah, New Jersey: Erlbaum).

—.   (2000), "Emotion, Art and the Humanities" in Lewis, M. and Havilland, J. M., (eds.) *Handbook of Emotion,* 2nd ed. (New York: Guilford), pp. 116–134.

Tan, Ed and Frijda, Nico H. (1999), "Sentiment in Film Viewing" in Plantinga, Carl and Smith, Greg M. (eds.) *Passionate Views:*

Film, Cognition, and Emotion (London and Baltimore: The Johns Hopkins University Press), pp. 48–64.

Tarkovsky, Andrey (1986), *Sculpting in Time: Reflections on the Cinema,* trans. Kitty Hunter-Blair (London: The Bodley Head)

Taylor, Sue Parker (1984), "Playing for Keeps" in Smith, Peter (ed.) *Play in Animals and Humans* "New York: Blackwell), pp. 271–293.

Thompson, Kristin (1988), *Breaking the Glass Armor: Neoformalist Film Analysis* (Princeton, New Jersey: Princeton University Press).

Thomson, George (1966), *Aeschylus and Athens: A Study In The Social Origins of Drama* (London: Lawrence & Wishart)

Thorndyke, Perry (1977), "Cognitive Structure in Comprehension and Memory of Narrative Discourse" in *Cognitive Psychology,* 9 , pp. 77–110.

Tinchon, Hans-Jörg (1999), "Ein psychologischer Messplatz zur Untersuchung medienpsychologischer Fragestellungen" in *Medienpsychologie* 11, 2 , pp. 69–95.

Todorov, Tzvetan (1972), "Die Grammatik der Erzählung" in Gallas, Helga (ed.) *Strukturalismus als interpretatives Verfahren* (Darmstadt and Neuwied: Luchterhand), pp. 57–71.

—. (1990), *Genres in Discourse* (Cambridge and New York: Cambridge University Press).

Trabasso, Tom, Secco, Tom and Van den Broek, Paul (1984), "Causal Cohesion and Story Coherence" in Mandl, Heinz, (ed.) *Learning and Comprehension of Text* (Hillsdale, New Jersey: Erlbaum), pp. 83–111.

Tröhler, Margrit (2002), "Von Weltkonstellationen und Textgebäuden. Fiktion—Nichtfiktion—Narration in Spiel- und Dokumentarfilm" in *montage/av* 11, 2, pp. 9–41

—. (2006), "Plurale Figurenkonstellationen: Die offene Logik der wahrnehmbaren Möglichkeiten" in *montage/av* 15, 2 , pp. 95–114.

—. (2007), *Offene Welten ohne Helden. Plurale Figurenkonstellationen im Film* (Marburg: Schüren).

Truffaut, François (1967), *Hitchcock by François Truffaut*, with the Collaboration of Hellen G. Scott (New York: Simon and Schuster).

Tynianov, Juri N. (1982), *Poetik: Ausgewählte Essays* (Leipzig and Weimar: Kiepenheuer).

VandenBos, Gary R., (ed.) (2007), *APA Dictionary of Psychology* (Washington, DC: American Psychol. Ass.).

Varela, Francisco J. (1981), "Autonomy and Autopoiesis" in Roth, Gerhard and Schwegler, Helmut, (eds.) *Self-Organizing Systems: An Interdisciplinary Approach* (Frankfurt am Main and New York), pp. 14–23.

—. (1990), *Kognitionswissenschaft—Kognitionstechnik: Eine Skizze aktueller Perspektiven* (Frankfurt am Main: Suhrkamp).

Vertov, Dziga (1960), *Dsiga Wertow—Publizist und Poet des Dokumentarfilms,* ed. Hermann Herlinghaus (Leipziger Dokumentarfilmwoche).

Viano, Maurizio (1999), " *Life is Beautiful*" in *Film Quarterly* 53, 1 , pp. 26–34.

Vinterberg, Thomas (1999), "Wir haben einen Stein ins Wasser geworfen: Interview mit Thomas Vinterberg von Marcus Rothe" in *Neue Züricher Zeitung,* 05.02.1999.

Von Trier, Lars (1996), "Director's Note—This Film is About 'Good'" in Björgman, Stig, (ed.) *Breaking the Waves* (London: Faber & Faber), pp. 20–22.

—. (1998), "Die Freude zurückgewinnen: Interview mit Lars von Trier" in Forst, Achim, *Breaking the Dreams: Das Kino des Lars von Trier* (Marburg: Schüren), pp. 187–196.

Vorderer, Peter, Wulff, Hans J. and Friedrichsen, Mike, (eds.)(1996), *Suspense: Conceptualizations, Theoretical Analyses, and Empirical Explorations* (Mahwah, N.J.: Erlbaum).

Vygotsky, Lev (1965), *Psichologija iskusstva* (Moskva: Iskusstvo).

—. (1980), "Aus den Vorlesungsskripten Wygotskis zur Psychologie des Vorschulalters" in Elkonin, Daniel, (ed.) *Psychologie des Spiels* (Berlin: Volk und Wissen Verlag), pp. 430–441.

Wajda, Andrzej (1964), "Stanislaw Janicki: Gespräch mit Andrzej Wajda" in Kotulla, Theodor, (ed.) *Der Film: Manifeste— Gespräche—Dokumente,* Vol. II (München: Piper), pp. 345–361.

—. (1987), *Meine Filme* (Zürich: Benzinger).

Wekwerth, Manfred (1960), *Theater in Veränderung* (Berlin and Weimar: Aufbau).

White, Murray (1999), "Representation of Facial Expressions of Emotion" in *American Journal of Psychology,* 112, 3, pp. 371–381.

Wollen, Peter (1976), "'North by Northwest': A Morphological Analysis" in *Film Form* 1, 1 , pp. 19–34.

Wong Kar-wai (2000), "Die Musik ist immer der Ausgangspunkt: Interview von Daniel Bax mit Wong Kar-wai" in *Die Tageszeitung* (Berlin), 30.11.2000.

Wright, Will (1975), *Six Guns and Society: A Structural Study of the Western* (Berkeley, Los Angeles and London: University of California Press).

Wulff, Hans J. (1996), "Suspense and the Influence of Cataphora on Viewers' Expectations" in Vorderer, Peter, Wulff, Hans J., and Friedrichsen, Mike, (eds.) *Suspense: Conceptualizations, Theoretical Analyses, and Empirical Explorations* (Mahwah, N.J.: Erlbaum), pp. 1–17.

—. (2002), "Das empathische Feld" in Sellmer, Jan and Wulff, Hans J., (eds.) *Film und Psychologie—nach der kognitiven Phase?*

(Marburg: Schüren), pp. 109–121.

—. (2003),"Empathie als Dimension des Filmverstehens: Ein Thesenpapier" in *montage/av*, 12, 1 , pp. 136–161.

Wuss, Peter (1968), *Problema oč uždenija i sovremennaja kinoiskusstvo,* Avtoreferat dissertacii (Moskva: VGIK).

—. (1979), "Zur Anwendung des Verfremdungsbegriffs bei der Filmanalyse" in *Brecht 78. Brecht-Dialog "Kunst und Politik"* (Berlin: Henschel), pp. 266–271.

—. (1986), *Die Tiefenstruktur des Filmkunstwerks: Zur Analyse von Spielfilmen mit offener Komposition* (Berlin: Henschel).

—. (1987), "Hypothesen zu einer werkorientierten Filmwirkungsforschung" in *Beiträge zur Film- und Fernsehwissenschaft,* 29 , pp. 64–90.

—. (1990a), *Kunstwert des Films und Massencharakter des Mediums: Konspekte zur Geschichte der Theorie des Spielfilms* (Berlin: Henschel).

—. (1990b), "Narration and the Film Structures for Three Learning Phases" in *Poetics,* 19 , pp. 549–570.

—. (1992), "Der Rote Faden der Filmgeschichten und seine unbewussten Komponenten: Topik-Reihen, Kausal-Ketten und Story-Schemata—drei Ebenen filmischer Narration" in *montage /av,* 1, 1, pp. 25–36.

—. (1993), *Filmanalyse und Psychologie: Strukturen des Films im Wahrnehmungsprozess* (Berlin: Edition Sigma).

—. (1996), "Narrative Tension in Antonioni" in Vorderer, P., Wulff, H.J. and Friedrichsen, M., (eds.) *Suspense: Conceptualizations, Theoretical Analyses, and Empirical Explorations* (Mahwah, N.J.: Erlbaum), pp. 51–70.

—. (1998a), "Originalität und Stil: Zu einigen Anregungen der Formalen Schule für die Analyse von Film-Stilen" in *montage/av,* 7, 1 , pp. 145–167.

—. (1998b), "Träume als filmische Topiks und Stereotypen" in

Dieterle, Bernhard, (ed.) *Träumungen: Traumerzählungen in Film und Literatur* (St. Augustin: Gardez! Verlag), pp. 93–116.

—. (2000), "Cinematic Narration, Conflict and Problem-solving" in Bondebjerg, Ib, (ed.) *Moving Images, Culture and the Mind* (Luton: University of Luton Press), pp. 105–116.

—. (2002), "'Das Leben ist schön'—aber wie lassen sich die Emotionen eines Films objektivieren?" in Sellmer, J. and Wulff, H.J., (eds.) *Film und Psychologie—nach der kognitiven Phase?* (Marburg: Schüren), pp. 123–142.

—. (2003), "The Documentary Style of Fiction Film in Eastern Europe: Narration and Visual Style" in Hojbjerg, Lennard and Schepelern, Peter, (eds.) *Film Style and Story: A Tribute to Torben Grodal* (Copenhagen: Museum Tusculanum Press, University of Copenhagen), pp. 215–238.

—. (2005), "Konflikt und Emotion im Filmerleben" in Brütsch et. al., (eds.) *Kinogefühle: Emotionalität und Film* "Marburg: Schüren), pp. 205–224.

—. (2006), "Konflikt, Emotion und Genre—Einige Hinweise aus Film- und Emotionstheorie für eine empirische Wirkungsforschung" in Stiehler, Hans-Jörg and Mikos, Lothar, (eds.) *Die Kunst des Betrachters: Jugendsoziologie, Kinderfilm und Medienkompetenz. Festschrift für Dieter Wiedemann* (Leipzig: Leipziger Universitätsverlag, 2006), pp. 79–106.

—. (2007), "Overcoming Conflicts by Play: Play on the Screen and in the Viewer's Mind" in Anderson, J.D. and Fisher Anderson, B., (eds.) *Narration and Spectatorship in Moving Images* (Newcastle: Cambridge Scholars Publishing), pp. 222–236.

—. (2008), "Film und Spiel: Menschliches Rezeptionsverhalten in Realität und Rezeptionsprozess" in Schick, Thomas and Ebbrecht, Tobias, (eds.) *Emotion—Empathie—Figur: Spielformen der Wahrnehmung,* BFF 62 , pp. 217–248.

Zillmann, Dolf (1991), "Empathy: Affect from bearing witness to the emotions of others" in Bryant, J. and Zillmann, D., (eds.) *Responding to the Screen: Reception and Reaction Processes* (Hillsdale, N.J.: Erlbaum), pp. 281–304.

Acknowledgements

This book is a result of the research that I carried out parallel to my teaching work at the Konrad Wolf Film & Television Academy (HFF) in Potsdam-Babelsberg. Parts of these studies have already been printed as individual articles in German, but the HFF gave me financial support for a translation into English of some of them. I would like to express my gratitude to this institution, because the translated versions became the basic texts for a rewriting and the elaboration of the present coherent treatise. The translation for one of the articles, which led to chapter VII, was made by Brian Currid; most of the other chapters were translated by Stephen Lowry, who created the basic texts for the chapters II, IV, VI, VIII and IX. I am extraordinary thankful to him for this extensive work which he realised in a careful and sensitive way despite the burden of his teaching work and his own creative projects. Sometimes, indeed, I have a sense of guilt towards him because, in my drive to establish my own technical terms in his native language, I did not follow some of his friendly advice. I am greatly indebted to my colleagues Barbara Fisher Anderson, Joseph D. Anderson and Torben Kragh Grodal, of the Society for Cognitive Studies of the Moving Image, for their stimulating interest in my work, even though for many years its results were accessible to them only through a few seemingly unconnected articles in English. Birgit Hansen has provided precious help by correcting considerable parts of my English text, and her advice regarding language and style has often led to a clarification of my thoughts.

I am immensely grateful to Christine Noll Brinckmann, whose invitations to deliver some keynote lectures for the Seminar in Film Studies at the University of Zurich encouraged me to summarize my ideas about central topics of our métier. That my colleague, despite her own workload, found time to thoroughly go through a late version of the manuscript, moved me deeply. To her generous solidarity I owe a constructive in-depth criticism of the book's content, as well as an amicable linguistic revision of the text.

In the tiresome last phase of writing I have received immeasurable help from Johannes Leisen, who was the first reader of the whole effort and provided intellectual inspiration as well as practical encouragement in finishing the work, reliably standing by my side during the final textual revision and the technical procedures regarding the manuscript. I owe to him the concept and manufacturing of the picture component of the book and also the technical preparation of the paper for going to press.

If the publication, despite all support and advice from friends and colleagues, still includes various insufficiencies, then, of course, the responsibility lies with me entirely.

Berlin, February 2009

Peter Wuss

Permissions

Chapter I and II are partly adapted and translated from pages 52–224 of *Filmanalyse und Psychologie: Strukturen des Films im Wahrnehmungsprozess*, (Berlin: Edition Sigma, Rainer Bohn Verlag, 1993, 1999). Adapted with permission.

Major parts of chapter IV are translated from "Konflikt und Emotion im Filmerleben", in Mathias Brütsch, Vinzenz Hediger, Ursula von Keitz, Alexandra Schneider, and Margrit Tröhler, eds., *Kinogefühle: Emotionalität und Film* (Marburg: Schüren Verlag GmbH, 2005), pp. 205–222. Adapted with permission.

Central parts of chapter V are translated from "Ein kognitiver Ansatz zur Analyse des Realitäts-Effekts von Dogma-95-Filmen", in *montage/av* 9, 2 (2000), pp. 101–126; copyright 2000 by Schüren Verlag GmbH, Marburg. Adapted with permission.

Chapter VII is a translation from the German version of the article "Träume als filmische Topiks und Stereotypen", in Bernard Dieterle, ed., *Träumungen: Traumerzählung in Film und Literatur*, (St. Augustin: Michael Itschert, Garde! Verlag, 1998), pp. 93–116. Adapted with permission.

Chapter VIII is for the most part a reprint of "Overcoming Conflicts by Play: Play on the Screen and in the Viewer's Mind", in Joseph D. Anderson and Barbara Fisher Anderson, eds., *Narration and Spectatorship in Moving Images*, (Newcastle-upon-Tyne: Cambridge Scholars Publishing, 2007), pp. 222–236.

Chapter IX contains some central ideas from pages 303–400 of *Filmanalyse und Psychologie: Strukuren des Films im Wahrnehmungsprozess* (Berlin: Edition Sigma, Rainer Bohn Verlag, 1993). Adapted with permission.

Figure 7 contains an adapted reproduction of curve-charts from Monika Suckfüll's unpublished pilot study on the heartbeat analysis of spectators during the reception of the film *Father and Daughter*. Printed with permission.

Keyword Index

Film Title Index

Person Index